Fodor's

E X P L O R I N G

FRANCE

FODOR'S TRAVEL PUBLICATIONS, INC.

NEW YORK • TORONTO • LONDON • SYDNEY • AUCKLAND

Published in the United States by Fodor's Travel Publications, Inc.
Published in the United Kingdom by AA Publishing.

Fodor's and Fodor's Exploring Guides are trademarks of Fodor's Travel Publications, Inc.

ISBN 0-679-02902-8
Second Edition

Fodor's Exploring France

Author: **Adam Ruck**
Additional writing and research by: **Fiona Dunlop, Lindsay Hunt, Michael Ivory, Ingrid Morgan, Judith Samson, David Shepheard**
Series Adviser: **Ingrid Morgan**
Series Editor: **Nia Williams**
Cover Design: **Louise Fili, Fabrizio La Rocca**
Front Cover Silhouette: **Catherine Karnow/Woodfin Camp**

Special Sales
Fodor's Travel Publications are available at special discounts for bulk purchases (100 copies or more) for sales promotions or premiums. Special editions, including personalized covers, excerpts of existings guides, and corporate imprints, can be created in large quantities for special needs. For more information write to Special Marketing, Fodor's Travel Publications, 201 East 50th St., New York NY 10022.

Manufactured in Italy by LEGO SpA, Vicenza.
10 9 8 7 6 5 4 3 2 1

Impressions of France: The Artist's Garden at Vetheuil, *by Claude Monet (1880)*

Adam Ruck is the author of *The Holiday Which? Guide to France* and *The Holiday Which? Guide to Greece*. He is a regular contributor to British national newspapers, including *The Daily Telegraph*, *The Sunday Telegraph*, *The Guardian*, *The Sunday Times* and *The Observer*.

The best way to appreciate France: taking time to watch the world go by in a Pyrenean village

About this book

This book is divided into three principal sections.

The first part of the book discusses aspects of life today and in the past. The second part covers places to visit, including drives and walks. The Focus on... and Close-up sections, also in this section, look at subjects in greater detail. The third and final part is the Travel Facts chapter, which includes both practical day-to-day information for the traveler and the Hotels and Restaurants section which is a selective list of accomodations and places to eat.

Some of the places described in this book have been given a special rating:

  Do not miss

  Highly recommended

  See if you can

General Contents

Top: Queyras Regional Park
Below: Flowers and wine in Alsace

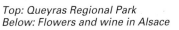

My France
by Jean-Marc Cholet

Why do French people like to stay in France? Anyone who is sharp-eyed enough can find beautiful places all around world. Without doubt, Italy or Spain, bathed by the sun and its vivid colours, can provide a harbor of peace for the traveler. But after a couple of days, the Frenchman or woman begins to feel slightly nervous about this profusion of light and heat. Turn to the north and you can be touched by the mists and mystery of the British Isles. But the French visitor is unlikely to spend more than a few days in a country so strange that it is impossible to find a regular baguette or a decent morning croissant. Germany is too big, and there are too many rules for a native of the Homeland of Human Rights. Emigrate to America? What for? We don't speak the language!

Traveling may ennoble the mind but the best journeys are the ones you take at home – especially when you live in France. The landscape is varied and sweet. Generations have nursed the countryside, cutting trees to open the views, building hedges to curb the winds, breeding cattle to add life to this work of art. And meanwhile, the French continued to cultivate a certain *art de vivre*. In the smallest village you can find a restaurant to delight you with its *cuisine du terroir*, and offer wines to make you fall in love.

We have cut off some heads in our time but nobody will oppress you here. However strong the desire to see the world, *Douce* France will always be the best place to live.

Why should the French go traveling anywhere else, when France has so much to offer?

Jean-Marc Cholet is a journalist and broadcaster living in Paris. He works as the rural affairs correspondent for France-Régions 3 television, and as a teenager made a brief foray into movie acting.

FRANCE

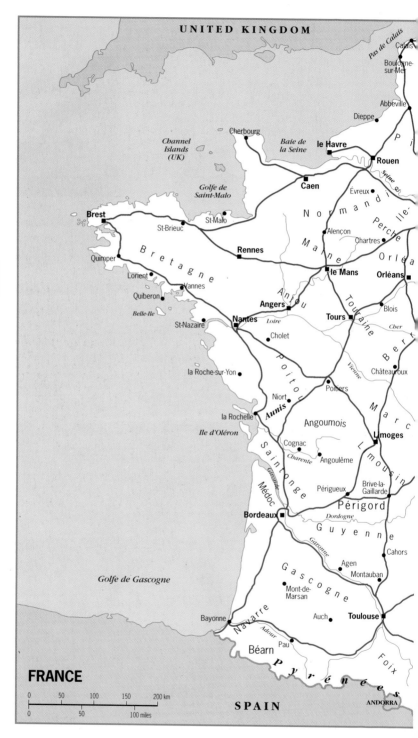

FRANCE

| 0 | 50 | 100 | 150 | 200 km |
| 0 | | 50 | | 100 miles |

UNITED KINGDOM

Pas de Calais
Calais
Boulogne-sur-Mer
Abbeville
Dieppe
Cherbourg
Baie de la Seine
le Havre
Rouen
Channel Islands (UK)
Caen
Évreux
Golfe de Saint-Malo
Normandie
Île-
Perche
Orléa
St-Malo
Brest
St-Brieuc
Alençon
Chartres
Bretagne
Rennes
Maine
Anjou
le Mans
Orléans
Quimper
Lorient
Vannes
Angers
Touraine
Tours
Blois
Quiberon
Nantes
Loire
Cher
Belle-Ile
St-Nazaire
Cholet
Berr
la Roche-sur-Yon
Poitou
Vienne
Châteauroux
Niort
Poitiers
Marc
la Rochelle
Aunis
Angoumois
Limoges
Ile d'Oléron
Cognac
Charente
Angoulême
Limousin
Saintonge
Médoc
Périgueux
Brive-la-Gaillarde
Gironde
Périgord
Bordeaux
Dordogne
Guyenne
Golfe de Gascogne
Garonne
Cahors
Agen
Montauban
Gascogne
Mont-de-Marsan
Bayonne
Navarre
Auch
Toulouse
Adour
Pau
Béarn
Pyrénées
Foix
SPAIN
ANDORRA

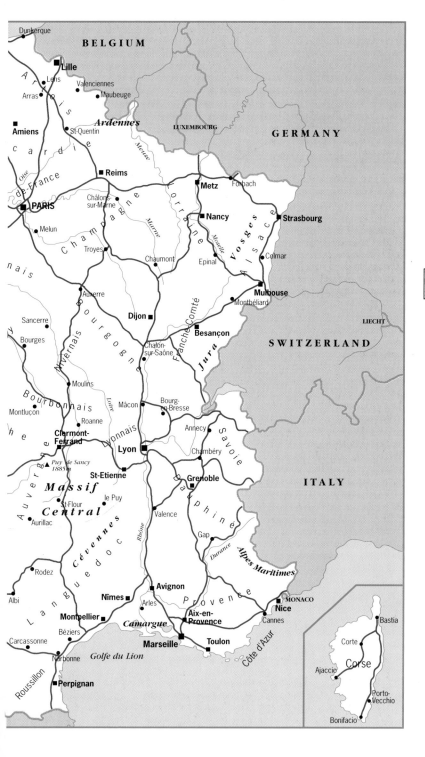

■ **Unruly, rebellious, the French nature is such that their revolutions and uprisings come and go as often as their governments. Over the past two centuries France has been ruled by about a dozen constitutions; political stability is only a recent phenomenon, introduced by de Gaulle with the Fifth Republic and relayed by the quiet strength of Mitterrand. ...■**

12

Monarchies, republics and empires have all had their turn over the past 150 years, interrupted by the traumatic four-year German occupation during World War II. Yet today France is regarded as one of the most powerful Western democracies, and with European unity becoming a reality, her influence is spreading.

Who governs? Far from being a mere figurehead, the French president in the Fifth Republic has considerable powers. Head of the army, responsible for nuclear force, nominator of the prime minister, he can call referendums or dissolve Parliament. Strangely aloof in the gilded cage of the Elysée Palace, he is not allowed to set foot in the National Assembly and is only answerable to the **Conseil Constitutionnel**, an independent elected body that judges the validity of every law passed and guarantees the Rights of Man. The prime minister, who leads a Council of Ministers, answers to the **National Assembly** (lower house) and **Senate** (upper house), which together make up the body of Parliament.

Elected for seven years, the president's mandate can adversely cross the fortunes of Parliament, whose deputies are elected every five years. Twice during the last decade (1986 and again in 1993) the Socialist Party's popularity has slumped, resulting in periods of 'cohabitation' between a Socialist President and a right-wing Prime Minister.

The General If the French president's powers are seen as top-heavy, it is thanks to Charles de Gaulle, who formulated the constitution in 1958 after the Algerian War of Independence had wrought havoc in French political life. Long periods in power are always dangerous, and the inimitable figure of *Le Général* was eventually driven out by the uprisings and strikes of 1968. Times have changed and France has since moved resolutely into the high-technological age, adroitly steered since 1981 by the sphinxlike Mitterrand. Yet even his popularity has waned. His wings are now clipped by a Gaullist majority in Parliament and a center-right Prime Minister, Edouard Balladur.

Many worlds make up the Republic: a rural idyll near Chartres

■ **Of all Western European countries, France has undergone possibly the most radical social transformations since the 1950s.** Previously an agriculturally based society and economy, slowly undergoing industrialization, it had a highly intellectualized, cultivated middle class as its top stratum. The nobility had all but disappeared with the Revolution, but certain of their values had been adopted by the haute bourgeoisie, one of which was an abhorrence of commercialism. This left the field wide open for the rise of the petit bourgeoisie. ...■

Property-owning, relatively well educated, set in their ways, the petit bourgeoisie were also xenophobic, proud of their regional identity and suspicious of intrusion from the centralized government or beyond. Since the 1950s rural areas have lost both the lower middle classes and the land-working peasantry to the big cities: Today only 5 percent are employed in agriculture (before the war, the figure was 33 percent). Moving into the high rises of the suburbs like over 80 percent of the population, they have renounced their historic individualism and become wage earners. Highly conformist, they have values that are materialistic and centered around the family unit.

Religion and morality Traditionally and still nominally a Catholic nation, France separated the church from the state in 1905. Today maybe 14 percent of the population are churchgoers, and religion is no longer a burning issue. Yet the moral character of the nation remains Catholic and sensual.

Ever pleasure-loving, the French were as influenced by the swinging '60s as the rest of the world. Although women only obtained the vote in 1946, their movement had its effect, legalizing the Pill and, much later, abortion. Two-thirds of women now work and many hold key posts in government and business (despite Edith Cresson's unhappy spell as Prime Minister from 1990). Yet, unlike American and British feminists, they cling to a feminine image while adroitly manipulating a still male-dominated society. Diane de Poitiers, Madame de Pompadour, Marie-Antoinette, Josephine—the tradition is long.

French morality is very much an individual's private business. The whole nation is often aware that a public figure has a mistress—but who cares? *Everyone because it's wrong & evil*

Only 5 percent now work the land *I'm sure there's many more*

Whoever wrote this is not a Christian

<< Over 47 million French people belong to the Roman Catholic Church. Other denominations include Protestants (950,000), Jews (700,000) and over 3 million Muslims, many of whom live in Marseille. >>

■ The tapestry of France's population, which has always included regional identities (Bretons, Corsicans, Alsatians) is becoming increasingly rich. Xenophobia and racism have come to the fore, as the immigration issue is tossed to and fro by political parties, each trying to win maximum electoral support. The 1990 census recorded a foreign population of 3.58 million (out of a total of 56.6 million), which does not include 1.5 million with French nationality and countless illegal immigrants. Well over 10 percent of the French population is of foreign origin—a proportion that demands attention. ...■

As elsewhere in Europe, immigrants were brought in from former colonies after World War II to cope with unwanted low-paying jobs. Joined by Portuguese, Italians and Spaniards, the main colonial influx came from the Maghreb: Algeria, Tunisia and Morocco. Lesser numbers arrived from central and West Africa, while French citizens from the DOM-TOM (overseas *départements* in the Caribbean and Pacific) also left their shores searching for work. The 1960s suburban *bidonvilles* of cheap prefabs were soon replaced by unplanned high rises, which in their turn became immigrant ghettos.

Racism Today the situation has hardly improved, despite various government attempts to rectify an incendiary situation. Politicians of every party try to divert support from Le Pen and his overtly racist tirades, via Chirac's bungled sympathy for those "driven crazy" by their immigrant neighbours, or via Edith Cresson, as the then Socialist prime minister, talking of the need to "fly planeloads home." Rising unemployment has sharply exacerbated French xenophobia, and

<< Of the 5 million or so children of immigrants, 4.2 million are French nationals. >>

"accidental" deaths or gang attacks on immigrant teenagers are on the increase.

No man's land Never socially welcome, naturalized French Algerians now find themselves completely stranded between two cultures. Immigrant women, more than men, suffer from restrictive Muslim laws that separate them from French society.

<< In October 1989, a French headmaster banned three Muslim schoolgirls from class because they insisted on wearing their scarfs. The incident developed into a major political confrontation. >>

However, all is not negative. A new youth movement, **SOS Racisme**, started in the 1980s and led by the dynamic Harlem Désir, has become a respected voice on immigrant issues. As support for the extreme right party, the Front National, runs as high as 30 percent in some regions (particularly in the south), immigrants feel understandably threatened, and SOS Racisme has created a forceful lobby. In the 1980s, the movement was so strong that young French people could be seen wearing badges in the shape of a human hand, inscribed with

Touche pas mon pote ("Hands off my friend"). Young Algerians born in France are also forging a new identity, calling themselves *les beurs* and successfully creating their own alternative music.

Jewish communities Although France's oldest immigrant group, the Jewish population, has played a major role in French culture and politics over the last two centuries, it too suffers from racism. About 700,000 Jews (the largest community in Europe) originated from central Europe, and they were joined during the 1960s by an influx into France of Sephardic Jews from North Africa.

As well as revitalizing the Jewish community, the Sephardim have underlined its distinct identity. The sense of separation from "mainstream" French history is

<< After a government commission noted in March 1990, that racism was on the increase Prime Minister Rocard asked that all political parties meet up to fight "this threat to our national heritage." >>

heightened by the memory of the deportation of over 117,000 Jews to concentration camps during World War II.

The American factor Until the late 1960s the French were at odds about the Americans, their insidious influence on French and world culture and their economic dominance. Tourists were laughed at and brash commercialism held in contempt. Yet the French secretly admired many of their commercial and cultural inventions (media styles, Westerns, rock and roll, fast food). However much French presidents (Mitterrand included) may rant about the spread of American cultural hegemony and support the Académie Française in its unyielding crusade to keep all words pure French, much of the U.S. influence is welcomed.

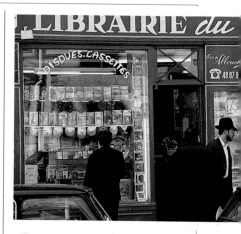

The well-known rue des Rosiers, in Le Marais, Paris...

<< One of the great marketing successes in recent years has been a clothes and accessories company selling goods closely modeled on American army-surplus styles—for 10 times the price. >>

With their newly acquired self-respect and high-tech society, the French are ready to accept the "winners"—whether foreign and speaking a different language or not—but not always those who are regarded as society's losers.

...is the heart of the city's lively Jewish quarter and is packed with Mediterranean-style restaurants and specialty shops

15

■ **For France, the 1980s was a decade of economic progress by leaps and bounds, reaping rewards from the near past and establishing a new, high-profile identity. State controls and centralized planning proved hard to maintain in the complexities of this newly wealthy society, despite the fact that the decade kicked off with a spate of nationalizations and rigorous controls. ...■**

Yet the face of both society and the economy was transformed, bringing a newfound prosperity on most levels. Recession (*la crise*) has since hit, but seems unlikely to bite as deeply as elsewhere.

It is hard to remember that the Socialist government's first steps in 1981 included controlling credit allocations, wage increases, exchange and prices. Furthermore, the strings of industrial strategy were still tightly held by central government, and nationalization steamed ahead. Countless banks and mega-industries were taken over, and the state share of industrial production rose from 15 percent to 30 percent virtually overnight.

Today France is the fifth industrial power of the West, and its per capita income for 1991 stood at $18,100 (compared with $20,060 in the United States, $23,400 in Japan and $15,649 in the United Kingdom). At just over 2 percent, the inflation rate is the lowest in the industrialized world and growth is respectable, but unemployment matches that of other European countries at more than 10 percent.

Nor can the gilded face of France conceal a widening rift between rich and poor: French workers on the bottom rung have seen hardly any change in their spending power over the last decade, whereas the top quarter in the table have seen a 20 percent increase. The compulsory minimum wage stands at 55 percent of the average wage, but as social security taxes are unenticingly high, the lowest-paid workers often find themselves paid *au noir* (off the books) and well below the minimum wage.

Reversed policy But where has this surprising upturn in wealth come from? After Mitterrand's initial steps, mentioned above, a *volte face* took place, leading to fiscal and monetary rigor, tax reductions, some privatizations (under Chirac's two-year government) and, above all, much financial deregulation. Further boosts were given by locking the French franc to the deutsche mark, and by the falling oil prices of the mid-1980s.

Not only that: A new generation of entrepreneurial French managers also appeared—a contrast to the old elitist breed of the *Grandes Ecoles*—and modern high-tech industries benefited as much from government aid as from real market effectiveness.

Future strategies Known today as much for the TGV, Minitel, Ariane and Concorde as for camembert and Château Margaux, France has caught up with a vengeance to the 20th century and seems set to dominate the next within the European context. Moving to the forefront of modern technology—whether fast-breeder nuclear reactors or offshore oil techniques—it has become a pacesetter in Europe.

Telecommunications, transportation, biotechnology and aerospace are fields where French know-how is recognized, although there is often a chasm between the world of pure research and its industrial applications.

Following the American example, French firms have invested heavily overseas. **St-Gobain** has factories in over a dozen countries, while **Renault, Peugeot, Thomson-Brandt** and **Michelin** all have a strong overseas presence. In the 1980s the foreign trade deficit was reduced by three-quarters, much thanks to the efforts of the armaments industry (**Dassault, Matra**), which accounts

A nuclear power station at Civaux. Nuclear power now provides most of the energy that is required in France

for a revenue of 25 billion francs annually (its influence often reflected in French foreign policy), and to France's growing self-sufficiency in energy.

New energy For years France depended on coal, gas, hydro-electricity and imported oil. Between 1960 and 1973, oil imports quadrupled, and when the oil crisis hit, it was importing nearly 75 percent of its energy needs. Since then, homegrown nuclear power has taken over and now accounts for three-quarters of national electricity requirements. Curiously, despite the ominous presence of nearly 50 nuclear power stations dotted over the country, there is little public outcry at this dependence. Even after Chernobyl (when French authorities solemnly declared that the radioactive cloud dispersed at the French border), 51 percent of the population remained in favor of developing nuclear energy. Somehow, the EDF (French electricity board) public relations department convinces the public that French reactors are more sophisticated and less prone to accidents. Time will tell whether they are right.

> << Visitors to France are contributing to France's greatest industry – tourism – which in a decade has tripled to represent an income of over 57 billion francs a year. >>

■ **It was Christian Dior's New Look that set the tone for postwar Paris's fashion hegemony:** Women all over the world tossed away the masculine, practical clothes that had dominated the war years and bowed to Dior's new feminine style. Despite repeated offensives from Milan, New York, London and Tokyo, high French style still maintains a monopoly on the successful marketing of thousands of signed accessories—the bread and butter of every top couturier. ...■

Twenty-one fashion houses make up the Chamber of Parisian Couture. But for many couturiers, their collections are simply a necessary public relations parade, all the better to sell their perfume. For your more average punter, life is far from the gilded chairs surrounding the catwalks. Luckily, another stratum of high fashion designers was formalized in 1974 to keep up with the growing rejuvenation of the fashion industry. Much influenced by England's Biba and Mary Quant, the new group of 24 members was labeled *créatures de mode* and now includes **Chloë, Kenzo, Montana, Gaultier, Mugler, Azzedine Alaïa, Cerruti**, names whose fame is often greater than that of the more obscure couturiers (ever heard of Lecoanet Hemant?). Wilder, racier, younger, the fashion creators' style can be outrageous, but when their twice-yearly collections are presented in the Cour Carrée of the Louvre (now in a specially designed space beneath the pyramid), Parisian hotels are taken by force.

Mixed influence As in every other field, the French shrewdness in realizing the scope and power of fashion extends to the acceptance of talented foreigners into their midst. Among the *grands couturiers* are four Italians, one Spaniard, one Japanese and one Norwegian. The fashion creators include the Japanese **Kenzo**, the influential Tunisian **Alaïa**, several Italians and even an American, **Patrick Kelly**. Strict rules govern production and marketing, and only those with a strong businessperson behind them succeed. **Yves St-Laurent** would never have survived without the astute Pierre Bergé, nor **Dior** without the textile giant, Boussac.

In total the prestigious French fashion industry generates an annual turnover of around 24 billion francs, though the number of regular *haute couture* customers is estimated at only 2,000 worldwide. Skilled craftspeople dedicated to the creation of luxury can only be found in Paris. But as their ages advance, parallel with those of the couturiers, fewer young people replace them in a laborious and traditional field.

Cut of the cloth The rest of French fashion is heavily dependent on

A glimpse of Parisian style, worn off the catwalk

impetus and inspiration from the upper echelons. No designer can exist outside Paris, but textile manufacturers are scattered all over the country. Much of French elegance depends on fine quality fabrics, and the "backward" French textile industry specialized for years in producing small runs of divine, costly cloths. **Lyon** was until recently the center of the silk industry. Inventive weaving techniques were part of the French prowess.

However chic the average Frenchman or -woman seems to be, much of his or her style emanates from a high degree of self-confidence. Head high, a good strut, and over half an hour a day spent on a careful toilette—the

<< The sturdy denim actually originated in Nîmes (hence the name de Nîmes). Today Nîmes is ruled by the fashion industry of Cacharel, and Hong Kong seems to supply the rest. **>>**

result is assured. Trying to keep up with the latest trends is an expensive affair, but most people manage to acquire the latest accessories. It is this innate sense of what is suitable and an eternal desire to seduce that ensure an impeccable turnout.

Good to look at, but it might break the budget: stylish display in the Boutique Christian Dior

■ "France is the most brilliant and dangerous nation in Europe, best suited to become in turn an object of admiration, hatred, pity, terror, but never of indifference." The words were those of Alexis de Tocqueville and the period was the 19th century, but the thought is still relevant today. This nation spawns thinkers from generation to generation, most of whom end up in Paris and on the Left Bank. Joined by artists, film directors and diverse literati, they should be providing some hot discussion toward the end of the millennium...but do they? ...■

Ever fashion-conscious, the French are drawn to new abstract ideas like moths to flames; the national passion for debate starts at school, where verbal dexterity is encouraged. Postwar thought was governed by existentialism, with **Camus** and above all the rolling-eyed

Shakespeare and Company: English words for sale in the Latin Quarter of Paris

Sartre as gods. Every intellectual was strongly influenced by their disenchanted voices and expressions of man's freedom to choose his destiny. But by the late 1960s a new approach began to take over, broadly called structuralism, bringing to the fore theorists such as **Barthes**, **Foucault**, **Lacan** and **Lévi-Strauss**, all of whom rejected the bourgeois view of history and saw man as the prisoner of a determined system. Relaying this rationalist approach

today are philosophers such as **Derrida**, **Deleuze** and **Lyotard**, who explore the concept of post-structuralism but remain well beyond the bounds of general understanding and concerns.

Mental hiatus Apart from the *nouveaux philosophes* such as **Glucksmann** and **Bernard-Henri Lévy** in the late 1970s, no new figures have appeared. Thus in the 1990s there is a gaping intellectual void, linked with general mental apathy and the gradual erosion of left-wing ideology. One colorful eccentric, **Jean-Edern Hallier**, still plays a provocative role, organizing his own kidnapping and even publishing his own satirical newspaper, *L'Idiot*, but he is hardly taken seriously. Apparently the fires of intellectual thought are hard to keep burning when a Socialist government is in power and a world economic crisis monopolizes attention. Disillusionment spreads as social problems increase.

<< The greatest advance in the literary world has come via TV, hardly France's pride and joy. "Apostrophes," reigned over by a genial Bernard Pivot, influenced public book taste for over 15 years, creating best-sellers and introducing reserved intellectuals to the general public. >>

Literary low The world of literature has followed a similar pattern. The famous old literary reviews, through which you could hear the rattle of gunfire between intellectuals, have given way to an epoch of fact-based news magazines. Authors with the universal appeal of Proust, Gide or Sartre have not been replaced, and the exponents of the *nouveau roman* of the 1960s have virtually retired from the stage—Marguerite Duras being a notable exception. Publishing is monopolized by three major companies that also control the juries of the main literary prizes, while their editors nearly all hang out with the critics at Lipp or La Closérie.

Cinema is still going strong and channels much of French creative talent. Since Louis Lumière directed the first films ever made in the 1890s, the French capital has maintained a monopoly on a specific genre: Poetic, intimate, intelligent and sensitive, the films focus on human relations and life. Although the heyday of a recognizable style such as the 1960s Nouvelle Vague is over, the *cinéma d'auteur* still maintains a monopoly. Godard, Chabrol, Truffaut, Rohmer, Resnais and Malle all left their indelible stamp, while one of the most engaging directors of more popular films was the comic genius Jacques Tati. More recently, Beineix (*Diva, Betty Blue*), Besson (*Subway*) and Bérri (*Jean de Florette*) have hit cinematic headlines. On screen, Gérard

Depardieu and Catherine Deneuve are among the most widely recognized French stars. Benefiting from substantial state subsidy, French cinema retains a strongly Gallic flavor and it is still the third-largest producer in the world.

Cinema is still big business

Art in crisis The same thing cannot be said for art. After dominating the world for 40 years, Paris lost to New York when World War II broke out. Since then, the hoped-for comeback has never materialized, despite public interest and government backing. Galleries and museums carpet the country, but there is a crisis of creativity and few contemporary French artists have achieved world renown. **Buren? César? Boltanski? Garouste?** Although big at home, they contribute little to the advance of 20th-century world art. It is almost as if the French are waiting for the 21st century.

■ **French cuisine in all its glory epitomizes the complexities of the national character. Science, sensuality and creativity combine to produce, at its best, food fit for ~~the gods~~. Every region of France has its specialties, proudly refined from generation to generation, and in the 1990s these are being enthusiastically revived by chefs weary of the two-carrot nouvelle cuisine. ...■**

Twenty years of invasion by a lighter, fresher diet has left its mark: The nouvelle cuisine school has been assimilated into a new approach to cooking that puts as much emphasis on nutrition as on inventive flavors and presentation.

Quick cuisine Don't believe that every French family sits down to a gastronomic orgy every evening. The advance of the 20th century has brought with it a rushed lifestyle, and the French have adopted convenience foods like every other Western nation. Food is no longer a priority.

Over the last decade fast-food joints have invaded every town center, and the young, ever attracted to the

French bread comes in many delicious varieties

American way of life, find these budget victuals the ultimate in trendiness. Old habits of lengthy, elaborate preparation do survive, above all in rural working-class homes, whereas the more monied urban strata, if not dining in a restaurant, are more likely to knock together some pasta and a salad than indulge in preparing a *blanquette de veau.*

Dinner talk Food and wine are still serious topics, talked about at length and with at least 15 national magazines devoted to them. Diners are choosy about the restaurants they frequent, whether the world-famous havens of top chefs like **Joël Robuchon, Paul Bocuse, Guy Savoy** and **Michel Guérard** or a neighborhood bistro.

Foreign influences have made themselves felt, too, and the recent assimilation of nouvelle cuisine has led to a boom in Japanese restaurants, and avant-garde treatments of seaweed. A new consciousness of ecology and dietetics in the '60s and '70s nurtured Michel Guérard's famous *cuisine minceur,* but countless Japanese apprentice chefs in the top Paris kitchens emphasized texture and meticulous presentation. The largest cookery school in the world is now in Tokyo.

<< Only 30 years ago the French spent an average of 40 percent of their household budget on food; today it is half as much. >>

Foodies' news However easily this new style of cooking was adopted by France's most famous chefs, it would not have been so widespread without the influential gastronomic magazine and guide, the *Gault Millau*, launched in the 1970s. Daring to confront on its own terrain the long-standing little red book, the Michelin guide, the innovative *Gault Millau* preached and praised an innovative approach, setting the pace with its own journalistic style. Chefs were encouraged to sweep away old rituals and prejudices, take risks, marry the unmarriageable; and thus a new generation of diners was brought up on flourless sauces, fish, delicate vegetable mousses and harmoniously arranged plates. Classic table service disappeared and a more balanced, nutritious gastronomy shifted into top gear.

Good old days Some may look back with nostalgia to the last days of *grande cuisine*, which really ended with World War I. But who has time these days to sit down to a five-hour, 16-course lunch? The line of illustrious historic chefs is long, from **Taillevent** (who wrote the first treatise on cooking) to **Beauvilliers** and the master of modern French cooking, **Carême**, author of five volumes about 19th-century French cuisine. Today's masters can no longer doggedly follow tradition: They must invent and personalize, while returning to products and techniques born from regional cooking. Forgotten are the *turbot aux kiwi* or the *rouget à la framboise*.

Home ground Paul Bocuse, unofficial French gastronomic ambassador, is himself descended from a line of chefs going back to 1765. After the necessary apprenticeship at Paris's top restaurants, he returned to Collonges-au-Mont-d'Or just outside Lyon, where diners still lap up his black truffle soup. France's gastronomic capital, Lyon, has the most varied supply of fresh produce at its doorstep. As the French couturier uses the richest fabrics, so the chef's priority is to show off the fresh, flavorsome, perfectly ripe ingredients of his region.

La nouvelle cuisine de terroir, led by **Roger Vergé**, **Jacques Maximin**, **André Daguin** or **Lucien Vanal,** is to be found scattered all over this varied country, and even if your purse doesn't stretch to the greats, there's little to beat a traditional regional dish in a family restaurant.

Eating at a bistro: not necessarily a very private affair

Work and Play

■ **Although their priorities apparently lie firmly in the camp of pleasure and leisure, the French are actually a hardworking nation. Since the working week is officially 39 hours long, and there are five weeks' vacation a year (the longest in Europe), as well as 11 days of public holidays, this can be hard to believe. Yet executives often start work at 8 am and finish 12 hours later. Weekends have therefore become sacrosanct, and are often spent at a weekend home, and holidays are calculated to the minute. "Work hard, play hard" seems to be the maxim. ...■**

It was not until the 1936 Front Populaire government that social reforms were made, stipulating two weeks' annual paid vacation, a 40-hour week and compulsory collective bargaining. The new paid vacations changed the face of the nation and, when extended after the war, led to that familiar sight of entire cities closed down for the month of August, the main roads being taken by storm on the 1st and 31st. Recent changes in school vacations and state encouragement have now spread vacations over July and August, and the traditional month duration is often reduced to allow skiing holidays in February and/or a break over the Christmas period. Further short vacations are astutely concocted by bridging a public holiday with a nearby weekend (*le pont*). This means that the month of May, which carries three separate holidays, becomes a complete wipeout in terms of economic productivity .

Homely holidays Where do all these itchy-footed French go? They are never particularly adventurous, and 48 percent don't actually leave home. Only a small percentage crosses the border to Spain or Italy. One vacation in six is taken abroad, with distant exotic destinations becoming popular with the more affluent. Begun in 1950, the **Club Méditerranée** vacation villages have been influential in opening up destinations where previously no Frenchman dared to tread. This formula of controlled individualism suits French needs: Once a year they let their hair down in some exotic spot without running any risks. And more recently the charter company **Nouvelles Frontières** has successfully herded groups of middle-class people around Indian temples or paddled them up the Amazon.

Sports vacations are increasingly popular. Bicycling has always been a French sport, followed closely by rugby (in the southwest) and soccer. But along with the rise in leisure time and spending power, the French are taking up tennis—inspired by idols **Guy Forget** and **Henri Leconte**—horseback riding, sailing, golf and the ubiquitous urban gyms. Previously their only national sport had been *boules,* and leisure time was spent mainly over long voluble meals, in dance halls, at the cinema or chatting at a local café.

Boules is now more a retirement sport, cinemas are losing audiences to TV, nightclubs attract only a very young urban crowd, and even cafés are losing their clientele and being forced to close.

Le weekend Conversely, with one family in nine owning a weekend home, the French are rediscovering the joys of nature and returning to their rural origins. *Bricolage* (do-it-yourself) has become a national pastime, and bucolic villages resound to the happy sound of thousands of hammers and drills every Saturday and Sunday.

They are not likely to spend Sunday morning at mass: Even before World War II the French were losing their faith and seeing Catholicism merely as a form of social conformism. Only 14 percent of the population regularly attends mass (10 percent in Paris), and half the newborns are baptized. But spirituality has not completely gone out the window: 65 percent still claim to believe in God.

Following the rules Back at work the French are, on the whole, a law-abiding lot. Strikes are rarely more than one-day token gestures of discontent, and the number of days lost annually is minimal compared with other countries. Since the unrest of 1968, when 9 million went on strike, labor relations have become less rigid and workers have more rights. Union membership is

Weekend leisure: punting on the Charente River

low—less than 15 percent of the work force (compared with 70 percent in Sweden and 40 percent in Britain); this is shared by the Communist-dominated **CGT** and the Socialist-inclined **CFDT**, which has an ongoing dialogue with the government. **FO** (Force Ouvrière) represents the white-collar workers, but most voluble of all is the **FNSEA**, the farmers' union. Despite its often extravagant demands, this union has adroitly managed to draw the country's attention to an endangered species, threatened by the transformation of French society.

■ **After two postwar decades of frenetic growth and mindless modernization, France has finally developed a more rational approach to town planning and, above all, consideration for the quality of life. Since the 1970s numerous town councils have switched their emphasis away from building monolithic housing developments toward concentrating on plans of a more ecological or aesthetic nature. ...■**

With more power in the hands of local authorities, architecture and urbanism have become political status symbols: Throughout France towns vie with one another to design the most avant-garde pedestrian zone, museum or conference hall, or to carry out the most ambitious program of restoration.

Changing conditions Somewhat belatedly, the French have recognized the importance of welfare and leisure amenities and the dangers of high-rise ghettos. Earlier this century millions moved from the land to embrace city life, but very often their housing conditions were basic: In 1954, for example, only 10 percent of French homes had a bath or shower and only 27 percent had flushing toilets. But a crash program of public housing (called HLM, *habitation à loyer modéré*), which by 1975 peaked at 550,000 homes a year, soon encircled every French town with modern apartment buildings. Today basic home comforts are available in nearly all houses: By the mid-1980s only 12 percent were without a bath or shower and 10 percent without a toilet. Public housing now looks to individual *pavillons* springing up on the outskirts of every town, and to more intelligent inner-city projects.

Changing tastes Despite radical building programs developed by every French president since de Gaulle, it was really in the 1980s under President Mitterrand that public awareness of architecture blossomed. Visitors to Paris are unlikely to miss seeing what has become the granddaddy of them all: the controversial Centre Pompidou, commonly known as **Beaubourg**. Built in 1977, its polychromatic high-tech design, rising out of the heart of historic Paris, upset many. But it set the tone for a new generation of architects and a new attitude toward public building, and today attracts more visitors than the Eiffel Tower.

Big ideas At his election Mitterrand followed Pompidou's example and immediately announced plans for his *grands projets* while completing others initiated by Giscard d'Estaing (**La Villette**, **Musée d'Orsay**). As Paris became a building site and a new billion-franc project hit the drawing board daily, the French realized that modern architecture was not just a rectangular block. It was becoming more subtle, as were its implications. Accused of harboring a Louis XIV complex, Mitterrand commissioned monument after prestigious monument, while his arch rival, Jacques Chirac, the Gaullist mayor of Paris elected in 1977, played a vanguard action with less visible urban projects, many of which are finally bringing some green to the city. As a result of this rivalry, Paris has become a window of contemporary design—and not only by French architects. La Grande Arche looms in the west; the four pinnacles of Dominique Perrault's **Bibliothèque de France**, rise over eastern Paris. At the same time, behind the scenes, slum clearance continues, historic districts like Le Marais are renovated, rents rise and

Paris becomes an increasingly bourgeois city. But will this activity turn it into a stultified museum and strip it of its essential local color?

Regional style Not slow to follow the capital's example, the provinces have also scrubbed their facades and invested heavily in presenting a modernized image to Europe. Since the autonomy of the 22 regions was increased in the 1980s, their self-consciousness and individual ambitions have rocketed. Obsessed by city status, towns such as **Montpellier**, **Saint-Etienne** or **Bordeaux** all compete in attracting foreign investment and in exporting a contemporary image. Every city seems to have its *technopole*, a concentration of high-tech skills, or its international airport, while modern art museums mushroom. Apart from massive rebuilding of city centers,

<< The most extraordinary city project is that of Montpellier, where Catalan architect Ricardo Bofill has designed neoclassical medium-rent public housing that is, in the local mayor's words, "the Rome of tomorrow." >>

many places were spruced up for the 1993 European ball. **Rouen** has been superbly restored, although the pedestrian precinct is ever-present, while the medieval streets of **Rodez** are gentrified to an almost absurd degree. And this is the danger: If renovation and rebuilding continue at such a rate, France risks losing much of its unique character for the sake of a bland, pristine Euro-face.

La Géode, the spherical cinema in the Parc de la Villette, Paris

Paris vs Regions

■ **If Napoleon, let alone Louis XIV's minister Colbert, could see the political structure of France today, he would certainly roll in his grave. Decentralization gathers momentum and devolution is a reality in a nation that was once the most centralized of all. This policy really came to fruit in 1982 when the administration of Mitterrand granted far greater autonomy to the restructured 22 regions, further increased by direct elections for regional councils in 1986. At the same time, the reorganization cut across traditional and cultural boundaries, causing bitter controversy. ...■**

City scene Today, France has a handful of burgeoning cities that are at last able to stand on a par with European equivalents, from Barcelona to Turin, while at the same time containing any separatist sentiments.

The French provinces were long seen as sleepy, narrow-minded, bourgeois backwaters where only the priest or boule-playing mayor had any importance. Inhabitants of any intelligence were destined for instant intellectual death in what was known as *le désert français*. Anyone with ambitions or initiative headed for Paris, leaving the provinces to Madame Bovary and company.

Industrial magnets This rural exodus continued until the last war and well into the 1950s, leaving behind an already underpopulated countryside, as people flocked to the growing industrial centers and, of course, to the cultural and economic metropolis of Paris. But the tide had started to turn under German occupation, when the government was moved to Vichy, and the southern provinces, cut off from the north, were forced to act for themselves. This was also the chance for the provincial press to play a role in daily life.

Postwar policies concentrated on catching up, modernizing, urbanizing and gearing up a backward industrialization. Communication was one of France's greatest drawbacks: even in 1970 it had fewer telephone lines than Greece and half as many as the United Kingdom or Germany. Tunnels (Mont Blanc), bridges, motorways and railways were built, which opened up new investment possibilities and increased mobility. Now nearly all French households have a phone, the railway system is one of the best and most technologically advanced in the world, and motorways, though costly for the user, crisscross the former *désert*.

About face Thus the pattern has changed and even Parisians are

A new look: modern civic buildings in Carnac

<< In 1992 Strasbourg set the example of the new clean city living by creating a car-free center — certainly a more attractive prospect than the centers of industrialized Lille or St-Etienne. **>>**

moving to the provinces. Increasing inner-city congestion, urban tensions, pollution and a high cost of living have lessened the appeal of the big centers. Looking for a calmer, less neurotic rhythm and more living space at a lower cost, the French are transferring to Montpellier, Lyon, Bordeaux, Toulouse or Grenoble. Government plans initially showed the way for the postwar shift: Atomic and space research centers were set up in Brittany, mass tourist projects in the Languedoc, Aérospatiale developed the Concorde and Airbus in Toulouse, and France's own silicon valley, Sophia Antipolis, grew up out of the lavender fields of Provence. Aid often came from the government agency **DATAR**, created in 1963 to stimulate new economic ventures and help with the infrastructure for these emerging regions. Today its concerns are directed more to patching up the problems of aging industries (steel, textiles, mining), usually in the north, where unemployment runs high.

Living options However rich the economic life of a town may be, few people want to live there without a reasonable choice of leisure activities. Here, again, the map of France has been radically transformed, first with Malraux's famous **Maison de la Culture** in the 1960s and more recently with a flood of prestigious new museums, concert halls and cultural centers. Jack Lang, Socialist minister of culture throughout most of the 1980s, stimulated local decision making and created specialized schools and major arts festivals throughout the country. **Montpellier** is now seen as the center for contemporary dance, **Arles** and **Lyons** for photography, **Montbéliard** for video, **Grenoble** and **Bordeaux** for contemporary art. Yet old habits die hard: Every artist, however well received in the provinces, *has* to come to Paris for consecration.

Regional rediscovery

Psychologically, medium- and large-size towns have thrown off the cloak of central state influence and in some cases their populations have tripled over the last 30 years. As the government transfers entire departments of civil servants to the regions and exorbitant rents in Paris create a surfeit of empty office space, the relationship between capital and regions continues to adjust.

ANGLIAE

PARS

London

Douer

Mia

Duyncke

Calis

Pican

die

Roan

on
Hano

Caez

Paris

Fra

nce

S. Malo

Alencon

Vendosme

bret aigne

Mans

Loir

un nes An

Tours

Orleans

ou

Loire flu

Angiers

Bourges

Nantes

Poictou

Poictiers

Molin

Rochelle

Limog

Saintes

Clermo

Limolin

Bordeaulx

Guien

Agen

R

rcacon

ne

Cahors

Montau
ban

Monreal

Baiona

Toulouse

Carcas
sone

Gualcoigne

Narb

■ **The first evidence of human life in the area now known as France goes back nearly ~~half a million~~ years, to a time when the ancestors of modern man left traces of their occupation in the form of stone tools and weapons. Eventually, these people were replaced by the first ~~Neanderthals~~. ...■**

Neanderthals were skilled hunters and workers in stone, but they were unsophisticated in comparison with the next wave of migrants, known now as Cro-Magnon people after the cave where a skeleton was excavated in 1868. The subtlety of Cro-Magnon culture is revealed in the still vibrant wall paintings of the Lascaux caves in Dordogne. This society was gradually subsumed into an age known as Mesolithic, when the nomadic way of life probably gave way to permanent settlements. Some time around 4500 BC, men began to grow food rather than gather it, and to enclose and tame animals rather than manage wild herds. All of this was made possible by the cultivation of grains to feed humans and animals all year. This, the Neolithic Revolution, led to the transformation of the landscape into something approaching the one we know today. The most obvious legacies of the Neolithic era are the complex ceremonial sites such as Carnac, in Brittany.

These monuments were developed by Bronze Age settlers, who introduced metalworking skills. The Neolithic and Bronze Ages spanned nearly 5,000 years, and much of that time was peaceful: the bronze weapons that remain may only have been ceremonial.

The disruption of this peaceful society seems to coincide with the arrival of Celtic tribes. Their culture and ironworking skills mark the beginning of a much more fully documented period of history – due largely to the written records of a new wave of invaders: the Romans.

Roman vs. Gaul The Celts became known as Gauls to the Romans, who set out to halt their advance into

31

<< A famous Gallic uprising against the Romans was led by the chieftain Vercingetorix, who in 52 BC was captured at Alesia and taken to Rome and executed. Caesar came to be both ally and conqueror of the Gauls, at once helping them to defend themselves in their turn against invaders from across the Rhine and enabling Rome to exploit new territory with trade and taxation. >>

Carved megaliths in Gavrinis

northern Italy. In 190 BC, the Romans came to the defense of the then Greek-owned port of Marseille, and advanced to **Narbonne, Aix, Arles** and **Nîmes**. In 58 BC, Julius Caesar finally crushed the Gauls.

■ In 43 bc, the Romans established their central government at Lyon, and trade to the north, with Britain, and to the south, with Spain and Italy, flourished. The new conquerors built stables (Arles), amphitheaters (Nîmes), circuses (in the Latin Quarter in Paris), baths, and aqueducts (Pont du Gard), and founded schools (Autun and Reims), and the whole country was crisscrossed by an efficient network of roads. ...■

The Gauls themselves became increasingly Romanized, benefiting from the new political and economic stability. Many educated Gauls, now speaking a form of Latin, were assimilated into the Roman Empire, and held positions of power within the imperial administration, later being entitled to Roman citizenship.

Christianity It was during the Roman period that Christianity was first introduced into France, from the 2nd century AD. Early Christians were persecuted: The great Saint Denis of Paris was beheaded at **Montmartre** (Martyr's Hill) in AD 262. The turning point came, however, with the conversion of Emperor Constantine in the year AD 312, when Christianity became the official state religion. Priests such as Martin of Tours were then eager to drive out the old pagan ways of the Celts, and many monasteries and churches were founded. By the year AD 500, the church had established itself as a powerful presence alongside the state, and exerted an influence that has continued to the present day.

Tribal invasions From AD 300 onward, the Roman Empire was in decline, and successive emperors were hard pushed to secure Gaul against the incursions of the marauding tribes from Germany. The Romans repeatedly fought back, but when, after 400, the great invasions of the Vandals began, the collapse of the empire was inevitable.
Attila the Hun advanced into eastern France and the Romans withdrew to Orléans, Tours and Bordeaux, so that when Rome itself was sacked and finally overrun in 455, Gaul was abandoned to the conquering tribes of Visigoths, Burgundians, Alemanni and Franks. In 481, Clovis became the first Merovingian king of the Salian Franks, who ruled the area between the Rhine and the Seine, and the foundations were laid of a recognizably modern France.

<< The Vandals overwhelmed the Romans with their brilliant horsemanship; they fought with bow and arrow from horseback – but according to St. Jerome they "could not walk on foot, and once dismounted, count themselves dead." >>

The Roman theater in Orange

■ **During the 500 years of Frankish rule, there was a constant struggle to expand territorial control. The south remained Romanized, with *patricii*, or the local aristocrats, holding most of the land. The walled cities were governed by bishops, and religious schisms showed how skin-deep was Christianity's hold over the population. ...■**

Clovis's own conversion to Christianity and his political marriage to Clotilda, a Burgundian princess, helped to secure Frankish power over a broader area. This power was under the regime of feudalism in which vassals pledged allegiance to their overlords and provided services, taxes and military support in return for protection and benefices. After Clovis, civil strife between warring robber barons was rampant, and successive Merovingian kings, like Dagobert I (628–37), tried in vain to impose law and order. The Frankish kings became *rois fainéants* (do-nothing kings) as power was effectively passed to their administrators, the so-called "mayors of the palace."

The Carolingians In 732, one of these mayors, Charles Martel, usurped royal power and became the first of the Carolingian kings. Martel led forays against the Arabs, the Burgundians, the Aquitanians and the Saxons, and by confiscating lands and giving these out as fiefs to his followers, established a wide influence.

The long-term project of uniting Gaul was virtually realized by Martel's grandson, Charlemagne, who was crowned in Rome by the pope on Christmas Day 800, and became the founder of the Holy Roman Empire, an entity that was to last officially for 1,000 years.

Charlemagne was a great warrior and cunning politician, and it was his own personal energy and frequent ruthlessness that held together a vast amalgam of lands in central and western Europe. His capital at **Aix-la-Chapelle** became the center of a cultural renaissance whose reputation attracted scholars from many lands.

Division of empire The feudal cohesion that Charlemagne imposed on Gaul, with a set of counties and marches, was short-lived. On his death in 808, the empire was divided among his sons, and the western section, Francia, fell prey to the ambitions of neighboring dukes.

Meanwhile, a flourishing civilization had arisen in the Languedoc, around the counts of Toulouse, and Viking Norsemen, or Normans, as they became known, established themselves at Rouen. The Church had also acquired tremendous authority and great wealth, often using its assets to thwart the policies of the kings. A state of aristocratic anarchy prevailed, and only lip service was paid to the sovereignty of the Carolingians.

33

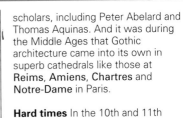

■ In 987, Hugh Capet was anointed king of France, founding a new dynasty of Capetian kings. Like his predecessors, his range of influence was largely confined to the Ile de France, and for some centuries, royal power was relatively limited. The Church, meanwhile, came under pressure to put an end to corruption. The order of Benedictine monks at Cluny, founded in 909, tried to provide a new moral discipline, claiming a direct link to the pope in a bid to sidestep the powerful bishops. ...■

The papacy itself had reformed, and in 1095 Pope Urban II launched the First Crusade to "liberate" ~~Palestine~~ Israel from the domination of the Saracens. The Crusades galvanized thousands of French men and women from all classes in a renewal of faith and devotion, in which princes and kings often participated for a mixture of religious and political purposes. Louis IX (1226–70), later canonized, was himself taken captive in Egypt on a crusading expedition and ransomed at an exorbitant fee.

Age of learning The Church also promoted learning and scholarship in the new schools and universities. The University of Paris was set up around the year 1200, and soon became the intellectual center of Europe, attracting famous teachers and

La Rochelle in 1372: Medieval France was a nation at war

scholars, including Peter Abelard and Thomas Aquinas. And it was during the Middle Ages that Gothic architecture came into its own in superb cathedrals like those at Reims, Amiens, Chartres and Notre-Dame in Paris.

Hard times In the 10th and 11th centuries, although trade and commerce had blossomed, the costs of war at home and abroad forced princes to raise taxes. In the early

<< The Holy Order of the Knights Templar, founded in 1120, had its headquarters in Paris; the Templars' wealth was a coveted prize, and Philip IV brutally suppressed them in 1307 amid appalling torture and execution, seizing their assets, temporarily, for himself. >>

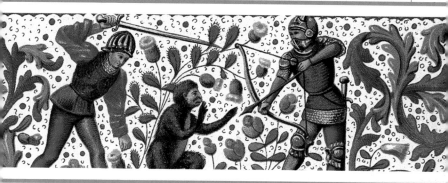

14th century, poor harvests led to famine and disease; meanwhile, a new class of mercenary knights emerged, regularly switching allegiances between lords.

Struggle for supremacy Philip Augustus (1180–1223) consolidated royal power, driving the English out of their Angevin Empire, which had grown up in Aquitania, Brittany, Gascony and Normandy. The king strengthened **Paris** as his capital city and backed the church against the Albigensian heretics (Cathars) in the Languedoc. When, in 1245 under St. Louis, the siege of the hilltop fortress at **Montségur** ended in the burning of hundreds of Cathars, the independence of the south was broken. From 1309 on, the popes were in exile at Avignon, a city under the control of the French king. So the Capetians were looking strong at the start of the 14th century. But in 1328, Charles VI died with no male heir. At first the crown passed to Philip IV of Valois, but soon the young King Edward III of England, a grandson of Philip IV, also laid claim to the throne. This dispute led to the devastating Hundred Years' War.

The Hundred Years' War The war had three main phases. In 1338, Edward seized back lands in Gascony. The English advanced into Poitou, took Caen, and won the historic battle of Crécy in 1346. To add to French misfortunes, the Black Death now swept the land, killing nearly a third of the population and leading in turn to peasant uprisings,

or *jacqueries*. In 1360, the new king, John II, was captured at Poitiers, and the French were forced to cede Aquitania and Calais to the English.

The second phase of the war followed the death of Edward III and his son the Black Prince, when the English position had begun to weaken. In 1415, Henry V returned to defeat the French at **Harfleur** and **Agincourt**, and Aquitania, Normandy, Brittany and Anjou became English territories. Henry married the French king's daughter, but both he and his wife died in 1421, and the quarrel over the throne passed to their infant son, the future Henry VI, and the dauphin, the future Charles VII.

The third phase of the war brought the shepherdess and saint, Joan of Arc, to raise the siege of **Orléans** and help Charles to be crowned in the cathedral at Reims. Soon after this, Joan was captured and burned at the stake in Rouen in 1431, but Charles went on to win decisive victories over the English. When the English withdrew from Normandy in 1453, the Hundred Years' War was finally over.

The aftermath War and disease had shaken the foundations of feudalism. Aided by a civil service drawn from the emerging bourgeoisie, Louis XI was now able to end the factionalism of the Middle Ages. When he died in 1483, Burgundy, Normandy, Brittany, Picardy, Anjou, Provence and Roussillon were all subdued, and France had begun to develop into a modern nation-state.

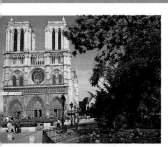

■ The Renaissance was the time of an explosion of tremendous creative energy in the arts, literature, philosophy and science. The city-states of 15th-century Italy had been its birthplace, but the revived knowledge of the ancient peoples and the developing concerns of humanism, together with a new consciousness of exploration and experiment, spread across the whole of Europe. ...■

François I (1515–47) presided over the patronage of the arts in France. Many of the beautiful châteaus of the Loire Valley, like those at **Chambord**, **Chenonceau** and **Azay-le-Rideau**, were built at this time. Art collections and libraries were expanded and artists were attracted to the court, including the Italians **Benvenuto Cellini** and **Leonardo da Vinci**, who spent the last years of his life working in France and is buried at Amboise. Literature also flourished, under a group of poets known as the *Pléiade*; the love poetry of **Ronsard** and **du Bellay** is among the most beautiful in the French language. **Rabelais** wrote his farcical novels *Pantagruel* and *Gargantua* during this period, and the retired mayor of Bordeaux, **Michel de Montaigne**, composed his essays on knowledge and the enigmas of the human condition.

The Wars of Religion François built France into the new system of European diplomacy, and negotiated a set of carefully arranged marriages to check the age-old rivalries with England and the powerful Habsburg dynasty that ruled Spain, the Netherlands and the Holy Roman Empire. The picture became more complicated, however, once the Reformation in Germany gained momentum. When, in 1517, **Martin Luther** was excommunicated, the many German princes took sides in theological debates on trans-substantiation and papal authority—by championing the Protestant cause if, for political reasons, they opposed the Habsburg emperor, Charles V, who was a Catholic Spaniard.

This political dimension was slow to emerge in France because of the tradition of Gallicanism, which meant that the clergy were more directly linked to the king than to the pope. Nevertheless, in 1523, the *Parlement* of Paris seized and burned Luther's books, and, after some hesitation, the king decided that the Lutheran heretics were a threat to be stamped out.

Repression of the Protestant Huguenots remained ineffectual. In 1536, **Jean Calvin** published his *Institutions of the Christian Religion*, and many Frenchmen sought instruction in his teachings in the independent Swiss state of Geneva. Protestant churches continued to spring up throughout France, and in 1560, Charles IX went so far as to issue an amnesty against religious persecution.

However, civil war eventually broke out as the members of the royal household divided between the two faiths in a fight for power. The **prince de Condé** headed the Huguenot Montmorency faction against the **duc de Guise**, who defended the royalist Catholic cause. The war was fought at different levels, with some full-scale military engagements (at Dreux and Jarnac) and a terrorist campaign of political murders (the duc de Guise, the prince de Condé and Henry III were assassinated). But the frequent outbreaks of crowd violence were the most horrifying; on August 24, 1572, thousands of Huguenots were murdered in riots in what became known as the Saint Bartholomew's Day Massacre.

Henry IV Supported by the traditionalist Catholic League, Henry of Navarre became the first Bourbon king (1589–1610). He was an ex-Huguenot turned Catholic, and, with his chief administrator Sully, he tried to restore political and social harmony. In 1598, he issued the Edict of Nantes, which guaranteed the right of worship to the Protestants. Although this helped to heal the wounds of civil strife, Henry was himself assassinated by a Catholic extremist while out one day in his carriage.

The reign of Louis XIII (1610–43) saw the rise to power of the great **Cardinal Richelieu**. Richelieu was a wise and wily statesman, whose strength lay in a dedication to the French national interest. Richelieu set about creating a complex balance

Cardinal Richelieu by Henri Toutin

of power in Europe, negotiating often-secret treaties with different heads of state, playing off the German Protestants against the Catholic Habsburgs during the Thirty Years' War, and contracting alliances via royal marriages, including that of Charles I of England. At home, he helped Louis cultivate the patronage of dukes and princes, overrode the various *parlements* and sent out his *intendants*, or agents of the crown, to collect taxes and manage the fiscal affairs of the state. Richelieu was a prime mover in assuring a strong central government, and did much to resolve the centuries-old antagonism between the nobility and the crown by paving the way for absolute monarchy.

■ **Louis XIV (1643–1715) was France's most glorious and longest-reigning king. Only five years old when he ascended the throne, his first task was to secure his position against *La Fronde*, an alliance of discontented nobles who sought to overthrow him. Louis successfully broke down the opposition, and from 1661 onward he was determined to exercise absolute power. He believed in his God-given right to govern the country and saw the welfare of the state as embodied in his own person: *L'état, c'est moi*, became the motto that characterized the Sun King's attitude. ...■**

Under his rule, France rose to new heights of prosperity and glory. The rise of mercantilism, masterminded by his minister of finance and loyal supporter **Colbert**, saw new industries grow up, and imports from the colonies in Canada, Louisiana (named after the king), and India brought massive wealth to the country. By contrast, however, much of this affluence was squandered by the lavish lifestyle of the royal household and by the wars that Louis waged against his European neighbors.

In the 1670s, construction began on the huge and magnificent palace at Versailles. Versailles became the new seat of the court and a symbol of national unity. Everyone jostled to take up residence there and enjoy the endless round of feasts, balls, and concerts, the elaborate rules of etiquette and social frivolities that Louis staged to divert the aristocratic families from more serious political concerns. Everything good, it seemed, emanated from the Sun King.

Warrior king Louis also headed an impressive war machine, built up by **General Vauban**, which he launched into several ill-fated campaigns. In 1672 Louis declared war on Holland, and in 1685 he revoked the Edict of Nantes. These actions incensed the Europeans. The Germans rose up at the hostility that Louis, a staunch Catholic, had shown toward Protestants; in 1688, William of Orange, himself a Dutch Protestant, became king of England, and soon most of Europe was ranged against France. Yet in 1689 Louis invaded the Rhineland, and many years of war ensued, in which France suffered eventual defeat. Undeterred, Louis sparked the War of the Spanish Succession by insisting that his grandson be settled on the throne of Spain as Philip VI. The Europeans again objected, and after a series of humiliating defeats in the years 1701–13, notably at Blenheim, the French were forced to retreat. The terms of the Treaty of Utrecht involved permanent renunciation of Bourbon claims to rule Spain and the loss of France's main colonies in the Americas.

Age of order Louis's reign saw the rise of classicism, in which order, reason, and elegance were major features. **René Descartes**, in his *Discourse on Method* (1637), had laid the foundations for modern science by emphasizing the importance of rational argument from observable facts. Love of order is reflected in all the arts of the period, whether in the architectural symmetries of Baroque *hôtels* (town mansions) and châteaus, in the design of parks and ornamental gardens, in **Pascal**'s mechanical "computers," or in the harrowing precision and logic of **Racine's** tragedies.

The Enlightenment These trends in science, culture and the life of the mind led, in the 18th century, to the Age of Enlightenment. French philosophers such as **Voltaire**, **Diderot** and **Rousseau** turned their thought to the practical applications of knowledge and the possibilities of social change. The absolutism of the monarchy had grown out of the 1,000-year-old traditions of feudalism, but now its structures were outliving their usefulness. The established *ancien régime* of kings and princes was becoming increasingly alarmed by the spread of revolutionary ideas.

But the storm was brewing. Under **Louis XV** (1715–74), France was brought closer to the brink of chaos. Rivalries between noble families, the

The Sun King: a miniature of Louis XIV, the longest-reigning French king

<< One of the most unpopular of the many taxes in the 17th century was the salt tax, *la gabelle*. In some provinces, where salt was a government monopoly, it was compulsory to buy a fixed amount. >>

corruption of officials, the widespread abuse of privileges, the division between Paris and the provinces, the incompetent management of the economy—all contributed to the widening gap between rich and poor. Taxation was high, famine and squalor were rife across the land, while a privileged minority lived in the lap of luxury. In the early years of the reign of **Louis XVI** (1774–93), food riots were commonplace, the monarchy was bankrupt, the financial and bureaucratic institutions were rickety and ineffectual, and the time was ripe for massive social and political upheaval.

Revolution and Empire

■ In 1789 began one of the most dramatic episodes in France's history. In a last-ditch effort to resolve the country's pressing problems, Louis XVI summoned the Estates General, representing the three states of the nobility, the clergy and "the rest." The Estates had no real political power, and had not convened since 1614, so their negotiations soon got bogged down over questions of procedure. The Third Estate, representing over 95 percent of the 20-odd million people of the country, decided to form a breakaway National Assembly. ...■

One morning, finding the door to the meeting hall inexplicably locked, the Third Estate withdrew to a nearby tennis court and swore an oath not to disperse until they had established a new constitution. The king, in a panic, dismissed them, and in the ensuing unrest, the crowds in Paris, fearing a military crackdown, stormed the prison of the Bastille on July 14.

The Revolution The National Assembly, composed mainly of liberal Girondins and radical Jacobins, issued the Universal Declaration of the Rights of Man. France was divided into a set of administrative departments; feudal duties and hereditary titles were abolished. At first, the king went along with this new order of things, but in June 1791, he foolishly tried to escape.

<< Legend has it that Louis XVI was captured at Varennes because he was recognized from his likeness on a coin. >>

In September 1791, a constitutional monarchy was officially declared, but there was a growing fear that the *émigrés* (exiled aristocrats), helped by European heads of state, were going to invade. To preempt this, France declared war, and won an immediate, astounding victory at Valmy against the Austrians and Prussians.

First Republic The imprisoned Louis could no longer be trusted. A new Convention abolished the monarchy and proclaimed the First Republic. In 1793, Louis was put on trial for treason, convicted and guillotined. Unfortunately, none of this revolutionary activity had really helped to solve the severe domestic problems of food shortages and money. In April 1793, a Committee of Public Safety was created to impose social reforms, ensure law and order and protect the Revolution. A power struggle among the revolutionary leaders led to the Jacobins ousting the Girondins. **Robespierre,** who emerged as virtual dictator, unleashed a Reign of Terror. The Revolution now span out of control and turned into a bloodbath of executions, wiping out thousands of former nobles, clergy and ordinary citizens. Even the original leaders, **Desmoulins, Danton, Saint-Just** and the incorruptible **Robespierre** himself, were sent to the guillotine.

The Emperor Napoleon

In 1795 a Directory, politically conservative and backed by the army, attempted to restore order, but its efforts remained futile, until the opportunistic Corsican, **General Napoleon Bonaparte**, mounted a surprise coup d'état in 1799.

Napoleon and Empire Napoleon immediately established his own brand of personal dictatorship. He was immensely successful. At home, he reformed taxation, confirmed the post-revolutionary property rights, set up a Bank of France to help the economy, developed the *Code Napoléon* to administer the law of the land, and restored the Church. He then launched into a series of brilliant military campaigns that swept across Europe. In the decade 1800–10, the French won victories at the battles of Marengo, Austerlitz, Jena and Wagram, and gained control over Italy, Spain, Germany and Poland. In 1804, Napoleon had himself crowned emperor in Rome.

Europe fought back. Britain and Spain counterattacked in the Iberian Peninsula, while a sea blockade starved France of important trade and supplies. In 1812, Napoleon launched an ill-fated Russian campaign, prevailing at the hard-fought battle of Borodino and marching into a tactically deserted Moscow. The severe Russian winter proved fatal. Napoleon's lines of communication and supplies were badly overstretched, and the *Grande Armée* was forced into ignominious retreat. Thousands of soldiers perished in the snow. At Leipzig, the French suffered a crushing defeat, and eventually, in March 1814, Napoleon abdicated.

Exile Even this was not the end of the irrepressible *petit caporal*. In 1815, Napoleon escaped from exile on the Mediterranean island of Elba, and staged a brief comeback, only to be conclusively overcome at the Battle of Waterloo. This time, his captors banished him to remote Saint Helena in the southern Atlantic, where he remained until his death in 1821. The man was dead, but the Napoleonic legend, and the legacy, lived on.

Napoleon at the head of his staff

>> During his crowning ceremony, Napoleon seized the imperial crown from the hands of the pope and placed it on his own head. >>

■ **After Napoleon, the Bourbon monarchy was restored. Under Louis XVIII (1814–24) France settled into a period of much-needed peace, while Charles X (1824–30) tried to turn the political clock back to reinstate the old ways. Such reaction was in vain, however, for the bourgeoisie were hungry for power, and the momentum of industrialization created new aspirations that backward-looking policies could not hope to fulfill. In the summer of 1830, the barricades went up in Paris, the king abdicated, and Louis Philippe was made head of the July monarchy. ...■**

42

Now a rapid industrial revolution took place. Output in coal, iron and textiles multiplied, and a national railway system was developed. As the money-grabbing middle classes grew rich, however, the working classes felt increasingly oppressed. Romanticism gave expression to the complex feelings of dislocation France was experiencing. Writers such as **Châteaubriand**, **Vigny**, and **Hugo** evoked a nostalgia for the past, and the value of individual imagination and emotion was invoked against the constraints of reason and routine. Socialist philosophies also sprang up, with thinkers like **Saint-Simon** and **Fourier** offering visions of an alternative social order often prefiguring much in Marxism.

The 1848 Revolution By 1848, the specter of revolution again haunted Europe. Food shortages and a recession had starving peasants on the rampage in the countryside, and the crowds in Paris again took to the barricades. Armed insurrection forced Louis Philippe to abandon his throne, and the Second Republic was proclaimed. Once again, heady idealism failed to effect any substantial changes; then out of the turmoil emerged **Louis-Napoleon**, the emperor's nephew, who managed to get himself elected France's first president. He first took steps to enhance his popularity, and then, in 1851, seized his chance to

mount his own coup d'état and crowned himself emperor.
Napoleon III, as he now was, steered a course between competing political factions and enabled France to prosper. The right to vote was extended, trade unions were made legal, schools educated more of the young. In 1869, the Suez Canal, a vast engineering project backed by the French, opened the way to increased trade with the Far East. **Baron Haussmann** undertook the systematic modernization of the capital, clearing slums and laying out the boulevards, squares and gardens that have made Paris so renowned a metropolis.

Tipping the balance Across the Rhine, Chancellor Bismarck was busy unifying Germany and

Henri Toulouse-Lautrec...

destabilizing the balance of power. In 1870, diplomatic provocation gave way to war. France lost battles at Metz and Sedan, and Napoleon III was himself taken prisoner. Paris fell to the advancing Prussian army. After the calamity of defeat, a new National Assembly clung to nervous conservative policies. In March 1871, a more radical municipal council was elected in Paris; the Commune rose up against the national government, which sent in troops to besiege the capital. After six weeks of fierce guerilla-style urban warfare, the uprising was crushed, and some 20,000 Communards were either summarily shot or deported.

Fin de siècle In 1875, France made a new start with the Third Republic. The political division between left and right persisted. Socialism gained ground, with a growing labor movement led by **Jaurès**, and for a time it was feared that the conservatives, under **General Boulanger**, might try another coup. Meanwhile, investment abroad brought great wealth from the colonies in Indochina, northern and southern Africa, and the Near East. France boasted an empire second only to Great Britain's.

Deep social divisions became manifest in the Dreyfus affair. In 1896, Captain Alfred Dreyfus, a Jewish army officer, was accused of espionage. On forged evidence, he was deported to the notorious penal colony at Devil's Island. The whole of France split into two camps over the question of his innocence. Among the traditionalist Catholics, anti-Semitic feelings ran high, and **Emile Zola**, in his famous article "*J'accuse,*" denounced a miscarriage of justice. Eventually, Dreyfus was acquitted, but the bitterness the affair aroused was long-lived.

Revolutions in art During this time, a wave of experimentation broke in the arts. In literature, the realism of the great novelists **Balzac** and **Flaubert** gave way to **Proust**'s meditations on time and memory, while the sensual poetry of **Baudelaire** was followed by the ethereal symbolism of **Mallarmé**'s sonnets. In the visual arts, Impressionism outraged the traditional salons, as new techniques in composition and color were developed by **Manet**, **Monet**, **Cézanne**, **Gauguin**, **Pissarro**, **Renoir** and **Van Gogh**. In music, too, new textures of sound and tonal harmony were introduced by **Debussy**, **Satie**, **Saint-Saëns**; and the new arts of photography, developed by **Daguerre**, the cinema, developed by the **Lumière** brothers, and the commercial poster art of **Toulouse-Lautrec** captured the popular imagination as the century moved into a mood of fin de siècle decadence.

Meanwhile, superpower rivalries loomed large. Germany's attempts to isolate France were outmaneuvered by a defense pact with the czar and the Entente Cordiale with Britain. Austria-Hungary's interventions in the Balkans threatened access to Suez, and to oil. The spiral of the arms race brought the European imperialists to an unavoidable showdown.

...celebrating a new age in French art and decadence

■ **The assassination of Archduke Franz Ferdinand of Austria, in Sarajevo in June 1914, was the trip wire that plunged Europe into war. Austria declared war on Russia; and when Russia responded, Germany in turn declared war on Russia, and then Britain and France declared war on Germany. The well-rehearsed Schlieffen plan allowed German forces to move swiftly through Belgium and penetrate into northeastern France. ...■**

The battle of the Marne halted the German advance, and years of trench warfare followed. Thousands fell, at Ypres, at Passchendaele, defending a few yards of mud in fields where once poppies blossomed. In 1916, **Marshal Pétain** held the symbolic stronghold of Verdun against persistent attack before launching a counteroffensive on the Somme. The stalemate was only broken by the intervention of the Americans, who entered the war in 1917, finally forcing the Germans to capitulate in November 1918.

The cost of the war A generation of young French men had been sacrificed, with over a million dead and 3 million wounded. Large areas of Flanders and the Ardennes were devastated. Inflation and the national debt had rocketed. The gains were comparatively slight: Alsace and Lorraine were returned to France, and the Treaty of Versailles, signed in 1919, imposed massive war reparations on the Germans. After the horrors of the trenches, many Frenchmen turned to promoting the cause of peace, and France contributed significantly to the newly created League of Nations and international conferences on disarmament. In the 1920s, reconstruction was initially paid for out of the reparation money from Germany; when the Germans stopped paying, French troops were sent to occupy the Ruhr. In spite of a series of unstable governments, things were relatively buoyant until the Wall Street crash of 1929 provoked a world recession. In the

1930s, unemployment rose, and the French economy nose-dived. Some feared, and others hoped, that there would be a Communist takeover, but the socialist Front Populaire, elected in 1936 under Léon Blum, was short-lived.

Appeasement and war Meanwhile, the Nazis were gaining strength in Germany. In 1935 Hitler broke the terms of the peace and ordered German rearmament. The French, fearing a collision course, sought to contain Germany with a series of fragile alliances, and even agreed to German expansion to the east. In 1938 Hitler annexed Austria and the Sudetenland in Czechoslovakia, and,

Greed, Revenge and other devils sign the Treaty of Versailles, 1919

General de Gaulle makes his comeback in 1946

signing a nonaggression pact with the Soviet Union, invaded Poland. Finally, both Britain and France abandoned their policy of appeasement and declared war.

World War II The quiet months of the so-called "phony war" were shattered by the Blitzkrieg of April 1940: Hitler invaded Belgium, Denmark and Holland, and dodged the Maginot Line, in which France had invested heavily after 1918 to prevent another German attack. After the panic evacuation from the beaches of Dunkerque, Nazi storm troopers marched into Paris.

The collapse of France was a deep humiliation. The country was divided

> **<<** "The French will only be united under the threat of danger. Nobody can simply bring together a country that has 265 kinds of cheese." —Charles de Gaulle **>>**

into occupied territory in the north and a "free" zone in the south, with a seat of government at Vichy headed by Pétain. Many fell into collaboration with the Nazis; the authorities deported Jews to the concentration camps and betrayed agents working in the French resistance. On the other side, underground resistance groups, like **Combat** and **Libération** and the famous **Maquis**, courageously helped prisoners of war to escape or planned attacks on military installations. They were aligned with the Free French Forces headed by **General Charles de Gaulle**, based in London, who acted as rallying point and a symbol of hope.

Liberation As the war progressed, Hitler's forces were worn down on the eastern front, and the United States and Great Britain united to prepare an invasion. In June 1944, the first landings on the beaches of Normandy were launched and the Nazis were steadily driven back out of France.

In August, Paris was liberated, and de Gaulle led a victory parade along the Champs-Elysées. Former collaborators were shot or publicly humiliated or, like Pétain, sentenced to prison. De Gaulle founded a provisional government to bring back to life a country once again ravaged by war. A national referendum opted for the creation of a new state, and in May 1946 the constitution of the Fourth Republic was declared. After 40 years of strife, France was ready to set itself on the road to reconciliation and recovery.

45

■ **In the aftermath of war, France had to rebuild itself and forge a new national identity. This involved a constant tension between the desire for traditional independence and the harsh realities of the modern world. It was with the aid of the Marshall Plan, for example, that Jean Monnet's Four-Year Plans were able to relaunch French industry. ...■**

In 1951 the European Coal and Steel Community linked France to West Germany, Italy and the Benelux countries, and this formed the basis of the European Economic Community. In the realm of defense, French wishes for a European column were overridden by the American-led NATO, which dominated as the Cold War developed.

Overseas France now entered the traumatic era of decolonialization. French paratroopers had been fighting Communist insurgents in Indochina since the close of the war, but the final rout at Dien Bien Phu in 1954 dealt a severe blow to the nation's morale. In 1956, when Egypt seized the Suez Canal, Britain and France invaded to protect navigation rights, but this turned into a fiasco after American intervention and Soviet threats persuaded them to withdraw.

Algeria Although Syria, Lebanon, Tunisia and Morocco were all granted independence peacefully, it was Algeria that focused political tensions. Since 1945, the Algerian National Liberation Front had kept up a campaign of terrorism, but the large number of settled French colonists were unwilling to relinquish power. More and more troops were dispatched to keep law and order, though there were sinister reports of unlawful torture and bombings. The generals commanding the army in Algeria threatened rebellion, and even a coup, and for a time seized Corsica. The crisis caused the collapse of the government, and with it the Fourth Republic.

The Fifth Republic General de Gaulle was recalled from retirement to help solve the dilemma. He instituted the Fifth Republic, giving him, as president, increased powers, and opted first for a version of Algerian self-determination. His decision was unpopular among the members of the *Organisation de l'Armée secrète*, composed of disgruntled officers and colonists, who mounted a terrorist campaign of their own. But de Gaulle stood firm, and in 1962 Algeria was granted independence.

Under de Gaulle, the 1960s became a time of rapid modernization. A wilting economy was boosted as France espoused consumerism, and shops filled with luxury goods. De Gaulle himself was all for traditional *grandeur*. His dream was for a united Europe stretching "from the Atlantic to the Urals." He resented American influence, and in 1966 he withdrew from NATO and forged ahead with the development of the independent nuclear *force de frappe* strike force. He ensured that France would continue to play a leading role in the Common Market by twice saying *Non!* to entry by the United Kingdom.

Uprisings For all his experience and political astuteness, de Gaulle was unprepared for the events of May 1968. Students and workers took to the streets to protest against the Vietnam War, wage settlements and the "system"; riot police stormed the barricades with tear gas and truncheon charges, and within days a general strike brought the whole country to a standstill. Somewhat at a loss, de Gaulle called for fresh

François Mitterrand addresses the Socialists in 1973

elections, but when his proposals for reform were rejected in a national referendum, he retired.

In the 1970s, Presidents **Georges Pompidou** and **Valéry Giscard d'Estaing** continued to pursue broadly Gaullist policies. The oil crisis of 1973 brought inflation and recession, and the alliance between the socialists and the communists gained ground. In 1981, finally, the Socialist **François Mitterrand** was elected to the presidency. Sweeping social changes were expected, and new legislation provided for more nationalization, ensured a minimum wage, and ended capital punishment.

Part-Dieu station at Lyon. The national rail network symbolizes modern France

But harsh economic realities forced the government to backtrack into a policy of austerity, and disillusionment set in. In 1986, France weathered another constitutional crisis when, a Conservative prime minister, **Jacques Chirac**, was appointed to "cohabit" with a Socialist president. In 1988, Mitterrand was elected to a second term, and the political situation remained stable until 1993, when the electorate swung right again.

In recent years, France has adopted a thoroughly modern outlook, building high-speed trains, a Channel tunnel, nuclear reactors and space rockets, while not neglecting to restore its Gothic cathedrals, tend its vineyards and expand its art galleries. This is a country that has settled into its new role as a major postindustrial nation with long traditions and a rich culture.

PARIS - PERIPHERIQUE

Two of the world's most celebrated monuments: Notre-Dame...

Parisians are a country if not a race unto themselves, notorious for their superior manners, high fashion, argumentative qualities and speedy approach to life. Paris is certainly not where the expression *douceur de vivre* originated. But it is an intellectual and artistic hotbed that has always enjoyed exporting its ideas, while happily importing and absorbing those of visiting foreigners. Although long vilified for their offhand attitude to tourists, Parisians have actually become more approachable. And the face of the city itself is also being transformed: Scrubbed, renovated, relandscaped, rebuilt, it has hardly stopped to breathe over the last 20 years and looks ambitiously to the future.

Charmed circle Nestling in the thickly forested saucer of the Ile de France, the *intramuros* population of Paris is just over 2 million; but if you count a growing number of satellite towns and the suburbs of the Ile de France, it exceeds 10 million. Yet however accessible the suburbs become, Parisian snobbery reigns supreme; the true Parisian lives inside the circle of 19th-century *portes* which contain its 20 *arrondissements*. Outside that limit are the *banlieusards*, the suburbanites, commuting into the center by RER. Over 75 percent of suburban dwellers use cars, since their local transport, excluding the limited RER network, is abysmal, and there is no other choice. Monstrous traffic jams in Paris and on the *périphérique* (ringroad) are part of their daily lives—sometimes stretching the 25 km as far as Roissy airport. Amenities are still being developed, and much thoughtless suburban planning of the 1960s and '70s has left a whole generation of lost souls and a few

...and the Arc de Triomphe

delinquents. Many of France's North African immigrants live in these characterless areas and have become targets for increasingly frequent racist attacks.

The new look At the same time some of the most adventurous architecture of Paris is gradually appearing in satellite towns such as **Noisy-le-Grand, St-Quentin-en-Yvelines** or **Cergy-Pontoise.** Cultural facilities have grown from the days of Malraux's famous Maisons de Culture, and inner suburbs such as Bobigny, Gennevilliers, Nanterre or St-Denis now boast modern theaters staging international productions.

For visitors driving around the Ile de France and coming into Paris, the landscape is not always as expected. Often resembling a New Jersey highway peppered with an unplanned array of billboards and advertisements, the *routes nationales* can be a shock. But turn off suddenly to follow the road to a château and you may find yourself in rolling, forested terrain. When not a spread of instant bungalows, villages are spruce, no stone out of place, and more than likely half the houses belong to Parisian weekenders. Avoid routes entering the capital on a Sunday night: Traffic jams are guaranteed.

Paris life In the center of Paris locomotion is easy if you stick to the excellent public transportation system or your own two feet. Distances are not great, and by metro it is unlikely to take more than 30 minutes from one end of a line to the other. Join in the Parisian way of life in the cafés of **St-Germain** or the new haunts of **Les Halles;** dine in animated brasseries or bistros where shared tables give an opportunity to chat with fellow diners.

Parisians lead fast lives, spending freely, and in consequence have to earn well to keep up. Time is valuable, and at the end of the day tempers can be frayed. But underneath the gruff exterior is a converted peasant dying to crack a joke, or a radical intellectual ready to chew the fat. The spirit of Paris, as well as its illuminated monuments, well deserves the description "city of light."

PARIS

BLVD BERTHIER

AVE DE LA PORTE DE CHAMPERRET

PERIPHERIQUE

Cimetière de Montmart

RUE DE ST_OUEN

RUE DE CLICHY

BL

Station Pont Cardinet

Square des Batignolles

AVENUE DE VILLIERS

BOULEVARD MALESHERBES

17

BOULEVARD DES BATIGNOLLES

SAINT-CYR

AVENUE DE WAGRAM

Porte des Ternes

BOULEVARD

BLVD DE COURCELLES

Parc de Monceau

Palais des Congrès

Musée Jacquemart André

St-Augustin

Gare St-Lazare

RUE D'AMSTERDAM

RUE DE CLICHY

CHAUSS D'ANTIN

RUE DE LA PEPINIERE

RUE DE HAVRE

RUE ST-LAZARE

AVENUE DE LA GRANDE ARMÉE

AVE DE FRIEDLAND

BOULEVARD HAUSSMANN

Porte Maillot

Arc de Triomphe

Lido

PLACE CHARLES DE GAULLE ETOILE

8

Opéra

AVENUE FOCH

VICTOR HUGO

Office du Tourisme

AVENUE DES CHAMPS ELYSEES

Palais de l'Elysée

PLACE DE LA MADELEINE

Ste-Marie Madeleine

RUE TRONCHET

BLVD DES CAPUCINES

AVE DE L'OPÉRA

AVENUE D'IENA

16

AVENUE MARCEAU

AVENUE D'IENA

AVENUE

Grand Palais

Petit Palais

RUE ROYALE

PLACE VENDOME

Jeu de Paume

PLACE DE LA CONCORDE

RUE DE RIVOLI

St-Roch

Palais Galliera

Palais de Tokyo

COURS ALBERT 1 ER

DE NEW YORK

PONT DE L'ALMA

Seine

COURS LA REINE

RUE DES INVALIDES

Orangerie

Jardin des Tuileries

Coméd

Palais de Chaillot

QUAI D'ORSAY

QUAI D'ORSAY

QUAI DE LA CONCORDE

QUAI DES TUILERIES

Jardins de Trocadéro

AVE BRANLY

PONT D'IENA

QUAI

Tour Eiffel

AVENUE DE BOSQUET

7

Esplanade des Invalides

ANATOLE FRANCE

Palais Bourbon-Assemblée Nationale

BLVD ST-GERMAIN

Musée d'Orsay

QUAI VOLTAIRE

Musée d Louvre

PONT DE BIR HAKEIM

Parc du Champ de Mars

BLVD DE LA TOUR-MAUBOURG

Hôtel des Invalides

Musée Rodin

RUE DU BAC

Ecole des Beaux-Arts

AVE DE TOURVILLE

RUE DE VARENNE

BOULEVA

QUAI DE GRENELLE

BOULEVARD DE GRENELLE

École Militaire

AVE DE LOWENDAL

Hôtel Matignon

RUE DE BABYLONE

BOULEVARD

BLVD DES INVALIDES

RUE DE RENNES

UNESCO

AVE DE BRETEUIL

6

AVENUE EMILE ZOLA

BLVD GARIBALDI

15

BLVD PASTEUR

RUE DE VAUGIRARD

BOULEVARD DU MONTPARNASSE

RASPAIL

RUE LECOURBE

RUE DE VAUGIRARD

BLVD DE VAUGIRARD

Tour Montparnasse

BLVD RASPAIL

RUE LEBLAND

Gare Montparnasse

RUE DU MAINE

BOULEVARD VICTOR

Porte de Sèvres

Parc des Expositions

BOULEVARD LEFEBVRE

14

Cimetière du Montparnasse

RUE FROIDEVAUX

AVE DENFERT ROCHE

RUE ERNEST RENAN

PERIPHERIQUE

Porte de la Plaine

GEN LECLERC

AVENUE DU MAINE

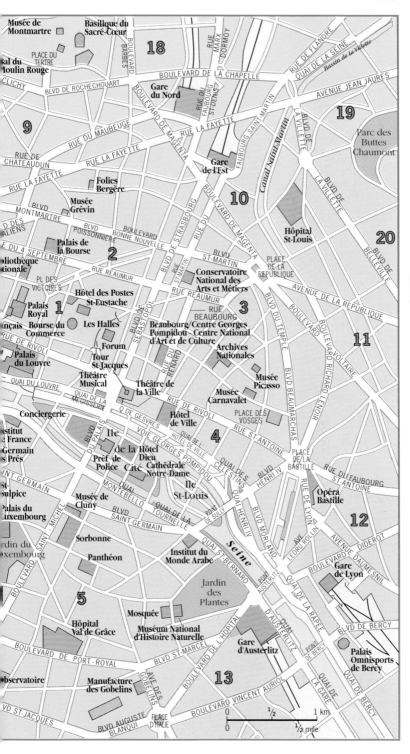

Musée de Montmartre
Basilique du Sacré-Cœur
al du Moulin Rouge
PLACE DU TERTRE
BOULEVARD BARBÈS
18
RUE MARX DORMOY
RUE DE FLANDRE
QUAI DE LA SEINE
Bassin de la Villette

CLICHY
BLVD DE ROCHECHOUART
BOULEVARD DE LA CHAPELLE
AVENUE JEAN JAURÈS

9
RUE DU MAUBEUGE
Gare du Nord
RUE DU FAUBOURG ST-DENIS
BLVD DE LA VILLETTE
19
Parc des Buttes Chaumont

RUE DE CHATEAUDUN
RUE LA FAYETTE
BOULEVARD DE MAGENTA
FAUBOURG SAINT-MARTIN
Canal Saint-Martin
BLVD DE LA VILLETTE

RUE LA FAYETTE
Folies Bergère
Gare de l'Est

BLVD MONTMARTRE
D DES LIENS
Musée Grévin
BLVD POISSONNIÈRE
BOULEVARD BONNE NOUVELLE
10
Hôpital St-Louis
20
BLVD DE BELLEVILLE

E DU 4 SEPTEMBRE
Palais de la Bourse
2
RUE REAUMUR
BLVD DE STRASBOURG
BLVD ST-MARTIN
PLACE DE LA RÉPUBLIQUE

iothèque tionale
PL DES VICTOIRES
Hôtel des Postes St-Eustache
Conservatoire National des Arts et Métiers
RUE REAUMUR
AVENUE DE LA RÉPUBLIQUE
51

Palais Royal
1
Les Halles
RUE BEAUBOURG
3
Beaubourg/Centre Georges Pompidou - Centre National d'Art et de Culture
BLVD DU TEMPLE

çais Bourse du Commerce
Forum
Archives Nationales
11

RUE DE RIVOLI
Palais du Louvre
Tour St-Jacques
Théâtre Musical
RUE DU RENARD
Musée Picasso
BLVD BEAUMARCHAIS
BOULEVARD RICHARD LENOIR
BOULEVARD VOLTAIRE

QUAI DU LOUVRE
QUAI DE LA MÉGISSERIE
Théâtre de la Ville
RUE DE RIVOLI
Musée Carnavalet
PLACE DES VOSGES
RUE ST-ANTOINE

Conciergerie
Q DE GESVRES
VOIE GEORGES POMPIDOU
Hôtel de Ville
4

stitut France
Germain Prés
BLVD DU PALAIS
Ile de la Cité
Hôtel Dieu
HOTEL DE VILLE
QUAI DE L
QUAI DES CÉLESTINS
PLACE DE LA BASTILLE

INT-GERMAIN
ulpice
Préf de Police
Cathédrale Notre-Dame
QUAI DE LA TOURNELLE
Opéra Bastille
RUE DU FAUBOURG ST-ANTOINE

alais du uxembourg
Musée de Cluny
QUAI MONTEBELLO
BLVD SAINT-GERMAIN
Ile St-Louis
PONT DE SULLY
QUAI HENRI IV
BLVD HENRI IV
12

rdin du xembourg
Sorbonne
Panthéon
Institut du Monde Arabe
QUAI ST-BERNARD
Seine
PONT D'AUSTERLITZ
BLVD MORLAND
AVE LEDRU ROLLIN
AVENUE DAUMESNIL
Gare de Lyon

BOULEVARD SAINT-MICHEL
5
Mosquée
Jardin des Plantes
BOULEVARD DIDEROT
QUAI DE LA RAPÉE

VD ST-JACQUES
Observatoire
Hôpital Val de Grâce
Muséum National d'Histoire Naturelle
BLVD SAINT-MARCEL
Gare d'Austerlitz
BLVD DE BERCY
Palais Omnisports de Bercy

BOULEVARD DE PORT-ROYAL
Manufacture des Gobelins
AVE DES GOBELINS
BOULEVARD DE L'HÔPITAL
13
BOULEVARD VINCENT AURIOL
QUAI D'AUSTERLITZ
QUAI DE LA GARE
QUAI DE BERCY

BLVD AUGUSTE BLANQUI
PLACE D'ITALIE

0   ½   1 km
0   ½ mile

Viewing one of the 30,000 works of art in the Louvre...

...and then recovering near the great Arc de Triomphe

Rive Droite

Covering a much greater area than the Rive Gauche, the Rive Droite governs the north, east and west of Paris in a curved sweep north of the Seine. This is where most museums and monuments are concentrated as well as regal squares and boulevards, often the results of Baron Haussmann's frenetic urban transformations in the mid-19th century.

The Louvre Hard to miss in its central riverside location is the Louvre, rapidly becoming the world's largest museum (due to be completed in 1996) and now entered through I. M. Pei's controversial glass pyramid. Symbol of seven centuries and 17 rulers, the Louvre developed from 12th-century fortress origins, and was rebuilt and extended in Renaissance style by François I and classical style by Louis XIV, who completed the awesome Cour Carrée. The royal art collection was first displayed to the public during the revolutionary period; today 30,000 works are exhibited, while many more remain in storage. Archaeological treasures found during recent excavations have added to the permanent display. The marble entrance under the pyramid skylight leads to the three wings, with categories and popular exhibits (*Venus de Milo*, *Mona Lisa*, etc.) well signposted. Be ready to wait in line in the summer months and expect certain sections to be closed during renovation and rehanging.

In the same Louvre complex is the less frequented **Musée des Arts Décoratifs**, entered from the rue de Rivoli, which displays furniture, decorative objects and reconstituted period rooms from the Middle Ages to the present. Its immediate neighbor is the **Musée des Arts de la Mode**, a museum of fashion, while in contrast the arcades of the **rue de Rivoli** outside offer wares designed solely for the visiting masses.

Unique viewpoint Looking through Napoleon's **Arc du Carrousel** due west, you see one of the city's great perspectives: through the **Tuileries gardens** to the **place de la Concorde**, up the **Champs-Elysées** to the **Arc de Triomphe** and beyond to the new office buildings of **La Défense** and the **Grande Arche**. The Tuileries house both the Orangerie, with Monet's spectacular large-scale series of *Nymphéas*, and the renovated **Jeu de Paume**, now a contemporary art exhibiton center. The terrace outside provides an unbeatable view looking across the place de la Concorde with its swirling, snarling traffic, its Egyptian obelisk, neoclassical mansions and view across the Seine to the **Palais Bourbon**, home of the National Assembly, while in the distance loom the **Tour Eiffel** and the glass domes of the **Grand-Palais**.

The Grand-Palais was built for the 1900 Exposition Universelle and epitomizes the iron and glass architectural style, while the **Petit Palais** opposite is more Baroque in style. Both are used for major historical retrospectives, while the sheer scale of the Grand-Palais allows it to house gigantic book and art fairs as well as a permanent science museum.

Walk Concorde to the Palais Royal

53

Starting at the place de la Concorde, walk up to the Jeu de Paume, then back to the terrace where steps lead to road level. Turn left off the rue de Rivoli up the rue de Castiglione to the place Vendôme. Cross the square and turn right down the rue Casanova, which becomes the rue des Petits-Champs. After the Bibliothèque Nationale turn right to the rue de Beaujolais, which leads to the Palais Royal; pass the 1806 restaurant, Le Grand Véfour. Walk through the gardens, past the back of the Comédie Française. Emerging on the place du Palais Royal, enter the Louvre or turn left along the rue Saint-Honoré to Les Halles.

The Champs-Elysées is no longer what it was. Invaded by fast-food joints and shopping arcades, its main attraction lies in large-screen cinemas and Napoleon's arch, which crowns the crossroads, **l'Etoile**. Its summit platform is accessible by elevator. To the north of the Louvre, on the **place du Palais Royal**, stands the theater, the **Comédie Française**, and behind this are the **Palais Royal gardens**. The palace was built in 1642 and the adjacent apartments in 1780, their arcades soon sheltering fashionable cafés. In the front courtyard are Daniel Buren's controversial 1986 striped columns.

Running northwest from the Palais Royal, the avenue de l'Opéra culminates in the opera house. Garnier's lavishly ornate design, completed in 1875, comes into its own inside, with a grand stairway of breathtaking magnificence. Leading off the place de l'Opéra is the **rue de la Paix,** lined with top jewelers; this runs into the **place Vendôme** (1715), home to the Ritz and crowned by a column commemorating Napoleon's victories.

The nearby **rue Saint-Honoré** epitomizes the Rive Droite: Its western end, the Faubourg, boasts luxury boutiques, while to the east are echoes of the "belly of Paris," **Les Halles**, a meeting-place for itinerant youth.

Above: Les Halles

In pre-Revolution days the Parisian population was 600,000. Its annual consumption was the following: 60,000 bullocks, 15,000 – 20,000 cows, 200,000 calves, 420,000 sheep: estimated total of 42 million kilos of meat.

Rive Gauche

Stretching from the **Quartier Latin** (5th) in the east across the increasingly bourgeois hub of St-Germain-des-Prés (6th) to the sedate 7th arrondissement and its pinnacle, the **Tour Eiffel**, the heart of the Rive Gauche is part officialdom, part academia, part bohemia and part aesthetics. Some inhabitants claim never to cross the Seine, and it is easy to understand why. Narrow streets lined with fascinating shops, cinemas, galleries and inviting bistros combine with major monuments and literary cafés to create an atmosphere more of *farniente* than of a hectic capital city.

The Sorbonne Students have traditionally monopolized the 5th since the Sorbonne was founded in the 13th century. Now joined by numerous other colleges, it seems impervious to time: This is where you will find twisting streets full of bookshops, cheap eateries or historic churches, culminating in the **Panthéon** at the summit of the Montagne Ste-Geneviève. To the east is the Jardin des Plantes, home to the pretty botanical gardens, the natural history museum and a mangy zoo.

54

Art: the street version, as practiced on the Left Bank

Musée de Cluny On the crossroads of boulevards St-Michel and St-Germain, the Musée Cluny clearly represents the span of the Quartier Latin's early history: Don't miss the Roman baths integrated into this superb Gothic mansion. Its collections include the famous *Dame à la Licorne*, a series of six allegorical 15th-century tapestries; the Gallery of Kings, sculpted heads lopped off Notre-Dame by an angry mob in 1793; and a rich panorama of other medieval treasures.

St-Germain Beyond boulevard St-Michel, the whole atmosphere changes as the 6th arrondissement begins. Rising over the central crossroads of the rue de Rennes and the boulevard St-Germain is the Romanesque tower of the 1163 church, worth visiting for its architecture and evening concerts. Although it was once a powerful Benedictine monastery, its fortifications disappeared in the late 17th century to make way for the residential Faubourg St-Germain. Close by are the **Brasserie Lipp**, the **Café de Flore** and the **Deux Magots**, all intellectual havens. Beyond streets of fashion boutiques is the church of **St-Sulpice**, famous for its gigantic 6,588-pipe organ and murals by Delacroix.

Ideal for promenading, jogging or sunbathing, the Luxembourg gardens, redolent of Nouvelle Vague films, stretch south from Marie de Médicis's **Palais du Luxembourg**, now home to the Senate, as far as the boulevard du Montparnasse.

Musée d'Orsay Back down at the Seine, linking the 6th and 7th arrondissements, is the Musée d'Orsay. Once a hotel and railway station, it is now a spectacularly renovated museum devoted to art and applied arts, 1848–1914. Beneath Laloux's soaring 1900 shell are galleries taking you from Romanticism through monumental academic works to Symbolism, the Ecole de Barbizon and finally to the jewel in the Orsay's crown—the Impressionists.

The sculptor Auguste Rodin (1840–1917) has his own delightful museum, south of the boulevard St-Germain. Set in one of the 7th arrondissement's loveliest gardens, the **Musée Rodin** has a strong collection of bronzes and marble works. The **Assemblée Nationale** is situated to the north, glowering across the bridge at the Concorde.

Les Invalides The most impressively scaled monument of the Rive Gauche was built under Louis XIV to house 6,000 invalid soldiers—hence its name. Inside this massive group of buildings is the vast military collection of the **Musée de l'Armée**, while towering over it all is the magnificent Baroque church, **l'Eglise du Dôme**. Some of France's greatest soldiers are entombed here, including Napoleon, encased like a Russian doll in six coffins. Leading west from the military academy are the formal gardens of the **Champ-de-Mars**, crowned at their end with the **Tour Eiffel** (984 feet), built for the 1889 Exposition Universelle by the engineer Gustave Eiffel. Much criticized at the time, the technical ingenuity of the tower was soon recognized. Walk below it, climb it, dine at it, gaze from it, day or night: you won't forget it.

Inside the Musée d'Orsay

Walk Pont des Arts to rue Soufflot

Starting from the Pont des Arts, walk east along the Quai de Conti, past the Institut de France, home to the Académie Française, and turn right at the Hôtel de la Monnaie. The narrow rue Guénégaud leads past galleries to the rue Mazarine. Turn left here, following it to the boulevard St-Germain, passing Paris's first café, Le Procope. At the three-pronged fork leading south from Odéon, take the left street, the rue Monsieur-le-Prince, which winds uphill to the rue Racine. Turn right here to arrive at the Théâtre de l'Odéon, behind which unfolds the Jardin du Luxembourg. Return to the northeast corner and emerge onto the boulevard St-Michel. Straight ahead is the rue Soufflot, which conceals a Gallo-Roman forum and ends at the Panthéon.

Street-level shopping at Les Halles

Le Marais and the Ile de la Cité

The transformation of Les Halles and the Marais is a phenomenon barely 20 years old. Stretching from Les Halles eastward to the Bastille, the renovated **Marais** has almost completely recovered the fashionable identity of its mainly 17th-century origins. Although geographically bordered to the south by the Seine, its historic character spills over onto the **Ile St-Louis**. Linked by a tiny footbridge, the other, larger island, the **Ile de la Cité**, is the historic heart of Paris.

Beaubourg Officially known as the Centre Pompidou, Beaubourg is the king of Les Halles. Completed in 1977 and soon due for a much-needed facelift, its multicolored high-tech architecture reigns over a completely renovated quarter that includes the site of the former vegetable market, now an underground shopping center incorporating an express RER station. Beaubourg itself shelters the **Musée d'Art Moderne** and a host of other cultural activities, and its precinct below buzzes with crowds drawn to a ragged army of street artists.

Le Marais Immediately east starts Le Marais, now bristling with trendy restaurants and bars, art galleries and boutiques. Propelled to its zenith in the 17th century when aristocrats vied with one another to build the most elegant mansion, it became home to literary salons, duels and power struggles. Today some of its narrow streets shelter jewelry wholesalers, replacing traditional craftsmen, and a lively Jewish quarter dating from the 13th century, the **rue des Rosiers**. The **rue Rambuteau**, leading into the **rue des Francs-Bourgeois**, is the main east–west axis along which are located monuments such as the magnificent **Hôtel de Soubise**, now housing the Archives Nationales, and the **Hôtel Carnavalet**, which contains a fascinating museum covering the history of Paris, as well as superb period rooms, including those of illustrious former resident Madame de Sévigné. One block north stands the beautifully renovated Hôtel Salé, which in 1985 opened as the **Musée Picasso**.

Notre-Dame, from the river

Place des Vosges The Marais culminates in the east in the perfect symmetry of the place des Vosges, completed in 1612. Once the site of a royal palace, its 36 redbrick mansions soon housed the crème de la crème of Parisian aristocracy and literati, today replaced by successful designers and artists. One former resident, Victor Hugo, has left a museum well worth a visit. Across the rue St-Antoine, the Marais claims further landmarks such as the medieval **Hôtel de Sens**, the **Hôtel de Sully** and, behind the **Hôtel-de-Ville**, the church of **St-Gervais-St-Protais**. This church was founded in the 6th century, but its present form dates from the 15th to 17th centuries.

Bastille Indelibly marked as a symbol of the Revolution, the Bastille is today an animated district dedicated to a youthful avant-garde, whether in its galleries, nightclubs or bars. Only 15 years ago it was resolutely working-

Walk **Beaubourg to the place des Vosges**

Starting from Beaubourg, take the rue Rambuteau and cross the rue des Archives. On your left is the vast courtyard of the Hôtel de Soubise. Continue along rue des Francs-Bourgeois past the 1510 turret of the Maison de Jean Herout before turning left into the rue Payenne. Walk past some typical Marais gardens and the Parc Royal, which adjoins the Musée Carnavalet. Turn left, then right to enter the rue de Thorigny and pass the Hôtel Salé (Musée Picasso). Walk around to the garden at the back, turn left down rue Vieille du Temple as far as the rue des Rosiers on your left. Walk to the end, turning left up rue Pavée and right back into the rue des Francs-Bourgeois. Continue to the end of the street and the place des Vosges.

class, home to furniture craftsmen, but its identity changed as artists moved into abandoned workshops and the new "people's" opera opened in 1990. A marina now terminates the Canal St-Martin.

The islands Floating midstream between the Rive Gauche and Rive Droite, the Iles are as different in character as the two banks they separate. The village-like **Ile St-Louis** grew up as a successful property development in the 17th century and has always been densely inhabited by wealthy businesspeople and successful writers, from Helena Rubinstein to Baudelaire and Balzac. The adjoining **Ile de la Cité**, famous for **Notre-Dame**, **Sainte-Chapelle** and the **Conciergerie**, is a mixture of the sublime and the banal. Alongside its medieval monuments stand government symbols such as the **Palais de Justice**, the **Hôtel Dieu** (a massive hospital) and the **Préfecture**, the central police station. The spectacular stained-glass windows of the 13th-century **Sainte-Chapelle** and **Notre-Dame**'s intricate sculpture and rose windows yearly bring millions to visit.

Monopolizing the northern stretch of the Ile de la Cité, the turreted walls of the Conciergerie are a grim reminder of the Revolution, when over 4,000 citizens, including Marie-Antoinette, were imprisoned there.

Beyond the centre

The winding path of the Seine, aligned with blissfully shady quays and massive monuments, tends to monopolize visitors' attention. But don't forget that there is more to Paris than the Louvre and Notre-Dame. Today's city gates, encircling the 20 arrondissements, were built in the mid-19th century, while Haussmann was still busy laying out a modern city, and included what were then outlying districts such as **Montmartre**, **Montparnasse** and **Père-Lachaise**. As the years pass, Paris spreads farther. Urban developments have provided new poles of attraction at **La Villette** and **La Défense**, where La Grande Arche now stands as the western gateway to the capital. Meanwhile, **Vincennes** and **Boulogne** (both parks), former royal hunting grounds, are lungs for the west and east of the city.

Palais de Chaillot Built for the Paris Exhibition of 1937, the grandiose Chaillot completes a monumental axis sweeping across from the Ecole Militaire, down the Champ-de-Mars, under or over the Tour Eiffel and across the Seine to the gardens below. Its other facade dominates the **place du Trocadéro**, a famous haunt for well-heeled local residents, housing no fewer than four museums, a theater, a cinema and a restaurant. Close by, down the avenue du Président Wilson, stand the twinned forms of the **Palais de Tokyo**, a photography and film center, and the municipal **Musée d'Art Modern de la Ville de Paris**.

Bois de Boulogne Immediately to the west, through Passy, beyond the glories of the Musée Marmottan, is one of the many entrances to the extensive Bois de Boulogne. Donated by Napoleon III to the city, it was soon remodeled by Haussmann to resemble London's Hyde Park. Rent bicycles or rowboats, wander in the rose gardens of the Jardin de Bagatelle, amuse your children in the Jardin d'Acclimatation or recuperate in the luxurious restaurant of the pretty Pré Catalan.

La Défense Western Paris no longer ends here. Since the late 1950s the business center of **La Défense** has sprouted anarchically skywards, leaving as many architectural horrors as marvels. The monumental **Grande Arche**, completed in 1989, has at last given a focus to the high rises, and its roof views are stupendous – as is the ascent in transparent elevators.

Montparnasse Another tower dominating Paris's skyline is the Tour Montparnasse, a 1970s oversight, which was part of a massive urban development, signifying the birth of an entirely renovated quarter that includes the city's most confusing railway station. Although no longer the artists' mecca that it was in the 1920s, it retains a few symbols, particularly the rebuilt bar and brasserie of **La Coupole**. Side streets like the **rue Vavin** or **rue Campagne-Première** are essential relics.

La Villette Attempts at creating another cultural island have over the last decade been concentrated in the northeastern corner of Paris at **La Villette**. Completed in

Grandeur, 1930s-style – the Palais de Chaillot

1993, this multicultural park complex contains an impressive museum of science and technology, a spherical cinema (**La Géode**), the renovated 19th-century cattle market christened **La Grande Halle** (used for concerts and exhibitions) and a music academy.

Eastern Paris Here are two more popular promenading areas: the cemetery of **Père-Lachaise** and the **Bois de Vincennes**. The former, spreading over a hillside, must contain the greatest density of celebrated writers, musicians and artists in the world. Armed with a plan, visitors set off in search of the tombs of Piaf, Jim Morrison, Modigliani, Chopin or Oscar Wilde. More mundane, the Bois de Vincennes is the eastern equivalent to Boulogne, and is similarly equipped with lakes, woods, rose gardens, a zoo and, its pride and glory, a severe medieval fortress once home to French kings. Vincennes will no doubt regain popularity with the important urban developments currently under way in nearby Bercy and immediately across the Seine in Tolbiac. Here the controversial new **Bibliothèque de France** is rising from the ground.

Montmartre The backdrop to many a Belle Epoque legend, Montmartre's charming winding streets and steps climb up to the white Roman-Byzantine cupolas of **Sacré Coeur**. Built as atonement for the massacred victims of the 1871 Franco-Prussian War, it attracts millions for its spectacular view across Paris. Montmartre also means throngs of fake artists, but its back streets cannot shake off a unique, peaceful character. Meanwhile, at the bottom of the hill, tourist buses line the boulevards and sex shops ply their trade—more proof of the city's eternal contrasts.

The first heated baths in Paris were built in 1761 and were floating affairs, moored along the Seine. In 1785 Deligny opened his still-famous establishment, the first swimming school in the world. In the early 20th century, 20 floating baths existed, but the last one was closed and sunk in 1976.

59

Montmartre lights up at night

Building started on Beauvais cathedral in 1227, but the choir collapsed a few days after completion under the weight of its ambitious design. A replacement was completed in the late 14th century, but remained roofless for two centuries. More disaster struck in 1573 when the new 502-foot spire tumbled, leading to the closure of the cathedral in 1605.

Ile de France

▶▶▷ Anet, Château d'
28260 Anet, on D928 south of Rouen
No direct train line

In 1548 Diane de Poitiers, Henri II's ambitious mistress, commissioned the architect Philibert Delorme to expand and rebuild Anet. Some of the greatest Renaissance artists, Jean Goujon, Germain Pilon and Cellini, created a magnificent home for this powerful woman. She later moved to the fabulous Loire château of Chenonceaux, but after Henri's death in 1559 she was ousted by his widow, Catherine de Médicis, and returned to Anet. An extravagantly decorated chapel containing her tomb is one of the few remaining features alongside one wing, the beautifully sculpted front entrance and a lovely park.

Open: March to October, 2:30–6:30. Closed Tuesdays. In winter open Sundays only.

▶▷▷ Astérix, Parc
60128 Plailly

Only 35 km north of Paris, this park, based on the antics of the Gallic cartoon hero Astérix, is packed with replicas of Roman monuments, gladiators, slaves and an imaginative range of related games, amusement rides and gastronomy (fancy a head of wild boar?). Nor is his pal Obélix forgotten. It is well organized and very popular on weekends, so be prepared for lines.

Open: daily, July to August, erratically at other times. Closed winter.

▶▷▷ Beauvais
In the flat Picardy landscape, the bulky medieval cathedral of Beauvais rises above the surrounding roofs. Apart from the incredible scale of the choir, its most astonishing features are the stained glass, the sculpted stone portals and the remains of the Basse Oeuvre, a rare 10th-century Carolingian church incorporated into the cathedral.

▶▶▷ Chantilly, Château de
Musée Condé, 60500 Chantilly; take Survilliers exit off A1
Rail: Chantilly

Famous for its forests, racecourses and whipped cream, Chantilly also boasts a château. Its mixed architectural styles reflect a lively history, from Renaissance origins through destruction in the Revolution to rebuilding in the 19th century. The magnificent grounds were transformed by Le Nôtre, who added lakes and canals. Inside the château the **Musée Condé** displays Italian and French Renaissance furnishings, a remarkable art collection ranging from Raphael to Delacroix and a reproduction of the illuminated medieval manuscript, the *Très Riches Heures du Duc de Berry* .

Open: Wednesday to Monday, 10:30–5, till 6 in summer.

The Temple of Love, one of the ornaments to be found in Le Nôtre's grounds of the Château de Chantilly

▶ ▶ ▶ Chartres

A11 southwest of Paris
Rail: Chartres

"The Acropolis of France" (Rodin), Notre-Dame de Chartres, replaces five successive churches, the last built in 1021 to house the relics of the Virgin Mary. Numerous fires culminated in the devastating flames of 1194, which inspired the community to build a new cathedral—accomplished in 25 years. The lower half of the facade remains pure 11th-century Romanesque, while the rest of the cathedral represents the transition to Gothic. Inside the cathedral, 176 luminous stained-glass windows attest to the talents of the Chartres craftsmen.

▶ ▷ ▷ Compiègne

Château de Compiègne, 60200 Compiègne; on A1
Rail: Compiègne

Surrounded by thick forests, the elegant town of Compiègne was a favorite retreat for French kings from the 14th century onward. Louis XIV gave some spectacular parties there; both Louis XV and XVI extended the château and Napoleon I and III also enjoyed its splendor. In the château, twenty lavish rooms are arranged according to period, the most impressive being Empress Josephine's bedroom, the Grand Salon and the ballroom. The obligatory guided tour lasts 45 minutes.
Open: Wednesday to Monday, 10–11:15, 1:30–4:15; till 6 in summer.

▷ ▷ ▷ Dreux

Its forest long preserved as hunting ground, Dreux became the personal property of the royal family in the 16th century and still has strong royalist connections. In recent years it has controversially supported the extreme right party, the Front National. The main monument of this market town is a hilltop chapel built by Louis Philippe's mother as the mausoleum for the Orléans family, who are still the French pretenders to the throne.

▶ ▶ ▷ Ecouen, Château d'

This superb château, on the edge of the Parisian suburbs, was built in the mid-16th century for the Constable Anne de Montmorency. Artists Jean Goujon and Jean Bullant were among those employed in the château design. Today it houses a museum devoted to the Renaissance period.
Open: Wednesday to Monday, 9:45–12:30, 2–5:15.

▶ ▶ ▷ EuroDisney

77777 Marne-la-Vallée; autoroute A4 east of Paris
RER: Line A from central Paris

The fourth Disney theme park opened its doors in 1992, an American paradise in the heart of Europe. Six hotels grouped around a lake allow visitors to explore the Magic Kingdom, from the vaguely medieval castle of Sleeping Beauty to a science fiction environment à la Jules Verne. Despite catastrophic first-year losses, this plastic universe is undeniably bigtime entertainment.

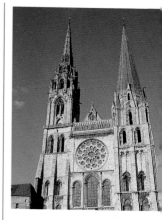

Notre-Dame de Chartres

61

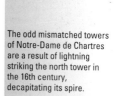

The odd mismatched towers of Notre-Dame de Chartres are a result of lightning striking the north tower in the 16th century, decapitating its spire.

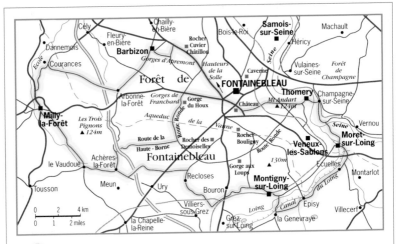

Drive **The forest of Fontainebleau.**

Start your tour at the sprawling Château de Fontainebleau.
The largest forest in the Ile-de-France is that of **Fontainebleau.** Rich in natural wonders (6,000 species of insects, 200 kinds of birds), as well as a wide variety of flora and fauna, it was originally a 12th-century hunting lodge. The château was transformed in the 16th century by François I and later used by the emperor Napoleon (*open:* Wednesday to Monday 9:30–12:30, 2–5). The gardens, relandscaped by Le Nôtre, are crisscrossed by canals.

Leave Fontainebleau by the N7, which takes you to Barbizon.
On your left are the **Gorges d'Apremont,** which invite a stop to climb up. Below stretches a spectacular gorge. **Barbizon** itself was home between 1825 and 1870 to landscape painters who created their own movement. Corot, Millet, Rousseau and Daubigny all worked here, painting in the open air and spending their evenings at the Auberge du Père Ganne. Today it is full of commercial galleries but remains pretty; and there is memorabilia in the houses of Millet and Rousseau.

From Barbizon follow the D64 to
Arbonne-la-Forêt. Take a tiny road on the right to reach Courances.
The **château** is sometimes open to the public, and the pure classical gardens and canals are exceptional (open in summer on weekends and public holidays 2:30–6:30).

Drive south to Milly-la-Forêt.
Milly-la-Forêt was once the home of Jean Cocteau; he is buried in the 12th-century church. The enormous beamed wooden market hall in the main square is 15th century.

Leave Milly, passing the church, via the D16 and drive to Le Vaudoué. On your left is the 407-foot hill of **Les Trois Pignons,** one of the most beautiful parts of the forest.

Continue to Achères-la-Forêt, from where you can either circle back to Fontainebleau via the Gorges de Franchard, another notable climbing and panorama spot, or continue toward the very pretty River Loing. Drive south of the Loing to Moret. This small fortified medieval town was once home to the Impressionist Sisley. Its Grande Rue is lined with historic houses, both medieval and Renaissance.

Return to Fontainebleau via Champagne-sur-Seine.

▶▶▷ **Rambouillet, Château de**

Château de Rambouillet

Lying about 55 km southwest of Paris, the château of Rambouillet has been the country retreat for French presidents since 1897. Originally 14th-century, it really came into its own when François I died there, taken ill while hunting in the forest. It was later much appreciated by Louis XVI, less so by Marie-Antoinette, who called it a "toad pond;" to appease her a dairy was built inside an English-style garden. The park is magnificent, landscaped over several centuries with rare trees, canals and islands. Guided tours of the château include Rococo bedrooms and Napoleon's bathroom, decorated with neo-Pompeii frescoes.

Open: only in the president's absence; hours are limited.

▶▶▷ **Saint-Denis**

The daunting necropolis of French kings, a metro ride from the center of Paris, is often overlooked by visitors. The Christian martyr St. Denis, who was decapitated at Montmartre, is said to have staggered northward carrying his head to a rural burial. A church rose on this site in the 5th century, but today's basilica was built by Suger in the early 12th century, its Gothic beauty inspiring similar edifices at Chartres, Meaux, Senlis and Notre-Dame. Following the example of the 7th-century Dagobert, St. Denis was for over 12 centuries the royal burial ground. Restored from revolutionary pillaging, it remains an incredible museum of funerary sculpture.

Open: daily 10–5; till 7 in summer.

▶▷▷ **St-Germain-en-Laye**

The main interest of this chic Parisian suburb lies in its medieval fortress, much rebuilt by François I in the 16th century. The 13th-century Sainte-Chapelle actually preceded its Parisian counterpart by 10 years, and although it has since lost its stained glass, the structure and details are magnificent. The château now houses the Musée des Antiquités Nationales (open: Wednesday to Monday 9:45–noon, 1:30–5:15), a unique collection of archaeological artifacts that includes the first known image of a woman's face, over 22,000 years old. Le Nôtre's gardens give fabulous views over the Seine valley.

> "Many men, not all of them French, have loved France like a woman, seeing in it, according to each context, their mother, their mistress or the woman of their dreams."—André Fontaine, *Le Monde,* 1982.

63

The Grand Terrace of St-Germain-en-Laye's fortress

The ceramics museum at Sèvres

The Musée National de Céramique in Sèvres (*open:* Wednesday to Monday 10–5) displays valuable examples of porcelain from Sèvres, Vincennes, Saxe and copies of Oriental pieces, Italian majolica and Islamic ceramics.

▶▷▷ Sceaux

A favorite for promenading or picnicking Parisians, the well-tended park at Sceaux once surrounded a 1677 château used for lavish receptions. Those days came to an end with the Revolution, when it was completely destroyed. Today's château was built in 1856; the grounds were restored to Le Nôtre's design earlier this century. Inside, the **Musée de l'Ile de France** displays paintings, costumes, royal porcelain and other objects relevant to the history of this region (*open:* Wednesday to Monday 10:30–6; 5 in winter). The park is open from sunrise to sunset. The Orangerie has a program of music recitals.

▶▷▷ Senlis

Formerly a Roman settlement, Senlis became home to a remarkable Gothic cathedral in 1153; building was not completed until 1560. The sculptures of the main entrance are devoted to the Virgin Mary and the lateral porches are typical of the Flamboyant Gothic style. Full of original Renaissance houses and 17th- to 18th-century town houses and devoid of a railway thanks to local lobbying in the 19th century, the cathedral town exudes a timeless atmosphere. Numerous Gallo-Roman ruins remain, too. Some have been integrated into the remains of the medieval castle (*open:* Thursday to Monday 10–noon, 2–6); others (such as the fortified wall) are still visible: 16 towers have survived from this period.

▶▷▷ Sèvres

Between Versailles and Paris lies the pretty old suburb of Sèvres (the Baroque composer Lully lived here, as did Balzac), which borders on the 392-hectare park of St-Cloud, with its Le Nôtre-designed waterways and infinite views over the city. Home to the royal porcelain factory, moved from Vincennes in 1756 by Madame de Pompadour, Sèvres has become synonymous with exquisite French craftsmanship, examples of which can be seen in its museum (see panel).

▶▶▷ Vaux-le-Vicomte, Château de

Domaine de Vaux-le-Vicomte, 77950 Maincy
Without Vaux, Versailles would never have happened. It was here that Louis XIV's shrewd, power-hungry minister of finance, Fouquet, decided to build a monument to the artists of the epoch—and to himself. Between the architect Le Vau, the painter Le Brun and landscape gardener Le Nôtre, a château and park of unrivaled extravagance and beauty were created. Unfortunately for Fouquet, Louis XIV was only too aware of its value and soon clapped his minister into prison, then proceeded to build Versailles. A victim of the vagaries of French history, Vaux-le-Vicomte was saved by an industrialist and has undergone extensive restoration over the last century. The formal gardens are a masterpiece of French style with terraces, fountains, statues and ponds leading away toward a concealed canal.
Open: 10–1, 2–6 in summer; 2–5 in winter.

*The Water Gardens
in Versailles*

▶ ▶ ▶   Versailles

Château de Versailles, 78000 Versailles

Every imposing avenue of Versailles converges on the palace, the town's raison d'être, Louis XIV's greatest creation and a world unto itself. In 1661 Louis decided to move his court and government to this swampy area, an astute way of isolating them but also of marking the flowering of French Baroque in an area with unlimited space for expansion.

The garden facade best epitomizes the Sun King's ambitions. Faced in stone, lined with Ionic columns and capped with ornamental balustrades and carved trophies, the central section is part of the "envelope" that Le Vau designed around the original hunting lodge.

The Royal Apartments are divided into the Grands and the Petits. The Grands, laid out in the 1670s by the King's chief painter, Le Brun, were the luxurious public rooms. The jewel of this stretch is the Galerie des Glaces, the largest, most magnificent and last public room to be completed. Le Brun's painted ceilings depict the king himself, while the 17 great mirrors once reflected candelabra, damask and precious furniture. Beyond is the Queen's Apartment and a series of dull picture galleries built later by Louis Philippe.

Before entering the Grands, don't miss the **royal chapel**, a perfect combination of elegance and grandeur, laid out on two levels. The Petits Apartements can only be seen with a guided tour. These were the royal family's real living quarters.

The gardens The severe symmetry of the largest palace gardens in Europe, another Le Nôtre masterpiece, is relieved by hundreds of statues, follies and fountains, not to mention the canals. If your time is limited, a small train will take you through the park to the **Trianons**, two more modest kingly residences. The Grand Trianon was built for Louis XIV to escape from the palace routine; the neoclassical Petit Trianon was built by Gabriel for Louis XV. Its grounds were later entirely transformed for Marie-Antoinette to play at milkmaid in a theatrical village, the *hameau*. For visitors similarly wanting to escape palace tedium, bicycles and rowboats are for rent at the Grand Canal.

Open: Apartments and Trianons Tuesday to Sunday 9:45–5; till 7 in summer. Park open sunrise to sunset.

In 1678 Hardouin-Mansart filled in the terrace to create the almighty Galerie des Glaces and added two blocks north and south to make the garden front of Versailles the longest in Europe.

Shopping

> "Paris is complete, Paris is the ceiling of humankind . . . It has no limits, Paris does more than make the law, it makes fashion. Paris can be stupid if it wants, it sometimes allows itself this luxury. The clouds of smoke from its chimneys are ideas of the Universe. A pile of mud and stone if you like but, above all, a moral being. It is more than great, it is immense. Why? Because it dares."—Victor Hugo, *Les Misérables.*

The perennial problem of Paris is how to escape without running up an almighty overdraft. Temptations lie in wait round every corner, many outrageously expensive but some just within a normal budget.

Markets For food and wine, go straight to the main market streets (closed on Mondays), which have a vast array of fresh produce and clusters of specialized shops. The most touristy, the **rue de Buci**, is the least impressive. Go instead to the **rue Montorgueil** (1st), traditionally part of Les Halles; the popular **rue Mouffetard** (5th); the **rue Poncelet** (17th); the picturesque **rue du Poteau;** or the **rue Lepic** in Montmartre (18th). For North African specialties, head for the back streets of Belleville or try the colorful **Marché d'Aligre** (12th). Nearby, at the **Bastille**, an immense, generous Sunday morning market is held. Lovers of Asian delicacies should go to **Chinatown** (13th), where numerous shops and supermarkets are concentrated among the restaurants south of the place d'Italie.

Fashion For cheap and cheerful, always stylish clothes, your best bets are the boutiques of the **rue de Rennes**, not forgetting the ubiquitous, unbelievably cheap **Tati** at No. 140, and the **boulevard St-Michel**, a favorite with students. Slightly more upmarket, the boutiques of the **boulevard St-Germain** and **Les Halles** always stock the latest crazes. Designer prêt-à-porter, from Kenzo to Mugler or Dorothée Bis, is best chased around the **rue Etienne-Marcel** and the **place des Victoires** (1st). Top shoe designers such as Stephane Kélian have also homed in here. And for the very top end of the market go straight to the **Faubourg St-Honoré** and the **avenue Montaigne:** You may find some affordable gifts at Hermès or Au Bain Marie. Don't forget **Galeries Lafayette.**

Bric-a-brac and antiques are relegated to the flea-markets, from the **Porte de Clignancourt** (open Saturday to Monday) to the **Porte de Vanves** (weekends only) or the daily auctions held at **Drouot.** A wonderful variety of valuable pieces can be seen at the enormous **Louvre des Antiquaires** (Metro: Palais Royal) or in the world-famous **Carré Rive Gauche**, a grid of streets behind the Quai Voltaire (7th) chockablock with priceless objects and paintings. Antiquarian book and print lovers could spend a lifetime exploring the back streets of the **Quartier Latin** and the secondhand bookstores lining the quays.

For the best in fresh food, go to market

Food and Drink

The choice of eating places in Paris is almost disarming —where to start. All depends on your budget: You could spend every evening in the 17th arrondissement's top restaurants, move down a notch to the rather staid 8th or bourgeois 7th or just head straight for the smoky bistros of the Latin Quarter and St-Germain.

Even if your pocket does not stretch to **Michel Rostang** or **Guy Savoy**'s establishments, you can try their more affordable bistros, both near the Etoile. There is a gamut of famous brasseries from **Flo**, **Julien** and **Terminus Nord** in the 10th to the **Vaudeville** or the **Grand Colbert**, both near the Bourse in the 2nd. The two giants of this style are the stunning 19th-century **Bofinger** at the Bastille, or the Art Deco artists' monument in Montparnasse, **La Coupole**.

If your aim is for a more intimate tête-à-tête that is not ruinous, go straight to **Le Marais**, where reasonably priced bistros and restaurants offer very acceptable cuisine. The side streets of **St-Germain-des-Prés** have equally inviting pickings, particularly near the metro Mabillon. For limited budgets try the **rue de l'Echaudé**, the **rue St-Benoît** and the **rue Monsieur-le-Prince**. In the 5th, low-budget travelers should go to the **rue des Boulangers**, while the **rue Mouffetard** has a heavy concentration of Greek, Italian and Asian.

Night food Riding on the crest of the Opéra wave, the newly developed Bastille area has become a nocturnal haunt. Small idiosyncratic restaurants and bars abound along the **rue de la Roquette**, the **rue de Lappe** and the **rue de Charonne**. Similarly colorful is the range in Les Halles, from trendy designer restaurants to American-style hamburger joints.

Ethnic-food enthusiasts should go to the 13th (China-town) or 20th (Belleville) for Asian food, for Japanese the **rue Ste-Anne** (2nd) and for North African any of the couscous restaurants scattered all over the capital.

See also **Directory**, page 276.

In 1991, 63 percent of the French thought they ate too much, compared with only 50 percent in 1971; 66 percent think they drink too much. Of all foreign cooking, 66 percent of the French prefer Italian, 51 percent North African, 35 percent Chinese, 32 percent Vietnamese, 20 percent Greek, 17 percent Indian, 16 percent Japanese and a mere 6 percent English cooking.

Nightlife

It is unavoidable: When in Paris, you have to partake of the nocturnal forbidden fruits. Part of the myth and part of the fun, there are haunts for all generations and tastes.

Pigalle is still hot, still changing since the days of Toulouse-Lautrec. Around the **place Blanche** are a multitude of haunts, from the **Moulin Rouge** to vast underground nightclubs like **La Locomotive**, concert halls such as **La Cigale**, trendy bars like **Le Moloko**, an all-nighter called **Le Dépanneur** or a combination of food, drink and dancing at **La Poste**. And that is just for day-to-day tastes. There are plenty of ~~strip joints as~~ well as "shows" aimed straight at tourists' wallets.

Late night Les Halles offers plenty of jazz bars and late-night haunts. For peep shows and tackiness the northern section of the **rue St-Denis** has it all, but for a late drink with good live or recorded music go to the **rue des Lombards**. Try **Au Duc des Lombards**, or tango at the **Trottoirs de Buenos Aires**. The **rue Berger** has another stretch of popular music bars, and you can always go for an early-morning pig's trotter at the **Pied de Cochon** opposite. This is without forgetting the long-standing, ultra-trendy nightclub, **Les Bains**.

Another nocturnal zone circles around **Le Palace**, the notorious theatrical disco in the Faubourg Montmartre. Not far away is the **Folies-Bergère**, and opposite is a jazz bar, the **Passage du Nord-Ouest**, where Piaf and Chevalier once sang. The **Rex** pulls in crowds for its rap and major concerts, while north of the boulevard jazz aficionados should track down the **New Morning** live jazz bar or the **Caveau de la Huchette** in St Germain.

Light fantastic Concentrated around the **rue de la Roquette** and the **rue de Lappe** at the Bastille are renovated old dance halls (**Le Balajo**) and crowded bars open till the early hours. Young and burgeoning in spirit, the revival of this area now spreads east to **rue Faidherbe**.

For more mature visitors the **Champs-Elysées** area has several rather select nightclubs, including **Régines** and **Olivia Valère**, and smart cocktail bars away from the flashing lights guiding tourists into the **Lido** and the **Crazy Horse Saloon**.

The rhythms of 'bebop' started in postwar Saint-Germain at the Tabou Club in rue Dauphine, which opened in 1947 with Juliette Greco, Boris Vian and Jacques Prévert. Sacrilegious in tone, exuberant in expression, these infamous night owls were reacting to the severe restrictions of the war years. They were soon named the "cellar rats."

The Moulin Rouge

Accommodations

With 1,500 or so hotels and an average of 18 million tourists spread among them annually, Paris caters for all tastes and budgets. It is one of the rare European capitals that offer quite acceptable and affordable accommodations in central areas, while a dozen or so establishments maintain standards of luxury straight out of another epoch. Unfortunately, France has the smallest minimum legal size of bathrooms and bedrooms in Europe, and in Paris, where real estate does not come cheap, many hoteliers exploit this to the full.

High style The 8th arrondissement (**Champs-Elysées, avenue George V, avenue Montaigne, Faubourg St-Honoré** and surrounding streets) is by far the most chic neighborhood, with a high concentration of luxury and 4-star hotels. This is where you stay if you need to pop out for another fitting at Dior's or to shop at Hermès. Some of the top hotels are also renowned for discreet call girl systems. *Prostitution*

Following closely in the luxury stakes is the 1st arrondissement (**Tuileries, Louvre, place Vendôme**), convenient for high-class jewelry and for culture, yet whose back streets have a sprinkling of affordable two- and three-star hotels. The adjacent 9th (**Opéra, Grands Boulevards**) has the densest concentration of hotels, over half of which are budget two-star establishments. The **Faubourg Montmartre** claims the majority; many are used by tour operators, but farther north toward **Pigalle** and **Montmartre** are some characteristic family-run hotels.

What's left The area most visitors should and do head for is the Rive Gauche, the 5th, 6th and even 7th arrondissements. Less businesslike in atmosphere than the Right Bank, the **Quartier Latin** and **St-Germain-des-Prés** house a host of reasonable one-, two-star and some very attractive three-star hotels. In general, prices are lower on this side of the Seine. Becoming increasingly similar in style is the Rive Droite's **Marais** district (3rd and 4th): lively, full of history, restaurants, galleries, boutiques and bars and within easy reach of other quarters. Youthful in temperament, it also borders the **Bastille**, where new hotels are opening yearly.

May, June, September and October are the hardest months to find rooms—be warned!

See also **Hotels and Restaurants**, pages 274 and 276.

"Paris is a vast studio of putrefaction where misery, plague and disease work together, where neither air nor sun penetrates. Paris is a terrible place where plants wilt and perish, where out of seven children, four die within the year."—Victor Considérant, 1848.

Practical Points

Air Paris has two international airports: **Orly** (14 km south) and **Roissy/Charles-de-Gaulle** (23 km north). Both are served by international and domestic airlines. The terminals of **Orly-Sud**, for international flights, and **Orly-Ouest**, for domestic flights, are best reached by Air France bus from the Invalides or, more cheaply, by Orlybus, which leaves from outside the Denfert-Rochereau RER station. **Roissy I** (foreign airlines) and the expanding **Roissy II** (Air France and Air Inter) can be reached by Air France bus leaving from Etoile or Porte Maillot, or by RER line B (Roissy-Rail) from Châtelet and Gare du Nord; this involves a brief, free shuttle ride at the other end.

Car If you arrive in Paris by car, you will eventually end up on the *boulevard périphérique*. This ring road encircles the city center with exits at each of Paris's gates—the *portes*—and avoids crossing unnecessary stretches of the center. However it can get disastrously jammed up, particularly during the evening rush hour (between six and seven). If arriving from the west of Paris, you may be confused by signs for *voie express Georges Pompidou*. This expressway is what you should follow to be spirited along beside the Seine into the heart of Paris.

Driving in Paris is not advisable, nor will it save you time. Parking has become a real problem, and even if you imitate Parisian pavement parking, it is still difficult. There is an increasing number of central underground car parks where you can safely leave your car for a few days while touring the city by public transportation. If you insist on driving, keep out of the bus lanes and remember to give priority to the right.

Train Paris is served by six mainline stations, each covering a different part of France or Europe. The **Gare du Nord** is for northern France, Belgium, Holland, Germany, Scandinavia and England; the smaller **Gare St-Lazare** serves Normandy, Holland and certain trains to England. For eastern France, Germany, Austria, Switzerland and onward, the **Gare de l'Est** will be your destination. Trains to western France, Brittany and the Atlantic coast leave from the **Gare Montparnasse**, a modernized station with a TGV terminus but seemingly without any logic. The **Gare de Lyon** speeds you south by TGV to the Côte d'Azur and southeast to Italy; the **Gare d'Austerlitz** serves the southwestern regions, Spain and Portugal. All are on the Paris Metro and close to the center. Be careful about choosing the correct section of the station: *banlieue* means suburbs; *grandes lignes* designates mainline trains. And always punch (*composter*) your ticket before boarding.

Inside Paris Finding your way around Paris is not complicated. The arrondissement system starts at the heart (Louvre, Châtelet) and curls outward, snail-like, to end in the 20th, the eastern quarter of Belleville. Street numbers start at the Seine, working outward. Walking around Paris is a pleasure, and safe; for longer distances the Métro is easily mastered. Buy a *carnet* (book) of 10 tickets or a *Paris-Visite*, valid for three or five days. *Formule I* is another system giving you one day's

Take a three-hour trip along Paris's Canal Saint-Martin, above and below ground and through a couple of locks. Boats run between the Bastille's Port de l'Arsenal or the Musée d'Orsay and La Villette, taking you along a leafy itinerary in eastern Paris, past the famous Hôtel de Nord and around the Parc de la Villette. (tel: 42 39 15 00 or 42 40 96 97).

transport, which can include the airports. Métro tickets are also valid for central sections of the RER and for buses; punch them (*composter*) as you board.

The Metro runs from about 5:30 AM to around 12:30 AM. Be *very* careful about wallets and handbags: pickpockets abound, particularly on Line 4, and have great professional finesse.

Taxis are not Paris's greatest asset. Be prepared for extras to be added to any fare from stations or airports and don't be surprised if they refuse to take four passengers. Several radio-taxi firms exist (**Taxis Bleus**, tel: 49 36 10 10; **G7**, tel: 47 39 47 39; **Alpha**, tel: 45 85 45 85) but this makes for a more expensive ride.

Emergency purchases A useful Parisian institution that has hardly changed since the 1960s is the network of drugstores. Open till 2 AM daily, they sell items from newspapers and magazines, books and records to medicine, camera equipment, gifts, wine, cigarettes, a snack or a meal. You can find them at the top and bottom of the Champs-Elysées, at Opéra or St-Germain-des-Prés.

Traveling in style

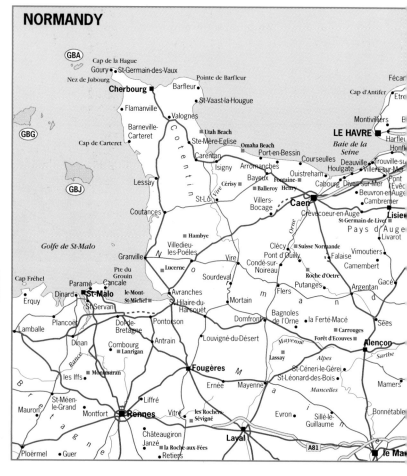

NORMANDY

72

Normandy emerged from an era of conflict and invasion. Viking invaders sailed up the Seine in the 9th century, wreaked their usual havoc and won themselves a handsome duchy, from which their vigorous descendants exported well-ordered Norman rule and architecture to England and the Mediterranean.

After William the Conqueror's invasion of England in 1066, Normandy was passed to and fro between English and French rulers. More recently, Normandy was the setting for the D-Day landings in 1944. The Battle of Normandy inflicted terrible damage on many old towns and villages.

Art and beauty Northwest of Paris, the Seine meanders through the heart of Normandy past fortresses, abbey ruins and the beautiful old city of Rouen, as if in no hurry to reach the sea. This is a region rich in artistic associations (Impressionists, Flaubert, Proust) from the period when the Normandy coast, easily accessible by train from Paris, was the height of fashion. To the west of the mouth of the Seine, the resorts of the Côte

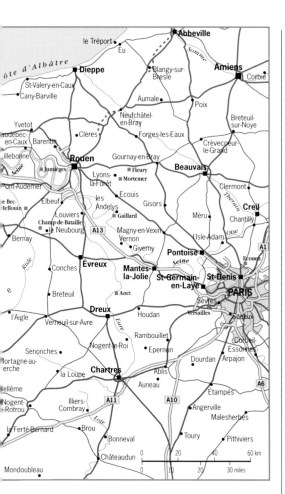

Fleurie still have plenty of chic, especially Deauville, with its golf and horses. Inland, the Pays d'Auge is Normandy at its most fruitful: Camembert and Calvados territory, with colorful timbered manor houses, fat cows in the orchard, and a diet of cream and butter, with no skimming.

Poorer country Western or Lower Normandy is poorer, more rugged land, geologically of a piece with Brittany. It keeps its quiet charms to itself – fortunately for those who love it.

▶▷▷ Albâtre, Côte d'

This 100-km stretch of once-fashionable coastline between Dieppe and Etretat was named after its chalky cliffs and milky waves. **Etretat** is the best place for cliff walks, beautifully set on a shingle beach with cliffs, pillars and arches on both sides. A small museum commemorates the fatal first attempt to fly the Atlantic by two French aviators in 1927. **Fécamp** is a larger town and busy commercial port, famous for the Benedictine liqueur made by the monks of its abbey. The drink has a museum to itself and the great abbey church (La Trinité) has interesting works of art in the chancel and crossing. Pilgrims venerate a marble tabernacle said to contain the blood of Christ (behind the altar). A stone in the south transept has an "angel's footprint," imprinted in 943.

▶▷▷ Alençon

A handsomely restored old market town in fertile agricultural and horse-breeding country north of Le Mans, Alençon has interesting Gothic buildings: a fat feudal fortress with bulging towers, now a prison; the 14th- to 15th-century church of Notre-Dame, with a beautiful porch and good stained glass; the 15th-century merchant's town house Maison d'Ozé, now the tourist office. But Alençon's great fame is its lace industry, by appointment to Louis XIV. Both the art museum and the lace museum have superb lace collections. Musée Leclerc focuses on World War II.

▶▷▷ Alpes Mancelles

Considering no summit rises higher than 1,368 feet, "Alpes" overstates the mountainous nature of this part of the Normandy/Maine regional nature park, southwest of Alençon around the Sarthe valley. But it is a picturesque and colorful region of fast-flowing streams, rocky gorges and slopes covered in heather and broom. **St-Léonard-des-Bois** is the best base: a picturesque village with accommodations, a very old church, good walks and fishing. Interesting frescoes can be seen at the former hermitage of **Ste-Céneri-le-Gérei.**

▶▷▷ Balleroy, Château de

This supremely elegant low 17th-century château was lucky to survive the last war intact. The château remained in the family for three centuries until bought by an American multimillionaire, the late Malcolm Forbes. It has sumptuous interior decoration and contents, and a hot air balloon museum in the stables.

74

The sticky drink Benedictine is still made according to the original recipe, involving 27 plants growing on the local cliffs, and was first concocted by a monk in 1510. The 19th-century neo-Gothic Palais de la Benedictine is no longer the main production center, but there are guided tours of a distillery and cellars where the liqueur matures in oak casks, with tastings.

The Benedictine distillery at Fécamp

Bayeux Tapestry

■ Having beaten off French invaders in 1054 and 1058, William, duke of Normandy, turned his attentions to lands across the Channel. In 1066 England's new king, Harold, was crowned; in the same year he was defeated and killed by William's forces in Hastings. On Christmas Day 1066, William the Conqueror was crowned king of England. ...■

A few years after the conquest of England, Bishop Odo of Bayeux commissioned a work of embroidery to adorn the choir of the cathedral on feast days, illustrating the Battle of Hastings and events leading up to it: a moral tale of Harold's perfidy punished. Traditionally known as Queen Matilda's Tapestry, the 230-foot-long work (colored wool on linen) was in fact produced in 10 years (1070–80) by English nuns.

Touring tapestry The story is told in 58 scenes bordered by friezes of mythical beasts and enlivened by a wealth of incidental detail, with captions and names of the main actors in Latin. Napoleon so appreciated the story, with its stylized depiction of the English as long-haired villains and the Normans as clean-cut heroes, that he took the tapestry on a tour of France as part of the marketing for his planned invasion of England.

Political propaganda, exquisite work of Romanesque art, medieval comic strip or valuable historical document, the tapestry can be enjoyed on many levels—provided you can get near enough to see it. It has a museum to itself in Bayeux and is one of the town's main sights. The strip of linen is surprisingly narrow (only 16 inches wide), and although it is well displayed, lines are often a problem. But there is an excellent slide show, audio guides and a photographic replica.

Bayeux itself, a few miles inland from the invasion beaches of the Calvados coast, was the first town to be liberated in 1944 and came through World War II unscathed. The center is pretty and a popular holiday base, with good hotels; one of its finest old timbered houses is now the tourist office. The beautiful cathedral is mostly 13th-century Gothic, but has Romanesque towers and arches in the nave, decorated with splendid reliefs. The carvings over the south doorway tell the story of the murder, by Henry II of England's soldiers, of Thomas à Becket, archbishop of Canterbury, in 1170.

The duke of Normandy's fleet lands at Pevensey—as depicted in the Bayeux Tapestry

■ **The short stretch of coast from Honfleur at the mouth of the Seine to Cabourg at the mouth of the Dives is the smartest, indeed about the only remotely fashionable, section of the north coast of France. The landscape is less rugged than to the north of the Seine, with long sandy beaches briefly interrupted by mini-cliffs, and a lush hinterland of orchards, thatch and timbered manor houses (the Pays d'Auge). ...■**

Apart from the view of Le Havre across the estuary, **Honfleur** is at heart a picturesque fishing port and artists' colony, with tall slate-hung houses overlooking the old harbor. St-Cathérine is an unusual 15th-century wooden church built by shipbuilders (it shows); and there are several good museums, one devoted to Boudin and other local marine artists, who got together at the Ferme St-Siméon (now an exclusive hotel). The sea has receded and Honfleur now has gardens where once there was a beach.

Different styles Separated only by the waters of the Touques, **Trouville** and **Deauville** lie at the heart of the Côte Fleurie. Both have big sandy beaches with duckboard promenades and ornate turreted villas, but there is a marked difference of style. Trouville, the first to become fashionable (in the 1850s) is now the poor relation, but has a year-round community. Deauville grew from nothing in the last quarter of the century, to become an affluent sprawl of big hotels in typically Norman timbered style, with a casino, spa, airport and other trappings of high society. It likes to be known as the Monte Carlo of the north, but bears a closer resemblance to Biarritz.

Quieter scene West of Deauville lies a series of quieter resorts, all with good beaches: **Blonville**, **Villers-sur-Mer** and **Houlgate**, the last two separated by cliffs that force the road inland. The former port of **Dives-sur-Mer**, where William the Conqueror set sail, has kept its 15th-century wooden market hall near the Guillaume le Conquerant shopping mall. On the opposite bank lies **Cabourg**, a stiflingly pretentious resort where most things are dedicated to the memory of Marcel Proust, who stayed often at the Grand Hotel, and wrote about Cabourg (as Balbec). At the Grand, time is not lost: merely arrested.

The son of a Honfleur ferryman, Eugène Boudin (1824–98) was the young Monet's mentor at Le Havre, and influenced Impressionism through his methods (painting outside and often recording the date, time and wind speed) and subject matter: bright, breezy Normandy seascapes, with a foreground of doll-like figures, indulging the new taste for seaside leisure. Boudin's use of color remained more traditional.

The harbor at Honfleur

▶ ▶ ▷ Caen

A big city and river port, mostly rebuilt after intense bombardment in 1944, Caen is not the most obvious tourist magnet. It has its appeal, however: great churches, albeit more imposing than endearing, and excellent museums, including the Caen Memorial-Musée pour la Paix (at the northwest edge of town, near the D22 exit to Creully), a presentation of life during World War II.

Town sights Caen owes its importance to William the Conqueror and his wife, Matilda, who made it their base. William and Matilda were cousins, and their marriage led to excommunication, lifted only when they founded an abbey each, for men and women, at Caen. The two churches, St-Etienne (gents) and La Trinité (ladies), survive, sited well apart to the east and west of the central fortress. Both show Norman Romanesque architecture at its most severe. A plaque marks William's empty tomb at St-Etienne. The 18th-century men's abbey buildings and cloister, partly occupied by the town hall, are open to visitors.

Between the two abbeys, reconstructed fortress ramparts, with a walkway, now enclose gardens and the outstanding fine arts and regional museums. Outside the walls (via the Porte sur la Ville) the 15th- to 16th-century church of St-Pierre contrasts sharply with the abbey churches, with a wealth of Renaissance ornament. A few old timbered houses, including the tourist office, survived the war, as did much of the 18th-century Place St-Sauveur, near St-Etienne. In the same part of town the deconsecrated 11th-century church of St-Nicolas is worth a visit. Rue du Vaugueux (east of the ramparts) is the café life and shopping center.

▷ ▷ ▷ Carrouges, Château de

A vast brick château of many periods, like a moated village turning its back on intruders. As well as the moderately interesting guided tour of the château itself, there is an information center for the Normandy Maine regional park and a good crafts center in the old chapel.

▶ ▷ ▷ Champ-de-Bataille, Château de

This is not a landing beach, but a magnificent late 17th-century château, comprising twin symmetrical brick and stone wings—one for the duke, the other for guests. There is varied decoration and contents, and a fine park.

Originally reluctant to accept a bastard's suit, Matilda was persuaded to change her mind when William dragged her round Lille by the hair, a wooing tactic that even then must have seemed primitive.

I would have killed him, not married him! The Jerk

Dieppe's attractive fishing port

Dieppe's trade links with Africa and the Far East led to the rapid growth of ivory carving in the home port. At the height of its 17th-century prosperity, 350 craftsmen were engaged in transforming tusks into portrait medallions, crucifixes, fans, caskets and other luxury baubles. The museum has a splendid collection and a model workshop.

▷▷▷ Cherbourg

A vast harbor for naval and passenger ships at the head of the Cotentin Peninsula, Cherbourg was efficiently destroyed by its occupiers in 1944, but remained a vital supply line for the Allied forces. Buildings and setting are equally uninspiring and there is little to detain the traveler.

▶▷▷ Cotentin

The rocky head of this anvil-shaped peninsula is at its most impressive in the west, with granite cliffs at **Cap de la Hague** and **Nez de Jobourg** and a splendid sandy bay between them; accommodations at **St-Germain-des-Vaux** and tiny **Port Racine**. In the sheltered northeast, **Barfleur** and **St-Vaast-la-Hougue** are fishing ports with some charm. To the south stretch the dunes of Utah Beach (see opposite). There is better bathing on the peninsula's west coast, on either side of the Flamanville nuclear power station. The best base is **Barneville-Carteret**, a merger of villages on an estuary sheltered by the Cap de Carteret: good cliff walks, beaches and excursions to the British island of Jersey. There are bigger resorts (notably **Granville**) farther south, without much charm. The best thing about the Cotentin interior is the town of **Bricquebec** – unpretentious, unspoiled and with an excellent market on Saturdays.

▶▷▷ Dieppe

A Roman seawater spa and the leading port of Renaissance France, Dieppe developed into a seaside resort when bathing caught on in the 19th century. Today it is a busy fishing port, with an excellent Saturday market and good shopping. From the cross-Channel ferry terminal, the pedestrianized Grande Rue leads into the heart of the old town, around the Gothic church of St-Jacques. The long pebble beach is overlooked by the 15th-century castle, now a museum showing ivories and items illustrating Dieppe's seafaring history. The Square du Canada has memorials to the thousands of Canadians who died in ill-fated Operation Jubilee in August 1942.

▷▷▷ Domfront

This former fortress town in Lower Normandy commands a river gorge. Fragments of castle ruins stand in public gardens at the top of the town. There are more substantial remains of old ramparts, and picturesque old streets around the modern church (St-Julien). Across the river stands the truncated Romanesque church of Notre-Dame sur l'Eau.

■ **As early as the summer of 1943 Churchill and Roosevelt decided that Normandy would be the bridgehead for the liberation of France under Generals Montgomery and Eisenhower. After months of intensive air attacks to destroy the occupying armies' communication lines, and a day's delay because of bad weather, a fleet of more than 4,000 landing craft set sail during the night of June 5, 1944, for the beaches of the Calvados and Cotentin coast, landing at dawn on the 6th, D-Day. ...■**

Above: Pegasus Bridge

Airborne troops were simultaneously dropped behind the coastal defenses at both ends of the invasion front. On the beaches, initial losses were heavy but the defenders lacked air support and a vital toehold was soon won.

79

Joint landings With Caen as their objective, British, French and Commonwealth forces landed in the east, on beaches code-named Sword (**Colleville-Plage, Lion-sur-Mer** and **St-Aubin**), Juno (**Bernières** and **Courseulles**), and Gold (**Ver-sur-Mer** and **Asnelles**). On D-Day itself the invading force took Arromanches and began to install an enormous artificial or "mulberry" harbor, towed across the Channel. Two and a half million soldiers and 4 million tons of equipment landed at Arromanches in the next three months.

Farther west, American forces landed at Omaha (**St-Laurent, Colleville** and **Vierville-sur-Mer**) and Utah Beach on the Cotentin coast. Fierce defensive resistance inflicted heavy losses, especially around **St-Laurent** (Omaha Beach).

Arromanches and the lively fishing port of Port-en-Bessin are the best places to stay in this area; Courseulles, best known for its oysters, and Riva Bella are beach resorts with numerous hotels.

Coastal route The D514 runs the length of the Calvados section of the invasion coast, passing numerous memorials, small museums and eloquent graveyards. War debris still litters the dunes and beaches: Tread carefully.

Museums and memorials The 50th anniversary of D-Day in 1994 refocused attention on the area. Both Caen and Alençon have new World War II museums. Others can be seen at Bayeux, Cherbourg, Pegasus Bridge, and Arromanches, all of which played a key role in the Battle of Normandy. At **Arromanches** remains of the mulberry harbor are still visible, and a British graveyard lies between Ryes and Bazenville. **Colleville** and **St-Laurent** have monuments by the sea and the biggest U.S. graveyard (Omaha Beach). **Utah Beach** has an American memorial at La Madeleine. This whole area is a focus of pilgrimage for veterans of World War II landings and the relatives of those who fell.

Claude Monet was born in Paris in 1840 but grew up at Le Havre, where Boudin persuaded him to paint landscapes. After studying in Paris and soldiering in Algeria, Monet settled in Paris in the 1860s, escaping to London during the Franco-Prussian war. His Le Havre painting *Impression, Sunrise* (exhibited in 1874) prompted a critic to coin the term Impressionism. Monet moved to Giverny in 1883 and died there in 1926. His dedication to his art was total. When his wife was dying, he painted her. "Just an eye, but what an eye!" said Cézanne.

▶ ▷ ▷ Ecouis

This small village north of Les Andelys is grouped around the 14th-century collegiate church of Notre-Dame, an unusual, broad, brick-vaulted building with many beautiful sculptures and carved wood paneling.

▶ ▷ ▷ Evreux

The departmental capital of the Eure has risen from the ashes many times, most recently after 1944 air raids. The cathedral spires melted, but the rest of the building survived, a surprisingly elegant mixture of styles from all periods from the 12th to 17th centuries, with richly decorated north and west facades, beautiful windows, an iron grille and carved wooden screens in the choir. The old bishop's palace is now the town museum, and the former abbey church of St-Taurin has a marvelous 13th-century reliquary of Taurinus, Evreux's first bishop.

▶ ▷ ▷ Falaise

The birthplace in 1027 of William the Conqueror, son of the 17-year-old duke of Normandy and a tanner's daughter, Arlette, was devastated in August 1944. But impressive castle ruins have survived, with the restorers' help. A guided tour reveals the window from which the lustful prince watched Arlette washing clothes at a riverside fountain below, and the room where William the Bastard was born. The main round tower dates from the 13th century.

▶ ▶ ▷ Gaillard, Château

Superbly sited castle ruins command a meander of the Seine and the pretty little town of **Les Andelys**, which has two small riverside hotels. Richard the Lionheart built the castle in less than a year (1196–97) to defend the Seine against the king of France. There is a steep path up to the ruins from the river, and a long way around by car, passing Grand Andelys's interesting late Gothic and Renaissance church (Notre-Dame).

▶ ▷ ▷ Giverny

In this small village near the confluence of the Seine and Epte, Monet spent the last 43 years of his long life turning out countless paintings of his gardens, including the water lilies series in the Paris Orangerie Museum. Only reproductions of Monet's paintings are on display, but the pink and green house is an original, with spectacular gardens and a lily pond. A modern building nearby houses a museum of American art.

Monet's pink and green house in Giverny

▷▷▷ Le Havre

Built for François I when the port of Harfleur became unnavigable, Le Havre was all but obliterated in 1944 and in its reconstructed form is no place to linger, except for the art museum at the port entrance, with works by Boudin and by Dufy, a native of Le Havre. The avenue Foch leads from the beach to one of Europe's largest squares, the place de l'Hôtel de Ville.

▶▷▷ Lassay, Château de

This imposing, well-preserved 15th-century military fortress, complete with barbican, drawbridge and pepperpot towers is on the main road from Bagnoles de L'Orne to Mayenne. The château's contents include the oven that baked the first porcelain from Alençon clay.

Château de Lassay

Born in Alençon in 1873, Thérèse Martin moved to Lisieux at age four and entered the Carmel there at 15 by special papal dispensation. The body was as fragile as the spirit was strong and responded badly to the hardships of life in the convent, where in winter only one room was heated to 10°C. After Thérèse died of tuberculosis in 1897, her autobiography, *The Story of a Soul*, was published. Its poignant account of pain and sacrifice in the quest for spiritual perfection ("my little way") proved enormously popular consolation, especially during World War I. Pilgrims came to Lisieux as early as 1899, miraculous cures were reported, and Thérèse was canonized in 1925.

▷▷▷ Laval

The departmental capital, once known for its linen, is still a textile town. The old quarter, huddled around its cathedral and château, still has some old walls and gateways. The naïf painter Henri (le Douanier) Rousseau was born in a tower of the Bucheresse gate (his father's workshop) in 1844; the château has a naïf art museum.

▷▷▷ Lisieux

This busy market town is a great place for cheese lovers on market day (Saturday). The gray Gothic cathedral (St-Pierre) houses the tomb of Bishop Cauchon, who played Pontius Pilate in the Joan of Arc story. But Lisieux's focus is the vast pilgrimage basilica of Ste-Thérèse. Millions come to ride the Petit Train that links Thérèse's family home of Les Buissonnets, with the Carmelite chapel and basilica, where mosaics illustrate her life.

▷▷▷ Lyons-la-Forêt

A flower-filled village in the thick of splendid beech woods, chosen as Yonville in a recent film of *Madame Bovary*. Flaubert's original model, Ry, lies to the west near Vascoeil, where the historian Michelet's château (Martainville) has interesting works of art. Lyons is a good base for exploring Normandy and the immediate forest. Its sights include the 131-foot Bunodière beech (signed from the N31), the ruined Cistercian abbey of Mortemer (south of Lyons) and the château of Fleury.

Norman Churches

■ **In Normandy as elsewhere in France, Benedictine monks of the Cluniac persuasion provided the main impetus for a wave of church building that followed the year 1000. Duke Richard II persuaded the Abbot of St-Benigne at Dijon to found a new monastery at Fécamp in 1003, and from then until the mid-12th century there was a frenzy of building in a distinctive style that spread to Britain, southern Italy and Sicily. ...■**

The basic elements of the architectural style, christened Romanesque (*roman* in French) in the 19th century because of its similarities with Roman (*romain*) architecture, are the barrel vault and round arch. Compared with some of the highly decorative styles that developed in the south of France, the Norman version was based on a sobriety verging on the austere.

Places to visit Caen's two abbey churches (St-Etienne and La Trinité) are fine examples on a grand scale,

Rouen (above and below)—filigree stonework

as are the Seine abbeys at **Jumièges** and **St-Martin-de-Boscherville**, and, simplest of all, **Lessay**'s reconstructed abbey church (north of Coutances). The truncated abbey church of **Cérisy** (southwest of Bayeux) is all the more impressive for its isolated setting in the fields on the edge of the village. **Lucerne** and **Hambye** are ruined sandstone abbeys in tranquil rural settings on the Cotentin Peninsula, between Coutances and Avranches. **Bayeux** cathedral has typically Norman decoration of geometric and foliate patterning. This is the style that was exported to England after the Norman conquest; in Britain all the Romanesque architecture is known as Norman.

Norman Gothic From the late 12th century the Gothic style (pointed arches, flying buttresses and bigger expanses of glass), born in the Ile de France area around Paris, gradually replaced the Romanesque style in Normandy.

Coutances cathedral, famous for its splendid octagonal lantern tower, and the later cathedral-sized church of St-Ouen at **Rouen** are superb examples of Norman Gothic at its most elevating and harmonious. Many other churches, if less admirably proportioned, have richer and more decorative detail to enjoy from the exuberant late Gothic (or Flamboyant) period, which continued to be used well into the 16th century: **St-Maclou** and the cathedral at **Rouen**, **Mont-St-Michel**, **Caudebec** and **Evreux** cathedral are all worth inspecting.

■ **A 262-foot granite island rises in glorious isolation from the muddy estuary of the Couesnon River, whose tortuous course at low tide, to the west of the rock, now places Mont-St-Michel in Normandy, rather than Brittany. There are quicksands in the notoriously treacherous estuary and water races across the 16 km of mud flats, occasionally flooding the parking lot. Explore the bay on foot at your peril. Assisted by the building of a road causeway, land is encroaching: Mont-St-Michel's days as an island are numbered. ...■**

The rock may have been a place of worship in pre-Christian times: Its early name, Mont Tombé, suggests use as a burial ground. In the 8th century the Bishop of Avranches built St. Michael's chapel there, and this was followed by increasingly splendid Carolingian, Romanesque and Gothic buildings, crowning the summit of the rock and supported by massive buttressed walls. A monastery was founded in the late 10th century, and throughout the Middle Ages played a dual religious and military role. As a fortress, Mont-St-Michel resisted the English throughout the Hundred Years' War.

Place of pilgrimage The pilgrim traffic began before the founding of the monastery. Today over half a million visitors a year file up the steep and narrow Grande Rue to La Merveille, as the abbey is known. The buildings are a combination of the finest sacred Gothic and Romanesque architecture. The most beautiful elements are the church itself (the incomplete nave is Romanesque, the choir soaring Gothic), the cloister and refectory. At the top of the 515-foot spire, the 19th-century figure of St. Michael has recently been rearmed, having lost his sword in a thunderstorm. This forms the apex of a multitiered citadel whose outlook is breathtaking, offering views of the Normandy and Brittany coastlines. Among all the souvenir shops, there is also a limited amount of

<< Legend has it that Aubert, bishop of Avranches, had St. Michael's designed according to instructions passed on in a vision by the Archangel Michael. **>>**

accommodation on the rock itself, and an overnight stay is well worthwhile, giving the chance to explore the sanctuary at its most evocative and least crowded – at dawn and dusk.

Visitors crowd into the narrow streets of Mont-St-Michel

The Pays d'Auge village of Le Bec-Hellouin

▶ ▶ ▷   **Pays d'Auge**

The fertile hinterland of the Côte Fleurie, between the Rivers Risle and Dives, is Normandy at its most delightful: the heartland of cider, Calvados and cheese. There is also plenty for the eye to enjoy, notably colorful manor houses like toy châteaus with moats, red tile roofs and patterns of timber, brick and stone. Traditional thatched roofs planted with flowers are less common than tourist office pamphlets suggest, but they do exist. **Cambremer** (west of Lisieux) and **Livarot** are at the hub of cider and cheese routes. Local tourist offices can supply maps of the routes and details of farms you can visit on the way.

The towns of the Auge did not escape war damage and cannot match the charm of their surrounding countryside. **Lisieux** is the main industrial and market center of the region (see page 81). **Pont-Audemer** is prettier: an old tanning town with timbered houses on its central island between branches of the Risle. The church of St-Ouen is a mixture of Romanesque and Renaissance, with beautiful 16th-century windows.

In the Middle Ages the abbey of **Le Bec-Hellouin** was an important center of learning and supplier of eminent churchmen, including Lanfranc, William the Conqueror's right-hand man and first abbot of St-Etienne in Caen. Only one tower survives of the medieval buildings. The rest is modern restoration of 17th- and 18th-century buildings, but the visit is interesting, the abbey being very much alive. Other village attractions are a vintage car museum and an excellent hotel/restaurant.

Manor houses For a good manor house tour (combining sections of the cider and cheese routes), head south from Lisieux along the river before turning west to

Vimoutiers and Livarot (see below) and returning north to the coast at Dives, via Crèvecoeur and Beuvron-en-Auge. The jewel of the manor houses is **St-Germain-de-Livet** (south of Lisieux), a fairy-tale vision with pepperpot turrets, arcaded courtyard and pink and white check stonework like a gingham tablecloth. The timbered wing is older than the rest (15th-century), but discordant. There are guided tours of the interior.

The manor crawl continues to **Fervaques**, its moat also fed by the Touques; **Bellou, Coupesarte** (a delightful moated farmhouse, with patterned brickwork and corner towers supported on wooden buttresses) and **Grandchamp**, all between Livarot and Crèvecoeur. **Crèvecoeur** has a fine collection of moated manor house, timbered dovecote, gatehouse, chapel and farm buildings, and a museum devoted to the Schlumberger family's contribution to the oil business. On the way north to Cabourg, **Beuvron-en-Auge** is an exceptionally pretty timbered village; there is also a 16th-century manor house at Cricqueville.

Cheese country Normandy produces over a quarter of the nation's meat and dairy produce, including the celebrated pungent cheeses of **Livarot** and **Pont-l'Evêque** and the more recently elaborated and milder **Camembert**, which is now produced throughout France in insipid imitation of the real thing. You can watch the manufacture of all three at the Musée du Fromage in Livarot. **Vimoutiers** (south of Lisieux) has a Camembert museum and a statue to Marie Harel, who launched Camembert after sheltering a priest during the Revolution in exchange for his cheese recipe. Cheese lovers will head for the hamlet of Camembert itself, south by the D16/246, where farms offer tastings.

Cider orchards proliferate in the Auge, thanks to the dampness and clay soil. Normans prepare meat and fish in cider sauce and drink cider, corked and wired like champagne, with their food. Calvados, the best known of many local apple brandies, does not reach its best for 15 years. Normans no longer pour "calva" down their infants' throats in the hope of producing another Conqueror (or perhaps to get some sleep), but still drink a nip with coffee, between courses (a habit known as *Le Trou Normand*), and after the meal. A distillery at Coquainvilliers (north of Lisieux) offers tastings.

Carvings and flowers in Rouen

Gustave Flaubert (1821–1880), misanthropic and merciless chronicler of his age (*Madame Bovary*, *Education Sentimentale*) was the son of a surgeon at Rouen's Hôtel Dieu, where young Gustave observed disease and death at close quarters. After giving up law for literature, he based himself in a riverside villa at Croisset (right bank, a few miles downstream of Rouen), now a museum, as is Flaubert's birthplace in Rouen, which doubles up as a museum of medical history. Both have a stuffed parrot purporting to be the bird Flaubert kept on his desk while writing *Un Coeur Simple*.

▶ ▶ ▶ **Rouen**

The capital of Normandy is a big industrial port spanning the Seine. The river is not one of the city's most beautiful features, but the fascinating center of tall, timbered houses and great Gothic churches has been carefully restored since Rouen was bombed during the war.

City center The two focal points of the city are the cathedral and the place du Vieux Marché, where Joan of Arc was burned at the stake on May 30, 1431. As well as a memorial cross and a modern church with 16th-century stained glass, the square has a parking lot; it makes a good starting point for a tour on foot.

The pedestrian rue du Gros-Horloge, a main shopping axis, is spanned by a one-handed gilt 14th-century clock mounted on a sumptuously carved Renaissance arch. The nearby Palais de Justice (take rue Thouret), much restored after war damage, is the city's most splendid Renaissance palace.

One of the great churches of France, from all periods of Gothic (mostly 13th- to 15th-century), the **cathedral** has a wealth of intricate carving on the outside. Inside, there are superb Renaissance tombs in the lady chapel (admission charge).Take the rue St-Romain to St-Maclou, a masterpiece of late Gothic (15th- to 16th-century) art on a cobbled square of timbered houses. A covered alley leads to the Aitre St-Maclou, a 16th-century court, originally a cloister used as a charnel house. Timbers are decorated with skulls and other death motifs.

Rue Damiette leads north to the 14th- to 15th-century St-Ouen, which purists consider the most harmonious and elegant of Rouen's churches, apart from the 19th-century facade; little ornament interrupts the soaring architecture.

Museums Another of Rouen's most picturesque streets, rue Ganterie, leads west to a cluster of the city's best museums: Fine Arts, Ceramics, and Metalwork (Le Secq des Tournelles). Rue Jeanne d'Arc leads back to the clock. The **Museum of Antiquities**, north of St-Ouen, has a rich and varied collection, including tapestries and mosaics; the **Flaubert/History of Medicine Museum** is west of Vieux Marché; and the **Corneille Museum** (dedicated to the Rouennais playwright Pierre Corneille, 1606–84) is near Vieux Marché.

▶ ▷ ▷   Sées

A peaceful, small town on the River Orne north of Alençon and the Ecouves forest, Sées scarcely seems to justify a grand 18th-century bishop's palace and cathedral. This is a fine twin-spired 13th- and 14th-century Gothic building visible from afar, with good stained glass in the crossing and a sweet 14th-century marble Virgin. On the other side of the river is a no less surprising 19th-century market hall, in grand classical manner. Several good hotels make Sées ideal for an overnight stop en route.

▶ ▷ ▷   Suisse Normande

The likeness to Switzerland is not unmistakable, but on its way north to Thury Harcourt the Orne dives and weaves through gorges and wooded valleys, and energetic visitors indulge their taste for a wide range of Alpine activities, from rafting to rock climbing. At a more leisurely level, there is good fishing and attractive walks to rocky belvederes above the river. For campers who do not require the sea, this is a good area. The main tourist center is **Clécy**, a good base for exploring the valley on foot, by car or in a canoe. There is a small local crafts museum in a 16th-century manor house and a miniature railway museum. **Pont d'Ouilly** is a possible alternative, a few miles downstream from the Roche d'Oëtre, about the most impressive of the viewpoints in Norman Switzerland, overlooking the wooded gorge of the Rouve valley. To the south, the Orne is dammed near **Putanges** to form the long **Lac de Rabodanges** (bathing and water sports).

▷ ▷ ▷   Vire

The not very interesting capital of the not very remarkable *bocage* area, which is characterized by hedges sited on raised earth banks. These proved effective defenses and made the area a nightmare through which to advance during the Battle of Normandy. Vire's specialty is a sausage (*andouille*) of pigs' intestines, the small wrapped in the large. Scanty castle ruins command a good view of the River Vire winding through a wooded gorge known as the Vaux de Vire. A medieval laborer and songwriter of the locality gave rise to the term *Vaux de Vire* (later Vaudeville) songs. There is a museum of *bocage* crafts and traditions.

The long-distance path GR36 follows the Orne from near Argentan to Caen. The section on the right bank opposite Clécy makes a good half-day's walk from the village. Take the minor road north from Clécy to join the GR36 just before the river bridge and railway crossing. The path forks right and climbs to the Pain de Sucre (sugarloaf), a good viewpoint high above a river bend, before descending south to the bridge and riverside cafés at Vey. Legs permitting, you can continue south to the Rochers des Parcs cliffs, popular with rock climbers.

The 19th-century market hall at Sées

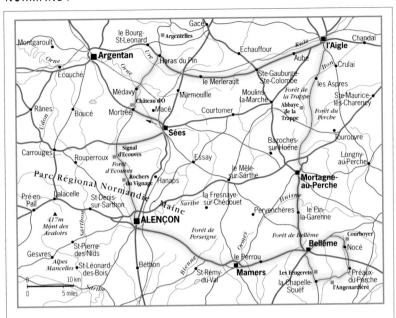

Drive A tour of the Perche

Start from Sées.
The Perche is a region of forests, undulating hills, powerful Percheron workhorses and manor houses.

Take the N158 to Château d'O.
Built on an island in a lake, **Château d'O**'s fanciful turrets would not be out of place in the Loire.

D26/16 to Haras du Pin.
Haras du Pin is the national stud farm founded by Colbert in the 17th century and housed in gracious classical buildings and park. Guided tours, by a groom, are free.

N26 to l'Aigle; D930 to Abbaye de la Trappe and Mortagne-au-Perche.
La Trappe's 17th-century Abbot de Rance launched the strict Trappist rule of abstinence, silence and hard labor. The abbey's setting is lovely but the buildings are of little interest. **Mortagne-au-Perche** has an interesting Renaissance church.

D938 to Bellême; circuit to Courboyer, l'Angenardière and Les Feugerets (D920/9/277/7).

Southeast of Bellême, **Courboyer, l'Angenardière** and **Les Feugerets** are among the finest of Perche manor houses.

Returning to Bellême, take the forest road and D210 to Mamers; the D311 to Alençon; and the D26/226/908 to Sées via the Ecouves forest.
The biggest and most impressive of the Perche forests is part of the Normandy Maine regional park (information center at Carrouges), well provided with marked paths. Denizens include boar, deer, snakes and multitudinous insects, so walkers should set off prepared (for the insects, anyway). Near the D26 and D226 crossroads, where there is a war memorial, the **Signal d'Ecouves** (1,368 feet) is the summit of Normandy. The GR36 path leads south from here to the Croix Madame crossroads, whence another path descends (east) to the Vignage rocks (good views), rejoining the D26 5 km south of the war memorial.

See pages 74 and 89 for **Alençon** and **Sées**.

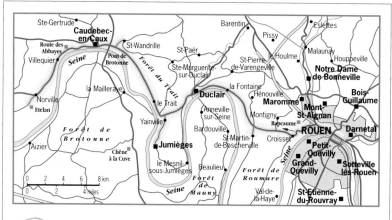

Drive The Lower Seine Valley

Start from Rouen.
The Seine probably derives its name from its sinuous course, nowhere more evident than on either side of Rouen: from Elbeuf to Jumièges is about 20 km as the crow flies, but 75 km for a fish. This tour follows the main road along the right bank, passing abbeys founded as early as the 7th century. It does not follow the meandering river, but there are minor roads that do. There is no bridge across the Seine between Rouen and Caudebec, but there are ferries at La Bouille, Le Mesnil-sous-Jumièges, Duclair, Jumièges and Yainville. On the outskirts of **Rouen**, Flaubert's no longer rustic pavilion at Croisset has memorabilia.

Take the D982 from Rouen to St-Martin-de-Boscherville.
At **St-Martin-de-Boscherville**, the 12th-century abbey church (St-Georges) has typical Norman geometric decoration on the facade and interesting capitals within, including jousting knights.

D143 to Jumièges and back.
Quietly set away from the main road, **Jumièges** is the greatest of the Seine Valley abbeys and the most ruinous, having been sacked in the 17th century and since used as a quarry. But the roofless ruins of the 11th-century church (the porch and the towers survive) and its still older

neighbor (St-Pierre, 10th century) are wonderfully romantic.

Take the D982 to St-Wandrille.
After centuries of changing fortunes, during which it was used as a mill and a private home and was much damaged, altered and restored, **St-Wandrille** abbey is once more inhabited by monks, known for their singing (daily services open to the public) and jam. The present church is a medieval barn brought from La Neuville, 50 km away in the Eure.

Continue to Caudebec-en-Caux.
Caudebec-en-Caux has a lively Saturday market beneath the beautiful late Gothic church (Notre-Dame), which has good stained glass and stonework.

Take the D81 to Norville (Etelan).
The late Gothic **Château d'Etelan** is open in summer.

<< At Villequier, just over 4 km from Caudebec, Victor Hugo's daughter and son-in-law were killed in a boating accident in 1843, victims of one of the fierce tidal currents that were a feature of the river at this point. There is a Hugo museum in the house on the quay, where Hugo used to live. **>>**

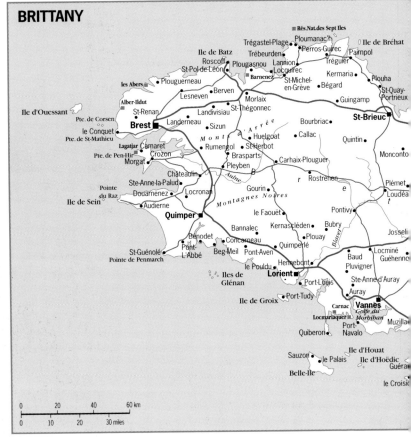

BRITTANY

Before it was named "little Britain" by invading Franks in the early Middle Ages, Brittany was Armorica: the land of the sea. For the visitor, the region's great attraction is its long coastline of sandy beaches, muddy estuaries, small fishing ports, villages of low gray and white houses; and, in the extreme west, rocky capes battered by Atlantic storms.

Inland Brittany is no longer a wasteland of heath, rocky hills and subsistence farmers but one of the most dynamic agricultural regions of France. This is good news for the Bretons, though it does not make compelling tourism. Brittany's big towns are dull and incursions from the coast are for specific points of interest—richly decorated village churches and fortresses marking the long-disputed frontier between France and the duchy of Brittany, independent until 1547.

A land apart As part of France, Brittany has been a backwater, physically remote (Brest is farther from Paris than are Bordeaux and Grenoble), poor and ignored. As a result, Brittany has kept, and recently tried hard to revive, its culture, traditions and the Breton language that, although scarcely flourishing, survives in western

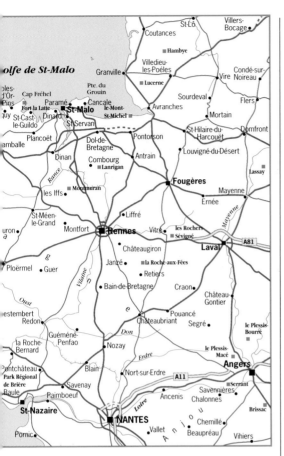

Traditional Breton dress

Brittany. This is a region of deep religious feelings, interwoven with a rich tissue of pagan myth and Arthurian legend. The combination of an intricate coastline, folklore and a good climate makes the southwest, around Concarneau and Quimper, the most picturesque corner of Brittany today.

BRITTANY

Remarkable shutters in Les Abers

Aber Ildut marks the boundary between the Channel and the Atlantic, and the nearby Pointe de Corsen is the westernmost point of mainland France.

Bélons de Bélon is an increasingly rare entry at the top of a French menu, promising a plateful of slithery delight. Bélons are the most prized of flat oysters. The estuary of the Bélon River, which joins the Aven at the sea, is their traditional but not their only place of origin—hence the distinction between Bélons de Bélon and any old Bélons.

▷▷▷ **Les Abers**

On the northwest coastline of Finistère, the many estuaries and shallow muddy inlets are known as *abers*. It is a low-lying, bleak and somewhat drab stretch of coast, rich in seaweed, artichokes and cauliflower. But the small port of **Aber Wrac'h**, on a promontory between the two main abers, has charm, small hotels and dunes at the end of the peninsula.

▶▶▷ **La Baule**

No longer officially part of Brittany, La Baule is the last resort before the mouth of the Loire, and the most fashionable of the long Breton coastline. Its 5 km crescent of south-facing pine-sheltered sands, promoted as the best beach in France, boasts 2,000 hours of sunshine a year. The sprawling resort behind the beach is geared up to the young, affluent and sporty.

▶▷▷ **Belle-Ile**

The largest of the Breton Islands is also the most lively and varied, with rocky coastal scenery on one side, good beaches on the other and picturesque villages, notably the little yacht harbor of Sauzon and fortified Le Palais, the main port and island capital. On the so-called Côte Sauvage (fairly tame, unless you coincide with a storm), Port Goulphar has two good hotels. The biggest sandy beach is Grands Sables, south of Le Palais, but there are prettier sandy coves (Herlin, near Bangor). The ferry from Quiberon is very busy in high season. Car rental can be arranged on the island, but this too needs advance booking in season. (See also page 93.)

Bélon see panel.

▷▷▷ **Brest**

France's great Atlantic naval base has little to offer tourists except the beauty of its setting, on a huge natural harbor: The bridge over the Elorn linking Brest and Plougastel Daoulas is a good viewing place. Rebuilt since World War II, the city is modern and gray, but its history, including the building of the 17th-century port by forced labor, is well evoked in the waterside Château and the Tanguy tower on the other side of the River Penfeld (Old Brest Museum). A sea center, the Oceanopolis, at the Moulin Blanc marina, Port de Plaisance, has 28,000 square feet of exhibits.

Islands and Capes

■ **The many islands dotted along the Breton coastline are rich in fascinating legendary, folklorish and historical associations but are, in general, fairly bleak and unrewarding to visit. The wilder the islands, the more intriguing the folklore, as a rule: Belle-Ile (see page 92) is the great exception. ...■**

Sein (access from Audierne) is no taller than a big wave ~~and will be an early victim of global warming.~~ A druids' refuge and burial ground, the island's entire active male population (130) answered de Gaulle's call by setting sail for Britain in 1940, and the island was later decorated for its support of the Free French cause.

Storm-lashed **Ouessant** (access from Brest) is an important dot on the shipping charts and notorious for shipwrecks. One of its lighthouses can be climbed; another contains a museum. Here, as on some of the other islands, women work the land (little of which is workable) and propose marriage. In the more sheltered waters off the south coast, Belle-Ile's neighbors **Houat** and **Hoëdic** (Duck and Duckling) are also accessible from Quiberon; Duck has excellent beaches.

Groix (access from Lorient) is like a smaller Belle-Ile, with a similar mixture of rocky and sandy coast. Its main village, Port Tudy, once a tuna fishing port, sees a little tourism.

Desert isles Off Concarneau, the nine uninhabited **Glénan** islands are a nature reserve with a big sailing school. Despite its northern location, **Bréhat** (access from L'Arcouest, near Paimpol) has a famously mild climate and exotic vegetation. With an intricate coastline of pinkish rocks, it is a better island for gentle walks than swimming.

The two most spectacular capes of threepronged Finistère (which means "the end of the world") are **Pointe Penhir**, on the cross-shaped tongue of the Crozon Peninsula, and the more celebrated **Pointe du Raz**, at the tip of Cape Sizun in the extreme southwest. There is not much to choose between them: cliffs of about 230 feet in both places and an overall effect whose savagery depends chiefly on the weather and crashing waves.

93

Between the Pointe du Raz and the less visited cliffs of the Pointe du Van, the little Baie des Trépassés is one of the candidate sites of the legendary city of Is, which was swallowed up by the sea as a result of King Gradlon's beautiful daughter Dahut's carrying on with the devil. She has since haunted the coast in mermaid's guise, luring sailors to their death.

Belle-Ile's town hall

BRITTANY

People have lived on the Brière's boggy marshes, communal land of 21 parishes, since the 17th century. The Brierons make clogs, punt around in flat-bottomed boats, spear eels, shoot game and cut peat, of which they enjoy a not tremendously lucrative monopoly for nine days a year. They harvest reeds to make their mattresses, baskets and thatch for their houses. And, in considerable number, they abandon the Brière for an easier life elsewhere. The Regional Park was created to encourage interest in the traditions of the region and thereby help to keep them and it alive.

94

▶▷▷ Brière Regional Park

North of St-Nazaire, the D50 runs from Montoir up through the Grande Brière—an area of peaty bogs, canals and villages on granite mounds that are islands in winter when the bogs flood. There are several of these around St-Joachim, which has accommodations and an information center for the Regional Park. The most interesting is Ile de Fédrun, a ring of white cottages, each with a punt berth. Punting excursions on the reedy canals can be organized. Much of the Brière is a bird reserve.

▶▷▷ Cancale

This is a cheerful port and gourmet pilgrimage, with fine views of the bay of Mont-St-Michel. Cancale has the most extensive oyster beds on the Channel coast, well viewed at low tide from the harbor jetty or the rocky spur that separates oyster park from beach. A museum just outside the town is devoted to oysters. Cancale's flat oysters, which were appreciated by Julius Caesar, Louis XIV and Napoleon, are now brought in from southern Brittany and planted at Cancale.

▶▶▶ Carnac

Most famous for its lines of standing stones (see page 95), Carnac is also a busy seaside resort with a splendid beach. Between Plage and Préhistoire is an ordinary town center, with an excellent museum.

▷▷▷ Combourg

This is a small lakeside town beneath a mighty feudal fortress. The great Romantic author Chateaubriand spent a short but gloomy period of his youth here, sleeping in a tower haunted by a previous lord of Combourg's cat. A few rooms have been made into a Chateaubriand museum, but the view is the main thing. A number of other châteaus and churches nearby make an interesting outing from Dinan: Lanrigen, Montmuran, and Les Iffs, with its Renaissance stained glass.

▶▶▷ Concarneau

One of the great fishing ports of France, and one of the great tourist centers of Brittany, Concarneau's walled old town (*ville close*) sits on an island within the port. The *ville close* has 17th-century walls to walk around and an interesting fishing museum with an aquarium and numerous fishy curiosities. The outer town is less special, but there are plenty of good fish restaurants around the port.

Investigating the center of Concarneau

Megaliths

■ **Megaliths (big stones) are a Breton specialty, although by no means unique to the region. There are many in the north and west, but the main concentration is on the Gulf of Morbihan in the southeast. ...■**

Carnac, on the Gulf of Morbihan, has a unique series of over 3,000 stones in three alignments. The stones were raised over a long period, possibly beginning in 5500 BC and lasting until about 1000 BC.

Brittany has no circles to compare with Britain's Stonehenge, but large numbers of **menhirs** (standing stones, from the Celtic *maen hir*, "long stone," as carried by Obelix). These either stand on their own or in lines. **Dolmens** are structures with roofs, probably used as graves, and **tumuli** are earth-covered burial mounds with stone-walled tunnels and chambers. Carnac has an interesting tumulus, as well as its lines, and a museum about pre-historic civilization that, unusually, has high entertainment value.

Mystery system It is argued that the Morbihan megaliths form an integrated system of astrological observation points, established over a period of hundreds of years and centered at **Locmariaquer** (east of Carnac, at the mouth of the gulf), the site where the greatest of all standing stones, weighing over 350 tonnes, stood 60 feet high. The argument leaves many experts unconvinced, and the significance of

the standing stones remains a mystery. Several theories have been put forward for the alignments at Carnac; traditional explanations are the most colorful, including windbreaks for Roman tents, and petrified legionnaires miraculously arrested while in pursuit of an early Christian pope, Cornelius, the patron of Carnac church.

Selected sites Outside Carnac, sites of prehistoric stones include:
Barnenez (eastern side of Morlaix estuary). Tumulus.
Gavrinis Island (access from Larmor Baden). A half-covered tumulus here has beautiful patterned carving.
Lagatjar (Crozon Peninsula, near Camaret). Alignments of 100 stones.
Locmariaquer. Doubters say the great menhir never stood, but a 17th-century sailor's description confirms that it did, before crashing and breaking into five pieces (four still in situ). There is a fine dolmen (Merchants' Table) with carvings nearby.
La Roche Aux Fées (southeast of Rennes). A massive 42-stone monument.

Dolmens are the exposed inner chambers of burial mounds

95

Ask most visitors to France where crêpes come from, and the most likely answer is the boulevard St-Michel in Paris, where street vendors smear them with gooey chestnut purée (or whatever), roll them into floppy cones and serve in a paper napkin. The buckwheat pancake is, however, a Breton export, and every village on the coast has its crêperie, where pancakes with a variety of fillings are served at tables, preferably with Breton cider. Wheat flour is often used instead of traditional buckwheat flour.

▶ ▶ ▷ **Corniche de l'Armorique**

This short stretch of scenic wooded coast road runs around a W-shaped bay, from **Locquirec**—a whitewashed resort with beaches on both sides of its narrow promontory—to **St-Michel-en-Grève**. The great feature of the bay is the enormous (4 km) beach at Lieue de Grève, punctuated by the **Grand Rocher**, a good viewpoint reached by a short but steep path from the road. There are interesting churches at **Plougasnou** and (on the coast west of Locquirec) **Ploumilliau**, east of St-Michel. The **Pointe de Primel** is an impressive granite headland in the manner of the Breton Corniche (see below), which adds to the confusion between the two Tregastels. **Primel-Trégastel** is a more modest resort than Plage of that ilk, but has a good beach. **Lannion**, the main town of this area, is not a bad place for a rainy day, with picturesque old houses around the central square and a fine hilltop church. A few miles south of the town, the isolated 16th-century Kerfons chapel has a calvary and beautiful rood loft.

▶ ▶ ▷ **Corniche Bretonne**

Scenically, the best thing about the north coast of Brittany is the zone of strangely eroded pink granite rocks scattered along the shore, between **Trégastel-Plage** and the fishing port and busy beach resort of **Perros-Guirec**. The locals, inspired by the curious eroded rock formations, have conjured some evocative names for them: Napoleon's Hat, Death's Head, the Pancake, the Torpedo, and so on. There are good views of the shoreline from the lighthouse at **Ploumanach**—a small fishing port between Trégastel and Perros—and from the coastal path **Sentier des Douaniers**, between Ploumanach and Perros, a beautiful 5-km walk. Ploumanach itself is divided by a municipal park—a kind of rock reserve. From Trégastel-Plage, the coast continues to **Trébeurden**, a small resort with good beaches split by a rocky promontory. From Perros-Guirec there are boat trips to the bird sanctuary archipelago of the **Sept Iles**.

The Corniche de l'Armorique

Parish Closes

■ **Breton sightseeing has its limitations, but the parish close (enclos paroissial) is a fascinating local specialty, best seen in Léon (northern Finistère). In 16th- and 17th-century Brittany, as nowhere else, the buildings around the village graveyard developed into an elaborate architectural complex. ...■**

St-Thégonnec offers a particularly elaborate example of the traditional Breton parish close

Traditionally, the close consists of triumphal arch (the churchyard gate); a highly decorated church porch, where parish councils met; a separate ossuary, where exhumed bones were stored to make room for new dead; and, as the focal point, a freestanding calvary swarming with carved granite figures in modern dress, illustrating Bible stories and popular morality tales.

Origins To the obvious question—why?—the best answers are probably local rivalry between villages, the survival in Brittany of passion plays, the use of the calvaries for popular religious instruction, and the singular Breton preoccupation with death. Many of

the church interiors have richly carved and painted wooden altarpieces, pulpits, or even complete rood screens.

Close competition Rivalry played an important part in the development of the two most spectacular and complex parish closes, at St-Thégonnec and Guimiliau, near Morlaix. Other outstanding examples of Breton church art of the period (not all complete parish closes) can be enjoyed at **Lampaul-Guimiliau** (wood carvings in the church); **La Roche** (ossuary, screen); **St-Herbot** (screen and ossuary); **Sizun** (arch and ossuary); **Le Folgoët** (a big pilgrimage church with a magnificent 15th-century granite screen); **Brasparts** (a carved Virgin in the church); **Berven** (screen); **Plougastel-Daoulas** (calvary); **Ploumilliau**, southwest of Lannion (a wooded sculpture of Ankou, the Breton Father Time, with scythe) and **Kerfons** chapel (rood loft and calvary).

Church Trail Farther afield, making a church route from west to east, notable closes can be seen at **Pleyben** (church and calvary); **Notre-Dame du Crann** (stained glass); **St-Fiacre**, near Le Faouët (an outstanding screen) and **Kernascléden** (15th-century frescoes).

   Guéhenno, south of Josselin, has a parish close with a remarkable story. Its great calvary was destroyed during the Revolution and pieced together laboriously and expertly by the villagers. In the north, near Paimpol, the chapel at **Kermaria** has a remarkable series of Dance of Death frescoes.

97

BRITTANY

A view of Dinan, strung along the banks of the Rance

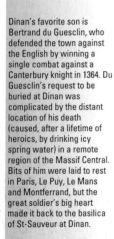

▶▶▷ Dinan

This is a wonderfully preserved medieval town, surrounded by 600-year-old ramparts and guarded by an impressive fortress, high above the Rance. Its few museums are a less powerful magnet than the cobbled streets, timber-fronted houses, crafts shops and weavers' workshops. There are good views from the Jardin des Anglais (Dinan had a large 19th-century British colony) and the small port.

The Rance estuary One of the longest and most beautiful of Breton inlets, the Rance sees huge tides of up to 43 feet. A short distance upstream of its mouth at St-Malo and Dinard, it is bridged by the world's first tidal-power dam, which uses both ebb and flow to generate electricity. You can walk along the dam, which makes a long narrow reservoir of most of the steep-sided inlet, drive over it, and sail through it. Boat trips go up the Rance from St-Malo to Dinan.

▶▷▷ Dinard and the Emerald Coast

Facing St-Malo across the mouth of the Rance, Dinard was crowned "Queen of the Emerald Coast" by English Victorians, who "discovered" the resort and its sheltered crescent of white sand. Its claims to rival La Baule as a fashionable Breton resort should be treated with some skepticism, but Dinard retains a certain style, with neo-Gothic villas and formal hotels, gardens and coastal walks.

Between Dinard and Cap Fréhel the coast weaves an intricate course up inlets and back along rocky promontories, with the finest cliff scenery between the medieval **Fort de la Latte** and **Cap Fréhel**. To the west lies a succession of family resorts: **St-Cast-Le-Guildo** and **St-Quay-Portrieux** (both mergers) are the liveliest, both good for water sports. **Sable d'Or Les Pins** lives up to its name, with shady pines and long golden sands, and **Erquy** is a small fishing port with everyday Breton charm, good seafood, and a beach. The big town of the area, **St-Brieuc** has an unusual fortified 14th-century cathedral.

▷▷▷　Dol de Bretagne

Once a bishopric, once beside the sea, Dol now overlooks land reclaimed from the Bay of Mont-St-Michel since the Middle Ages. St. Samson's cathedral is a massive 13th-century granite structure, with splendid views from the tower. Champ-Dolent is a fine menhir (see page 95) to the south, near the Rennes road.

▶▷▷　Fougères

One of the most impressive of all fortresses marking the medieval border between France and Brittany is eccentrically located below this substantial town. Perhaps for this reason its defensive record was not spotless. A great benefit of the arrangement is marvelous aerial views of the castle from a number of vantage points, including the garden terrace of the place aux Arbres.

The first Rohan at Josselin was the wife of Jean de Beaumanoir, who captained the winning side in 1351 when the forces of Josselin and pro-English Ploërmel agreed to a hand-to-hand fight. At the scene of combat, the two lanes of the N24 part to skirt a commemorative column.

▶▷▷　Josselin

An old town named after the younger son of the baron who began building its castle in the early 11th century. In striking contrast to the powerful round towers and wall rising from the waters of the Oust, most of the building is in ornate Renaissance style, much restored.

▶▶▷　Locronan

Between Quimper and the Crozon Peninsula, the small village of Locronan has a grand ensemble of Renaissance buildings around its central square, a reminder of the days of wealth derived from sailmaking. Every second Sunday in July, Locronan has a *pardon* (pilgrimage) following the course of St. Ronan's daily barefoot walk. The village is now a thriving arts center.

Lorient　See panel.

Lorient prospered with the Compagnie des Indes, which built its shipyards opposite Port Louis on the sheltered Blavet estuary. Louis XVI and Napoleon transformed the port into a naval base. Lorient's occupying German garrison held out until May 1945, by which time little remained standing. The modern town holds a festival of Celtic culture in August.

Dol de Bretagne

Drive **Visiting the hill country: Monts d'Arrée**

Start at Huelgoat.
Huelgoat is a rare inland resort, beside a lake at the heart of Brittany's hill country, the **Monts d'Arrée**, now one section of the fragmented Armorique Regional Park. The *goat* in the name, meaning "forest," is no longer appropriate after centuries of deforestation and severe storm damage in October 1987. The main walking area is to the northeast of the village; Arthur's camp is genuinely ancient if not Arthurian.

D764 to Roc Trévézel; D785/30 to St-Rivoal and St-Cadou.
The route skirts the reservoir and much-resented nuclear power station of **St-Michel**, a surprising landmark at the heart of a regional park. Near the crossroads of D764 and 785, the **Roc Trévézel** (1,260 feet) is the summit of Brittany, a wild and bleak rocky crest. ~~Hundreds of millions of years ago~~ these mountains stood as high as the Alps do now. A few miles west, on the Sizun road (D764), the old hamlet of **Kérouat** has been restored as a rural ecomuseum. **St-Rivoal** has been similarly revived as a museum dedicated to local crafts and traditions. South of St-Cadou is the **Ménez-Meur** wildlife reserve and

regional park information center.

D130/342/42, Forêt du Cranou, to Le Faou.
Le Faou is an attractive estuary port, with good hotels on the main square.

D791 Corniche de Térénez road; excursion to Ménez-Hom (D60/47/83).
Ménez-Hom (330 m) is the western bastion of the Monts d'Arrée, a splendidly isolated hump at the base of the cruciform Crozon Peninsula. A steep road climbs to a viewing platform. At a crossroads near **Trégarvan**, north of Ménez-Hom, the old village school has been restored (Musée de l'Ecole Rurale). There are sandy beaches along the south side of the peninsula, between **Ste-Anne-la-Palud** and **Morgat**.

D47/21 to Brasparts, D14 to St-Herbot and back to Huelgoat.
Brasparts has a crafts center and an interesting church with Renaissance porch and calvary. **St-Herbot's** Gothic church has a 16th-century ossuary and calvary and carved wooden screen. Herbot is the patron saint of horned beasts; hoping for protection for their cattle, farmers traditionally deposit locks of tail hair in the church on pardon day.

▶ ▷ ▷   **Morbihan, Golfe du**

The Morbihan (Little Sea) Gulf forms an almost complete circle, including the **Vannes** and **Auray** estuaries and enclosing 40 inhabited islands: The entrance to the inland sea between Locmariaquer and Port-Navalo is less than 2 km wide. In the 1st century BC the gulf was the site of a sea battle between the local Veneti tribe and the forces of Rome. Julius Caesar watched the proceedings from the summit of a prehistoric tumulus on the shore near Arzon, on the southern arm of the entrance to the gulf.

Oyster country The best way to see the gulf is by boat, either a private yacht (tricky currents in the strait) or on a boat trip, for which Vannes is the main base. Low tide reveals huge expanses of mud flats and oyster beds. The gulf (especially the Auray Peninsula) is the breeding ground for flat oysters, which grow on lime-washed tiles until they are big enough to be transported to parks all around the Breton coast.

Driving around the gulf is long and not particularly rewarding. Of the two main towns, Vannes is more interesting to visit than Auray, except for one of the big pardons at **Ste-Anne d'Auray**. Locmariaquer, the island of **Gavrinis** (from Larmor Baden) and **Carnac** are the highlights of Breton prehistory (see page 95). On the southern arm of the gulf, the main points of interest are the old monastery of **St-Gildas-de-Rhuys**, with a part-Romanesque church (St. Gildas's tomb), and the splendidly wild 13th- and 14th-century fortress of **Suscinio**. **Port Navalo** has accommodations and summer boat trips.

Sailing on a private yacht or an organized trip is the best way to see the sights of the Golfe du Morbihan

The cobbled streets of Auray

After his amorous adventure with a young pupil, Héloïse, in Paris, the philosopher Peter Abélard withdrew to the lonely job of abbot of St-Gildas-de-Rhuys in 1126. In a letter to Héloïse he expressed his hatred of Brittany and his suspicion of the Breton monks. Abélard's attempts to impose discipline in the abbey went down very badly with men he referred to as savages, who spoke a language he was unable to understand. In 1138 the resentful monks rebeled and tried to poison Abélard, but he survived and escaped.

Nantes's history has its darker moments. Gilles de Rais, the original Bluebeard, was tried and burned at the stake in the ducal castle in 1440. Nantes later made fortunes out of the slave trade. And in 1793, it saw macabre ceremonies known as Republican Weddings, when Royalists were stripped naked, bound together in pairs and dumped in the Loire in order to make room in the city's prisons.

In the 19th century, Paimpol was the main base of France's long-haul cod-fishing fleet, immortalized in Pierre Loti's novel *Pêcheur d'Islande.* On February 20, most of the town's men would set sail for six months in the North Atlantic, returning in late summer. Refrigeration technology hit the industry and Paimpol is now a busy pleasure port and agricultural marketplace.

▶ ▶ ▷ Nantes

The former capital of Brittany is no longer part of the region and no longer a city of much charm. The old town, once pierced by branches of the Erdre and Loire, is now encircled by fast ring roads, and the town's chief monument, the 15th- and 16th-century dukes' castle, stands among tall modern buildings. Nevertheless, there are popular art, decorative art (fabrics) and maritime museums. The fine arts museum (behind the cathedral) is outstanding: it includes works by Perugino, Ingres and de la Tour; and the late Gothic cathedral has the beautiful Renaissance tomb of the last duke of Brittany, François II.

▶ ▷ ▷ Quiberon

This is a lively port and resort with a good beach, at the end of the long sandy isthmus linking the former island to the mainland. There are good walks along the rocky west coast. Fresh sardines used to be a specialty, but supply has dwindled recently. Ferries to Belle-Ile and the other Quiberon islands (see pages 92–93).

▶ ▶ ▷ Quimper and Cournouaille

Cournouaille's 6th-century King Gradlon made Quimper his capital after the destruction of Is, and a statue of him stands between the twin spires of the Gothic cathedral, which changes direction at the crossing. Quimper takes tradition seriously, and is full of well-kept charm: cobbled streets, timber-framed houses, costumed and coiffed old ladies making lace. It has a moderately interesting fine arts museum, a Breton museum in the old Bishop's Palace and even a crêpe museum. There are boat trips down the Odet estuary.

At the mouth of the river, **Bénodet** is the largest of several family beach resorts in the camper's favorite corner of Brittany. **Beg-Meil** is the other focus for camping.

The rest of the southwest corner of Brittany is disappointingly dreary. **Pont l'Abbé** is a town of needleworkers and the home of the tallest of all Breton *coiffes* (caps), here not kept for special occasions. **St-Guénolé** has a good beach, a prehistoric museum and splendid rocky coast at the back of the port and at the nearby Pointe de Penmarch. **Audierne** is ideal if you prefer fishing ports to beach resorts. Masses flock to the **Pointe du Raz**, Brittany's most spectacular rocky cape (see page 93).

A stall selling lace in Quimper

Pont-Aven

■ The name of Pont-Aven has become inextricably linked with that of Paul Gauguin, the 38-year-old Paris stockbroker who gave up everything (job, wife and five children) to settle there in 1886, with his fellow artist Emile Bernard. ...■

Gauguin and Bernard did not discover Pont-Aven (southeast of Quimper), which was already full of artists, mainly Scandinavian and British. It was picturesque then as now, with walks in the Bois d'Amour by the river, and watermills outnumbering dwellings 15 to 14. There were several inns: the Julia (French academic artists), des Voyageurs (Americans, some of whom stayed all year) and the more bohemian Pension Gloannec, where Gauguin and friends holed up at 60 francs a month, including two good meals a day and cider; more often, paintings were accepted in lieu.

Model neighbors Pont-Aven was a thoroughly pretty place, added to which the locals readily agreed to pose in their quaint costumes for a few sous a day. Gauguin, Bernard

> << "When my wooden shoes ring on this granite, I hear the muffled, dull, powerful tone I seek in my painting."—Paul Gauguin >>

Paul Gauguin's Gossipers

and disciples, including Sérusier and Maurice Denis, were not insensitive to these aspects of Breton charm but looked beyond them and the naturalistic aims of Impressionism. They launched a new, more mystical art, using the local chapels for their sense of rural piety, interwoven with myth and superstition. Within walking distance of the village, the Trémalo Chapel's wooden *Christ* inspired Gauguin, as did Nizon's *Calvary* (*Yellow Christ* and *Green Christ* paintings).

Grand exit In 1889 Gauguin and friends moved from Pont-Aven, which they found overrun, to Le Pouldu on the coast, where Gauguin surprised walkers with his rough appearance—naked, with long hair and a spear at the ready. This caused less of a stir in Tahiti, which was Gauguin's next move.

Pont-Aven still has its walks, restored mills (no longer outnumbering dwellings) and various galleries, but no Gauguin paintings on permanent display.

The whole Léon coast is rich in seaweed: Roscoff has over 70 varieties, which it puts to medical, chemical and agricultural use. Ordinary seaweed is an excellent natural fertilizer for artichokes, cauliflower and onions. In a few places, especially on the more primitive islands (Batz, Molène), seaweed is still harvested on horseback in the traditional way.

▶ ▶ ▷ Rennes

The capital of Brittany was almost entirely demolished by fire in 1720 and subsequently rebuilt in a severe classical style. Only the area between the market square (place des Lices) and the city's two waterways escaped and remains old and higgledy-piggledy. The sumptuously decorated 17th-century Law Courts are open to visitors; the cathedral has a fine carved wooden altar in a south aisle chapel; and the regional museum is excellent.

▶ ▷ ▷ Roscoff

This port and pretty seaside resort, once renowned for its pirates, is now known for the sea cure. Roscoff boasts an enormous 17th-century fig tree and beautiful alabaster altar reliefs in the church near the harbor, whose Renaissance belfry bristles with cannon to warn off the English. The creation of a deep-water port was a key part of the strategy to revive Breton agriculture in the 1960s, under the dynamic leadership of Alex Gourvennec. Reestablishing old Celtic links, the farmers' ferry company, Brittany Ferries, exports vegetables to southwest England and Ireland, and welcomes ferryloads of British tourists on the return leg. Day trips go from the old port to the sandy island of **Batz** (pronounced "Baa"), often accessible on foot at low tide.

▶ ▷ ▷ Ste-Anne-la-Palud

West of Plonevez-Porzay is the sandy beach and seaside hamlet of St-Anne-la-Palud, host to the most famous *pardon* in Brittany on the last weekend in August; spectacular processions on Saturday and Sunday.

Roscoff's harbor at low tide

▶▶▷ St-Malo

This is a port with a long and proud history of nautical explorers, traders and swashbuckling corsairs (licensed pirates, effectively) who took the name St-Malo as far as the distant Falkland Islands (Malvinas to the Argentinians; Malouines to the Malouins). The heart of their home town at the mouth of the Rance is a walled citadel (St-Malo-Intra-Muros) at the entrance to the harbor. Although the town had to be rebuilt after destruction in 1944, the job was faithfully done, and Intra Muros deserves a rampart tour and a wander.

• **Stroll** *At low tide you can walk to two islands: a Vauban fort and Grand Bé, where the 19th-century author Chateaubriand, who spent his formative years at St-Malo, is buried.*

▶▷▷ St-Pol-de-Léon

This vegetable market town near Roscoff has two beautiful churches, the cathedral and slightly later Kreisker chapel, famous for its slender 183-foot belfry. The former seat of the barony of Léon, St-Pol is one of the seven old Breton bishoprics, a tour of which every Breton should traditionally make at least once. The saint in question is the 6th-century missionary Paul Aurelian, who lived here for 36 years before retiring to the island of Batz, where he is said to have tamed and expelled the local dragon.

▶▶▷ Tréguier

An old hillside town, well set above a deep oyster-rich inlet near busy north coast resorts, Tréguier has a celebrated pilgrimage (May 19) in honor of Brittany's beloved St. Yves, a 13th-century lawyer and poor man's champion. A splendid cathedral is set on the market square. Tucked into the rocky coast to the north, little **Port Blanc** has great charm and was appreciated by H. G. Wells and Bernard Shaw, among many other escapists.

▶▶▷ Vannes

This important town in Breton history (the act of union with France was finalized here in 1532) has old walls and fortified gateways intact, commanding the head of the Gulf of Morbihan. A canalized waterway reaches the foot of the town walls. The old town center is touristy and picturesque, with timbered and gabled houses overhanging the narrow streets around the cathedral, which houses the tomb of St. Vincent Ferrier, an itinerant preacher who died here in 1419.

▶▶▷ Vitré

Set at the foot of a fine turreted 14th-century castle on the River Vilaine, Vitré rivals Dinan as a medieval time warp. Lots of interesting old houses line the streets that run between the castle and the church of Notre-Dame, which has an external pulpit for open-air religious debate. Literary tourists may want to visit the nearby **Château des Rochers-Sévigné**, home of a great letter-writer of the 17th century, the marquise de Sévigné.

Pardons are a mixture of religious and pagan festival: pilgrimages undertaken to seek anything from forgiveness to a bumper harvest. These remain serious religious occasions, but also provide a chance for a costume display and, afterward, a bunfight. The most important are at Rumengol (August 15 and Trinity Sunday), Perros-Guirec (August 15), St-Jean-du-Doigt (June 23–24), Ste-Anne-la-Palud (last weekend in August), and Tréguier (May 19). The biggest pilgrimage centers are Le Folgoët (main event in early September) and Ste-Anne-d'Auray (June 29). Locronan has an extra-large *pardon* every six years (next in 1995) lasting a week.

"Vannes and his wife" look out over their home town

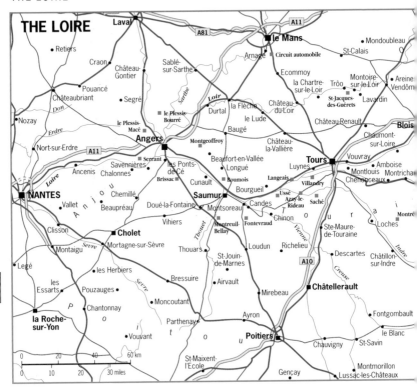

One of the most popular of the Loire Valley châteaus: Azay-le-Rideau

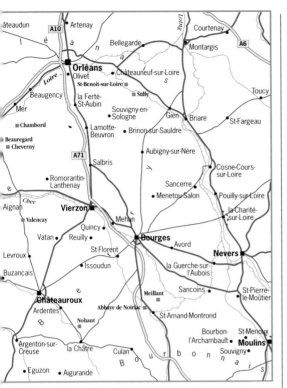

The Val de Loire, in the form of the ancient provinces of Anjou, Touraine, Orleanais and Berry, is the historic heart of France. As capital of the Plantagenet kings' Angevin Empire, which at its zenith stretched from the north of England to the Pyrenees, it was the focus of almost three centuries of war between the French and English, which culminated in the expulsion of the English in 1453.

Gracious living The resulting ascendancy of French pride engendered a period of fervent building, and as a result the countryside around the Loire Valley is incomparably rich in Renaissance châteaus, built of milky white tufa. With their turrets and towers, steep, gray slate roofs, galleries and pleasure gardens, they are a perennially popular part of the tourist itinerary. It may come as a disappointment to realize, during a lengthy guided tour (in French), that for many châteaus the main interest is in their historical associations. It pays to make a careful selection and to include one or two of the more intimate, inhabited châteaus.

The river The wide, shallow Loire flows sluggishly between mud banks and silt islets, past looming nuclear power stations and busy towns and highways. Its prettier tributaries are punctuated with white and gray villages and fringed by forests, orchards and fertile cultivations, justifying the area's claim to be the garden of France.

THE LOIRE

In 1516 François I, determined to lure to Amboise as many distinguished Italian artists as he could, persuaded Leonardo da Vinci to enjoy a quiet retirement as first painter, engineer and architect to the king. He thrilled the court with dramatic *son-et-lumières* (sound-and-light shows), fireworks displays and pageants, using mechanical special effects; he also drew up plans for a new Venetian-style town. The museum set up in his former home in Amboise, the manor of Le Clos Lucé, contains models constructed (fairly recently) according to his designs—including a parachute, helicopter and tank.

Detail from the cathedral at Angers

 Amboise

This small and attractive town was one of the earliest Loire settlements, and an important bridgehead in the Middle Ages. It became the site of one of the greatest royal châteaus after Charles VIII, inspired by the exuberant Renaissance buildings he had seen on an otherwise unsuccessful campaign in Italy, embarked on building a new style of palace—a far cry from the fortress strongholds that had hitherto characterized royal buildings.

Only fragments of the château remain today, but a guided tour is well worth taking in order to visit the superb Flamboyant chapel of St-Hubert, on the former ramparts, and the extraordinary Tour des Minimes, with a spiral ramp said to have been able to accommodate horses and carts.

▶▶▷ **Angers**

A large town on the banks of the Maine, Angers lies in the area known as Black Anjou on account of the local rock, which in contrast to the white tufa of Touraine, farther east, lends a forbidding tone to the buildings. The black shale fortress walls of the Château d'Angers are relieved by white stripes; 17 drum towers remain to evoke its military past, when Angers was an outpost of the French kings on the border of hostile Brittany.

Angers is well endowed with buildings of interest. Around the powerful early Gothic cathedral are many fine old houses; of particular interest are the 16th-century Maison d'Adam (place Ste-Croix) and the Renaissance Hôtel Pincé. Nearby, the Logis Barrault houses a good fine arts museum.

▶▶▶ **Azay-le-Rideau** see pages 112–113.

▶▷▷ **Beaugency**

Another important Loire bridgehead, delivered from the English by Joan of Arc in 1429, Beaugency is now a compact small town with a cluster of sights by the river: an evocative ruined keep (*donjon*), picturesque cobbled streets, a regional museum in the château, and a Renaissance town hall.

Tapestries

■ Tapestry weaving in Europe is believed to have started in the 12th century, although the techniques were probably used in classical Greece and Rome. From the 14th to the 17th centuries the art reached its peak. The main workshops were in Paris, Arras, Bruges, Tournai and Brussels; later, royal workshops were established at the Gobelins factory outside Paris, and at Aubusson. ...■

The most famous tapestry to have survived from the early period is the incomplete but superb series of 70 works illustrating the Apocalypse of St. John the Divine, commissioned by the duc d'Anjou in 1375, and made in Paris by Nicolas Bataille from cartoons by Hennequin de Bruges. These huge works (328 feet long and 16 feet high), intended for Angers cathedral, provide a graphic illustration of St. John's writings, depicting rivers of blood and whores of Babylon against a more gentle background of *mille-fleurs*, with humorous touches such as rabbits popping in and out of holes in the border.

Survival over the centuries The preservation of these tapestries is nothing short of miraculous, following haphazard storage (they were displayed only rarely in Angers cathedral) and disposal during the Revolution. In 1843, the bishop of Angers set about buying all the fragments he could find and having them carefully restored. Now they hang in a modern gallery in the Museum of Tapestries in the **Château d'Angers**.

Tapestries for today On the opposite side of the river, the **Ancien Hôpital de St-Jean** is the setting for a remarkable series of contemporary tapestries created in Aubusson by the painter and designer Jean Lurçat. Inspired by the Apocalypse, Lurçat created intense and colorful symbolic works entitled *Le Chant du Monde* (The Song of the World). Against a black background, he depicted his fears of the future of the world; the first four panels (including *The Man of Hiroshima* and *The Great Charnel House*) are more pessimistic in their outlook than the later ones.

Originally there were to have been 17 panels; only 10 were created, over a period of nine years, before Lurçat's death in 1966.

Detail from an Angers tapestry

■ ◀◀ Tapestries were used not only for wall hangings in churches and houses of the rich, but as covers for beds, chairs, tables and cushions, and as horse blankets and rugs. ▶▶

▶▷▷ Beauregard, Château de

Like Chambord, Beauregard was one of François I's hunting lodges. Unlike Chambord, this château is still inhabited, and although it is on the popular château trail (Cheverny is just up the road), it is relatively unfrequented, and is well worth visiting. There is a portrait gallery of 363 famous people, a delft tile floor, and some fine timbered and coffered ceilings.

▶▷▷ Blois

The busy town of Blois could be considered the tourist capital of the Loire Valley. Picturesque and lively, it makes a good base for visitors without a car (those, at least, who don't mind hills too much), who can choose from a selection of sightseeing bus tours on offer from the tourist office. Taking pride of place on a cliff top north of the river is the great royal château (see pages 112–113), whose architectural variety—with parts ranging from the 13th to 17th centuries—reflects its history as the favored royal residence until Louis XIV moved the court to Versailles.

The hilly town has its share of pedestrianized shopping areas and picturesque old streets by the river; the tourist office organizes guided walks.

Architectural detail at the royal château of Blois

▶▶▷ Boumois, Château de

A few miles northwest of Saumur, the Château de Boumois's early 16th-century fortress exterior hides a graceful Renaissance inner house and courtyard, and a fine Gothic chapel.

▶▶▷ Bourges

This large industrial town is notable for one of France's great Gothic cathedrals (mainly 12th- and 13th-century), famous for its double aisles, beautiful stained glass, and richly sculpted Romanesque side doors from a previous building. Bourges also possesses one of the most perfect examples of a Gothic mansion, which combined comfort with defense—the Palais Jacques Coeur, built for a 15th-century financier.

▶ ▶ ▷ Brissac, Château de

Between the Loire and the wine villages of the Layon, southeast of Angers, Brissac is yet another example of a château that combines medieval foundations and towers (which resisted all attempts at destruction) with a later building: In this case the more recent addition is an elegant 17th-century central wing, richly decorated.

▶ ▷ ▷ Candes

At the confluence of the Loire and the Vienne stands the quiet farming village of Candes, where the fortified church of St-Martin (12th- and 13th-century) has much of interest, including a richly sculpted facade and soaring Angevin vaulting (which differs from other Gothic styles in that the keys of the ogival arches are higher than those of the other arches). The steep path behind the church offers attractive river views.

▶ ▶ ▶ Chambord

At the western edge of the Sologne is the huge forest estate and hunting reserve of Chambord. There are public avenues and paths, and game observation posts (good times to catch sight of the deer and wild boar are said to be dawn and dusk). At the heart lies the

On the east bank of the Vienne, east of Poitiers, the small town of Chauvigny has a fine hilltop fortress. On the same hill, the church of St-Pierre has remarkable grotesque capitals; and to the south of the town, the little church of St-Pierre-les-Eglises has interesting frescoes.

Chauvigny market

memorable 440-room Château de Chambord, which was transformed by François I from a simple hunting lodge (see pages 112–113).

▶ ▶ ▷ Chaumont-sur-Loire

This small riverside town is overlooked by a hillside park whose tall cedar trees almost hide one of the finest early Renaissance châteaus in France, home for many years of the scheming Catherine de' Médicis after the death of her husband, Henri II. The château appears more like a medieval fortified castle than a royal residence, and the furnished interior illustrates the rather spartan lifestyle enjoyed by its noble inhabitants. There are very fine stables in the grounds.

■ The great age of château building in the Loire followed the campaigns of Joan of Arc and the subsequent expulsion of the English from France in 1453. A new feeling of national pride and optimism was engendered, which resulted in ambitious royal building programs. The failure of successive military forays to Italy by Charles VIII, Louis XII and François I between 1494 and 1525 was mitigated by their exposure to the Renaissance movement in that country. Italian architects, artists and gardeners were brought to the French court, and schools were established first at Amboise, then at Tours, Blois, and Fontainebleau. ...■

In the Loire Valley's ancient hunting grounds of kings and courtiers, the new climate of peace changed the need for fortification, and emphasis was placed instead on comfort and elegance. Massive walls, moats, machicolations, battlements and drawbridges were gradually to give way to ornamental details: open loggias, finely sculpted exterior staircases, mullioned and dormer windows, columns and pilasters.

Chenonceau, spanning the River Cher (right) and a detail from Blois (below)

Inspired designs In the transitional period of the early 16th century, Renaissance features were grafted onto Gothic ones; later influences were the Mannerist decorative architectural arts of Rome, providing inspiration for the school of **Fontainebleau**. This period was followed (in the 17th century) by a more dignified classical approach for exteriors, combined with brilliantly profuse interior decoration. No motif was too elaborate: Scrolls, nymphs, shells, luxuriant foliage and wreaths were applied in stucco, wood or papier-mâché to walls, ceilings and furniture.

Four of the most beautiful and most popular Loire châteaus from the Renaissance period are **Azay-le-Rideau**, **Blois**, **Chambord** and **Chenonceau**.

Azay-le-Rideau This graceful small white château, its image reflected in a moat formed by the River Indre, retains its medieval appearance, like so many buildings of the period, but combines this with the new ornamental style. It boasts a beautifully decorated internal staircase with straight flights, an innovative departure from the conventional spiral. The interior has been arranged as a Renaissance museum.

Blois The royal château of Blois is interesting for its variety of styles. From the 13th century onward, a succession of buildings was erected around a central courtyard. The most impressive is the elegant François I wing (adorned by a magnificent spiral staircase tower), which was partly demolished by François Mansart in order to build the Gaston d'Orléans wing, in sharply contrasting classical style.

A guided tour of the interior features heavily restored rooms and much historical detail, including a description of the bloody murder of the duc de Guise in 1588. More rewarding is a son-et-lumière performance in the courtyard.

Old stone and new dog at Chenonceau

113

Chambord Designed by an Italian architect, this monumental château was built as a superior hunting lodge by François I. Its size defies most camera lenses, and lends an air of fantasy to the building, which may seem to have more in common with Disney than the Renaissance. The most memorable exterior feature is the extraordinary sculpted roofscape, consisting of numerous chimneys, bell turrets, dormer windows, spires and capitals; it served as a viewing terrace from which to observe the start and finish of hunts, as well as tournaments and pageants, and was also a place for court assignations and intrigues.

Inside, the most outstanding feature is the very famous double spiral staircase, by which people can ascend and descend simultaneously without meeting each other. Its design was at times attributed to Leonardo da Vinci, among others. The château is sparsely furnished, and evokes little of the life of former times; but you can visit without a guided tour.

The exterior aspect of Chambord is best enjoyed before or after popular tourist visiting hours; at dawn or dusk, it assumes an almost magical quality. Son-et-lumière performances provide yet another opportunity for visual indulgence.

Created for the financier Gilles Berthelot in the early 16th century, Azay-le-Rideau is one of several in the Loire Valley where the building work was directed by a woman — in this case, Berthelot's wife.

Chenonceau A supremely elegant château whose arched gallery spans the River Cher. The building work was supervised by Katherine Bohier, the wife of Thomas Bohier, royal tax collector and embezzler. Following confiscation by François I, the château came under the influence of Diane de Poitiers and then (more significantly in architectural terms) of Catherine de' Médicis, who added a gallery on the bridge. The interior is well furnished, and it is possible to visit without a guided tour (explanatory notes are available). There are fine formal gardens and a park; other attractions include a waxworks museum that illustrates scenes from Chenonceau's past.

An onion seller in Chinon

▶▶▷ Chenonceaux

The village of Chenonceaux (note that the village is spelled with an *x*, the château simply Chenonceau) is well provided with accommodations and other tourist facilities, but not with charm. An overnight stay is worth considering, however, in order to beat the morning crowds at the château.

▶▶▶ Cheverny, Château de

This is a rigorously symmetrical classical château, supremely harmonious, whose interior has been largely unaltered since its completion. Sumptuously decorated and furnished in Louis XIII style, it is one of the few Loire châteaus to evoke the feel of a home; it is still privately owned and inhabited. There are likely to be long lines for the guided tour in high season.

Cheverny is famous for its liveried hunt; on the grounds of the château, the kennels and trophy room can be visited.

▶▶▷ Chinon

A busy and interesting small town and tourist center on the leafy Vienne is dominated by the ample ruins of its medieval castle, a royal residence best known as the place where in 1429 Joan of Arc first persuaded the dauphin Charles to let her take command of an army in order to drive the English out of France.

Chinon is an attractive base for a short stay (there are several hotels and restaurants, as well as a riverside campsite). The picturesque cobbled streets of the restored old town are lined with half-timbered houses; the principal center of activity is the Grand Carroi crossroads.

▶▶▷ Cunault

On the south bank of the Loire northwest of Saumur lies the beautiful Romanesque church of Cunault, part of a former Benedictine monastery. Tall and slender, the pure white of the tufa stone broken only by fragments of fresco, Cunault is renowned above all for its wealth of remarkable sculpted capitals, which can best be admired through binoculars.

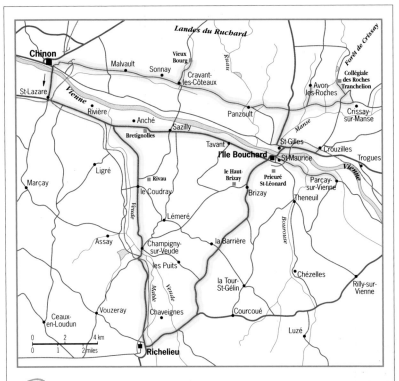

Drive **Discovering the River Vienne**

Start at Chinon.
The Vienne is an intimate and secretive river, bordered by gardens, orchards, willows and poplars.

D749 to Champigny-sur-Veude and Richelieu.
The chapel of Sainte-Chapelle at **Champigny-sur-Veude** is part of a former château demolished by Cardinal Richelieu in a fit of jealousy. Saved only by the intervention of Pope Urban VIII, it is a wonderful example of the marriage of Renaissance with Gothic. In the town of **Richelieu**, to the south, the cardinal's own château was demolished in the Revolution. Fine parks remain; of more interest, however, are the results of 17th-century classical town planning.

D757 to l'Ile-Bouchard. Take the D760 to Crouzilles or the D18 to Parçay-sur-Vienne or the D757/D21
to Avon-les-Roches, Les Roches-Tranchelion and Crissay-sur-Manse.
The area southeast of Chinon, along the Vienne valley, is rich in early churches. At **l'Ile Bouchard** fine capitals remain in the ruins of St-Léonard priory. Various detours offer the opportunity to visit the Romanesque churches of **Crouzilles, Parçay-sur-Vienne** and **Avon-les-Roches**, the Gothic/Renaissance collegiate church of **Les Roches-Tranchelion**, or the Carolingian church of **Vieux-Bourg-de-Cravant**.

Return to Chinon direct on D21 via Cravant-les-Côteaux, or go back to l'Ile-Bouchard and take the D760 via Tavant, Sazilly and Anché; rejoin the D749 to Chinon.
The tiny Romanesque church of **Tavant** has lively frescoes, full of realism (for access, apply to the caretaker, who lives nearby, or to the town hall).

THE LOIRE

Fontevraud Abbey was established in the early 11th century, catering for both monks and nuns, as well as fallen women and lepers. Each unit had its own church, cloister and living quarters. Headed by an abbess, the order became popular with noblewomen, and acquired great wealth under the patronage of the rich and the royal. It also became the chosen resting place for the Plantagenet Henry II, his queen Eleanor of Aquitaine, and their son Richard Lionheart, whose effigies lie in the abbey church.

Powder horns in the museum of hunting at Gien

▶ ▶ ▷ **Fontevraud**

Relatively little remains of the great 11th-century abbey of Fontevraud (even the few buildings that survived the Revolution had to serve for over 150 years as a national prison). Apart from the soaring abbey church, the most interesting part is the kitchen, a rare example of secular Romanesque architecture, flanked by apsidal chapels and topped by 20 chimneys.

▷ ▷ ▷ **Gien**

A bridgehead town and useful stop on the rather dull stretch of Loire east of Orléans, Gien is known mainly for its faience (items can be purchased from the large factory just to the west of town). The large redbrick castle contains a museum of hunting; next to it, the modern church of Ste-Jeanne-d'Arc fits in unusually well with its surroundings.

▶ ▶ ▷ **Langeais, Château de**

One of the most interesting late medieval royal châteaus to have come down to us largely unaltered, Langeais illustrates the transition from Gothic (fortress exterior, drawbridge and barbican) to Renaissance (interior). It contains a wonderful collection of contemporary furnishings and works of art that evokes the lifestyle of the time of Charles VIII and Anne of Brittany. The château lies in the busy center of an otherwise unexciting small town.

▶ ▶ ▷ **Loches**

Above the modern town of Loches lies the heavily fortified medieval city, whose fierce keep and dungeons served for many centuries as a state prison. The château is perhaps best known as the home of Agnès Sorel, well-loved and extravagant mistress of Charles VII; a guided tour (lengthy, and focusing heavily on history and architecture) reveals among other things the tiny prayer cell of Anne of Brittany. It's worth wandering around the walls and through the old quarter leading up to the medieval city, where there are some fine Renaissance houses.

▶ ▶ ▷ **Le Loir**

The confusingly named tributary of La Loire meanders slowly through a peaceful agricultural countryside. Although within easy striking distance of its more famous sister, Le Loir is off the main tourist track (with the exception of the **Château du Lude,** renowned for its son-et-lumière performances with a large cast of local actors). Its towns and villages preserve an everyday charm.

Church country All this does not mean that Le Loir is without sightseeing interest. Indeed (like the stretch of the Vienne described on page 115), it is of particular interest to lovers of early churches. Along its banks is a succession of small Romanesque buildings, most of which were on a medieval pilgrimage route leading to Santiago de Compostela in Spain. Orders of Benedictines, Cistercians and Knights Templar housed and fed the pilgrim travelers, and in **Montoire** and **Trôo** hospices and leper hospitals offered comfort to the sick. The Loir churches are of special interest for their brightly colored frescoes; some are remarkably well preserved. A good area for a church crawl is on the stretch of river between **Vendôme** and **La Chatre-sur-le-Loir.** Particular ones to seek out include the church in the little village of **Areines**, the site of a Roman settlement, on the eastern side of Vendôme (take the D917 east, followed by the first road on the left); St-Genest in **Lavardin**, which has especially fine mural paintings dating from the 12th to the 16th centuries; and **St-Jacques-des-Guérets**, on the south bank of the Loir just outside the village of Trôo, which also has a superb series of paintings.

Town sights The towns along this stretch of Le Loir offer plenty of interest, too. **Vendôme** not only has a fine Gothic abbey church (La Trinité), with a rich Flamboyant west front, but is also a picturesque place built on several islands, with waterside gardens. The attractive market square of **St-Martin** has a beautiful Renaissance belltower. **Montoire** possesses some of the best frescoes of all the Loir churches, in the tiny chapel of St-Gilles; it is also remembered as the site of a meeting in 1940 between Marshal Pétain and Hitler.

The Loir Valley's soft tufa stone has long provided accommodation, in conditions of constant temperature and humidity, for wine storage and mushroom cultivation. Along Le Loir, the banks are riddled with tufa caves that are used for troglodyte dwellings. Now no longer only simple peasant abodes, troglodyte caves are sought-after second homes, with central heating to supplement the log fire (the chimney sticks out of the ground above) and conservatories tacked onto the front.

117

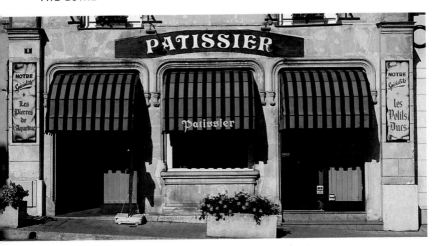

The Loire Valley produces every style of wine. The best appellations for dry whites are: Muscadet de Sèvre-et-Maine; Pouilly-Fumé and Sancerre, and the cheaper Reuilly, Quincy and Menetou-Salon; Savennières, and the individual vineyard appellations of Coulée de Serrant and La Roche aux Moines. For reds: Saumur-Champigny; Bourgueil and St-Nicolas-de-Bourgueil; Chinon. For sparkling whites: Saumur; Vouvray and Montlouis. For sweet whites: the superb Quarts de Chaume and Bonnezeaux, and the larger area of Côteaux du Layon; Vouvray and Montlouis.

In the village of Luynes

▶▷▷   Luynes

Just off the north bank of the Loire, west of Tours, the village of Luynes is overlooked by yet another of the valley's sentinels—the Château de Luynes (not open to the public). The current building (mainly 13th-century) replaced an earlier fortress, which in turn was built on the site of a Roman camp. The **aqueduct** that served this, and the town of Tours, can still be seen to the northeast of the village.

▶▶▷   Le Mans

Known mainly for its 24-hour automobile race, industrial Le Mans serves as a crossroads town between Normandy and the Loire Valley, a fact that is rather a shame in view of its many attractions. This ancient city still preserves its Gallo-Roman ramparts, and the beautiful Romanesque/Gothic cathedral is rich in interest: vivid stained glass, Renaissance tombs, and a 12th-century south doorway which could rival that of Chartres. In the old town within the ramparts there are more churches and several fine houses, some of which can be visited: the Maison de la Reine-Bérengère houses a local history and ethnography museum; the Tessé mansion has a rich collection of paintings.

On a different track Racing enthusiasts will not want to miss the 24-hour circuit (13.5 km of track, off the D139 to the south of the city) and the Automobile Museum, which houses an excellent collection of elegant vintage cars.

▶▷▷   Meillant, Château de

South of Bourges, the Château de Meillant is the finest in the Berry. Similar to many of the Loire châteaus in its combination of fortress and palace, Flamboyant Gothic and decorative Renaissance, Meillant rivals its better-known neighbors for the interest of its interior, beautifully decorated and furnished (and, unlike many others, still inhabited).

▶ ▷ ▷   Montgeoffroy, Château de

About 20 km east of Angers, this elegant and harmonious 18th-century château has remained in one family since it was built, and the Louis XVI furniture and wall hangings are the original pieces designed for it. The tour of the house includes a small series of beautiful rooms, as well as the kitchen garden, saddle room and the stables, with a collection of carriages.

▶ ▷ ▷   Montreuil-Bellay

Southwest of Saumur, the large hulk of the 15th-century Château de Montreuil-Bellay dominates the small village above the very leafy little Thouet River; the château comprises several parts, including a pyramid-shaped kitchen reminiscent of that at Fontevraud (see page 116), complete with cooking utensils. The former chapel is now the village church.

▶ ▷ ▷   Montrichard

This attractive little market town on the banks of the Cher has a beach, half-timbered houses by the river, and one of the many fierce keeps built in the 11th century by Foulques Nerra, count of Anjou. On the outskirts of town are stretches of former tufa quarries, now housing wine or mushroom cellars, or troglodytes.

The Château de Montreuil-Bellay

▶ ▷ ▷   Nohant, Château de

Near La Chatre, in the south of the Berry, this was the home of Aurore Dupin de Francueil, better known as George Sand; it is now a museum, with plenty of souvenirs of Sand and her lovers and friends, who included Chopin, Liszt, Flaubert and Balzac. The countryside in and around the *Vallée Noire* of this stretch of the Indre features heavily in her novels.

▶ ▷ ▷   Noirlac, Abbaye de

In the Berry, south of Bourges, this former abbey is a typical example of the simple, austere style of Cistercian buildings. Some of the living quarters are furnished, giving an idea of monastic life from the 12th century.

The cloisters of the Abbaye de Noirlac (see page 119)

Food specialties of the Loire include river fish, particularly pike (*brochet*), carp (*carpe*), shad (*alose*) and salmon (*saumon*), served with a sorrel sauce (*à l'oseille*) or a sauce of butter, vinegar, and shallots (*beurre blanc*); early vegetables, particularly asparagus, and mushrooms; game, particularly in the Sologne; cold, potted pork (*rillettes* and *rillons*) and pork with prunes, a specialty of Tours; fresh cream cheeses (*crèmets*), eaten with sugar and cream; goat cheeses, especially from Poitou; caramelized upside-down apple tart (*tarte Tatin*).

▶▷▷ Orléans

Indelibly associated with Joan of Arc, who delivered it from the English in 1429 after a siege of eight months, the industrial city of Orléans has long been the site of decisive battles. From the early days when Orléans stopped the hordes of Attila, through the Wars of Religion and the Revolution, and finally during the last world war, Orléans suffered much destruction. Now it is the regional capital and a lively university town, although it cannot be said to brim with charm. References to the Maid abound (road and house names, statues and a museum devoted to her); other sights include a much-altered cathedral with fine carved panels around the choir, and an arts museum.

▶▷▷ Plessis Bourré, Château du

This magnificent moated fortress is not only one of the finest houses in Anjou, but also one of the best examples of secular architecture of the late 15th century. Built by Jean Bourré (who was also responsible for Langeais) in the period that marked the transition from heavy feudal fortress to elegant abode for gracious living, Le Plessis Bourré has sumptuously decorated living quarters (including an exceptionally fine painted wooden ceiling in the guardroom) around a huge courtyard.

▶▷▷ Plessis Macé, Château du

On a hill some 13 km to the northwest of Angers, the château of Plessis Macé retains much from the days when it was a strategically important fortress, including ramparts, moat and keep. But the 15th-century additions are of much more interest, particularly the splendid Flamboyant Gothic courtyard balcony, which served as a ladies' viewing area during tournaments.

▶▷▷ Poitiers

An industrial and university city, much damaged during the last war, Poitiers is worth a visit for those interested in its Romanesque churches, and its high-tech theme park, Futuroscope. On the great pilgrimage route to Santiago de Compostela, a distinct school of Romanesque architecture emerged in the province of Poitou, notable for its very richly decorated facades; today, the finest example may be seen on the church of Notre-Dame-la-Grande, on Poitiers's market square. Another exceptional building is the very early baptistery, unattractively situated but worth seeking out for its medieval frescoes.

▶▷▷ St-Aignan

A small town on the Cher, St-Aignan has narrow streets of half-timbered houses climbing up wooded slopes below a Renaissance château (access only to the terrace). The Romanesque church has many features of interest, including beautiful capitals and frescoes in the crypt.

▶▶▷ St-Benoît-sur-Loire, Abbaye de

The site of St-Benoît was a druid place of worship before the monastery of St-Pierre-de-Fleury was founded in the 7th century. Renamed St-Benoît after receiving the relics of the saint, the abbey became an important place of pilgrimage and enjoyed increasing prosperity. The beautiful basilica seen today was built between the 11th and 13th centuries, and is one of the finest examples of Romanesque art and architecture in the country—tall and light, with harmonious proportions and wonderfully sculpted capitals. It has now been revived as a monastic community; daily services with Gregorian chants are held.

▶▶▷ St-Savin

Twenty kilometers east of Chauvigny, the abbey church at St-Savin-sur-Gartempe is another very beautiful Romanesque church, notable for its extraordinarily vivid life-size mural paintings. (Binoculars are available and well worth renting to appreciate the detail.)

In the countryside around Poitiers are many old and beautiful churches, including St-Jouin-de-Marnes and St-Pierre at Parthenay-le-Vieux (both northwest of Poitiers), and St-Savin-sur-Gartempe.

The village of St-Benoît-sur-Loire

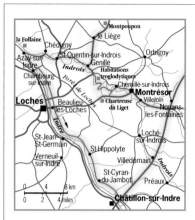

Drive **Tributaries of the Loire**

Start at Loches. East to Beaulieu-lès-Loches, then D92 along the Indre to Châtillon-sur-Indre. D675 to Nouans-les-Fontaines.

The Indre and Indrois are quiet and beautiful tributaries of the Loire, meandering through chalky escarpments, lined with willows, alders and poplars. Despite being less well endowed with grand châteaus than other parts of the region, the area is very rewarding for an unhurried tour on minor riverside roads through sleepy villages, past small churches, ruined abbeys and mills, and troglodyte caves. **Châtillon-sur-Indre,** on the northern fringe of the Brenne marshlands, is an important market town for agricultural produce and equipment, with views from the fortress-topped old town (and a beautiful Romanesque church). The 13th-century church in **Nouans-les-Fontaines** also merits a short detour to see the large and very fine altarpiece by Jean Fouquet.

D760 to Montrésor, then the D10 to Chemillé-sur-Indrois, and a short detour to Chartreuse du Liget.
For those suffering from withdrawal symptoms, the medieval fortifications and interior manor of the **Château de Montrésor** will come as a timely architectural injection; it's beautifully furnished by the Polish family who set about

restoring it in the mid-19th century. Montrésor is also notable for the elegant Renaissance doorway of its church. **Chemillé-sur-Indrois** has a small leisure complex on a lake. At the edge of the Forest of Loches lie the remains of the Carthusian monastery of **Le Liget**.

Follow the Indrois Valley west on minor roads to Genillé, and the D10 to St-Quentin-sur-Indrois and Azay-sur-Indre.
Azay-sur-Indre, St-Quentin-sur-Indrois, Genillé, Chemillé-sur-Indrois and **Villeloin** are all attractive villages with old houses, abbeys or small castles.

Follow the Indre southeast on the D17 back to Loches. Visitors leaving the area to head northeast via the Cher could additionally visit the Château de Montpoupon, on the D764 from Loches to Montrichard.

> **<<** Like several other monasteries, Le Liget was founded by Henry II in expiation for the murder of Thomas à Becket; it's worth trying to gain access to the frescoed Chapelle St-Jean, and to stop for a glance at La Corroierie, a former annex of the monastery, on the Montrésor road. **>>**

▶▷▷ Saumur

Not one of the Loire's most attractive towns, Saumur's main fame (apart from the pepperpot-towered castle that dominates the town and surrounding countryside) derives from the tufa that gives this area its name of White Anjou. The many caves and cellars carved out of the soft white chalk in and around Saumur shelter thousands of bottles of sparkling wine and around 70 percent of the country's cultivated mushrooms. This may be reason enough for visiting the town (guided tours and tastings are offered at many of the wine houses), but an additional attraction might be the equine interest offered by Saumur's celebrated cavalry squad, the Cadre Noir, which puts on an annual display in July (and which can be seen practicing at other times), and by no less than three museums devoted to various aspects of the horse and horsemanship (one in the château, which also houses a museum of decorative arts).

The château itself has been much altered since the days when it was depicted so beautifully in the book of miniatures *Les Très Riches Heures du Duc de Berry*, and has served as a prison and barracks. There are good views from the watchtower over the old and new towns.

▷▷▷ Serrant, Château de

Guided tours are given of this large and very imposing domed Renaissance-style château near Angers. They reveal opulent decor and furniture; in the chapel, designed by Hardouin-Mansart, is the Baroque tomb of the marquis de Vaubrun by Coysevox.

▶▷▷ Sologne

This area is an infertile plain of marshland and deciduous forest, bounded by the large loop of the Loire between Blois and Gien. The D922 between **La Ferté-St-Aubin** and **Romorantin** is signed as a tourist route, passing typical Sologne countryside and lakes bright with water lilies. Attractive village features include low brick and timber houses and galleried churches: Fine examples can be found at **Souvigny-en-Sologne** and **Brinon-sur-Sauldre**. An interesting ethnographic museum in the main town of **Romorantin** offers the opportunity to learn about Solognote life. The **Etang du Puis** is a large lake with water-sports facilities.

The Sologne's main activities have long been huntin', shootin' and fishin'. Local prosperity depended on royal popularity; when the court returned to Paris in the 17th century, there followed a period of neglect and stagnation. After reforestation, the Sologne began to thrive again. Thousands of pheasants are now reared to provide recreation for weekend gunslingers, and the lakes and rivers are rich in pike, carp and perch.

Looking at the Loire across the rooftops of Saumur

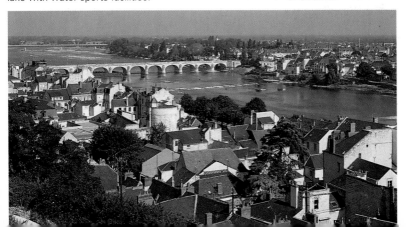

THE LOIRE

The Château d'Ussé

Born in Tours, the great novelist Honoré de Balzac (1799–1850) referred constantly to his beloved Touraine, encapsulating the charms of the countryside in *Le Lys dans la Vallée*. This novel, among many others, was written in the Château de Saché (near Azay-le-Rideau), in which he frequently sought refuge from the clamor of Parisian life. Balzac's rooms in the château have been arranged as a museum and contain manuscripts and proofs covered with such an abundance of notes that many a printer must have been driven to despair.

▶ ▷ ▷   Sully, Château de

This feudal fortress is notable for one of the finest medieval timber roofs in existence. It was fashioned out of chestnut (which had previously been seasoned for several years both in and out of water) by ships' carpenters.

▶ ▷ ▷   Tours

The capital of the department, as well as a thriving industrial and university city, Tours has high-rise outskirts that do not bode well for the intending visitor. But the city has managed to preserve (with much recent restoration) its historic heart, and the straight wide boulevards provide excellent shopping facilities. For tourists without a car, Tours makes a good base from which to take coach tours of the châteaus; and the lively old town is well provided with restaurants and bars. Sights include museums (devoted to medieval and fine arts, modern stained glass and wine) and a Gothic cathedral with beautiful stained glass.

▶ ▷ ▷   Ussé, Château d'

This is the classic fairy-tale château of one's dreams, used by the writer Perrault as the model for his setting of *Sleeping Beauty*. Ussé's woodland backdrop (at the edge of the dark forest of Chinon) is appropriately romantic. Topped by turrets and tall chimneys, the outside is rather more captivating than its interior, with the exception of the Renaissance chapel.

▶ ▷ ▷   Valençay, Château de

This vast domed château, in a well-stocked park to the south of the Cher in the Berry region, is a very fine example of the classical Renaissance style. Most famously associated with the 19th-century politician Talleyrand, to whom a small museum is devoted, the château is richly furnished in mainly Louis XV, Louis XVI and Empire styles.

▶ ▶ ▷   Villandry, Château de

A much-altered château that retains only the keep from its original fortress building, Villandry is notable above all for the re-creation of its 16th-century gardens, one of the finest examples of the formal style known as *à la française*. Arranged on three terraces, they combine symbolic designs and decorative effects with practical use (vegetables, herbs and fruit). The planting, clipping and pruning statistics are mind-boggling.

The French Garden

■ When Charles VIII returned from northern Italy filled with a desire to copy the ornamental architecture of the Italian Renaissance, he brought with him not only the best architects, artists and crafts-people, but also a very talented garden designer, Pacello da Mercogliano. French gardens before the 16th century were mainly of practical use (orchards and areas for vegetables and medicinal herbs), with only a rare concession to ornament. The château gardens at Amboise and Blois were to break new ground. ...■

Setting a trend Larger and more colorful than tradi-tional gardens (those at Blois covered an area five or six times that of the palace), with a greater variety of flowers, Amboise and Blois were to be the first of a series of royal pleasure gardens, which became increasingly decorative and fanciful as the century progressed.

Style change The other, more subtle change concerned the composition of the garden, which became symmetrical, conceived as part of the overall design of a building. The classical garden, *à la française*, was developed with genius by the great royal gardener **Le Nôtre**; at its best it was supremely ordered and, under Louis XIV, inescapably grand.

Using the elements Le Nôtre was one of the first gardeners in France to recognize the importance of trees in a landscape composition; he also used water, in the shape of tranquil ornamental ponds (unlike the Italian style of fountains or informal streams and lakes), to great effect. Three gardens sum up Le Nôtre's legacy: These are those at the **Tuileries**, **Vaux-le-Vicomte**, and **Versailles**.

The gardens at Versailles...

Le style anglais The French garden could be said to be the very opposite of the English garden (called "romantic"), whose natural rambling style, punctuated by architectural ornaments such as fake temples, pagodas and Gothic ruins, became increasingly popular in France. The style reached its peak in the 19th-century parks created by Napoleon III as a result of his long exile in London—most notably, the **Bois de Boulogne** and the **Bois de Vincennes**.

Gardens with a past On a more modest level, in town or village, the French garden of today betrays its ancestry: Formal and symmetrical patterns of bold and contrasting colors—red with blue, orange with white—are popular and widely employed; their discipline is far removed from the apparent disorder and subtle hues of the English cottage garden.

...and at the Château d'Ussé

THE ATLANTIC COAST

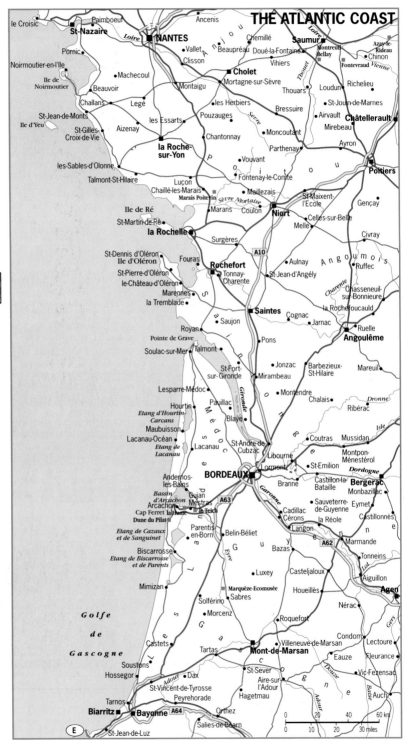

le Croisic
St-Nazaire
Paimboeuf
Pornic
NANTES
Ancenis
Loire
Chemillé
Saumur
Montreuil-Bellay
Azay-le-Rideau
Chinon
Fontevraud
Vienne
Noirmoutier-en-l'Ile
Ile de Noirmoutier
Machecoul
Beauvoir
Challans
Legé
Montaigu
Cholet
Mortagne-sur-Sèvre
les Herbiers
Vihiers
Doué-la-Fontaine
Beaupréau
Vallet
Clisson
Thouet
Loudun
Richelieu
St-Jean-de-Monts
Ile d'Yeu
St-Gilles-Croix-de-Vie
Aizenay
les Essarts
Pouzauges
Chantonnay
Bressuire
Thouars
Moncoutant
Parthenay
Airvault
Mirebeau
Ayron
Châtellerault
St-Joun-de-Marnes
la Roche-sur-Yon
Vouvant
Fontenay-le-Comte
Poitiers
les-Sables-d'Olonne
Talmont-St-Hilaire
Luçon
Chaillé-les-Marais
Marais Poitevin
Marans
Coulon
Maillezais
St-Maixent-l'Ecole
Gençay
Niort
Melle
Celles-sur-Belle
Civray
Ile de Ré
St-Martin-de-Ré
la Rochelle
Surgères
A10
St-Dennis d'Oléron
Ile d'Oléron
St-Pierre d'Oléron
le-Château-d'Oléron
Fouras
Rochefort
Tonnay-Charente
Aulnay
St-Jean-d'Angély
Angoumois
Ruffec
Chasseneuil-sur-Bonnieure
Charente
la Rochefoucauld
Marennes
la Tremblade
Saintes
Cognac
Jarnac
Ruelle
Royan
Saujon
Pons
Angoulême
Pointe de Grave
Soulac-sur-Mer
Talmont
St-Fort-sur-Gironde
Mirambeau
Jonzac
Barbezieux-St-Hilaire
Mareuil
Lesparre-Médoc
Gironde
Montendre
Chalais
Ribérac
Dronne
Hourtin
Etang d'Hourtin-Carcans
Pauillac
Blaye
Maubuisson
Lacanau-Océan
Etang de Lacanau
Lacanau
Médoc
St-Andre-de-Cubzac
Coutras
Mussidan
Montpon-Ménestérol
Dordogne
Andernos-les-Bains
Bassin d'Arcachon
Gujan-Mestras
Arcachon
Cap Ferret la Teste
Dune du Pilat
A63
Libourne
Lormont
St-Emilion
BORDEAUX
Branne
Castillon-la-Bataille
Bergerac
Monbazillac
Etang de Cazaux et de Sanguinet
Parentis-en-Born
Belin-Béliet
Cadillac
Cérons
Sauveterre-de-Guyenne
Eymet
Castillonnès
Biscarrosse
Etang de Biscarrosse et de Parents
Garonne
la Réole
Langon
A62
Marmande
Tonneins
Lot
Aiguillon
Mimizan
Luxey
Casteljaloux
Houeillès
Agen
Solférino
Sabres
Marquèze-Ecomusée
Morcenz
Roquefort
Nérac
Condom
Lectoure
Fleurance
Golfe de Gascogne
Castets
Tartas
Villeneuve-de-Marsan
Mont-de-Marsan
Eauze
Vic-Fezensac
Auch
Soustons
Hossegor
Dax
St-Sever
Aire-sur-l'Adour
Adour
Tarnos
Biarritz
Bayonne
A64
St-Vincent-de-Tyrosse
Peyrehorade
Hagetmau
Orthez
Salies-de-Béarn
St-Jean-de-Luz
E

| 0 | 20 | 40 | 60 km |
| 0 | 10 | 20 | 30 miles |

126

When the French mass-migrate for two months to the beach every summer, all roads to the Mediterranean are jammed, while on the Atlantic coast an infinity of pines, dunes and sandy beaches await. From Bordeaux to the Pyrenees, the map reveals only a scattering of resorts.

Family formula Do not expect pretty ports or charming coastal villages of the unspoiled "hidden gem" variety. Aquitaine provides huge horizons and wide open spaces, ideal for family vacations: a simple apartment or a campsite, sun and sand, lots to do but comparatively little to see. Lakes near the sea offer safe swimming and water sports. Surfers head for the ocean rollers.

The Northern stretch The Vendée and Charente coasts are more varied, with bays, fishing ports, islands and a rural economy of oysters, mussels, vineyards and salt pans. But here, too, the land is flat, and resorts are best for families requiring little more than a beach for the kids and French food and wine from the supermarket for mom and dad, who will almost certainly return home with fond memories of *mouclade* (mussels in white wine) and a souvenir bottle of Pineau des Charentes, the local cognac-based aperitif. Of the towns, only the old port of **La Rochelle** has much style and joie de vivre.

English links Northern and southern coasts are separated by the Gironde, a deep incision where most of the rivers in southern France reach the sea. **Bordeaux** was the capital of English territory in France after Louis VII rashly lost Eleanor of Aquitaine to the future king of England, Henry Plantagenet, in 1152. The English were not chased out until 1453, by which time bibulous Albion had acquired a taste for claret, as the English still call red bordeaux. The region has not severed its British links of trade, blood and vineyard ownership.

Wine country In the land of the most aristocratic of wines, connoisseurs can gaze with awe at the immaculate vineyards of **Latour**, **Lafite** and **Yquem**, whose precious grapes are picked one by one. Tasting is another matter: many of the châteaus are a bit sniffy about visitors. The wine villages are dull, with the notable exception of **St-Emilion**.

One of the more bizarre, not to say unsavory, traditions of Landais gastronomy is eating ortolan buntings. Having been caught in nets, the birds are nourished and gradually poisoned by a diet of milk mixed with a daily increasing quantity of armagnac. They are roasted in their own fat, served on paper and consumed by diners with napkins over their heads to ensure that no fume of the delicate bouquet escapes.

▶ ▷ ▷   Angoulême

In an area most travelers are content to cross as fast as possible, the motorway now gives the capital of Charente department a wide berth. This is no great shame: Angoulême is a big town of little charm. The 12th-century cathedral, which has a row of domes in the Périgord manner, suffered rather badly at the hands of its 19th-century restorer Abadie, but some of the carvings that can be seen on the facade are original, and of high quality.

▶ ▷ ▷   Arcachon and Côte d'Argent

The Aquitaine coast consists of two sandy beaches: 100 km from **Soulac** to **Cap Ferret**, 125 km from **Arcachon** to the outskirts of **Bayonne**. With dunes blocking the way to the sea, rivers feed a string of inland lakes. The River Eyre alone has broken through. Its estuary is the wide but tight-lipped bay of **Arcachon**, famous for its oysters and favored both by yachtsmen and migrant birds.

Between Arcachon and the smelly oyster capital **Gujan Mestras** is a theme park of medieval crafts (La Hume). **Le Teich** bird reserve has several marked walks and, if you're lucky, flamingos and storks in residence.

▶ ▷ ▷   Aulnay

This beautiful Romanesque pilgrimage church is set among cypresses on the edge of a small village between Poitiers and Saintes. It has outstanding stone carving on the west end and the south doorway and capitals inside the church. Note the Indian elephants (right transept).

▶ ▶ ▷   Biarritz

Biarritz was a small whaling port until Empress Eugenie brought Napoleon III for a six-week stay in 1854 and thereby launched the Atlantic coast's only rival to the Riviera. Her villa, later the Hôtel du Palais, has been sumptuously restored but other aspects of Biarritz's former splendor are sadly tarnished, and the summer population is an odd mixture of beachcombers and genteel older visitors.

The 12th-century cathedral at Angoulême

▶ ▶ ▷   Bordeaux

A seaport 100 km from the Atlantic, Bordeaux is the most formal and elegant of provincial cities, a creation of the Enlightenment dedicated to the civilized business of exporting fine wine. Like Paris, only a century earlier, it was rationalized with the creation of wide boulevards, public gardens and a colonnaded Grand Theater, the pride of the city. Eighteenth-century palaces along the Garonne are the city's noble facade, and the place de la Bourse is a splendid gateway to the heart of old Bordeaux. The place du Parlement is its focus. Other sightseeing is predictable: a vast cathedral and a well-stocked art museum. Rue St-Catherine and cours Clemenceau are best for shopping. The tourist office, Maison du Vin (with tastings) and a good wine shop are grouped together on the cours 30-Juillet near the theater. Vinorama is a new wine attraction on cours du Medoc.

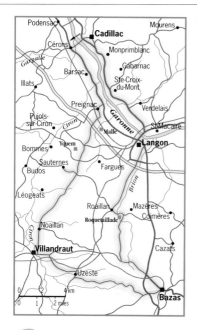

The crest of the Château d'Yquem, closed to visitors but visible from the road north of Sauternes

Drive Entre-Deux-Mers and Sauternes

Start at Cadillac. D11 to to Cérons; N113 to Barsac, Preignac.
Cadillac, an old walled village, is at the edge of the vineyards of **Entre-Deux-Mers**, about 40 km south of the medieval town of **St-Emilion**. Cross the Garonne into dessert wine country. Near Preignac the beautiful **Château de Malle** is the best Bordeaux château to visit.

D8/125 to Sauternes.
Barsac and **Sauternes** have Maisons du Vin with tastings and wine for sale. The prestigious **Château d'Yquem** is closed to visitors, but worth admiring from the road (D116E north of Sauternes).

D8 to Villandraut; D3/110 to Uzeste; Bazas; D3/223 to Roquetaillade; D125/D222 to Langon (cross the Garonne).
Bertrand de Got, the 14th-century Pope Clement V, built a fortress at Villandraut and lies buried in the church at Uzeste. His nephew built the **Château de Roquetaillade**, whose entrance ticket also covers a

rural museum. Bazas has an interesting church on an arcaded square.

D10 to Ste-Croix-du-Mont and Cadillac.
On a hill of fossilized oysters, Ste-Croix-du-Mont makes a sweet white wine modest only by Sauternes standards. It can be tasted in caves below the church.

Wine country: Sauternes

■ **The hinterland of the Aquitaine coast, between Bordeaux and the Basque country, is a vast triangle of flat pine forest, 200 km by 100 km, planted in the 19th century to stabilize shifting dunes and drain a marshy heath populated only by mosquitoes, bees, sheep and shepherds who went about on stilts. ...■**

New life Logging and resin tapping, followed by coastal tourism and a modest oil industry (on and around the Lac de Parentis) transformed the life of the region.

The Landes towns are on the edge of the forest. **Mont de Marsan** is a good place to watch a *course landaise* (a race) starring nimble *écarteurs* (literally "dodgers") who, among other tricks, leap over charging cows.

In the woods The forest itself is disconcerting, empty of spirit: no views, no flowers, little wildlife, few villages, just the smell and sight of pine trees and the piercing whine of cicadas. In small clearings there are low timber and brick farmhouses, each surrounded by a cornfield, a vegetable patch and a few farm animals.

Ecomuseum The best reason to venture inland from a Côte d'Argent campsite is the Landes ecomuseum at **Marquèze**, reached by train from Sabres. This is a fascinating all-around presentation of the pastoral life and ecology of the area in the pre-pine age, including a traditional farm. It is part of the regional park, where the River Eyre is also being opened up for canoeing.

Among the contents of the small museum at **Solférino**, an agricultural community founded by Napoleon III, is a cast of the emperor's bootprint (August 1857), made to commemorate this momentous initiative to tame the wilderness. **Luxey** has an ecomuseum with a display of resin products.

Recreating Landes life in the ecomuseum at Marquèze

Old-time travel to the Marquèze museum in the Landes region

▶▷▷   Dax

With hot water gushing from a fountain at the center of town, Dax is one of the oldest spas in France. Its specialty, mud baths for rheumatism, appeals to sufferers ancient and modern. The church of St-Paul-lès-Dax has good 11th-century reliefs on the apse.

▶▷▷   Marais Poitevin

Between Niort and the sea a maze of canals linked to the Sèvre/Niortaise drains a wide area of reclaimed marshland punctuated by "island" villages (**Marans, Chaillé**). Punts are the traditional means of transport for fishermen and can be rented with or without pilot at **Coulon**, west of Niort. Eels are a local specialty. **Maillezais**, with splendid abbey ruins, also has boats for rent.

▶▷▷   Pornic

A small town and fishing port on a rocky creek, Pornic has charm, unlike the owner of its château, Gilles de Rais (Bluebeard), who gave up a dazzling military career for satanism and infanticide. There are summer ferries to the small island village of **Noirmoutier**, also accessible by road (a toll bridge or a causeway practicable only at low tide).

▶▶▷   La Rochelle

One of the great trading ports of Renaissance France, and of Protestantism, La Rochelle is now a prosperous user-friendly city: No other French town places free bicycles at the disposal of visitors. In the old port, twin towers still guard the narrow harbor entrance. The nearby Tour de la Lanterne (a 15th-century lighthouse and prison) gives good views. The old center has kept its houses (rue des Merciers, rue de l'Escale), mostly 16th- and 17th-century. The Musée du Nouveau Monde relates La Rochelle's trading history; the aquarium in Les Minimes is excellent. Nearby Ile de Ré is now reached by an expensive toll bridge.

▶▷▷   Saintes

An ancient town on one of the main pilgrimage routes (and the modern auto route) to Spain, redbrick Saintes has a Roman arch gracing the right bank of the Charente. On the other side of town is a small Roman amphitheater (Arènes). St-Eutrope is only a fragment of a great pilgrimage church, with the tomb of the 4th-century martyred bishop of Saintes in its beautiful crypt.

131

The offshore islands of Ré, Noirmoutier and Oléron are all accessible by toll bridge from the mainland. Ré is the most interesting, with vineyards, farms, whitewashed villages and the fortified port of St-Martin. Noirmoutier mostly consists of salt pans, but the old village has pine woods and a good beach at hand; Oléron has vast oyster parks off the old port of Château d'Oléron. From Aix (ferries from La Rochelle, Fouras and Boyardville on Oléron) Napoleon left France in 1815; his house displays Imperial memorabilia. Yeu (ferries from Fromentine) is an island of granite cliffs, lobster pots and tuna fishing. Pétain was imprisoned there from 1945 until his death in 1951.

■ **The Bordeaux vineyard area is the most productive fine wine district in the world. The five main districts are Médoc (red), Sauternes (sweet white) and Graves (white) on the left banks of the Garonne; and St-Emilion and Pomerol (red) on the right bank of the Dordogne. Less prestigious wines (with exceptions) are produced between the rivers (Entre-Deux-Mers) and on the eastern side of the Gironde (including Côtes de Blaye and Côtes de Bourg). ...■**

132

Bordeaux vineyards: a treat for the eye as well as for the palate

Divisions and ranks Each region is divided into many appellations (**Pauillac** and **St-Julien** are two of the most famous in the Médoc, for example), and each appellation into estates, usually referred to as châteaus. The finest Médoc châteaus were ranked into five categories of *crus classés* in 1855 (from first to fifth); there have been only minor changes and additions since. This classification, varying slightly from region to region, is not an infallible guide to quality; many wines in the lower *crus classés*, or even the supposedly lesser *crus bourgeois*, are often as good and better value. The *crus bourgeois* of the appellations of **St-Estèphe** and **Haut-Médoc** are worth trying.

Along the D2 from **Bordeaux** to **St-Vivien-de-Médoc** are some of the most prestigious wine châteaus in the world: **Margaux**, **Latour** (south of Pauillac). Not all are open to the public. **Mouton-Rothschild** and **Lafite** (north of Pauillac). Good châteaus in the Médoc are:

Château Batailley near Pauillac: 18th-century château with gardens and cellars open (tel: 56 59 01 13).

Château Cos d'Estournel at St-Estèphe: by prior appointment (tel: 56 59 15 55).

Château d'Issan near Margaux: 17th-century moated château; by appointment (tel: 56 44 94 45).

Château Loudenne near St-Yzans: wine museum (tel: 56 09 05 33).

Château Margaux: by appointment; closed August and harvest time (tel: 56 88 70 28).

Château Mouton-Rothschild near Pauillac: wine museum; by appointment (tel: 56 59 22 22).

There are Maisons du Vin (information offices with sale of wine and exhibitions) at **Margaux, Bordeaux,** and **Pauillac**; and vineyard tours can be organized from **Bordeaux, Pauillac, Hourtin,** and **Lacanau**.

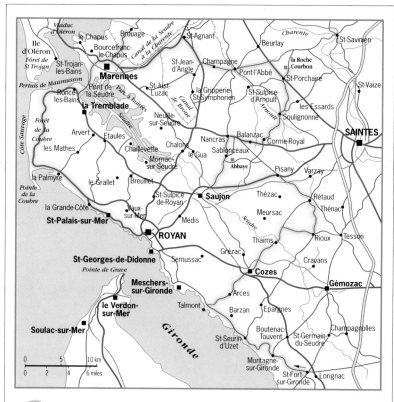

Drive   **Churches, beaches and the Gironde estuary**

Start at St-Fort-sur-Gironde.
St-Fort is 50 km north of Blaye, Louis XIV's key defensive position on the Gironde. In the vineyards north of Blaye there are roadside invitations to taste and buy *pineau* (a grape juice and cognac aperitif). **St-Fort** and nearby **Talmont** have interesting churches.

D114/136 to Rioux; D216 to Rétaud; D142/N150/D117 to Sablonceaux; D117/728 to Corme-Royal; D119 to St-Porchaire; D122 to La Roche Courbon and back.
Rioux and **Rétaud** are the highlights of the inland church tour, also featuring Sablonceaux Abbey and Corme-Royal. **La Roche Courbon** is a richly decorated moated château set in lovely gardens.

N137/D18/D7/D123 to Marennes;

D3 to Brouage and back; D25 to Ronce-les-Bains and Royan.
Brouage was a 17th-century salt port and mighty royal fortress, but the sea has retreated and left a somnolent village. Tablets commemorate Champlain, the locally born founder of Québec, and the sad affair of Marie Mancini, who came to Brouage after being spurned by Louis XIV in favor of a Spanish princess. At the mouth of the Seudre, **Bourcefranc-le-Chapus** and **Marennes** are the local oyster centers. There are beaches and campsites along the wooded Grande Côte and Côte Sauvage toward Royan, but swimming is often hazardous.

Royan is a big resort that has been developed in bleakest postwar functional style, redeemed only by its shallow beach.

DORDOGNE

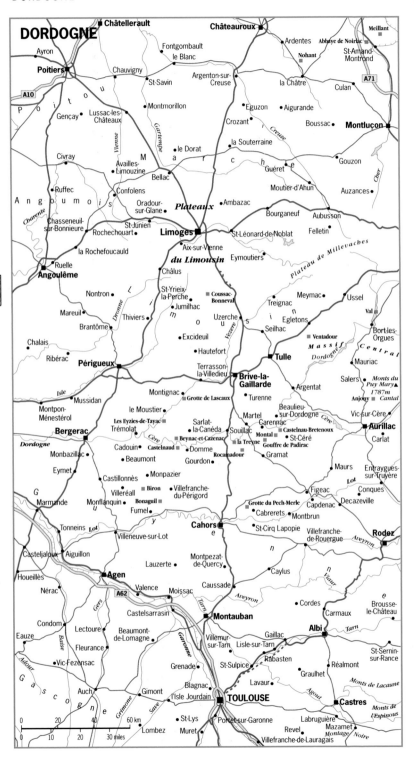

Bergerac, on the banks of the Dordogne

The Dordogne is a river flowing from the Massif Central to join the Gironde at Bordeaux, and an administrative department that includes a section of this river and an area to the north fondly known to the French as Périgord—home of the truffle, the walnut and the bloated liver of force-fed geese. It is also the region of Europe that has yielded most to students of prehistory; the area is uniquely rich in cave paintings.

To its many visitors, the Dordogne embraces a much larger and more diffuse area of southwest France, stretching from the undulating farmland of Limousin to the bleak limestone *causses* (plateaus) of Quercy and the orchards of the Lot Valley. It signifies French country life at its most delightful: old villages of golden stone with rust-colored roofs, fortress ruins on wooded riverbanks, market stalls groaning under the weight of fresh local produce, and small-scale cultivation. The typical Dordogne farmer has a handful of animals, an area of corn to feed them, fruit trees and walnuts, a small vineyard, and possibly a plot of tobacco. Less idyllic, but highly significant to France's economy, are the hydro-electric power installations along the rivers, and the rich uranium mines of the Limousin.

So irresistible is the Dordogne's charm that many visitors have made it a second home. Foreign money has pushed prices up and the hunt for a cheap French ruin to restore has moved on, but some of the prettiest villages now contain large colonies of expatriates, particularly British and Dutch. The favorite section of the Dordogne Valley, between **Sarlat** and **Trémolat**, may now seem too neatly restored, with too many foreign voices.

Protect and survive In the Middle Ages the land between the Lot and Dordogne valleys was a border zone between French territory and English-controlled Aquitaine. As well as isolated fortresses commanding the river valleys, the rival factions built fortified new towns (*bastides*). Some of these survive, little changed.

DORDOGNE

Count Henri-Marie-Raymond de Toulouse-Lautrec was born in Albi in 1864. His birthplace is open to visitors; here, at the age of 14, he fell and suffered the first of two leg injuries that contributed to his deformity. Toulouse-Lautrec went to study in Paris, where he immersed himself in the low life depicted in his paintings, drawings and posters. He died in 1901, aged only 37.

Flemish weavers imported the craft of tapestry making during the 14th century, and over the next two centuries the Marche towns of Aubusson, Felletin and Bourganeuf vied with each other for ascendancy. Crowned *manufacture royale* by Colbert in the 17th century, Aubusson enjoyed prosperity until Louis XIV's revocation of the Edict of Nantes in 1685 ushered in a new era of religious intolerance and forced many weavers (mostly Huguenot Protestants) to emigrate. During the 19th century the tapestry industry declined as wallpaper became the rage, but today several factories in Aubusson thrive and bold modern designs appear alongside classic patterns.

▷ ▷ ▷   Agen

Prunes are not often considered a gourmet item, but the succulent *pruneaux d'Agen*, stuffed with marzipan or marinated in cognac, are in a league of their own. Apart from its plum trees, this market town on a fertile plain between the Lot and Garonne has few charms except a cluster of narrow streets in its old quarter and a handsome aqueduct with 23 arches. Its museum has works by Goya, Sisley and Boudin, and a superb Greek marble Venus unearthed by a local farmer in 1876.

▶ ▶ ▷   Albi

A big, redbrick town beside the Tarn dominated by its warlike Gothic cathedral. Built with funds seized from heretics or alleged *pénitents* (reformed sinners), it was a defensive fortress in a time of inquisition, torture and simmering popular resistance. Instead of stained glass to illuminate the faithful, Ste-Cecile has narrow apertures like arrow slits. Only the delicate 15th-century doorway lightens the effect. Inside, gruesome Last Judgment scenes adorn the west wall. The bishop's palace (Palais de la Berbie) has a fine Toulouse-Lautrec museum. Formal gardens overlook a river spanned by an 11th-century bridge, now coping with modern traffic.

▷ ▷ ▷   Argentat

This sleepy village straddles the Dordogne just before it flows into a series of reservoirs among wooded gorges. Upstream is the Argentat dam and a hydro-electric power station. The left (south) bank is the prettier side: A terrace of ocher-fronted, *lauze*-tiled (stone-tiled) houses with chestnut balconies hangs over the water. Nearby are the ruins of the fortress of Tours de Merle.

▶ ▷ ▷   Aubusson

The tapestry town of Aubusson nestles between the steep slopes of the Creuse Valley, continuing the craft that began there during the Middle Ages. Weaving galleries and workshops can be visited all over the town. The Musée Départemental de la Tapisserie exhibits 500-year-old carpet-weaving techniques, and the Maison du Vieux Tapissier contains tapestries ancient and modern, and a reconstructed workshop. During the summer the Hôtel de Ville holds regular exhibitions, including tapestries by the modern master Jean Lurçat.

Aubusson still produces carpets and wall hangings; the Tapestry Museum shows weaving methods

■ **During the Middle Ages the English fought for centuries to gain control of this part of France. Countless reminders of this turbulent period can be seen on hilltops and strategic vantage points throughout the region, in castles, fortified churches, and bastide towns (see page 139). ...■**

War and peace Some grand châteaus date from or were rebuilt during later, less warlike centuries, and more closely resemble the pleasure palaces of the Loire. But the typical castle architecture of the Dordogne is unmistakably military. Grim fortresses glare at each other from either side of the river—English on one bank, French on the other—almost close enough to hurl insults. Much of the damage they have suffered dates not from the Hundred Years' War, but from the wars between Catholics and Protestants during the 16th century. Some castles have been restored, and are used as private residences, hotels or wineries. Others are open to the public; many of these can only be visited on lengthy guided tours (in French). There are *circuit des bastides* motoring routes: ask at the tourist offices (16 rue du President Wilson, Périgueux; 97 rue Neuve d'Argenson, Bergerac; place Liberté, Sarlat).

Beynac-et-Cazenac One of the Dordogne's most spectacular and memorable fortresses towers above a huddled village on a sheer cliff commanding a beautiful stretch of the Dordogne. The keep dates from the 13th century; the main building from the 14th.

Biron A massive and intimidating château perched on a volcanic crag, Biron has a huge view of surrounding countryside. The buildings date from the 12th century onward, gradually mellowing in more gracious times.

Bonaguil One of the best surviving examples of late 15th- and early 16th-century military architecture. The cruel Berenger de Rocquefeuil insisted on making his castle impregnable, even though he outlived the age when this was necessary.

Castelnaud Beynac's opposite number on the English (south) bank has almost equally splendid views. Now partly restored, it houses a military museum.

Coussac-Bonneval This interesting 14th-century castle has machicolated pepperpot towers and contains fine furnishings, tapestries and woodwork associated with Achmet-Pasha, the eccentric mercenary who was born here.

Montbrun Dating from the 12th century, this lovely moated castle was reconstructed in the 15th. It was besieged unsuccessfully by Richard the Lionheart.

Medieval siege warfare is explained in Castelnaud's military museum

Tobacco first appeared in France for medicinal purposes in 1560. Powdered into snuff, it was recommended by the Portuguese ambassador as a cure for Catherine de' Médicis's migraines. Pope Urban VIII excommunicated smokers; Louis XIII first taxed, then outlawed the habit, but the nation was hooked. And so it remains. In spring and summer the dark leaves fill plots around the valleys of Bergerac and the Lot-et-Garonne. Later they are dried before being dispatched to the state-controlled *Régie Nationale des Tabacs* for processing into that Gallic aroma.

A cigar holder becomes a work of art at Bergerac's Musée du Tabac

▶ ▷ ▷ Beaulieu-sur-Dordogne

This waterfront market town has as appealing a setting as its name suggests, and among its older streets are several well-preserved mansions. Its great glory, however, is the Benedictine church of St-Pierre, best known for its elaborate south portal, carved in 1125. Damaged in parts, this vigorous sculpture is still one of the region's best examples of Romanesque art. A Last Judgment takes up the tympanum. The old monastery buildings can be seen from place des Pères; the Chapelle des Pénitents from the riverside.

▶ ▷ ▷ Bergerac

Though now encased in suburbs of little interest, Bergerac's older quarter repays exploration. It's one of the Dordogne's largest towns, a former capital of Périgord, and is an important commercial and agricultural gateway to the Médoc plains. Bergerac's own wines are no mean rivals to its neighbors' products downstream, the most celebrated being the sweet dessert wine of Monbazillac, to the south.

Trading activities Bergerac always had strong Protestant connections from its Huguenot community and its geographical and trade associations with Britain and the Low Countries, and it was much battered in the religious conflict that swept through France. Though Bergerac lost political status to Périgueux, the town made a canny entrepreneurial living through the centuries from riverborne trade. Modern preoccupations are as diverse as tobacco (a principal local cashcrop) and nitrocellulose, used in paint and plastics. Rostand's hero Cyrano (he of the unfortunate nose) has only tenuous links with the town, but has been enthusiastically adopted as a citizen worthy of a statue.

What to see Bergerac's main sights and most picturesque buildings lie among the narrow streets north of the historic port area. The **Cloître des Récollets** is a lovely half-timbered convent where the Regional Wine

Council meets annually to deliberate the merits of the *vendange* (free tour around the spittoons, with a tasting afterward). The museum contains an interesting section on the river and port. The turreted 15th-century Maison Péyrarède houses France's only **Musée du Tabac**. Tobacco jars, pipes, snuffboxes and cigarette holders document the history of the weed. The Gothic church of **Notre-Dame** contains several valuable paintings and tapestries.

▶▷▷ Cadouin

This large village on the edge of the Besside forest was once an important place of pilgrimage. Its Cistercian abbey, founded in 1115, stood on the Way of St. James, the route to the Spanish shrine of Santiago de Compostela. During the Middle Ages kings and princes halted here to pay homage to its revered Holy Shroud, later discredited as an 11th-century Egyptian textile. With state help the massively buttressed golden stone monastery has been restored. Inside, the church is severe and dark, but the cloisters are beautifully carved in a mix of Flamboyant Gothic and Renaissance styles, indicating how long they took to complete.

▶▷▷ Cahors

Encircled by a natural moat, a *cingle* of the Lot, Cahors was a worthy prize to the English, who besieged it during the Hundred Years' War. They gazed at it without attacking, and the impregnable town was eventually ceded by treaty in 1360, to the great disgust of its inhabitants. Still the old town bristles with ramparts, battlements, barbicans and fortified towers, but access is easier today over several modern bridges. Much more interesting, though, is the unique 14th-century Valentré bridge (the only one still standing today), its curious proportions emphasized by three pointed towers from which unfriendly missiles could be directed at intruders. From a distance (the hilly banks make a good viewpoint) the seven graceful Gothic arches make a magnificent reflection in the water.

Local specialties Within this pleasant market town many shops display tempting local produce, particularly supplies of the robust local "black wine." The narrow streets leading from the main square toward the river ramparts make a fascinating area for unscheduled wandering. Worth seeing are the **Maison de Roaldès** (Henry IV's mansion) and the cathedral of St-Etienne, with Byzantine domes in Périgord style, a fine carved north doorway and interior frescoes.

▷▷▷ Carennac

This is one of the Dordogne's most charming and peaceful villages, where medieval and Renaissance houses overlook an island in the river, and orchards flourish. François de Salignac (Fénélon) wrote his masterpiece *Télémaque* here while he was the prior in the 18th century. Not to be missed is the splendid Romanesque doorway of St-Pierre, where *Christ in Majesty* occupies the tympanum, encircled in a strange oval halo known as a *mandorla*.

Southeast of Bergerac, the border country of the Hundred Years' War is studded with bastide towns. Their purpose was military: Besides massive fortress garrisons, both the English and the French created a permanent civilian guard. Built on a grid pattern, often with an arcaded market square and fortified church tower as a refuge during times of siege, the bastide towns had streets too narrow for a mounted knight to wield weapons effectively. Best of the bastide towns are Monpazier, Monflanquin, Villeréal, Villefranche-du-Périgord, Beaumont and Eymet. Sometimes over-restored, several of these towns now verge on the chic.

Interior of the Cistercian abbey at Cadouin

Drive River valley and open land

Start at St-Céré.
St-Laurent castle in St-Céré was the home of Jean Lurçat, the great tapestry designer of the 1930s. His work is displayed in the Casino.

D940 and D43 to Castelnau.
One of the Dordogne's most formidable castles can be found at **Castelnau**. Once this vast red pile of 11th-century masonry housed 1,500 soldiers; now it contains a museum and furnished chambers.

D43 and D30 to Carennac; D43 to Cirque de Montvalent and N140 to Gluges; D43 and D23 to Creysse and D114, D15 to Meyronne.
The River Dordogne curves through lush meadows dotted with villages. Most strikingly set is **Gluges**, at the foot of sheer cliffs; **Creysse** and **Meyronne** have castle remains.

D23 south to Grottes de Lacave.
At **Lacave**, an elevator and underground railway transport visitors to limestone caverns.

D23 to Belcastel; D43 to La Treyne.
The terrace of **Belcastel**'s mighty château offers a splendid panorama of a wooded river bend. A short way west is the **Château de la Treyne**, part 14th-century. It is now a hotel.

D23, D673, D90 to Gouffre de Padirac.
The **Gouffre de Padirac** is a giant sinkhole imbued with satanic associations and spoiled by crowds. An elevator descends the fern-lined walls; a boat tours the caverns.

Divert from D673 onto D14 and D118 to Loubressac or D38 to Autoire; then join D30 and D673.
Loubressac is a hilltop bastide, with a vast view from the 15th-century château. A long-distance footpath, the GR480, leads through Loubressac to **Autoire**, where farmhouses have been snapped up as second homes. Near the village is a scenic spot, the **Cirque d'Autoire**.

D673 to Montal and St-Céré.
The romantic Renaissance château of **Montal** was built by Jean de Balsac d'Entraygues as she waited for her son Robert to return from the wars in Italy. He never did, and the heartrending legend *Plus d'Espoir* ("Hope No More") is carved beneath one of the château windows. Inside, the Renaissance staircase is encrusted with sea monsters and shells, testifying to the dedication of Maurice Fenaille, a philanthropic historian who restored and later gave the château to the state.

▶ ▷ ▷ Creuse, Vallée de la

The River Creuse rises on the Millevaches plateau, on the granite foothills of the Massif Central. Dozens of small streams eventually form this picturesque waterway, beloved by George Sand, who set several of her novels here. From its infant course past the tapestry towns of **Aubusson** and **Felletin**, the river meanders through a varied landscape of gorges, reservoir lakes and farmland. Principal landmarks include the great fortress of **Crozant**, one of the biggest in the region, and the giant dam at **Eguzon**, behind which stretches the serpentine **Chambon Lake**. At **Fontgombault** an abbey founded by the hermit Gombault is worth seeing for its tall choir and decorated capitals. The Benedictine order has returned (it was suppressed in 1714), and goat cheese is sold in some of the outbuildings.

▷ ▷ ▷ Culan

A massive fortress clings to the overgrown rocks overlooking the Arnon Gorges. Among many illustrious visitors the castle numbers Joan of Arc, sheltering here after Orléans, and Louis XI. It is open to the public, and contains a collection of furniture and tapestries.

▶ ▷ ▷ Domme

Few fail to be impressed by Domme's picturesque location on a rocky cliff high above the Dordogne. A bastide town, its hilly setting proved too difficult for the classic grid-patterned rectangle, and getting around Domme, particularly in high season, involves serious bottlenecks and confusing maneuvers through the town's various gateways. It's best to enjoy the ocher-stone buildings on foot. In the main square is a covered market hall; below it is an entrance to some small stalactite caves, once used as a refuge for the townsfolk. Animal bones found in the caves are on display. From the Belvedere de la Barre there are stupendous views of the river looping through fields far below. Most striking of the surviving gateways is the Porte des Tours, whose burly round towers once imprisoned many hapless Knights Templar, falsely accused of heresy and perversion by Philip the Fair.

▶ ▷ ▷ Hautefort, Château de

The formidable silhouette of Hautefort Château, overlord of the Ans country from the 14th century, is a striking feature of the Périgord Blanc. Hautefort has been rebuilt several times since the Middle Ages, most recently after a disastrous fire in 1968. It has now been restored to its mostly 17th-century grandeur. The moat is dry, the drawbridge fixed, and the gray-gold walls enclose gardens and a few furnished rooms (guided tours).

Weaving baskets at La Rogue-Gageac

Domme's setting defeated the traditional geometric bastide plan

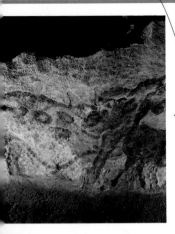

■ The limestone caverns of the Massif Central are famous for their beautiful formations; those in the Dordogne are better known for prehistoric animal paintings. The Périgord region has been inhabited by man since ~~Palaeolithic~~ times: The earliest skeletal traces of ~~Neanderthal type~~ were found at Le Moustier near Les Eyzies-de-Tayac in 1909. Many other remains (tools, tombs, bones, weapons, ornaments) have been unearthed, but by far the most exciting discovery occurred in 1940, when some boys out rabbiting with a dog stumbled by chance upon the cave of Lascaux, one of Europe's most important prehistoric finds. ...■

The Museum of Prehistory, set into the rock-face at Les Eyzies-de-Tayac

The paintings at Lascaux and other caves in the Dordogne are probably between ~~17,000 and 20,000~~ years old, and were executed by ~~Cro-Magnon~~ man, ~~a taller, vastly more sophisticated creature than the earliest flint-wielders~~. The most interesting prehistoric sites in the Dordogne lie around **Les Eyzies** and **Montignac** in the Vézère Valley, and near Cabrerets on the Lot, but there are many lesser caves dotted all over the region, some decorated with animal drawings, others naturally adorned with stalagmites and stalactites.

Collections of prehistory There are several ~~good~~ museums and exhibition centers of prehistory, notably at **Les Eyzies**, **Périgueux**, **Sarlat**, and **Le Thot** near Montignac. The major sites become very crowded in high season; advance booking of tickets to the site is advisable.

Damaging breath Lascaux itself was thronged with curious visitors from the end of World War II, and alarmed officials soon realized that just two decades of warm, carbon dioxide–exhaling tourists had done more damage to the paintings than ~~17,000~~ years of lying undisturbed. A film of greenish microorganisms was creeping steadily across the walls. Quickly the original cave was closed to all but a handful of privileged researchers. Meanwhile a replica cave, Lascaux II, perfect down to every last contour, with all the dyes synthesized from the same ingredients, was created nearby. It is fascinating and awe-inspiring to emerge from the air-lock system amid a herd of galloping bison, deer and horses in brilliant shades of red, ocher and black.

To visit the caves, you must book tickets in the attractive town of **Montignac**. At **Le Thot**, 7 km southwest, a prehistory center houses displays of cave art, audiovisual shows, and in the surrounding park wild animals (deer, wild boar, etc.) roam among ~~life-size animated mammoths~~.

Les Eyzies-de-Tayac Farther down the Vezère, Les Eyzies revels in its soubriquet "Cradle of Prehistory" because of the archaeological riches discovered in the immediate surroundings. The **Museum of Prehistory**, housed in a 13th-century fortress halfway up a rock face, is certainly worth a visit for background information, time charts and displays of bones and artifacts discovered locally. Just outside the town is the **Grotte de Font-de-Gaume**, where the highly sophisticated animal drawings are originals, not copies; among them are the marks of later "artists" of modern times. Numbers of visitors are restricted, so book early in the morning.

Smaller caves with animal drawings near Les Eyzies include the **Grotte des Combarelles** and the **Abri du Cap Blanc**, to the east. The **Roque-St-Christophe** is a series of rock galleries in a cliff used for millennia as a shelter from elements, wars and predators, where various traces of troglodyte inhabitants have been found. **La Madeleine** is an excavated Magdalenian village with cave dwellings and a display center. Visitors tour the caves at **Rouffignac**, northwest of Les Eyzies, in an electric train, through about 4 km of galleries decorated with hundreds of animal engravings.

On a lighter note, the Disney-like **Préhistoparc** presents an everyday story of cave people.

Horse at Lascaux

Pech-Merle Farther south, near the River Lot, is **Pech-Merle**, near Cabrerets: a huge series of caverns containing limestone formations and exquisite animal paintings. The tour leads through chambers decorated with the graceful outlines of horses, silhouetted handprints, and a frieze of bison and mammoths. Among curiosities are the mudprints of prehistoric feet.

DORDOGNE

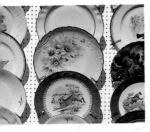

Limoges porcelain

The process of firing enamel dates back to the 6th century, but it developed to a much more sophisticated art at Limoges during the 12th century with the invention of the champlevé technique: successive coats of enamel are spread on engraved copper, each fired at decreasing temperatures, resulting in a deep, jewel-like luster. Painted enamels are still produced at Limoges. The porcelain industry in Limoges took off with the discovery of high-quality kaolin (china clay) at St-Yrieux in 1768; today Limoges produces about half of France's porcelain, mostly tableware.

▶ ▷ ▷   Limoges

The ancient crafts of enameling and porcelain making still figure largely in Limoges's economy, but the old medieval core has now spread far and wide along both banks of the Vienne. One of the most interesting parts of the older sector is the Quartier de la Boucherie, a web of narrow alleys once occupied by a guild of butchers. Several churches are worth a look; don't miss the cathedral of St-Etienne in ambitious Gothic. Two excellent museums chart the history of Limoges's major industries: the Musée National Adrien-Debouche is devoted to chinaware; the Musée Municipal contains a splendid collection of Limousin enamels.

▶ ▷ ▷   Martel

This quiet gray truffle town on Quercy limestone is rich in history and fascinating to explore. The town is named after Charlemagne's grandfather, Charles Martel, who defeated the Saracens in the 8th century and built a church here. From the 18th-century covered market, composed of a forest of timbers on stone stilts, streets full of ancient mansions stretch past the sturdy fortified church of St-Maur, the Mirepoises Cloisters and the Maison Fabri, where Henry Short-Coat, son of Henry Plantagenet, died a painful and penitent death after pillaging the shrine of Rocamadour.

▶ ▷ ▷   Moissac

Despite Moissac's river setting, surrounded by hilly orchards and vineyards, the modern town is unprepossessing. The reason to visit it is the ancient abbey church of St-Pierre on the right bank of the Tarn. It has suffered many vicissitudes since its Benedictine foundation in the 7th century, but still has a remarkable Romanesque south doorway depicting St. John's vision of the Apocalypse. The ornately carved capitals in the cloisters are among the best in France.

▶ ▷ ▷   Monbazillac, Château de

From the lovely hilltop château with its massive pepper-pot towers, well-combed vineyards stretch as far as you can see. The luscious white wine for which Monbazillac is famous is said by some to be sweeter and richer than Sauternes. The château dates from about 1550 and, though it looks robust enough, was designed more for leisured living than defense. Today it is looked after by the wine cooperative that produces Monbazillac, and houses a tasting center, restaurant and shop.

▶ ▷ ▷   Montauban

Modern suburbs do little for this pink brick bastide on the rich plains of the Garonne and Tarn, but its historical and artistic associations are impressive. A Protestant stronghold, Montauban resisted Louis XIII's besieging troops for over three months in 1621. The picturesque quarter surrounds the 17th-century arcaded place National, where rose-colored houses are linked by angled porticoes. The best thing in town is the Ingres Museum in the bishop's palace near the river, where the 19th-century artist's paintings and drawings are displayed; and the best event is the annual jazz festival.

▶ ▷ ▷   Montpézat de Quercy

Besides its agreeable old houses and arcades, this little Quercy town is worth a visit to see the Collegiate Church of St-Martin. Its main treasures are the lavishly worked tapestries in the sanctuary, depicting scenes from the life of St. Martin, and the tombs of the local great family, the des Prés, several of whom became famous clerics.

▷ ▷ ▷   Moutier d'Ahun

A church is again the main focus of interest here: The part-Romanesque, part-Gothic building dates originally from the 12th century, but later suffered many indignities at the hands of pillaging Protestants. Between 1673 and 1681 its finest feature was incorporated: a magnificent display of oak wood carving, which covers the walls of apse and chancel.

▶ ▷ ▷   Oradour-sur-Glane

Most French towns quickly repaired wartime damage, but what happened in Oradour was too dreadful to forget. So it has been left exactly as it was, an effective monument to the horrors of war. On June 10, 1944, a group of SS troops swept through the town on a mission of vengeance. They were still smarting from their humiliation after D-Day and angered by the deaths of two outriders at the hands of Resistance snipers in a neighboring village. They rounded up all the citizens of Oradour, putting women and children in the church, men in the surrounding outbuildings, and systematically massacred them. Many died in machine-gun fire; others burned to death when the church was torched. The total death toll was 642, of whom over 200 were children. Today the old village of Oradour is just the same as when the Nazis left: bullet marks on walls, charred shutters, old—now vintage—cars parked in garages, trailing telegraph wires. The ruins and the cemetery can be visited. Nearby new Oradour and its modern church have risen phoenix-like from the ashes.

History and tranquillity in the village of Martel

145

DORDOGNE

The faithful who visit Rocamadour climb the long stairway halfway up the side of the cliff to an assembly of seven chapels, where the ~~miraculous~~ shrine of St. Amadour is believed to lie beneath the altar of a smoke-blackened Virgin.

In 1956 several people were killed in rockfalls at La Roque-Gageac as the cliffs collapsed. Today the village is safely shored up.

Lush countryside surrounding Périgueux

▶▷▷ Périgueux

The capital of Périgord is a large, lively agricultural and commercial center, where truffles, foie gras, walnut sweets, honey, wine and liqueurs are stacked temptingly high in the windows of chic *épiceries* (grocery shops) in the old quarter. A regular market adds to this cornucopia. The pedestrianized narrow streets around the cathedral and the houses by the river offer fascinating architectural detail at every turn. The Romans who patronized the Vésone spring have left plenty of evidence, notably Vesunna's Tower, a stumpy cylindrical structure of yellowish stone. Other finds from the Gallo-Roman period can be seen in Périgueux's excellent museum. The St-Front cathedral's white domes and spiky turrets evoke some Islamic Levantine scene rather than a Catholic stronghold. It was much restored in the 19th century by Paul Abadie, the controversial architect of Sacré-Coeur in Paris. Inside it doesn't work well, and seems chilly and lifeless. The original cathedral, the massive St-Etienne-de-la-Cité, is now hemmed in by traffic.

▶▷▷ Rocamadour

Rocamadour's setting is irresistibly dramatic, particularly early or late in the day, when the light is indirect. Rocamadour clings to a sheer limestone spur rising from a dry canyon. An excellent view can be had from the belvedere at **L'Hospitalet**, across the valley. Close up, the fortified village loses some of its magic in an undignified scuffle for parking places and a clamor of souvenir cash tills. The town hall contains fine modern tapestries by Jean Lurçat. On the skyline is a château fortress, partly 14th-century. Falconry displays at the Rocher des Aigles make an interesting diversion.

▶▶▷ La Roque-Gageac

The crumbling cliffs of golden limestone into which La Roque-Gageac is built make it one of the most remarkable settings on the Dordogne. Traditional flat-bottomed *gabares* (boats) take tourists downstream, passing numerous châteaus. The **Château de la Malartie** is a 19th-century folly, the **Manoir de Tarde** genuinely 16th-century.

▶▶▷ St-Cirq-Lapopie

Huddled on its wooded limestone cliffs above the Lot, this golden-stone village is much frequented by tourists. Formerly a wood turners' colony, many of its houses are now owned by artists, and have been lovingly preserved with mullions and turrets intact. The 15th-century church juts out of the rock face to survey a dizzying sweep of Lot and Cère valleys.

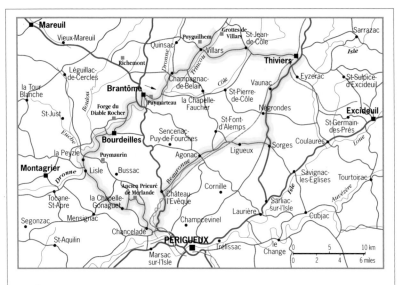

Drive Exploring Périgord Vert

Start at Brantôme.
Brantôme lies in the heart of Périgord Vert. Its riverside setting and good food make it a popular draw. An imposing Benedictine abbey is the main building of interest.

D78, D83, D82, D3 to Puyguilhem and D82 to Grottes de Villars.
Northeast lies the 16th-century château of **Puyguilhem,** restored after World War II. It is state-owned and open in summer. To the northeast are the **Grottes de Villars**, limestone caves decorated with animal engravings believed to be 30,000–40,000 years old.

D98 from Puyguilhem to St-Jean-de-Côle and D707 to Thiviers.
St-Jean-de-Côle has a typically Périgordian assembly of brown and gold stone houses. The 11th-century priory church and Château Marthonie are its most notable buildings.
Thiviers is an agreeable agricultural town. The Château Vaucocour offers views of the Isle, while the 12th-century church sports bizarre Romanesque carvings.

N21 to Sorges; then D74 and D3 to Agonac, D3E to Château l'Evêque and D939 and D2 to Chancelade.
Sorges has a museum, the Maison de la Truffe, in the local Syndicat d'Initiatif, devoted to the truffle; in winter you can join a truffle trail through nearby oak woods. Northwest of Périgueux lie the monastic ruins of **Chancelade**, where the abbey church and chapel of St-Jean remain of a once-great 12th-century community.

D2 and side road to Prieuré de Merlande; join D1 to Lisle, then D78 to Bourdeilles and Brantôme.
At **Merlande** an isolated chapel in a woodland clearing is all that remains of an associated priory, remarkable for its Romanesque carving. Heading back toward the swift-flowing Dronne, you will encounter the town of **Bourdeilles**, dominated by a high medieval and Renaissance castle. Hastily patched up to receive a proposed visit by Catherine de' Médicis (who canceled), it has excellent views over the rocky green river, and a fine collection of furnishings.

Follow the river upstream to return to Brantôme.

DORDOGNE

Périgord's buried treasure, truffles, look like lumps of coal, and their aroma is questionable. Yet these unappetizing fungi are the subjects of an abstruse Périgordian science, tales of aphrodisiac powers and gourmets' dreams. Truffles come in about 30 different species, weigh about 3½ oz, and flourish on the roots of sickly oak trees. Their sporadic appearance during November and December sends farmers and poachers with trained pigs or dogs to nose them out. Truffles figure regularly on Périgordian menus, but large samples are rare. Sorges is a noted center, and the Maison de la Truffe is full of fascinating truffle facts.

St-Léonard-de-Noblat

▷▷▷   St-Junien

Glove making is the local industry of this busy town on the Vienne, its other point of interest being the Collegiate Church of St-Junien, a fine Romanesque building in Limousin style. St-Junien's 12th-century limestone tomb stands behind the altar.

▷▷▷   St-Léonard-de-Noblat

Birthplace of the scientist Gay-Lussac, this hill town has prospered from agriculture and stock rearing. The belfry is the most notable feature of its church.

▶▶▷   Sarlat

This beautifully restored golden-stone town is now one of the most popular centers in the central Dordogne, and suffers accordingly from crowds. Sarlat stages many cultural events and holds an annual arts festival. Its buildings are of minor interest, but they form a harmonious grouping, despite the busy road known as the Traverse that now bisects the old town. The cathedral's belfry is 12th-century; the rest was rebuilt in the 16th and 17th centuries. The strange conical-towered building is the Lanterne des Morts, a funerary chapel. On the main square is a Renaissance house where the poet Boétie was born. Other noteworthy mansions include the Gothic Hôtel Plamon and the Renaissance Hôtel de Maleville.

▶▷▷   Souillac

A bustling commercial center, Souillac is also a popular resort and is often crowded. Just outside is one of the smartest campsites in the Dordogne. Its old quarter is quite limited, but the prize is the domed church of Ste-Marie and its fine doorway, now visible inside the nave. The carvings depict episodes from the life of Theophilus, who made a pact with the devil, then repented and persuaded the Virgin to annul his signature.

Drive Along the Aveyron Valley

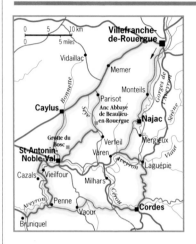

Many route variations are possible around the Aveyron valley. This long river follows a picturesque course toward the Tarn through a southerly spur of Quercy.

Start at Villefranche-de-Rouergue; then D47 and D149 to Najac. From Villefranche-de-Rouergue, a 13th-century bastide town with a fine central square, follow the river southward to Najac.
Of all the many medieval fortresses in France, **Najac**'s is a classic example. Set high on a cone-shaped bluff, its defensive walls are extended by a dizzy cliff plunge to one of the Aveyron's looping bends. To reach it, you walk along the one village street of ancient houses toward the castle keep on its promontory.

D564, D594 and D106; then D958 to Laguépie. D922 to Cordes.
Farther south, leaving the river temporarily, the beautiful hilltop bastide of Cordes has been well preserved and is now a popular artists' colony, resuming a tradition of craftsmanship dating back to the 14th century.

Head west along the D91 and take D33 to Penne.

At one of the valley's most beautiful sections, **Penne** reveals yet another ruined and rugged fortress on a hill. This village was batted to and fro like a shuttlecock during the Hundred Years' War, and also suffered during the Albigensian Crusade. Now its peaceful streets are lined with escutcheoned, half-timbered houses, leading up to the castle ruins.

D115 to Bruniquel.
The cruel Visigothic princess Brunhilda is said to have founded the castle; she was eventually tied to the tail of a wild horse and trampled to death. The castle still retains very early sections; the Knight's Hall and guardroom chimneypiece are worth seeing.

Return on D115 to St-Antonin-Noble-Val.
This ancient town is set opposite a sheer rock wall, the **Rochers d'Anglars**. Its tiered merchants' houses have roofs covered in round *lauze* tiles, and its town hall, one of the oldest in France, houses a prehistoric collection. Notice the 14th-century calvary on the market square.

Leaving the Aveyron to follow its tributary the Bonnette, head north on the D19 toward Caylus.
Caylus has a huge covered market and fortified church, which contains a striking modern crucifix.

An alternative route via the D75 and D33 leads to Beaulieu-en-Rouergue.
This route passes the Grotte du Bosc, a smallish cave in a dry underground riverbed with limestone formations. At **Beaulieu** the abbey church dates back to the mid-13th century and has a seven-sided apse. The dormitory now houses a modern art gallery.

Return to Villefranche-de-Rouergue via the D33 and D926.

149

DORDOGNE

All over the Dordogne, cheerful, healthy-looking geese roam the fields free-range, munching whatever they choose. These are the lucky ones—they haven't yet encountered the *gavage* process, in which corn is poured down their gullets through funnels to enlarge their livers. If you enjoy foie gras, visit, just for interest, a pâté farm to see what actually happens. Force-fed geese stay inside dark sheds, for they can hardly waddle, and endure five or six weeks' involuntary gluttony.

A relief at the basilica of St-Sernin

 Toulouse

Though it dates from Roman times, Toulouse reached its heyday during the Middle Ages, when it was a center of learning and culture. Its university is second in size only to the Sorbonne. A strategic location at the junction of several important trading routes guaranteed it a place in the sun; it was also an important stop-off point for pilgrims along the Way of St. James to Santiago de Compostela in Spain. It fostered some of the best lyric poets of its day, and the earliest literary society in Europe. Today Toulouse has much high-tech industry, a lively arts scene and horrific traffic problems. It is no longer a beautiful place, but its distinctive pink buildings include many attractive Renaissance mansions. The old quarter stretches south of the place du Capitole, on which stands the 18th-century town hall, now home to the theater and opera house. The main shopping streets are the rue d'Alsace-Lorraine and the rue St-Rome.

St-Sernin The basilica of St-Sernin is the biggest Romanesque church in France, dedicated to a saint martyred by bulls in AD 250. Its exterior features a five-story octagonal belfry and a grouping of small chapels around the apse and transepts. Inside, the 17th-century woodwork has been re-restored to its original splendor after Viollet-le-Duc's misguided "improvements."

Other sights The Eglise des Jacobins is a stern Gothic hall church with an unexpectedly flamboyant interior. Toulouse has two museums of note: the Musée des Augustins, containing medieval sculpture rescued from wantonly demolished churches; and the Musée St-Raymond, with a fine collection of Roman art.

▶ ▷ ▷   Uzerche

The "Pearl of Limousin" stands on a rocky spur above the waters of the Vézère, moated on three sides. Densely packed buildings sprouting belfries and turrets are linked by steps and interspersed with 14th-century fortifications. The 12th-century church of St-Pierre has capitals carved with animals and foliage, and an eerie crypt.

▶ ▷ ▷   Ventadour

These romantic castle ruins above the rocky Luzège gorge can be reached by foot from Moustier-Ventadour. Home of the viscounts of Ventadour before they grew weary of feudal plumbing and decamped to Ussel, this was also where the troubadour Bernard de Ventadour developed his talents. Of humble birth (some say the son of the viscount by a kitchen maid), Bernard wrote courtly love songs inspired by his illicit passion for the viscountess.

Drive **Between the Dordogne and the Corrèze**

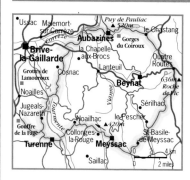

Start at Collonges-la-Rouge.
The buildings of **Collonges-la-Rouge**, fashioned from brilliant magenta sandstone, vie with one another for attention. The corbeled Maison de la Sirène bears a mermaid; whimsical turrets adorn the Hôtel de la Ramade de Friac and Hôtel de Beuges; the Castel de Vassignac sports mullions, watchtowers, and loopholes for firing missiles.

D38 and D150 west to Turenne.
Turenne is built of more typical pale limestone, but its vainglorious hilltop castle, reduced by the Revolution to two ruined towers, is striking. Turenne's bankrupt overlords were

forced to sell their birthright to Louis XV in 1738, but during the Middle Ages the viscounts of Turenne held sway over 1,200 villages, minted their own currency, collected their own taxes. Today the village is full of 15th- and 16th-century houses. Northwest lies the **Gouffre de la Fage**, a series of limestone caverns.

Take the D8, D38 (east), D162 (crossing the N121) and D48 to Aubazines.
The Cistercian abbey church of St. Stephen is **Aubazines**'s main feature of interest, originally dating from the 12th century. The church has amusing 18th-century choir stalls, and St. Stephen's splendid Gothic carved tomb. The restored abbey still houses a religious community but can be visited.

D48 to Gorges du Coiroux and Puy de Pauliac.
The summit can be climbed on foot for a panoramic view.

D48, D94 and D940 to Roche de Vic, and D10 and D38 to Collonges-la-Rouge.
The **Roche de Vic** is a hilltop vantage point crowned by a chapel.

THE PYRENEES

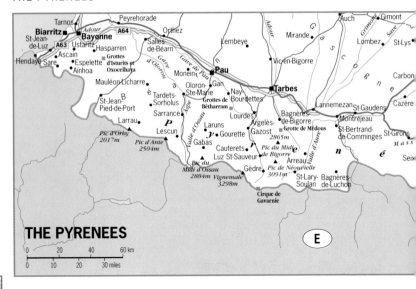

THE PYRENEES

E

```
0      20      40      60 km
0    10     20    30 miles
```

Climbing abruptly from the plains of Gascony, the Pyrenees—mountains rich in history, even richer in natural beauty—are a formidable natural barrier between France and the Iberian Peninsula. They are two mountain chains, overlapping for a few kilometers where the Garonne rises in the Valle d'Aran, a corner of Spain on the northern side of the watershed. Elsewhere, natural and national frontiers mostly coincide.

There is a marked contrast between the forests and pastures of the damp and cool Atlantic Pyrenees, and the vineyards and orchards of the sun-drenched Mediterranean flank, one of the driest corners of France. Proud Pyreneans are hypersensitive to suggestions that this is France's second-best mountain range and resent comparisons with the Alps. They do not like to be told that their highest peaks only nudge the 9,840-foot level, while the Alps break 13,120 feet; that there are only a few pocket-handkerchief glaciers and that winter sports development lags behind by a long way. The Pyrenees' many thermal and mineral springs made the region fashionable in the 19th century, with the result that many of its main resorts are slightly run-down old spas, reinforcing the contrast with the state-of-the-art sports resorts in the Alps.

For many visitors, the unfashionable nature of the Pyrenees is their great appeal. Prices are low, accommodations unpretentious, the welcome warm and unaffected. The mountains are mostly uncluttered by ugly modern resorts and cable-car pylons. The flowers are spectacular, the wildlife abundant (only the Camargue is better for bird-watching), a few species surviving only in the Pyrenees. A Grande Randonnée (GR) trail follows the range from coast to coast and takes hikers into a spectacular wilderness. If the resorts are disappointing, the Pyrenees are a backpacker's paradise.

There is also plenty for sightseers: pilgrimage places past and present, including Lourdes, the most popular invalids' pilgrimage place in Christendom; the showpiece

THE PYRENEES

fortified city of Carcassonne and dizzy citadels where medieval heretics sheltered from persecution; and a wealth of inventive art in the Romanesque churches of Catalonia. And the Basque country offers a beautiful coastline, picturesque old villages and the most fascinating of all Europe's fringe cultures, with an ancient and cherished language.

THE PYRENEES

▶ ▷ ▷ Andorra

Straddling the spine of the Pyrenees, Andorra is a small co-principality nominally subject to the French president and the Spanish bishop of Urgel. In practice it is proudly independent—and making a good living from tourism, generated by Andorra's tax-free status. Almost all Andorra lies on the Spanish side of the Port d'Envalira (7,895 feet), the highest main road pass in the Pyrenees. Although both francs and pesetas pass, Spanish currency and language prevail except at Pas de la Case (6,858 feet), a modern ski resort on the French border. Villages along the main road down the Valira valley have been ruined by modern development, and the capital, Andorra la Vella, is a traffic-jammed supermarket city. The Valira del Nord side valley is less developed. Andorra has some of the best skiing in the Pyrenees.

Houses in Bayonne

▷ ▷ ▷ Arles-sur-Tech

This market town makes a more attractive base than nearby Amélie les Bains. Its old abbey church has interesting Romanesque carving on the facade, a Gothic cloister and a Baroque altarpiece illustrating the story of the town's patrons, a pair of 3rd-century Kurdish martyrs. The Fou cascades down a narrow gorge (access only on foot) to join the Tech, 2 km above Arles.

▶ ▷ ▷ Aure, Vallée d'

The Neste d'Aure (*neste*, like *gave*, is a local Pyrenean word for river) flows from the slopes of the 9,840-foot massif de Néouvielle to join the Garonne at Montréjeau. The middle section of the valley is pleasantly rural, and the old gray village of Arreau makes a good base or overnight stop. The main alternative is St-Lary-Soulan, a fashionable and stylish resort by Pyrenean standards, with a cable car to good ski slopes. Above St-Lary the road narrows and climbs into wilder country on its way to the Bielsa road tunnel to Spain. From Fabian, it is a slow 14-km drive up to a cluster of high lakes (dammed and natural) beneath the snowy walls of the Néouvielle, some of the most impressive Pyrenean scenery accessible to motorists. Marked GR hiking trails lead over the massif to Barèges.

▶▶▷ Bayonne

An old river port on the Nive, the capital of the French Basque country is famous for its ham, chocolate and bayonets. On the left bank, the twin spires of its fine 13th-century Gothic cathedral dominate an attractive precinct of old shopping streets. The arcaded Rue du Port-Neuf has mouth-watering *confiseries* (confectionary shops) and old-fashioned tea shops (**Cazenave** is recommended); the place de la Liberté is the focus of café society. The right-bank half of the old town has the excellent Musée Bonnat, with a rich art collection, including works by Goya and Ingres.

▶▷▷ Bétharram, Grottes de

This 5-km complex of grandiose underground chambers, rich in stalactites and stalagmites, is reached by cable car and toured by boat and train. Bétharram would be a powerful attraction in any region; being so close to the pilgrimage site of Lourdes (14 km east), it is often dauntingly crowded.

▶▶▷ La Bigorre

The Bigorre is the heartland of the high Pyrenees and its main tourist area. The route from Arreau to Luz-St-Sauveur crosses the attractively pastoral Col d'Aspin and wilder Col du Tourmalet (6,934 feet), notorious as the most punishing climb in the Tour de France. From the pass a rough toll road (often not clear of snow till July) and cable car lead to the TV station and observatory on the **Pic du Midi du Bigorre** (9,397 feet), an incomparable viewpoint. **La Mongie** is a rather unsightly ski resort linked by ski lift to Barèges, a small resort with sulfur springs and summer campers. Madame de Maintenon brought the duc de Maine to Barèges in 1677, and Napoleon sent wounded soldiers there to recuperate. **Bagnères de Bigorre** is an older and larger spa—there are impressive stalagmites and stalactites in the nearby Grotte de Médous. Cauterets and Luz-St-Sauveur are the other main resorts (see separate entries).

▷▷▷ Le Canigou

Lonely eastern bastion of the Pyrenees 50 km from the Mediterranean, the Canigou (9,132 feet) is the ~~holy~~ mountain of the Catalans who come annually from France and Spain to light fires on its summit. From Vernet, Jeep trips are organized up the rough forest road to the Chalet-Hôtel des Cortalets (7,134 feet), two hours' walk (a slog, but not difficult) from the summit. There is a longer and slightly less difficult road up to the chalet from Prades. The classic Canigou experience is to stay overnight at the chalet and walk to the top in time to see dawn break over the sea.

A troupe of *chanteurs montagnards* (mountain singers) toured Europe in the 19th century, enchanting Second Empire society audiences with their recitals of Pyrenean songs, glorifying the delights of the Bigorre. The chorus still exists at Bagnères de Bigorre.

The Basque Country

■ Since the Basques swarmed down from the high passes to ambush Charlemagne's rear guard and kill Roland at Roncevaux in 778, they have been no friends of the French. However, the beret and the rope-soled espadrille are just two Basque contributions to the national way of life. Of obscure origin, the Basques speak an impenetrable tongue, once thought to have been the pre-Babel language. The devil is said to have mastered only three words of it after seven years of study. ...■

Most of the Basque country lies on the Spanish side of the Pyrenees and only one in ten of the half-million speakers of the Basque language is French. Although the Basques are conscious of their cultural and ethnic solidarity—*Zazpiak Bat* (the seven are one) is a favorite slogan—Spanish and French Basques have evolved differently. In Spain the mineral-rich region was quick to industrialize, and Basques have been prominent in the economic and political life of the nation. In France the Basque country, consisting of the three provinces of Labourd, Basse Navarre and Soule, was a remote backwater of farmers and fishermen until tourism reached the coast in the 19th century. They are a humble and traditionally reserved people who leave acts of separatist violence to their Spanish cousins. Even in France, however, town center demonstrations, usually about political prisoners, are not uncommon. It is hard not to view these processions with colorful banners and unintelligible chanting as another example of quaint Basque folklore, like the costumed displays of traditional Basque dancing and music.

Celebrating the Basque festival in Bayonne

The national game Basque pelota is not one game but many variations of the old *jeu de paume*, featuring a hard ball hit against a wall (*fronton*), which is a conspicuous feature of every village in the southwest. The fastest version of the game (*cesta punta*) takes place in an indoor court (*trinquet*); players wear long, curved scooplike gauntlets (*chistera*) to catch the ball and return it in a single swing of the arm. When played well, this is one of the most exciting and graceful of ball games. At a simpler level (as practiced by children against the village *fronton*), bare hands or a wooden bat (*pala*) are used. Most of the major championships and important matches are held at Biarritz. St-Jean-de-Luz is another good place for pelota watching.

Labourd Well watered to a fault, the Labourd is the prettiest of the three Basque regions, with a beautiful coastline of cliffs and sandy coves fronting a bumpy landscape of green hills and immaculately kept, red and white timbered villages. Sare, Ainhoa and Ascain are outstandingly pretty, with typical Basque churches, of which the main characteristics are sex-segregated seating arrangements (the galleries are for men only) and small circular gravestones bearing the Basque swastika emblem. On the coast, **Biarritz** (see page 128) is the grand resort and surfing capital of Europe. The old fishing port of **St-Jean-de-Luz** has a perfectly sheltered sandy beach (a rare commodity on the Atlantic coast), lots of good fish restaurants, elegant shops and plenty of Basque charm in the colorful streets of its pedestrianized center. The house where Louis XIV spent the month (May–June 1660) before his marriage to the Spanish infanta Maria Teresa of Spain stands by the harbor. His fiancée stayed in the beautiful house next door. Their marriage took place in the spectacularly ornate church of St-Jean Baptiste. After the ceremony, the door used by the royal couple was blocked. The border town of **Hendaye** is dreary by comparison, but has a vast beach.

Bayonne, the capital of Labourd, is the acknowledged capital of the French Basque country. It has a core of streets in typically colorful Basque style, and is worth a visit for sightseeing. In early August it hosts the largest Basque festival, with much dancing of fandangos and other dances to tunes played on the *txistu* (three-holed flute) and *ttun-ttun* (tambourine). ·

Inland From the Col de St Ignace, between Ascain and Sare, a railway ascends the Rhune (2,952 feet), a superb viewpoint commanding the coast and rolling hinterland.

Typical ingredients in Basque cuisine are tomatoes, peppers, garlic and onions: Mixed with eggs these make *piperade*, a Basque omelet. Chicken, kidneys and grilled tuna are often served *à la Basquaise*, with a sauce of red peppers, garlic and onions. Traditional *gâteau Basque* has lemon and black cherries from Itxassou (south of Cambo les Bains). The best Basque wine is Irroléguy, from the area around St-Etienne-de-Baïgorry.

157

Espelette has a pimiento festival and is a marketplace for *pottoks*, diminutive semi-wild horses that inhabit the local hillsides.

Soule (see page 166) cannot rival the coastal region for village prettiness but has magnificent countryside of forests and sheep pastures still managed, as they have been for centuries, by committees of communal representatives.

The red and white houses of Ainhoa

Carcassonne's magnificent defenses

Built in 1969, the Odeillo solar oven at Font-Romeu consists of 9,500 mirrors forming a concave surface area of 19,000 square feet, concentrating the sun's rays into a 30-inch oven where the temperature can reach 3,500 degrees Celsius (6,332 degrees Fahrenheit). Since 1986 it has not been used for power generation, but there are other highly technical scientific uses to which the mirrors are put, as explained in the permanent exhibition on site.

▶▶▶ Carcassonne

Set apart from a thriving modern town beside the Aude stand the towers and walls of a mint-condition medieval fortified city, one of the great sights of Europe. The defenses were of little use in 1209, when Carcassonne lasted less than a month before opening its gates to the crusading army of Simon de Montfort. Tourism rules in the narrow streets, but nothing spoils the time warp in the beautiful grassy area between the city's twin curtain walls. The massive towers buttressing the inner wall are a mixture of 13th-century and clearly visible Gallo-Roman masonry. The outer wall was built after the 1209 siege. Inside the city, the basilica of St-Nazaire has both a Romanesque nave and a Gothic choir.

▶▶▷ Cauterets

A 19th-century spa proud of its boiled sweets (*berlingots*), Cauterets is a good all-round resort: no great beauty as a village, but full of animation in midsummer and an excellent base for excursions into the Parc National des Pyrénées. The park information center has a good exhibition of Pyrenean ecology (with a section devoted to the bearded vulture). A cable car hoists skiers to the Cirque du Lys, known for the most reliable snow in the Pyrenees. For walkers, the classic excursion is by road past waterfalls to Pont d'Espagne, where trails lead up to the highest peak in the French Pyrenees, the Vignemale (10,817 feet).

▷▷▷ Cerdagne

Cerdagne/Cerdanya is the upper Segre valley, divided between France and Spain according to the terms of a postscript to the 1659 Pyrenean treaty. It is a famously sunny region and its main resort, **Font-Romeu**, a sprawling ski resort, claims 3,000 hours of sun a year and boasts a solar oven. Greatly used for high-level athletics training, it is also a Catalan pilgrimage site, with an 18th-century hermitage on the site of a spring where a miraculous statue of the Virgin was uncovered by a bull. There are other interesting churches at Llo, the most picturesque old village in French Cerdagne, and Hix, near the border at Bourg Madame.

Cathars and Fortresses

■ The Albigensian Crusade, launched by Pope Innocent III in 1209 to eradicate the Cathar heresy that flourished in south-western France, is one of the more compelling stories of internecine butchery and bravery in the annals of medieval history. Apart from wiping 400 villages off the map, it brought about royal control of Languedoc and the destruction of a multi-cultural civilization of great refinement, which had flourished at the court of Toulouse. ...■

Kill them all! Promised remission for all sins past and future and the cancellation of all debts in exchange for 40 days' service, an army of land-grabbing northern French crusaders went south. Even contemporaries were shocked when Béziers was singled out for exemplary massacre on July 22, 1209; Cathar and Catholic were slaughtered indiscriminately ("Kill them all, for God will recognize his own," cried the abbot of Cîteaux, no slouch with the sword); not even women and children sheltering in churches were spared.

Towns soon opened their gates to the crusaders but the Cathar *parfaits* and *parfaites* (the mystical corps of Cathar priests) retreated to remote fortresses in the foothills of the eastern Pyrenees. Their headquarters on the rock of Montségur, southeast of Foix, was besieged by 10,000 Catholics throughout the autumn and winter of 1243–44. A truce was eventually concluded but all 207 Cathars declined to abjure their faith or escape, and walked calmly into the flames of a huge bonfire on the morning of March 16, 1244.

The Cathar strongholds The two most exciting of these ridge-top aeries to visit are Peyrepertuse and Quéribus, north of the main Perpignan–Foix road (D117). **Quéribus** is set 1,640 precipitous feet above the main valley, with superb views of the Canigou and other high peaks to the south. Its siege in 1255, which succeeded only through treachery, was the last episode of the intermittent crusading effort. **Peyrepertuse** is a larger complex of ruins crowning a ridge, splendidly wild and overgrown and also commanding magnificent views. **Montségur** is equally impressive, but you are less likely to have it to yourself. There is a steep path to the ruins from the pass on its western flank. **Puivert** and **Puilaurens** are other good examples beside the Perpignan–Foix road near Quillan.

A stronghold formed by nature and by man: Peyrepertuse

St-Bertrand-de-Comminges (above)

The Devil's Bridge at Céret (right)

▶ ▷ ▷   Céret

An attractive, leisurely Catalan town at the heart of the fruit-growing region of the Tech valley, Céret attracted leading Cubist artists at the turn of the century and has an excellent modern art museum, with works by Chagall, Dali, Picasso, Dufy and Braque. A canopy of plane trees adds to the pleasures of a stroll through the old part of town, south of the place de la République.

▶ ▷ ▷   Le Comminges

The heart of the Comminges region is the upper valley of the Garonne. In 72 BC, Pompey founded a city, *Lugdunum Convenarum*, on an isolated hill at the entrance to the mountain valley. The old walled village of St-Bertrand-de-Comminges now stands on the site, dominated by its cathedral, which used to be an important stop on the pilgrimage road to Spain. All that survives of the original 12th-century building is the facade and three sides of the cloister, with beautiful capitals and an open gallery giving a fine mountain view. The choir has outstanding 16th-century carved wooden choir stalls and screen. At the foot of the hill there are some excavations of the Roman city and, beautifully set among cypresses near the quiet village of Valcabrère, the delightful 11th-century basilica of St-Just, largely built of recycled Roman masonry. Roman inscriptions and columns are easily identified.

▷ ▷ ▷   Le Couserans

Between the Pays de Foix and the Comminges, the Couserans is an out-of-the-way region of quiet valleys without major sights or spectacular mountain scenery. The traditional local ways of life have survived better than in most places, but depopulation is as great an enemy as overdevelopment. The Bethmale valley, well known for its local dress (including extravagantly upturned wooden footwear), is now quiet vacation home country. The only resort of any size is **Aulus-les-Bains**, a spa once known for its bear tamers, now well past its prime but set among beautiful mountains near the Spanish border ridge and a good base for hikes to mountain lakes and waterfalls (the 361-foot Cascade d'Arse, notably). **Seix** is a center for canoeing.

Drive **Pays de Foix**

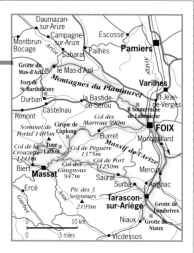

This tour combines the best Pyrenean caves with beautiful hill driving to the east of Foix.

Start at Foix.
Foix is less enchanting than a view of its picturesque three-towered castle suggests, but is a lively place with a good choice of restaurants.

Take the N20 to Tarascon-sur-Ariège. You can make excursions to Grotte de Niaux (D8) and Grotte de Lombrives (N20).
Niaux is one of the finest prehistoric painted caves in Europe, with black bison and ibex in its Salon Noir, "discovered" in 1906. The guided tour is in French only. Numbers allowed into the cave are limited; book a slot a day in advance or early in the morning. On the other side of the same mountain, **Lombrives** (2-hour guided tour and train ride) is an enormous network of caves used as a refuge and burial place since prehistory and covered with graffiti.

Take D618 to Massat and Biert, then D18/D17 via Col de la Crouzette, Sommet de Portel and Col des Marrous back to Foix.
The rest of the tour is a long scenic drive, 75 km of beautiful woods, pastures and panoramas from high passes. It can be abbreviated by taking the narrow road that climbs steeply from the Col des Caugnous

(6 km east of Massat) to the Col de Péguère near the Tour Laffon, a fine viewing tower a few minutes' walk from the road. The view from the Sommet de Portel (4,871 feet) is better still.

From Foix excursions can be made to Rivière Souterraine de Labouiche and Grotte du Mas d'Azil by D1 (30 km each way).
Visiting the underground Labouiche River involves a 1.5-km boat trip, with stalagmites, stalactites and a waterfall to admire. South of the village of Le Mas d'Azil, the D119 runs through a superb 1,380-foot-long tunnel carved by the River Arize. Before sheltering 17th-century Protestants, side caves (guided tour) were inhabited by prehistoric man for thousands of years. Finds are well displayed on site.

▶ ▷ ▷ Cirque de Gavarnie

The most celebrated mountain beauty spot in the Pyrenees is the huge theater of cliffs, waterfalls and snowy peaks to the south of Luz-St-Sauveur. The classic way to see the cirque is by donkey (or on foot) along the 5-km path from the car parks at the village of Gavarnie (where there are accommodations) to the foot of the cliffs.

▶ ▷ ▷ Isturits and Oxocelhaya (Grottes)

These two caves in the Basque country are within easy reach of the coast for a rainy-day outing. The higher chamber (Isturits) has yielded important evidence of occupation by prehistoric man; Oxocelhaya is more beautiful, with well-lit stalactites and stalagmites.

▶ ▷ ▷ Lourdes   *idolatry*

Lourdes is an astonishing manifestation of contemporary ~~faith~~. Lines of stretcher cases inch toward the ~~holy~~ taps, the candles and the screen of votive crutches at the entrance to the ~~miraculous~~ riverside grotto where a young country girl, Bernadette Subirous, saw the ~~Virgin~~ on February 11, 1858, and on 17 subsequent occasions. Shop after shop peddles plastic virgins, bottles of ~~holy~~ water and 35-kg candles at about 1400 francs apiece. The cavernous underground basilica has room for 20,000 ~~pilgrims~~.

Lourdes was once an important strategic stronghold. An impressive fortress overlooks the Gave de Pau and houses a good regional museum.

▶ ▷ ▷ Luchon

The Romans' favorite spa in the Pyrenees still has a certain chic, with tree-lined avenues, a casino and thermal baths set in a handsome park. At a junction of high mountain valleys, Luchon makes an excellent base for excursions. From the woods and waterfalls of the Val de Lys it is a splendid hairpin drive up to the miniresort and lofty belvedere of Superbagnères (5,904 feet). The Hospice de France refuge (10 km southeast) and the Port de Pierrefite (above Bourg d'Oeil, 22 km northwest) are better starting points for walks.

▶ ▷ ▷ Luz-St-Sauveur

This picturesque old village and modest resort between Lourdes and Gavarnie is an attractive alternative to the larger resorts in the area. Once the capital of a self-governing republic, it has an unusual fortified church. There is a national park information center next door.

▶ ▶ ▶ Niaux, Grotte de

See **Pays de Foix Drive,** page 161.

▶ ▷ ▷ Oloron-Ste-Marie and Vallée d'Aspe

Oloron is a busy market and chocolate-making town at the confluence of Aspe and Ossau Rivers, on the old pilgrimage route to Spain. Its showpiece is the 12th-century marble doorway of Sainte-Marie, richly carved with Biblical figures.

Running north from the Col du Somport (5,353 feet) is the beautiful Aspe valley. Its relative tranquillity and its

---

A tough three-hour walk from the Col de Gavarnie/Boucharo leads to the Brèche de Roland, a cleft in the rock wall where, according to the *Chanson de Roland,* Charlemagne's expiring lieutenant smashed his sword on the rock to prevent its falling into infidel hands.

The infrastructure for the world's leading pilgrimage is enormous: 400 hotels, 35 campsites, and scores of sanatoria, all dependent on voluntary helpers.

"Beastly dens ... sufficient to cause as many distempers as they cure."—Arthur Young, on Luchon, 1787

The Col d'Aubisque offers a scenic drive

dwindling population of bears are threatened by a road tunnel currently under construction under the Somport. Above the valley, the rough gray village of **Lescun** is a good hiking base with simple accommodations, beneath a superb circus of peaks including the Pic d'Anie (8,213 feet).

▶ ▷ ▷ Ossau, Vallée d'

One ridge east of the Aspe, the Ossau valley runs north to Pau from the Spanish border at the Col du Pourtalet (5,884 feet, open only in summer); the two valleys combine to make a circuit via Jaca in Spain. The upper Ossau valley is beautiful wild country, with a few bears lurking around Laruns, and rather more *isards* (Pyrenean chamois) on the slopes of the Pic du Midi d'Ossau (9,463 feet), centerpiece of the famous view from Pau. From Gabas a narrow road climbs steeply to the artificial Lac de Bious (4,658 feet); from here it is a two-hour walk to a cluster of natural lakes among splendid scenery at the foot of the Pic du Midi. Hiking trails link to form a full circuit of the mountain. On the other side of Gabas, a cable car and mountain railway lead to the Lac d'Artouste via the panoramic Pic de la Sagette (6,662 feet). There is a hiking trail back to Gabas from the lake. From Laruns, it is a beautiful drive east over the Col d'Aubisque (5,606 feet).

▶ ▷ ▷ Pau

The one-time capital of Béarn has two claims to fame: Henri IV (le Béarnais), best loved of all French monarchs, was born there in 1553; and the boulevard des Pyrénées gives a famous view of the mountain range, best when the distant peaks are snowy (from November to April).

At the western end of the boulevard des Pyrénées, the château is a mixture of medieval, Renaissance and Second Empire. The interior (guided tours) has a display of 17th- and 18th-century tapestries and many Henri-related items, including his cradle, a tortoise's shell.

THE PYRENEES

Henri IV's mother, Jeanne d'Albret, queen of Navarre, sang Béarnais songs when she was in labor in order not to produce a crybaby; her father rubbed the newborn's lips with garlic and Jurançon wine, to make him grow into a big strong man. Both strategies worked. The French crown fell to him when the Valois line expired with Henri III in 1589. Although the new king was a Protestant, his mother having abandoned the Roman faith, finding the gates of Paris closed to him, he renounced his Protestantism with the famously pragmatic words: "Paris is well worth a mass." ← *wrong*

163

Pau enjoyed a vogue in 19th-century Britain as a place to winter, or as a permanent residence. It has not entirely lost its sedate atmosphere. The fashion started when the duke of Wellington's soldiers, on their way home from war in Spain and a successful encounter with Marshal Soult at Orthez in 1814, were fêted as liberators at Pau. Many settled there, advertised the alleged curative powers of Pau's mild climate, and introduced racing, golf and fox hunting. Hunts still meet on winter Saturdays.

The High Pyrenees

■ **The high Pyrenees cover more than half the 400-km length of the range, from the Pic d'Anie (8,213 feet) above Lescun in the Aspe valley to the Pic Carlit (9,581 feet), east of Andorra. Apart from the Somport and Pourtalet passes in the west and the Garonne gap (the Spanish Valle d'Aran) where the two Pyrenean chains overlap to the south of Luchon, there are no easy frontier passes in this wilderness area of spectacular peaks and rocky cirques mirrored in mountain lakes. The area has a rich and fascinating ecology, with the best examples of high-mountain flora and fauna in Europe. ...■**

A legendary mountaineers' challenge: the Vignemale

A thin strip (110 km by 15 km at its widest) of the frontier mountains in the west, from Lescun to the Néouvielle massif above St-Lary, is part of the Parc National des Pyrénées.

Climbers' challenges The highest Pyrenees are in Spain (due south of Luchon, the Maladeta massif culminates at the 11,165-foot Pic d'Aneto), but the northern side has the most famous and beautiful peaks, including the Vignemale (10,812 feet), highest point of the frontier, the terraced cliffs and waterfalls of the **Cirque de Gavarnie** (see page 162), and the mighty **Pic du Midi d'Ossau** (9,463 feet), an isolated bastion that is the climber's favorite playground in the range. The Pic du Midi was first climbed in 1787 (the year after the first ascent of Mont Blanc) by a shepherd from the Aspe valley.

South of Cauterets, the uninterrupted 2,624-foot wall of the north face of the **Vignemale** is another formidable challenge for mountaineers. The Vignemale has the biggest glacier in the Pyrenees and was the adopted home of one of the more colorful characters in the history of mountaineering, Count Henry Russell (1834–1909), who dynamited seven caves (including one only a few meters below the summit) to inhabit and use for dinner parties. Russell climbed the Vignemale more than 30 times and had guides bury him to the neck in scree on the summit for closer communion with the mountain he described as his own. This was no exaggeration: Barèges gave it to him on a 99-year lease. Luchon's museum has a section devoted to Russell and there is a statue of him at Gavarnie.

Wild things Bears, the most celebrated specialty of Pyrenean wildlife, do not inhabit the high mountains but the fringe of human habitation at medium altitude (invariably below the tree line). Other denizens of the mountains include marmots (numerous), *isards* (Pyrenean chamois) and desmans, a nocturnal vole with webbed feet and a long trunk, found only in streams in

Stunning Pyrenean mountain scenery in the Parc National des Pyrénées

the Pyrenees and the Caucasus. Undisputed king of the Pyrenees, however, is the lammergeier, or bearded vulture, the largest of European vultures (over 3 feet long and with a wingspan of up to 10 feet) and a unique link in the food chain—its favorite food is bone marrow, which it obtains by dropping bones onto rock from a great height. Lammergeiers nest on mountain ledges in the wildest locations and shun the company of other vultures at a carcass. On the wing it is a magnificent sight, clearly distinguishable from other vultures by its size and narrow pointed wings and tail.

The hiker's Pyrenees An 8-km rough road leads from **Gavarnie** to the **Barrage d'Ossoue** reservoir, along a valley where you might glimpse *isards*, marmots and (if you're lucky) bearded vultures. From the lake it is about three hours' walk to the foot of the Vignemale's Ossoue glacier and one of Russell's caves.

The **GR10** hiking trail crosses from Atlantic to Mediterranean on the northern side of the chain, passing through the national park via numerous refuges. No rock climbing is involved, but in many places the isolation and the high altitude of the path brings it into the realm of mountaineering. A Pyrenean **Haute Route** (for experienced climbers only) takes a higher line along the crest of the frontier mountains, crossing into Spain in several places.

There are national park information centers at Cauterets, Luz-St-Sauveur and St-Lary-Soulan.

Pont d'Espagne, south of Cauterets, is the point of departure for some of the most celebrated, not-too-arduous walks in the Pyrenees. You can take a chair lift to the beautiful Lac de Gaube (otherwise an hour on foot). From the lake the GR10 continues up the valley to Les Oulettes refuge (7,055 feet) with increasingly impressive views of the north wall of the Vignemale. From there it climbs steeply to a high col (another two hours) on the mountain's eastern shoulder and down to the Barrage d'Ossoue. Another path from Pont d'Espagne follows the beautiful Marcadeau Valley to the refuge Wallon (6,120 feet, two hours from Pont d'Espagne). The trail, much used by travelers and smugglers down the centuries, continues over the mountains to Panticosa in Spain via the Port du Marcadeau (8,334 feet).

THE PYRENEES

From St-Jean-Pied-de-Port, the modern road to Roncevaux follows the Valcarlos defile, where Charlemagne's rear guard, under Roland, count of Blaye, with the valiant support of Olivier le Preux and Bishop Turpin, was ambushed and annihilated by rock-throwing Basques in 778. Legend, in the form of the great epic poem the *Chanson de Roland*, transformed Basques into Saracens and translated the action to the Ports de Cize route to the east, now open only to hikers (GR65).

St-Jean-Pied-de-Port

The edible scallop takes its French name, *coquille St-Jacques*, from the emblem of the medieval pilgrimage to Compostela, Spanish burial place of the crusaders' patron saint, Santiago (St. James or St.-Jacques), on the scallop-rich coast of northwest Spain. Wearing the pilgrim's uniform (cap with cockle badge, stick and gourd) pilgrims crossed France on set routes from Paris, Arles, Le Puy, Vézelay and Tours. Pilgrimages continued throughout the Hundred Years' War but the vogue waned by the 16th century. So-called pilgrims were mistrusted as spongers, and the term *coquelin* (now *coquin* in colloquial French) took on pejorative meaning.

▶▷▷ St-Jean-Pied-de-Port

An old Basque town with great charm and a long tradition of hospitality for passing travelers, St-Jean was where medieval pilgrimage routes converged before crossing the mountains (*port* means "mountain pass") to Roncevaux in Spain. Pilgrims walked down the still delightful cobbled rue de la Citadelle from the Porte St-Jacques to Porte d'Espagne. Old pink sandstone houses and a fortified church (Notre-Dame du Pont) built into the fabric of the ramparts overlook the right bank of the River Nive. The great military engineer Vauban added a citadel and a new system of defenses on the left bank in the 17th century. Although full of tourists in summer, St-Jean is a cheerful place and a good base, with hotels both plush and simple, excellent restaurants, folklorish displays of Basque singing and dancing, and shops full of berets and Basque walking sticks.

▶▷▷ St-Martin-du-Canigou

This much-restored abbey is spectacularly sited on the western side of the Canigou above Vernet-les-Bains (see page 167).

▶▷▷ Serrabone

The 11th- to 12th-century abbey church here sits in a wild setting among scented scrub-covered hills to the south of the Prades–Perpignan road (see page 167).

▶▷▷ Haute Soule

Soule is the easternmost province of the Basque country and, in terms of village charm, the least interesting. **Mauléon-Licharre,** the capital, manufactures typical Basque products—espadrilles and pelota bats. The churchyard at **Gotein** (3 km south) is characteristically Basque, with triple-crowned belfry wall and adjacent *fronton* (pelota court). Patient drivers can traverse the beautiful beech forests and wild pastures of the Haute Soule, still managed by the traditional collective syndicates of Soule communes, either driving 42 km from St-Jean-Pied-de-Port to Larrau (via the Col Bagargui, 4,353 feet) through the fringe of the Iraty forest, or 36 km from St-Jean to Tardets-Sorholus via Ahusquy, a more pastoral route. In wild country south of Tardets, the D113 leads past the entrance to the **Gorges de Kakouetta**, a narrow canyon accessible only to walkers (proper hiking boots are needed). At **Ste-Engrace**'s Romanesque pilgrimage church, the Queen of Sheba rides an elephant on one of the pillar capitals.

Romanesque Churches

■ Medieval Catalonia was a prosperous and cosmopolitan region, with trade links all over the Mediterranean. Its architecture from the Romanesque period, before the ~~lumpish~~ northern Crusaders descended on the southwest to snuff out ~~tolerance and~~ invention, seems to reflect its open society. There is a remarkable and fruitful fusion of influences, from as far afield as southern Spain (so-called Mozarabic style) and Lombardy in northern Italy, home of many specialized masons. ...■

Serrabone This is the most exciting church in the region, due to the contrast between the dour gray exterior of the 11th- to 12th-century priory church, which stands alone in sub-mountainous wilderness, and the wealth of delicate carving (lions, eagles, griffins, floral patterns) on roseate marble inside.

St-Michel-de-Cuxa The 10th- to 11th-century buildings of the powerful abbey are red-tiled, and there is a handsome four-story crenellated tower. The 11th-century crypt has a remarkable central pillar like a palm tree. The cloister was exported to The Cloisters museum in New York, but has been partly reconstructed. Look out for the delightful capitals. There is a long-winded guided tour and concerts in July–August.

Corneilla de Conflent Sainte-Marie here has good carved doorway and windows and 12th-century (wooden) and 14th-century (marble) Virgins inside.

St-Martin-du-Canigou This spectacularly sited rock-top monastery above Vernet has superimposed 10th- and 11th-century churches and a cloister of impressive rough simplicity. Much of St-Martin is obviously restored, but the spirit is authentic. It is best reached on foot (half an hour maximum) from Casteil above Vernet. There are guided tours.

Eus A small Romanesque chapel (St-Vincent) sits at the bottom of an old village up a sunny slope. Good view of the Canigou. North of Prades by D35.

St-Martin-de-Fenollar This small chapel, with wonderful 12th-century frescoes of Christ in Majesty, Evangelists, Magi, and so on, is signed from the N9, 6 km north of Le Perthus. It is open afternoons only.

St-Génis-des-Fontaines Stylized carvings of Christ and apostles stand over the doorway (dated 1020) of this church on the D618 between Le Boulou and Argelès.

Above: St Michel-de-Cuxa; below: detail at Serrabone priory church

PROVENCE

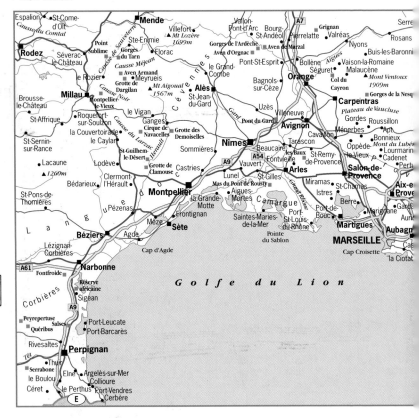

Espalion • • St-Côme-d'Olt
Causse du Comtal
Mende
Rodez
Séverac-le-Château
le Rozier
Millau
Brousse-le-Château
St-Affrique
St-Sernin-sur-Rance
Lacaune ▲1260m
St-Pons-Thomières
Béziers
Lézignan-Corbières
Narbonne
Fontfroide
Corbières
Peyrepertuse Salses
Quéribus
Rivesaltes
Perpignan
Thuir
Serrabone
le Boulou
Céret
le Perthus

Villefort
Ste-Enimie
Causse de Sauveterre
Point Sublime
Gorges du Tarn
Florac
Causse Méjean
Aven Armand
Meyrueis
Grotte de Dargilan
Causse Noir
Montpellier-le-Vieux
le Vigan
le Vigan
Causse du Larzac
Ganges
Cirque de Navacelles
Roquefort-sur-Soulzon
la Couvertoirade
le Caylar
St-Guilhem-le-Désert
Grotte de Clamouse
Lodève
Clermont-l'Hérault
Bédarieux
Pézenas
Mèze
Agde
Sète
Cap d'Agde

Mt Lozère 1699m
Mt Aigoual 1567m
Cévennes
le Grand-Combe
Alès
St-Jean-du-Gard
Uzès
Sommières
Nîmes
Castries
Lunel
Montpellier
la Grande-Motte
Frontignan

Vallon-Pont-d'Arc
Gorges de l'Ardèche
Aven d'Orgnac
Pont-St-Esprit
Bagnols-sur-Cèze
Pont du Gard
Villeneuve
Avignon
Beaucaire
Tarascon
les Baux
Fontvieille
Vauvert
St-Gilles
Arles
Mas du Pont de Rousty
Aigues-Mortes
Camargue
Saintes-Maries-de-la-Mer
Pointe du Sablon
Port-St-Louis-du-Rhône

Bourg-St-Andéol
Pierrelatte
Bollène
Séguret
Orange
Col du Cayron
Carpentras
Plateau de Vaucluse
Gordes
Roussillon
Ménerbes
Bonnieux
Mont du Lubéron
Lourmarin
Cadenet
St-Remy-de-Provence
Salon-de-Provence
Miramas
Istres
Pont-de-Bouc
Berre
Marignane
Martigues
Marseille
Cap Croisette

Grignan
Valréas
Nyons
Buis-les-Baronnies
Vaison-la-Romaine
Malaucène
Mont Ventoux 1909m
Gorges de la Nesq
Oppède-le-Vieux
Apt
Aix-en-Provence
Aubagne
la Ciotat

Golfe du Lion

68

Cap d'Antibes *by Claude Monet*

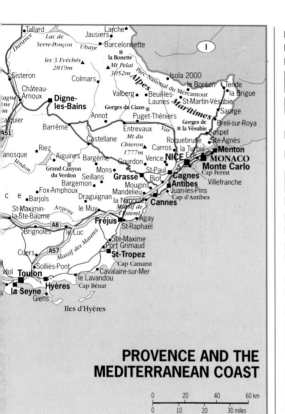

PROVENCE AND THE MEDITERRANEAN COAST

0   20   40   60 km
0   10   20   30 miles

The French call it le Midi, where the sun is high in the sky and hot. The winter sun is warm enough for lemons at Menton, and launched the south of France as a winter playground. Now tourists prefer the white heat of the summer. It is a harsh climate, prone to the howling mistral (north wind) that fans devastating fires every summer. Only the Riviera is sheltered from its forces.

It is an area of enormous diversity of life, landscape and history. The Mediterranean coast has the spectacular mountains, fashionable urban resorts (with urban traffic problems) of the Riviera, and the long tracts of featureless sands of the Languedoc coast.

The French make for the sea en masse in July and August. The marshlands of the Camargue and the high mountain country of the Maritime Alps have their own wilderness appeal. Between the two lies the hill country of rural Provence, an ideal retreat: bright colors and lavender-scented air, and scores of old villages that are ideal for sitting in the shade of a plane tree sipping *pastis* (aniseed liqueur) and watching a game of boules. The sightseeing glories of the south are Roman—great amphitheaters and triumphal arches to rival the best in Italy. There are medieval treasures, too—the papal city of Avignon—and a wealth of artistic associations: scenery made famous by Van Gogh and Cézanne, and great modern art museums. Artists follow money and the sun. In the south, there is plenty of both.

The Camargue

■ **The shifting marshy area, half land and half sea, of the Rhône delta is desolate but uniquely appealing. It is a wilderness full of potent, exotic images—wild horses; costumed cowboys (*les gardians*); migrant flamingos and flamenco festivals. ...■**

Here land and sea have an unstable relationship. A fragile ecosystem exists, where wildlife and society are threatened by irrigation, agriculture and (of course) tourism. The Camargue is an ornithologist's pilgrimage, with over 100 migrating species, including flamingos. The best chance of seeing them is in the spring at **Etang de Fangassier** in the southeast. There is a good information center at **la Capelière**, on the eastern side of the main lagoon (Vaccarès), with guided tours on request.

Several traditional Camargue ranches (*manades*) are open to visitors and run riding excursions. **Méjanes**, on the Etang de Vaccarès, has a highly commercialized example.

Towns and ports The main resort is **Les Saintes-Maries**, where the ~~Holy~~ Maries (Salomé and Jacobe) landed on the beach with a black servant girl, Sarah, the patroness of gypsies. On May 24 and 25 each year, gypsies flock from all over Europe for the pilgrimage, which is followed by a Camargue festival of dancing,

costume displays, bullfights and rodeos. Les Saintes-Maries is a rather seedy resort, but worth visiting for its church, a windowless fortress full of ex-votos. There is also a good sandy beach.

At the western edge of the Camargue lies **Aigues-Mortes**, purpose-built by Louis IX in the 13th century as a fortified port on wasteland bought from a monastery. The grid of old streets is encircled by ramparts, which you can climb and tour for views over the Camargue and empty marshes.

Two modern resorts nearby are **Port Camargue** and **Le Grau du Roi**.

Other points of interest
Mas du Pont de Rousty: an open-air museum beside the main Les Saintes Maries to Arles road. A 3-km walk through specimen Camargue-scapes.
Pont de Gau: a big bird sanctuary near Les Saintes-Maries.
St-Gilles: a small pilgrimage town on the northern edge of the Camargue, with an old church; the facade is decorated with beautiful but damaged sculptures dating from the 12th century.

▶▷▷ Aix-en-Provence

Chic and cultured, Aix is one of Europe's loveliest small cities, still seemingly inhabited by the spirit of Provence's last great ruler, *le bon roi* René d'Anjou (1409–80), who made Aix his base and a center for all the arts. Once a spa (Aix is from *Aquae*), it is still a fountain-rich city of classical town houses. The only nightmare is parking. Café life and traffic jams center on Aix's main boulevard, the cours Mirabeau, shaded by a magnificent canopy of plane trees and flanked by some of the best facades.

Old town To the north lies the old town, a maze of narrow cobbled streets, with a lot of restoration of old buildings under way. This is the most interesting part of town to explore, and there is an excellent market on Tuesday, Thursday and Saturday.

St-Sauveur cathedral has elements from all periods, from Merovingian (the baptistery) to Renaissance, and a delightful Romanesque cloister. The great treasures are the triptych *The Burning Bush*, painted by Nicolas Froment for King René, and the carved prophets and sibyls on the main doors. Both are kept shut, but a key holder is usually on hand.

Near the cathedral on the rue Saporta are two good museums. The former archbishop's palace has an excellent collection of 17th- and 18th-century Beauvais tapestries. The Museum of Old Aix's folklore collection includes *santons* (Christmas crib figurines, a Provençal specialty).

On the south side of the cours Mirabeau in the quieter Mazarin quarter, the Musée Granet has an outstanding collection of works by Ingres, Rubens, Bernini and Giovanni Bologna. A room is devoted to Cézanne, who was born at Aix in 1839 and died there in 1906. The nearby 17th-century Fontaine des Quatres Dauphins (rue Cardinale) is one of the most delightful of Aix's many fountains. (See also pages 174–175.)

▶▷▷ Antibes

This lively old port at the heart of a big modern town has narrow back streets, pretty squares and a good market. Overlooking massive 17th-century fortifications, the Grimaldi castle now houses a Picasso museum (see pages 174–175). The former cathedral dates from the 12th to 17th centuries and has a good Renaissance altarpiece (the local Brea school) in the south transept.

Detail of a fountain in Aix-en-Provence

The flower market in Aix-en-Provence

PROVENCE

In 1854 Frédéric Mistral and six fellow poets writing in the Provençal language of the medieval troubadours formed a group, *les Félibres*, dedicated to reviving the language. Mistral wrote two epic love poems, *Mireio* and the *Song of the Rhône*, spent 20 years producing a Provençal dictionary and founded the Provençal museum in Arles. In 1904 he won the Nobel Prize for literature.

Van Gogh dreamed of establishing an artists' colony in Arles, with Gauguin as its "abbot." The two shared Van Gogh's "yellow house," decorated with sunflower paintings, but after a quarrel and the severed-ear incident, Gauguin left. Van Gogh entered an asylum in 1889. His house, later a café, was bombed in 1944.

▶▶▶ Arles

Spiritually, if not officially, Arles is the capital of Provence. The Gallic Rome was a city of 100,000, a busy inland port linked to the sea by canal. Now it is half that size, but still an important town. It is one of the great tourist centers of the south, with spectacular Roman and medieval buildings, a beautiful old town center, good museums, cultural events, costume festivals and bullfights. Arles is also a good base for exploring, unless you want a rural retreat.

The heart of town is not the soulless place de la République, with its obelisk from Arles's Roman circus, but the leafy place du Forum, which has a statue of the poet Mistral, café tables under the plane trees, live music in the evenings and the simple delights of Mon Bar Tabac, where posters of Olympic Marseille soccer players and Camargue bullfighters vie for wall space. Most of the sights are covered by a global entrance ticket.

Amphitheater and theater See pages 188–189.

St-Trophime The 12th-century reliefs of the Last Judgment on the facade are a masterpiece of Romanesque carving. St-Trophime boasts one of France's most beautiful cloisters, a mixture of Romanesque and Gothic.

Museums The most unusual is the dusty old Muséon Arlaten (Arles Museum), the grandfather of folklore museums and still one of the best. Features include attendants in local costume, a 16th-century statue of the brotherhood of Camargue *gardians* (cowherds), a bullskin rug with horns and re-created interiors. Separate museums display pagan and early Christian antiquities.

Les Alyscamps One of the most famous burial grounds in medieval Christendom is now rather a letdown. Most of the tombs lining the shaded avenue, once a thought-provoking approach to Arles, have gone (some to the Christian art museum).

Espace Van Gogh An initiative has transformed the old Hôtel Dieu into a commercial and cultural center, painted in Van Gogh's favorite primary colors, with flower beds to match.

Pont de Langlois An old wooden bridge painted by Van Gogh survives, unobtrusively signed near the Sémence de Provence factory on the Salon road.

▶▶▶ Avignon

A historical heavyweight city beside the Rhône, its old center still enclosed by 4 km of medieval walls, Avignon is an essential stop on the Provençal sightseeing trail. It is often windswept and can seem a rather joyless place, but comes alive during the annual drama and dance festival (mid-July to mid-August).

Avignon owes its fame to the 12th-century bridge of the popular song, long reduced to four spans jutting out into midstream, and the 14th-century Babylonian

The Papal Palace at Avignon

In the 14th century Avignon was a Provençal city surrounded by papal land. Fed up with the insecurity of life in Rome, Pope Clement V brought the papal court to Avignon in 1309. Six French popes succeeded him, buying Avignon from the countess of Provence in 1348 and building the magnificent Papal Palace. In 1377 Gregory IX took the curia back to Rome but in 1378 a group of cardinals returned to Avignon with a French rival to the new Italian pope. Thus began the Great Schism, which lasted until 1417.

Away from the monumental center, the most picturesque part of Avignon is the old gypsy quarter, where the cobbled rue des Teinturiers was the home of the 19th-century calico cloth dyers. The focus of café life is the place de l'Horloge. The main north–south axis of the walled town, the rue de la République, has the best shopping.

Captivity, as the scandalous papal residence at Avignon was known. The popes gave Avignon its walls and the magnificent Papal Palace.

Town and gown Outside the rule of French law, the city was a haven for outlaws and assorted disreputables (as well as having a big ghetto), so the "town and gown" contrast of low life and the curia's ostentatious opulence was real enough.

The palace has a rock-solid facade, which defied all attempts to dismantle it after the Revolution. Its interior, though, was turned into a barracks. The rooms are unfurnished except for beautiful 14th-century frescoes, many inspired by *mille fleurs* tapestries.

There are good views from the nearby Rocher des Doms gardens and two excellent museums: the Petit Palais, an old papal guest house with an outstanding collection of Gothic and Renaissance art; and the Musée Calvet, in a fine 18th-century town house, with good 18th- to 20th-century art, furniture and wrought ironwork (closed for repairs until 1995).

Villeneuve-lès-Avignon On the opposite bank of the river, Villeneuve-lès-Avignon was an exclusive residential suburb much favored by cardinals. French kings built impressive fortifications (Philippe le Bel's tower at the end of the bridge and the Fort St-André, both commanding splendid views of Avignon) to remind the popes of French power. The handsome 19th-century buildings of Villeneuve's Carthusian monastery are now a cultural center (open to the public).

Modern Art

■ **Toward the end of the 19th century, artists made their way to southern France, attracted by its special light and color. Avant-garde artists followed Van Gogh's and Cézanne's example by coming south to paint, and society artists followed society to Nice and Monte Carlo when the Riviera hit the social jackpot in the last quarter of the century. ...■**

Rosary Chapel, Vence, designed by Matisse

In the first category, Signac discovered the old fishing port of St-Tropez in 1892; artists who followed him there included Bonnard and Matisse. In 1905, Matisse and André Dérain worked together at Collioure. "The light here is very strong," wrote Dérain, "the shadows very luminous. I am learning to rid myself of the whole business of the division of tones."

This approach earned Dérain, Matisse, Dufy and others working on the coast the name *fauves*—the wild beasts of color. One of many to fall under the influence of Cézanne was Georges Braque, whose landscapes at L'Estaque, in the first decade of the 20th century, first elicited the term "cubist." Matisse and Dufy settled in Nice and recorded all the brilliance and joie de vivre of the Riviera. Picasso settled in the south of France in 1946, revived the flagging ceramic industry at Vallauris, and lived there, at Cannes, at Vauvenargues beneath the Mont Ste-Victoire and finally at Mougins until his death in 1973. As well as providing inspiration for many great modern artists, the south is a rich store of their works in private and public collections. Ironically, the two founders of the new art, Van Gogh and Cézanne, so closely associated with the south, are not represented there.

Aix-en-Provence Cézanne's studio is open to the public, but it is a sadly inadequate memorial. To admire the Mont Ste-Victoire, Cézanne's favorite subject, take the Le Tholonet road east from Aix. A collection by op art master Viktor Vasarély is at the Vasarély Foundation to the west of town.

Antibes One floor of the Grimaldi château is filled with paintings, drawings, sculptures and ceramics by Picasso, most of it the output of a single year (1947).

Biot An interest in ceramics brought Fernand Léger to Biot shortly before he died in 1955. The museum of his work is one of the best modern museums in the south.

Cagnes Renoir painted on despite arthritis so severe he was unable to wield the brush unaided. His home and studios at Les Collettes are open to visitors. The château also displays collections of work by artists who worked and lived locally, including Dufy and Vasarély.

Fréjus The Chapelle de Jérusalem (4 km from Fréjus on

Nice is an art-loving center: its contemporary art museum is the latest addition

the N7) contains unfinished interior decoration by Jean Cocteau.

Menton Jean Cocteau designed a museum to himself in a section of the old harbor fortifications and also decorated the Salle des Mariages in the town hall with cheerful murals.

Nice Cimiez has outstanding museums devoted to Matisse (in the Roman arena) and Chagall (near the bottom of the Avenue de Cimiez). In the city center, there are temporary modern art exhibitions in Les Ponchettes, at the eastern end of the beach, and a contemporary art museum near the theater and acropolis conference/exhibition center. There is some Warhol, a squashed Renault, a portrait of a man via the contents of his wastepaper basket, and striking blue dye on bronze portraits by Yves Klein, who also created an exotic *Garden of Eden* on the roof.

St-Paul-de-Vence There are dozens of art galleries within the walls and, without, the exceptionally rich and architecturally intriguing Maeght Foundation modern art museum.

St-Tropez L'Annonciade museum has a small but select private collection of Postimpressionist paintings, many of St-Tropez, in a former chapel. Signac, Bonnard, Matisse and lots of local scenes by Camoin, who worked at St-Tropez for over 60 years.

Vence The Rosary Chapel, looking like a Provençal *mas* (farmhouse) from outside, was designed and decorated by Matisse between 1947 and 1951.

Villefranche A 14th-century chapel (St-Pierre) beside the port once stored fishing nets. In 1957 Cocteau decorated it with scenes from the life of St. Peter.

"The future of the new art lies in the South. The painter of the future will be a colorist such as never existed ." – Van Gogh, 1888

"Sunlight cannot be reproduced, but must be represented by something else – by color." – Paul Cézanne, native of Aix, 1876

PROVENCE

Troubadours were court poets in Occitan-speaking southern France during the 12th century. Some were noblemen, including William IX of Aquitaine, who wrote freely about his prowess in the lists of love. Most troubadours were more discreet, scarcely mentioning the object of devotion. As the French kings extended their control over the southwest, the poets retreated to Provence, where the fashion died out at the end of the 13th century.

A relaxing game of boules at Bandol

▶▷▷ **Bandol**

A lively weekend resort between Toulon and Marseille, with marina, sandy beaches and the best of Provençal red wines. It is a few minutes by boat to the small island of Bendor, a purpose-built leisure center with crafts village, sailing and diving schools and a museum of alcohol.

▶▷▷ **Les Baux**

"The Petra of France" (Augustus Hare) is a ruined citadel in a savagely romantic setting on a spur of the jagged Alpilles chain, almost invisible from below. Home of a notoriously rapacious medieval dynasty that included the star of Bethlehem in its coat of arms, Les Baux later became a Protestant refuge. Richelieu demolished the fortress and, having supported a population of 6,000 during the Renaissance, Les Baux was all but deserted by the 19th century. Les Baux now teems with visitors. To stand any chance of appreciating the ghostly beauty of the place, visit at sundown.

▶▷▷ **Béziers**

A wine center at the foot of the Minervois hills, Béziers stands for rugby, Spanish bullfights and the most savage atrocity of the Albigensian Crusade: on July 22, 1209, Simon de Montfort's crusaders massacred 30,000 inhabitants, not bothering to distinguish Catholic from Cathar. "Kill them all," said the abbot of Cîteaux, "for God will recognize his own." The main points of interest are the former cathedral, prominently placed high above the River Orb, and the two museums nearby: the Musée du Vieux Bitérrois et du Vin (local history, archaeology and wine) and the Musée des Beaux Arts (paintings).

▶▷▷ **Biot**

A picturesque and usually overcrowded old village in the scented hinterland of the Riviera, long famous for its ceramics industry and more recently for its glass and the Fernand Léger museum (see page 174). You can visit the main glassworks (Verrerie) and watch the blowing process. There are potteries and galleries in the heart of the village, which has kept its 16th-century gates and arcaded square.

176

Perched Villages

■ **Provence is hill country, and on almost every hilltop there perches a village, a rhapsody of crumbling honey-colored walls and pink tile roofs, and steep cobbled alleys too narrow for cars. A shady little square with a café and a fountain at the heart of the village, long views over vineyards, lavender fields, olive groves or the sea. Paradise on earth. ...■**

Hill villages evolved for defense in the lawless centuries that followed Roman peace. Since the 18th century many of the hill villages have gradually been abandoned by their inhabitants. Most have been revived by tourism and new residents seeking a peaceful alternative to the coast. The most picturesque have now evolved from artists' colonies to popular scenic spots. The most spectacularly sited villages overlook the sea high above the Riviera—**Eze, Gorbio, Ste-Agnès, La Turbie** and **Roquebrune**, with its 10th-century castle. Even **Monaco** counts as a perched village, naturally pretty but about the most tawdry of them all. Other picturesque spots near the coast, all often overcrowded, are **Biot** (famous for its pottery and glass), **Tourrette-sur-Loup** (a weaving center, **Gourdon** (a tourist trap) and **St-Paul-de-Vence**, the most famous of all the artists' villages. For all its fame, St-Paul remains a place of style and irresistible charm, with a plane-shaded boules pitch outside the Café de la Place at the gates of the old walled village. Opposite the café, the prestigious Colombe d'Or hotel is full of masterpieces of modern art, accepted in lieu of payment by the enlightened proprietor, M. Roux. Deeper into the mountainous hinterland of Nice, **Peillon** and **Luceram** are worth visiting for their church paintings. Strung across a precipice high above the Roya gorge, **Saorge**'s setting is the most startling of all. It is easier to reach by car than looks likely from below, and fascinating to explore on foot.

Farther west, the landscape of the interior is less wild, the hill villages more welcoming. **Bargème, Mons, Bargemon, Seillans** and **Fox Amphoux** all have great charm. In the fashionable Lubéron/Vaucluse area, **Gordes** and the red ocher village of **Roussillon** are the touristy scenic spots. Quieter villages include **Oppède le Vieux**, where the imposing Renaissance houses are now being rescued; and **Ménerbes**, recently invaded by Britons. **Le Barroux, Crestet** and **Séguret** are beautifully restored villages on the flanks of the jagged Dentelles de Montmirail.

Eze, one of the most dramatic of the Provence hill villages

PROVENCE

Baroness Ephrussi de Rothschild's collection is housed in the Ile de France Museum, Cap Ferrat

The coastal landscape between Marseille and Cassis is unexpectedly wild and beautiful: cliffs and inlets (*calanques*) of bleached gray rock, clear water and pocket handkerchief beaches, accessible only on foot (an arduous marked GR path follows the coast) or by boat. Surmiou and Sugiton calanques can be reached on foot from Marseille (start near the university). The three eastern calanques are served by boat trips from Cassis: Port-Miou (accessible by car); Port-Pin; and En-Vau, the prettiest of all.

▶▶▷ Cannes

Famed for its international film festival in May, Cannes is the year-round glamorous focus of the Riviera, with spectacular yachts and expensive beaches along the palm-lined promenade, La Croisette (see pages 182–183).

▶▷▷ Cap Ferrat

A beautiful walk makes a full circuit of this narrow rocky cape filled with luxurious villas. Set in a villa among superb gardens, the **Ile de France museum** has Baroness Ephrussi de Rothschild's rich art collection. The small resort and marina of **St-Jean-Cap-Ferrat** is in keeping with the cape's style of muted opulence.

▷▷▷ Carpentras

This is a busy medieval market town at the heart of the most fruitful area of Provence, famous for its truffles and sweets (*berlingots*). Sights include a 15th- and 16th-century cathedral, a small Roman triumphal arch, and the beautiful Hôtel Dieu.

▶▷▷ Cassis

A charming fishing port beneath the 1,312-foot cliffs of Cap Canaille. The waterfront cafés, fish restaurants and small hotels are a Mediterranean idyll. Boats travel to the rocky inlets, good for scuba diving and rock climbing.

▷▷▷ Esterel Massif

The 32-km coast road between La Napoule and St-Raphael offers the most spectacular scenery in the south. Flame-red porphyry mountains drop to the rocky shores, and rough and narrow forest roads lead into the mountains. A track branching south 3 km west of the **Auberge des Adrets**, a notorious brigand's hangout in the late 18th century, takes you within walking range of the Esterel's highest peak, the **Mont Vinaigre** (2,027 feet). The **Pic de l'Ours**, near the coast (1,627 feet), is also dramatic. Few swimming spots, but there is red sand at Agay, a small resort on a sheltered horseshoe bay.

▶▷▷ Fréjus

Fréjus was the first big Gallo-Roman port, with ruined aqueduct, theater and amphitheater (see page 188). An outstanding complex of cathedral buildings clusters round its town center: cloisters, a 5th-century baptistery, an archaeological museum, and the Gothic cathedral itself. The modern resort of Fréjus Plage has a big marina and good sandy beach.

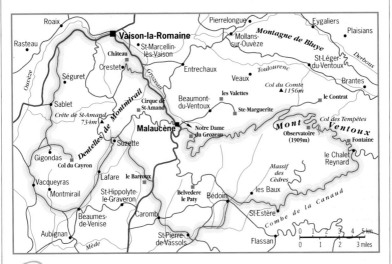

Drive The Dentelles de Montmirail and Mont Ventoux

Start at Malaucène.
Malaucène is a lively market town at the foot of **Mont Ventoux**, France's highest mountain outside the Alps and Pyrenees. Its bare scree slopes make the Ventoux look snowcapped all year; in winter it is, and there is skiing on both flanks.

D974 via Mont Ventoux.
The road loops round the summit (crowned by ugly towers and a café), giving enormous views. On the eastern side is a memorial where cyclist Tommy Simpson died during the 1967 Tour de France.

From Mont Ventoux continue to Bédoin.
The road down to Bédoin through thick woodland was long used for time trials and still has the skid marks to prove it. **Bédoin** is an attractive village with a nudist holiday zone nearby.

D138 as far as Caromb and Le Barroux.
Caromb and **Le Barroux**, dominated by an ill-proportioned Renaissance château, both have excellent small hotels.

Continue north to Suzette.

The slopes above Le Barroux lead to the dramatic jagged crest of the **Dentelles de Montmirail**. There are good views of the crags from **Suzette**.

D90 to Beaumes-de-Venise.
The tour now takes in some Rhône wine villages: **Beaumes-de-Venise**, **Vacqueyras** and **Gigondas**. The Dentelles de Montmirail are signed from Gigondas. The road surface soon turns rough, climbing through vineyards to a pass at the foot of the central spine of the Dentelles, the Col du Cayron. From here it is a steep 15-minute walk up an obvious path to a breach in the rocks, giving spectacular views. There are many possibilities for extending the walk: paths along the eastern flank of the rocky crest, or through the vineyards from the Col du Cayron, a long hike to Séguret (see below).

D23 to Séguret; then the D88 and 977 to Vaison, taking the D938 back to Malaucène.
The circuit continues to **Vaison-la-Romaine** via the restored village of **Séguret**. On the other side of the hill, **Crestet** has a medieval castle, an arcaded square and fountain, and a fine view.

Easily reached by boat from Hyères and Giens, the islands of Porquerolles, Port Cros and Levant offer forest walks, good beaches and no cars. The largest, Porquerolles, has a small village resort. Mountainous and luxuriant, Port Cros and surrounding waters are a national park. Its two hotels are booked months in advance. The Ile du Levant has nudists in the west, and a small resort (Héliopolis). The eastern half is a naval base.

▶ ▷ ▷ Fontfroide

This Cistercian abbey, set among the Corbières vineyards near Narbonne, was abandoned at the Revolution and was privately owned for most of this century. The buildings, a mixture of Romanesque and ancien régime styles, have been well restored and complemented by delightful gardens.

▷ ▷ ▷ Fontvieille

This unremarkable village is known for a pretty windmill on a wooded hillside to the south—the *moulin* of Alphonse Daudet's *Lettres de Mon Moulin*, although the author neither owned nor wrote from it. The mill has been restored to working order and houses a museum of Daudet memorabilia.

▷ ▷ ▷ Giens Peninsula

Two 5-km spits of sand enclose working salt pans and link the village of Giens to the motherland near Hyères. There are pine woods and some modest resort development (Hyères Plage) along the eastern sandbar. The biggish town of Hyères, once a health resort of some cachet, no longer attracts many tourists, although the old upper town around the place St-Paul has some charm and fine public gardens.

▶ ▷ ▷ Grasse

The world capital of the perfume industry is an old town in a sheltered, south-facing setting. Queen Victoria wintered here, but modern Grasse has no trace of Riviera glamour. The old town center has a tumbledown charm, though, with a narrow arcaded marketplace, the place aux Aires. Stalls surrounding the fountain are filled with local fruit, flowers and herbs.

The massive 12th-century cathedral boasts three Rubens and a rare religious work by Grasse's most famous son, Jean Honoré Fragonard (1732–1806). Fragonard left Grasse at six and returned only briefly in 1790, bringing with him a series of paintings, *The Pursuit of Love*, rejected as too frivolous by their intended owner. Copies of the originals are on display in the villa where he stayed, with one good self-portrait and a number of works by his son Alexander.

Several scent producers (including Fragonard) offer free factory tours. The International Perfume Museum charges for entrance and is less visited.

Grasse took to perfumery when scented gloves came into fashion in the 16th century. It takes 500 kilos of roses to produce a liter of essential oil; many local plants are still used and a few, like the pink sentifolio rose, are unique to the Var. Manufacturers still employ a specialist sniffer (*le nez*) to choose the fragrances.

▶ ▷ ▷ Lubéron

The 65-km mountain ridge between the Rivers Durance and Coulon is divided into Petit and Grand Lubéron by the only road over the ridge, between Bonnieux and Lourmarin. The Lubéron is wild country, protected by regional park status but developing nevertheless. Now ultra-fashionable, the quiet villages on the wooded north slope have become the latest corner of Provence to experience the questionable benefit of a second-home renaissance, spurred on by the phenomenal success of Peter Mayle's book. Ménerbes, Bonnieux, and the marquis de Sade's Lacoste are examples of reviving villages. Oppède-le-Vieux, a place of romantic ruins, is in the early stages of rescue from abandonment.

Drive The Vaucluse plateau

Start at Vénasque; take the D4 to Murs.

Vénasque is a fortified village on a ledge of the Vaucluse plateau. It was a bishopric in the early Middle Ages and gave its name to the papal territory, Comtat Venaissin. Beside the church is an intriguing ancient chapel. The road climbs through oak woods to the **Col de Murs** before descending into the fashionable second-home territory of the Vaucluse/Lubéron.

D102 to Roussillon.

The red village of Roussillon is a tourist trap, but not to be avoided for that. The vivid color of the buildings and the earth of the surrounding hills is astonishing.

D2 to Gordes; D177 to Sénanque and back.

Gordes is another busy scenic spot, carefully restored and expensive, at the heart of *borie* (stone dwellings) country. An imposing Renaissance château (now housing a Vasarély museum) and turreted church command the plain and the steeply terraced village. A narrow road winds to the Cistercian abbey of Sénanque, set among fields of lavender.

D2/N100/D24 to Fontaine de Vaucluse.

Fontaine de Vaucluse was made famous by its romantic associations with Petrarch's love poetry. The site and nearby village are now thoroughly commercialized.

Walk The Fort de Buoux

This complex of ruined medieval fortifications is on the site of a much older citadel, south of the hamlet of Buoux (turn off the D113 at a *colonie de vacances*, holiday camp); later used as a Protestant refuge, it was dismantled in the 17th century. Walking possibilities include a two-hour tour. For a longer haul, follow marked paths across the Lubéron to Lourmarin or Vaugines; or along the crest of the Grand Lubéron to the Mourre Nègre (3,690 feet), and down to Auribeau (north side) or Cabrières (south).

■ ***Menton's dowdy, Monte's brass,
Nice is rowdy, Cannes is class.***

The French Riviera has changed profoundly in the past few decades, primarily in becoming a summer instead of a winter playground. But the words of the old song still say plenty about the differences of style between the resorts that form an almost unbroken urban sprawl along the mountainous coastline between Cannes and the Italian border. This is the Riviera proper, although the term Côte d'Azur is often used to include the less densely developed coast between Cannes and Marseille. ...■

182

Cannes This is the Riviera at its most showy: the promenade of La Croisette, lined with palm trees and palatial hotels, is a perfect catwalk. Unlike many Riviera resorts, Cannes has a good sandy beach, parceled up into expensive private concessions, many of them attached to hotels and with classy lunch restaurants. There is a public beach at the west end of the Croisette, near the gleaming conference center separating the promenade from the port, which is full of expensive yachts. It is also naturally picturesque, overlooked by the trees and medieval towers of **Le Suquet**, a small hill where some traces of an old village survive. The Croisette, the rue d'Antibes and side streets between them have the best shops. Boat trips go from the port to the Lérins islands, Ste-Marguerite and St-Honorat, both with dense woods. St-Honorat is owned and occupied by a monastery; Ste-Marguerite has old prison buildings.

Juan-les-Pins A favorite with the Americans in the '20s – Frank Gould, Coco Chanel, Harpo Marx, Mary Pickford and many others – Juan-les-Pins is less smart now, a young place with fast food and discos. A monument at neighboring **Golf Juan** commemorates Napoleon's landing after his escape from Elba in 1815.

Antibes See page 171.

Nice The capital of the Alpes Maritimes and the Riviera is, if not rowdy, a big city. The Promenade des Anglais is now a roaring dual carriageway but has kept many of the domes and facades of its Belle Epoque buildings (notably the Hotel Negresco).

An Italian city (Nizza) until 1860, and the hometown of Garibaldi, Nice has kept more than a hint of Italian style in the gardens and arcaded neoclassical buildings around the place Masséna and the port, and especially in the narrow back streets behind the quai des Etats Unis and the broad plaza of cours Saleya. This is Nice's open market and the best place for cafés and restaurants.

Larger-than-life musicians at the Nice Mardi Gras

This old quarter is separated from the port by the so-called château—a hill with gardens and views.

Many of Nice's Victorian visitors (including the queen) stayed at Cimiez, a hill suburb and site of the Roman settlement, with good museums and ruins (see pages 174–175 and 188). The other museums are in the strikingly modern complex north of the place Garibaldi (see page 188) and, for old masters, the Masséna and fine arts museums. Nice goes mad for its two-week pre-Lent carnival, ending with fireworks and a battle of flowers.

Cap Ferrat See page 178.

Villefranche The most sheltered bay on the Riviera; an unspoiled fortified village above the fishing port (see also page 175).

Monaco/Monte Carlo Every inch of the Grimaldi family's tiny principality is occupied, and Monaco continues to grow upward (skyscrapers) and outward, on new man-made promontories. The old clifftop village of Monaco is now a toy-town pink and yellow tourist village with white-suited police officers, waxworks museums, the Grimaldis' marzipan palace (a Napoleon museum and some of the interior are open to visitors), a gruesome 19th-century cathedral with some good Renaissance paintings and an oceanographic museum. Traffic is strictly controlled: signs to Monaco lead into underground parking lots, with elevators to the center.

Monte Carlo is the heartland of Monaco: plush jewelers, luxury hotels and the exuberant casino and Hôtel de Paris. A 3-km circuit is used for the Grand Prix in May.

Menton Mild winters and lemons brought fame to Menton (it has a lemon festival in February). A Baroque belfry and high, pastel-painted houses overlook the beach. Summer concerts are held on the small piazza outside the church of St-Michel (see page 175).

Above: Menton

Three corniche roads hug the mountainous coastline from Nice to Menton. The lower (N98) runs through all the resorts: a 33-km journey of many hours in summer. The middle corniche (N7) is much quicker and passes the perched village of Eze; the upper or Grande Corniche (D2564) goes through La Turbie and over the Col d'Eze. Both upper and middle corniches by-pass Monaco. Above this there is now a fourth corniche, the A8 motorway. With its fast drivers, sharp bends, tunnels and multiple exits, the motorway demands full concentration.

▶ ▷ ▷ Marseille

The Mediterranean's biggest port and France's second city is an acquired taste—notorious for corruption and gangsterism, and a sure break from the tourist trail. The Greeks founded the city in the 6th century BC, but it is the modern life of the city that intrigues and repels in equal measure.

The city, which suffered extensive bomb damage, is a melting pot of Arab, African and Latin cultures, with France's biggest community of Algerians. Racial tension simmers—National Front leader Jean Marie le Pen has his roots here.

The once-celebrated Canebière is not what it was, but is still the main shopping street. There is an Arab market, a spectacular morning fish market at the old port (a good area for restaurants), cheap souks near the Porte d'Aix, and a splendid Sunday market at Gardanne (a suburb).

Marseille's most famous monument is a former prison—the rocky island of Château d'If (boat trips from the old port). There are some good museums: archaeology (strong on Egypt), fine arts, local history (near the old port in a beautiful Renaissance house), fashion and natural history. The best of the smaller museums are the Cantini (faience) and Grobet Labadié (near the art museum—a 19th-century collector's preserved house and contents). A hilltop cathedral dominates the port and city.

Local produce from the Massif des Maures

▷ ▷ ▷ Maures, Massif des

A hinterland of thickly wooded hill country between Fréjus and Hyères, named after its dark mantle of pines, chestnuts and cork oaks, whose trunks are still stripped of bark for commercial use. To the west of the resorts on the bay of St-Tropez (see page 190) are peaceful beaches with campsites.

Le Lavandou/Bormes is the main resort agglomeration, with a big marina. La Croix Valmer and Cavalaire are smaller centers. The interior is little visited, mainly because the roads over the hills are narrow and very slow (except the D25 from Ste-Maxime to Draguignan). The D558 Grimaud/La Garde crossing is more rewarding. There are ferries and boat trips in the Hyères islands (see page 180) from Cavalaire and Le Lavandou.

▶ ▷ ▷   Montpellier

A dynamic city of high-tech industry, bold new architecture and buzzing student life, Montpellier has cast off its traditional mantle of donnish stuffiness. One of the few big southern cities without a Roman history, Montpellier grew in medieval times because of trade with the eastern Mediterranean.

The 17th- and 18th-century promenade du Peyrou is an impressive ensemble of triumphal arch, statue of Louis XIV and water tower at the head of the aqueduct that quenches the city's thirst. The view from the terrace is splendid.

People prefer to congregate around the place de la Comédie, esplanade gardens and on the place Jean Jaurès in the old town.

Antigone, the new residential area, is a typically ambitious neoclassical project. The Musée Fabre has an outstanding collection of old master and 19th-century paintings. One of the benefactors was Alfred Bruyas, a rich patron of Courbet, Delacroix and others. There is a photography festival in May and an international wine fair in October.

▷ ▷ ▷   Narbonne and the Languedoc/ Roussillon Coast

This coastline, sandy from the Petit Rhône to the Pyrenees, is often thin strips separating sea from enclosed lagoons. The resort style is modern: The pyramid apartment blocks of **La Grande Motte** are an aggressive '60s monument, while more recent resorts have adopted a less obtrusive style. **Port Camargue** is an interesting marina-based design. The biggest development of all is **Cap d'Agde**, with a 62-court tennis club and a nudist area (Port Nature). Between Montpellier and Béziers is the fishing port of **Sète**, built at the end of the Canal du Midi in the 17th century.

Southern resorts Further south, **Port Leucate** and **Port Barcarès** are big new resorts with marinas, on a sandbar between sea and salt lake. For a short stretch before the Spanish border, after the concentration of campsites at Argèles sur Mer, the coast is mountainous. **Collioure** is an artists' favorite.

Other areas of interest:

Agde Founded by Greeks when it was a seaport, Agde has a fortified black lava church.

Elne Cathedral with beautiful 12th- to 14th-century cloister.

Narbonne A wine town that once hit the news because of race riots. The twin towers of an unusual, unfinished Gothic cathedral dominate the town and surrounding vineyards. There is a good archaeological museum near the cathedral.

Salses Well-preserved 15th-century fortress, altered by Vauban.

Sigéan Safari Park African wildlife; expensive.

Pre-Renaissance Europe did not read Greek, and medical knowledge filtered in from the east via the spice trade, of which Montpellier was a center. The university specialized in medicine and attracted Petrarch and Rabelais among its students. Herbs grow throughout the south of France; in Provence they are an important industry. Buis-les-Baronnies has an international herb market at the beginning of July.

All summer the Roman amphitheaters at Nîmes and Arles and the modern arena at Béziers are the setting for the *corrida*, the traditional gory Spanish bullfight. The Camargue specializes in a more informal and sporting encounter, the Provençal *course à la cocarde*. In makeshift arenas bullfighters (*razeteurs*) try to snatch a rosette (*cocarde*) from the horns of Camargue bulls, which survive to fight again. The *razeteur* escapes by vaulting over the ringside hoardings.

The Maritime Alps

■ **Between the mouth of the Var and the Italian border, the Alps drop abruptly into the Mediterranean with no transition between mountains and coast. This cramps life by the sea and offers plenty of escape routes from the heat and crowds into the cooler, cleaner air of the mountains. ...■**

Old perched villages of the immediate hinterland (**Eze, Peillon, Peille, Gorbio, Lucéram, Coaraze**) are the obvious short-haul targets. Longer journeys involve heading up any of the four main river valleys that have their sources high up near the Italian border: the **Tinée, Var** and **Vésubie** (which end up as one, the Var); and the **Roya**, which crosses into Italy about halfway down to the sea. Connoisseurs of river gorge drives will want to tick off the **Vésubie** gorges (between Plan du Var and St-Jean-la-Rivière) and the **Cians** gorge between Pont de Cian and Beuil (tight driving). The source of the Tinée is near the **Col de la Bonette** at the northern limit of the Maritime Alps; the **Bonette** road, Europe's highest, is a rugged and beautiful route north, for travelers not in a hurry.

The **Roya** valley is of more varied interest; either follow the river up from Ventimiglia (Italy) or drive up from Menton to Sospel and over the Col de Brouis, joining the Roya near **Breil**, a small town with simple accommodations. North of Breil, the Roya cuts impressive gorges, especially below the balcony village of **Saorge**, well worth a detour to explore on foot. **La Brigue** is the best base in the upper valley, with an interesting church and remarkable 15th-century frescoes in the nearby chapel. On the other side of the valley are **Lac des Mesches** and **Casterino**, the start of hikes to the Vallée des Merveilles around Mont Bégo—100,000 rock engravings from 1800 to 1500 BC. The valley is only accessible from July to early October.

The **Mercantour** is France's youngest national park, covering a long stretch of high mountain country along the Italian border. Gateways to the park (with information centers) include the summer and winter resort of **Valberg** and **St-Martin-de-Vésubie**.

Le **Boréon** (near St-Martin) is a good starting point for hikers.

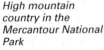

High mountain country in the Mercantour National Park

▶ ▶ ▷ Nice
See pages 174–175 and 182–183.

Swimmers in the Gardon River, near Pont du Gard

▷ ▷ ▷ Nîmes
The birthplace of denim (serge de Nîmes) is not one of the most charming towns of France, best known for extreme heat and its Roman amphitheater and temple (see page 188).

▶ ▶ ▷ Orange
Orange, gateway to the south, has a fine Roman arch that, with its still finer Roman theater, is the most compelling reason for a visit (see page 189). Orange is an important market town for the Rhône Valley's fruit and wine output. Its princely ruling family has exported the name, which has nothing to do with the fruit, all over the world.

187

▷ ▷ ▷ Perpignan
The capital of French Catalonia, redbrick Perpignan was the medieval headquarters of the kingdom of Majorca—an offshoot of the ruling house of Aragon. Their low-rise fortress covers a large area at the heart of the city. The streets around the cathedral (Gothic) and medieval town gate (Castilian) are more entertaining. Catalan is spoken here, and there is Hispanic music and even dancing in the streets on summer evenings. The most beautiful building in the town center, the Gothic Loge de Mer (a trading house), is now a burger restaurant.

▷ ▷ ▷ Pézenas
Now a small town of under 10,000 inhabitants, Pézenas once enjoyed a glorious reputation as the Versailles of the south. It flourished in the Middle Ages, thanks to special trade privileges, and later hosted the meetings of the Languedoc Estates General, which were the occasion for lavish festivities during the governorship of the Bourbon prince de Conti, an early patron of Molière in the 1650s. The old town center around the place Gambetta has kept many beautiful 17th-century houses. Outstanding among them are Hôtel Lacoste and the Hôtel d'Alfonce, where Molière's troupe performed in 1655. It is open in July and August.

In the 16th century the principality of Orange passed to the house of Nassau. The first prince of this house was William the Silent, who led the rebellion of the Netherlands against Spain, becoming the provinces' Stadtholder in 1580.

▶ ▶ ▶ Pont du Gard
A Roman aqueduct near Nîmes: one of the master-pieces of ancient Roman architecture in France (see page 189).

■ **The Romans enjoyed the south of France. They colonized it early, romanized it intensively and adorned it with temples, theaters, amphitheaters, aqueducts, monumental arches and bridges. There is no region outside Italy that is so rich in Roman remains. ...■**

188

Colonization began in 125 BC when consul Sextius responded to an appeal from the Greek port of Massilia (Marseille) and destroyed a native power base on the Entremont plateau. A new *Provincia* (Provence) was established in 118 BC. Marseille lost its privileges in 49 BC. Its commercial role was taken over by Arles, Fréjus and Narbonne, which became the capital of the renamed Provincia Narbonensis in 27 BC.

Aix-en-Provence The first Roman town in Gaul, founded as Aquae Sextiae by consul Sextius, has left little to show for itself, apart from the Musée Granet's items from the pre-Roman settlement at Entremont.

Arles Once the capital of Gaul and Constantine's favorite base, Arles has a spectacularly well-preserved amphitheater (Arènes) and theater, still in use for bullfights and real drama. The amphitheater (1st century AD) held more than 20,000 spectators, nearly half the town's present population. The structure was converted into a medieval fortress and later a town within a town, which was dismantled in the 19th century. The theater (1st century BC) seated 12,000. An obelisk from Roman Arles's racetrack stands on the main square. There is also a good museum of Roman art (Musée Païen) here.

Fréjus This Roman port has surviving fragments of theater, aqueduct and Gaul's oldest amphitheater, which now hosts bullfights and rock concerts.

Nice-Cimiez The hill town of Cemenelum was the capital of the Roman province of Maritime Alps. Between the monastery and the once-grand hotels of Victorian Cimiez is an area of excavations, including a small amphitheater, a museum and a large area of baths, thought to have been sex-segregated.

Nîmes The amphitheater (1st century AD) and temple known as the Maison Carrée (1st century BC) are the best-preserved buildings of their kind in the Roman world. The former survives as a full three-story structure and after a 1,500-year hiatus again echoes with the roars of fighting bulls and an excited public. It survived thanks to being converted into a fortress in the 5th century. The Maison Carrée has done service as town hall, private home, stable, church and now museum.

The 1st-century amphitheater at Nîmes

Orange As at Nîmes, two outstanding Roman buildings attract tourists to an otherwise uncaptivating town. Founded in 46 BC, Arausio was three times as populous as modern Orange. The Roman theater (1st century BC) is the only one with its backstage wall standing. A statue of Augustus fills a niche above the stage, still used for summer drama. The triumphal arch (1st century BC) is a traffic circle on the N7 at the northern gateway to town. In the interests of traffic flow, do not attempt to admire it from the wheel.

Pont du Gard A three-tiered section of the Uzès to Nîmes aqueduct, spanning the River Gardon, made of massive stones without mortar. You can drive across the lower tier and walk across higher up, either the unspectacular interior of the channel where the water flowed, or, vertigo and the mistral permitting, its 10-foot-wide unprotected roof, 160 feet above the water. The bridge's woodland setting is beautiful, but no longer wild.

St-Rémy-Glanum and Les Antiques Among trees to the south of St-Rémy, utterly uncluttered by fencing or graffiti, stand two beautiful Roman monuments (late 1st century BC). The triumphal arch has lost its top but not all its decoration of fruit and captives. Beside it stands a well-preserved and elegant memorial to two grandsons of Augustus. Not far away, on the other side of the road, lie the extensive excavations of Glanum, a pre-Roman town, probably a spa, which was later romanized, then abandoned in the 4th century.

La Turbie Trophée Only partial remains survive of the 160-foot Alpine Trophy, which was built in 6 BC to celebrate Augustus's successful Alpine campaigns. There is a good museum on site with reconstructions based on another trophy in Romania, and old engravings of the trophy as a medieval fortress.

Vaison-la-Romaine A Roman bridge spans the River Ouvèze and separates medieval Vaison from the dull modern town and the excavations of the affluent Roman Vasio, in two sectors separated by the place Novembre 11. Ruins include a shopping street, a villa, public toilets, a theater and a museum, all in a setting of rose beds and cypresses.

The many Alpine tribes resisted Rome longer than the rest of Gaul and were not conquered until the campaign of Augustus (24–12 BC). This success allowed the completion of the Via Aurelia from Rome to Arles and was commemorated with the 160-foot Alpine Trophy. Nîmes flourished throughout the first two centuries AD, while Arles emerged as the center of the new Christian religion.

The Roman theater in Orange

Various places where Van Gogh planted his easel in and around St-Rémy and the asylum of St-Paul have been furnished with explanatory notices and photos of the relevant paintings. The tourist office can provide maps and organizes tours of the *Lieux Peints* (places where Van Gogh painted) three times a week (Tuesday, Thursday and Saturday at 10 AM). More energetic hikers can tackle the marked path (GR6) from Les Antiques to the ruined town of Les Baux along the crest of the Alpilles.

St-Tropez still retains a sense of identity, despite its glamorous status

▷▷▷　Port Grimaud

The Venice of the Riviera is an ingenious modern resort at the head of the Gulf of St-Tropez, designed for a yacht-owning (or renting) clientele. Its streets are waterways spanned by footbridges linking clumps of vacation homes, each with its own mooring outside the front door. The architecture is inspired by the local style and, with shady squares on many of the accommodation clusters, Port Grimaud achieves the simulation of ordinary village life, except that there are no ordinary villagers.

▷▷▷　St-Raphaël

A big resort at the foot of the Esterel, popular in Roman times and revived a century ago. Modern St-Raphaël has no great cachet, but the Riviera ingredients are there—beaches, marina, palm trees, traffic jams and golf courses.

▷▷▷　St-Rémy

A cheerful little plane-shaded town at the foot of the mini-mountainous range of Alpilles, with Glanum and Les Antiques (see page 189) on its doorstep. The main square is a good place for a drink in the shade, except on Wednesdays when the market takes over. On the edge of town is the former monastery of St-Paul-de-Mausole, the asylum where Van Gogh lived for a year from 1889 to 1890. The restored Romanesque church and cloister are usually open to visitors, but there is nothing else to see: Even the bust of Van Gogh by Zadkine has been stolen.

▶▶▷　St-Tropez

Among an arty élite, the old fishing port of St-Tropez and its surrounding coast and mountains have been no secret since the turn of the century, when the painter Paul Signac settled there. But it was Brigitte Bardot in the 1950s who made "St-Trop" a cliché for liberated youth. This it remains, although the original habitués are graying and liberated youth arrives in herds from nearby campsites. The port has exorbitant hotels, low-rise and studiously informal; stars hiding in high-walled villas; fat yachts in the port; lots of denim and leather and loud rock music; and lots of blondes. Out of season and early in the morning, the close-knit old port remains its old self, as portrayed on scores of canvases in the excellent museum. In the evening the broad square at the back of the old town becomes a vast boules arena. The port has no beach to speak of, but the Ramatuelle Peninsula has long tracts of sand, which are part of St-Tropez mythology (Tahiti, Pampelonne). The old hill villages set back from the coast (Ramatuelle, Gassin and Grimaud) now have more chic and less hubbub than St-Tropez itself.

▷▷▷　Ste-Maxime

Facing St-Tropez across a wide bay, Ste-Maxime is a much quieter and more sheltered resort, originally a Phoenician colony. It has a fishing harbor, marina and a sandy beach. The bay provides safe sailing and windsurfing.

The well-preserved Château de Tarascon, sitting on the bank of the River Rhône

▷▷▷ Sisteron

Strategically placed on rocky slopes hemming in the Durance, Sisteron is one of the natural gateways of northern Provence, a fortress town with an impressive citadel, described by Henri IV as the most powerful in the realm and strategic enough to attract heavy bombing in 1944. The citadel has been restored and is used for summer drama. There is a 12th-century former cathedral in the town, and picturesque streets between it and the river.

▷▷▷ Tarascon/Beaucaire

Their imposing medieval fortresses confronting each other across the Rhône, Beaucaire and Tarascon vividly commemorate the medieval frontier between French Languedoc and Imperial Provence. The Château de Tarascon is one of the best preserved of its kind, and open to visitors; but there is not much to see inside. The next-door church has a Romanesque door, and the tomb of Saint Martha in the crypt. Tarascon also has a popular museum, the so-called house of the fictional Tartarin de Tarascon, anti-hero of Daudet's comic novels.

St. Martha found Tarascon terrorized by a monster with a lion's head, six twisted bear claws and an unhealthy appetite for women and children. She tamed the beast and led it back to the Rhône. King René organized a celebration in 1474, parading a model through the streets, knocking down anyone in its way. A less destructive version still takes place in June.

PROVENCE

The dukes of Uzès have been the official first dukes of France since the 17th century. King Louis XIII announced that all peers should get their titles confirmed by chancery and that future precedence would reflect the speed at which this was achieved. In the ensuing race the carriages of Uzès and Luynes converged at speed in the narrow rue St-Thomas du Louvre. The Luynes team was overturned and Uzès was the first duke home.

Fields of lavender are favorite aspects of upper Provence for a brief midsummer period between flowering and harvest: July is best. Lavender grows naturally above 1,968 feet and thrives on the climate and chalky soil. A hybrid plant (*le lavandin*, not *la lavande*) has been developed to grow at lower altitude. Provence produces 100 tons of lavender essence and 1,000 tons of lavandin essence each year.

▷▷▷ Toulon

France's main Mediterranean naval port features more in history books than on vacation itineraries. The young Captain Bonaparte covered himself in glory during the eight-month siege of English-occupied Toulon in 1793, and in November 1942, 60 French ships were scuttled in the harbor when the Nazis moved into Vichy France.

The dingy back streets of the old town center of Toulon may have louche appeal and certainly have cheap restaurants, and you can count on finding a hotel room when the rest of the south of France (except Marseille) is taken.

Otherwise, Toulon's main attractions are the Naval Museum at the eastern end of the arsenal complex and Mont Faron, the rocky mountain ridge dominating the city and reached either by cable car or a narrow hairpin road. As well as a splendid view, there is a museum devoted to the Allied landings in 1944, and a tatty zoological museum. The 19th-century fort on the summit is still occupied by the military.

▷▷▷ Uzès

This dignified old town, robbed of its fortifications by Richelieu because of its Protestant leanings, stands on a high plateau of rocky garigue, the southeastern ledge of the Massif Central. At the heart of the town, near the arcaded main square, is the ducal palace (Duché), still inhabited, with a medieval tower and a fine Renaissance facade by Philibert Delormé. The round 12th-century tower (Tour Fenestrelle) is all that remains of the Romanesque cathedral. In 1662 Jean Racine was sent to Uzès to forget dreams of a literary career and prepare for holy orders. Racine liked the town, but could not understand the people, who spoke southern dialect, not rhyming Alexandrine couplets. He returned to Paris, and the rest is tragedy.

Vence See page 193.

▶▶▶ Verdon Gorges

Between Castellane and Moustiers is the most spectacular gorge in Europe, with limestone cliffs plunging 2,296 feet to the narrow riverbed. The best way to see it from a car is by following the Route des Crêtes, a circuit that leads from La Palud on the north bank. The road passes the **Châlet la Maline**, one terminus of the tough day's walk (14 km) along the bottom of the canyon, via numerous tunnels (flashlight essential), to a parking lot near the Point Sublime. For a quick taste of the gorge scenery, park at this end of the path and walk down to the water.

The main tourist center is **Moustiers-Ste-Marie**, an interesting old village straddling a mountain ravine and waterfall. Long famous for its ceramics and lavender, Moustiers is well worth a stroll, if you can park. The church has an unstable look—bulging walls and unaligned Gothic choir and Romanesque nave. Below Moustiers the Verdon is dammed to form a vast reservoir. There are a few villages and campgrounds beside the lake: Only **Ste-Croix-du-Verdon** has any charm.

Drive   Vaison-la-Romaine, Nyons and the Baronnies

Start at Vaison-la-Romaine.
Vaison-la-Romaine is a good base
for excursions. The Ouvèze
separates medieval Vaison, beneath
a hill fortress, from the modern and
Roman towns.

D938/D538 to Nyons.
Nyons, a center of olive production,
has an olive museum and oil mills
open to visitors: most interesting
during the winter pulping season. A
jumble of vaulted lanes (Quartier des
Forts) climbs from the place Bufaven
to a tiny pilgrimage chapel.

*D94 to Curnier; D64 to Buis-les-
Baronnies.*
A beautiful drive over the **Col d'Ey**
to **Buis**, passing a riverside lavender
distillery at Ste-Jalle. Buis is the

main center of trade for the popular
lime blossom (*tilleul*) infusion.

D5 back to Vaison.

Drive   Vence, Col de Vence, Gourdon

Start at Vence.
Vence is a busy hill town that has
kept three medieval gateways and a
pretty square (place du Peyra) on the
site of the Roman forum. The former
cathedral has Roman inscriptions in
the facade. Matisse's **Rosary
Chapel** (see page 175) is near the St-
Jeannet road.

Follow D2 northwest to Col de Vence.
There are fine views from the 3,182-
foot **Col de Vence**.

D2 to Courségoules and Gréolières.
Beneath the impressive walls of the
Montagne du Cheiron, **Gréolières**
and **Courségoules** have good
Renaissance paintings in their
churches. Enthusiasts of mountain
motoring can continue toward the
ski resort of **Gréolières les Neiges**
or around the **Cheiron massif**.

D3 to Gourdon and Gorges du Loup.
Gourdon is a former Saracen
stronghold in a superb setting
dominating the Loup valley and
surveying the coast. The Loup has
impressive views, but few safe
stopping places except at a café that
charges for a sight of a waterfall, the
Saut du Loup.

D2210 via Tourrettes-sur-Loup.
Tourrettes-sur-Loup is a pretty old
hill village, a center of cut-flower
industry and now a thriving arts and
crafts center.

Return on D2210 to Vence.

MASSIF CENTRAL

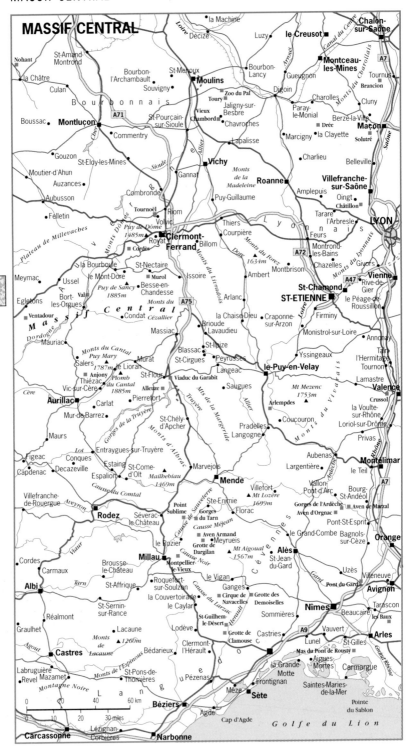

MASSIF CENTRAL

la Machine
Décize
Luzy
le Creusot
Chalon-sur-Saône
Loire
Canal du Centre
A7
Montceau-les-Mines
Montsau Charollais
Tournus
Brancion
Nohant
St-Amand-Montrond
Bourbon-l'Archambault
St-Menoux
Bourbon-Lancy
Gueugnon
Digoin
Charolles
Cluny
la Châtre
Souvigny
Moulins
Zoo du Pal
Paray-le-Monial
Drée
Berzé-la-Ville
Mâcon
Culan
Toury
Jaligny-sur-Besbre
Marcigny
la Clayette
Solutré
Boussac
Montluçon
A71
St-Pourçain-sur-Sioule
Vieux Chambord
Chavroches
Saône
Commentry
Cher
Lapalisse
Charlieu
Gouzon
St-Eloy-les-Mines
Sioule
Vichy
Monts de la Madeleine
Roanne
Belleville
Villefranche-sur-Saône
Moutier-d'Ahun
Auzances
Gannat
Amplepuis
Oingt
Châtillon
Aubusson
Combronde
Puy-Guillaume
Tarare
l'Arbresle
LYON
Felletin
Tournoël
Riom
Volvic
Thiers
Courpière
Feurs
Montrond-les-Bains
Plateau de Millevaches
Puy de Dôme 1485m
Royat
Clermont-Ferrand
Billom
Monts du Forez 1634m
A72
Chazelles
Monts du Givors
Vienne
Meymac
Cordes
Monts Dore
la Bourboule
St-Nectaire
Murol
Issoire
Ambert
Montbrison
A47
Rive-de-Gier
Ussel
le Mont-Dore
Besse-en-Chandesse
Arlanc
St-Chamond
ST-ETIENNE
le Péage-de-Roussillon
Egletons
Bort-les-Orgues
Val
Puy de Sancy 1885m
Monts du Lembron
A75
la Chaise-Dieu
Craponne-sur-Arzon
Firminy
Annonay
Ventadour
Massif
Central
Condat
Cézallier
Brioude
Lavaudieu
Monistrol-sur-Loire
Tain l'Hermitage
Tournon
Mauriac
Dordogne
Massiac
St-Ilpize
Yssingeaux
Lamastre
Monts du Cantal
Puy Mary 1787m
Murat
Blassac
St-Cirgues
Peyrusse
Langeac
le Puy-en-Velay
Mt Mezenc 1753m
Valence
Crussol
Salers
le Lioran
St-Flour
Viaduc du Garabit
Sauges
Arlempdes
la Voulte-sur-Rhône
Anjony
Thiézac
Plomb du Cantal 1885m
Alleuze
Coucouron
Loriol-sur-Drôme
Vic-sur-Cère
Cère
Pierrefort
Mts de la Margeride
Privas
AURILLAC
Carlat
St-Chély-d'Apcher
Pradelles
Langogne
Aubenas
Largentière
le Teil
Montélimar
Maurs
Mur-de-Barrez
Gorges de la Truyère
Marvejols
Vallon-Pont-d'Arc
Bourg-St-Andéol
A7
Figeac
Conques
Entraygues-sur-Truyère
Gorges de l'Ardèche
Aven de Marzal
Capdenac
Decazeville
Estaing
St-Côme-d'Olt
Mende
Villefort
Mt Lozère 1699m
Aven d'Orgnac
Pont-St-Esprit
Villefranche-de-Rouergue
Espalion
Mailhebiau 1469m
Ste-Enimie
Florac
le Grand-Combe
Bagnols-sur-Cèze
Orange
Cordes
Rodez
Séverac-le-Château
Point Sublime
Gorges du Tarn
Aven Armand
Meyrueis
Alès
St-Jean-du-Gard
Uzès
Villeneuve
Avignon
Carmaux
Brousse-le-Château
le Rozier
Grotte de Dargilan
Mt Aigoual 1567m
Pont du Gard
Albi
St-Affrique
Millau
Montpellier-le-Vieux
le Vigan
Ganges
Cirque de Navacelles
Grotte des Demoiselles
Nîmes
Beaucaire
les Baux
Tarascon
Roquefort-sur-Soulzon
la Couvertoirade
le Caylar
Sommières
Arles
Réalmont
St-Sernin-sur-Rance
St-Guilhem-le-Désert
Castries
A9
Vauvert
Graulhet
Lacaune
Monts de Lacaune 1260m
Bédarieux
Lodève
Grotte de Clamouse
Clermont-l'Hérault
Lunel
St-Gilles
Aigues-Mortes
Castres
Mas du Pont de Rousty
Carmargue
Labruguière
Mazamet
Monts de l'Espinouse
St-Pons-de-Thomières
Pézenas
la Grande-Motte
Saintes-Maries-de-la-Mer
Revel
Montagne Noire
Frontignan
Mèze
Sète
Pointe du Sablon
Béziers
Agde
Cap d'Agde
Golfe du Lion
Carcassonne
Lézignan-Corbières
Narbonne

0 20 40 60 km
0 10 20 30 miles

The Massif Central is no single mountain range, but an enormous highland region between the Loire and the Mediterranean, covering about one-sixth of France. More southern than central, it is certainly massive. Diversity comes as no surprise.

High ground The highest peaks are in the northern region, Auvergne, a land of rich pastures and a mountain diet of ham, hard cheese (Cantal, St-Nectaire) and dark bread: food built to last through a long winter of isolation. Its villages are gray and, as a vacation area, so is its image. The main resorts are spas and, by Alpine or Pyrenean standards, the mountains are unimpressive, with no glaciers, no snowcapped peaks in summer, few rock faces to excite climbers, and no great lakes. Just big hills, ugly hydroelectric reservoirs, and dreary old spas.

Quiet simplicity On the other hand, Auvergne tourism is quiet, prices are low, and the value in simple hotels is often outstanding. There is a little skiing (more than a little, for cross-country skiers) but in general the slopes and rough old mountain villages have escaped the ravages of ski development. Summits are accessible to walkers and are quite high enough to be rewarding. With good fishing and canoeing, Auvergne is a fine area for an active outdoor vacation, with some sightseeing thrown in—hilltop castle ruins, beautiful old churches and a range of extinct volcanoes, small but perfectly formed.

Wild country Farther south, the Causses and Cévennes form less high but wilder and not as well-trodden country. For fishing rivers and green valleys, substitute white water and rocky gorges; for cow pastures, windswept limestone plateaus with no spring water, only dew ponds and sheep; and for creamy St-Nectaire, razor-sharp Roquefort. This is wilderness France, an area of enormous appeal to a growing minority of travelers, second-homers and permanent refugees from the comforts and stresses of town life, who take their escapism seriously. If you find the charms of rural France a bit tame, try the southern Massif Central.

Canoeists flock around the Pont

The Massif de l'Aigoual has an annual rainfall of over 2 m; over 60 cm of rain fell in 24 hours on October 30 and 31, 1963.

▷▷▷ Aigoual, Massif de l'

Aigoual means "wet." For reasons to do with the convergence of Atlantic and Mediterranean air currents, the southern bastion of the Massif Central (5,140 feet) is the wettest place in France. The slopes have been reforested in an attempt to reduce flood damage. There are roads to the summit from north and south, big views from the top and an arboretum (**Hort de Dieu**) just below it, signed from the road. **Meyrueis** is a popular tourist base, well placed for excursions to **Aven Armand** and **Dargilan** grottoes and drives along the **Jonte** and **Tarn** gorges. It has a Cévennes National Park information center.

▶▷▷ Allier, Gorges de l'

West of Le Puy, the Allier runs north through dark gorges of granite and volcanic rock, best seen from the train, between tunnels. It is an area for simple accommodations and outdoor vacations—riding, fishing, canoeing (information from the tourist offices at **Brioude** and **Langeac**). There are interesting churches (usually locked) with frescoes near the river north of Langeac—**Peyrusses**, **St-Cirgues**, **Blassac**. **St-Ilpize** is a picturesque old village with ruined fortress.

▶▷▷ Anjony, Château d'

A well-preserved 15th-century fortress overlooks the village of Tournemire (north of Aurillac) and its colorful volcanic-stone church, proud possessor of a thorn from Christ's crown. The château's four slender towers make an impressive landmark, and there are interesting Renaissance murals inside.

▶▶▷ Ardèche, Gorges de l'

The D290 from Vallon Pont d'Arc to Pont St-Esprit is the great Ardèche road, a succession of roadside belvederes hundreds of meters above the river. Objects in view include a natural archway (the **Pont d'Arc**) spanning the river and, usually, a dense traffic of canoeists doing the Ardèche properly. In summer, the pace of the river is comfortable; operators at **Vallon** rent out two-person canoes and organize return buses from **Sauze**, near **St-Martin d'Ardèche**, 32 km and about six hours' paddling and drifting downstream, via many good sunbathing and picnic places. To the south of Vallon is the magnificent **Aven d'Orgnac** pothole (guided tours, long staircases; underground group photos on sale by the time you resurface). **Aven Marzal** is a shorter detour from the Ardèche road, and is almost as spectacular.

Drive The Cévennes and Mont Lozère

Start at Florac.
This long circuit through some of the wildest country in France is easily abbreviated by using the D998 Florac/Pont de Montvert road along the upper valley of the Tarn. **Florac, Mende** or **St-Jean-du-Gard** will do as overnight stopping places. Mende is the largest, a quiet old cathedral town beside the Lot. Florac is the headquarters of the Cévennes National Park and is the starting point of the classic drive down the Tarn gorges.

Take the D907 and Corniche des Cévennes road to St-Jean-du-Gard.
The western leg between **Mende** and **St-Jean-du-Gard** includes the panoramic Corniche des Cévennes road, which runs through *camisard* country (see box below).

Follow D983, 984 and 29 (crossing the N106), and the D35 to the Col de la Croix de Berthel, and Le Pont de Montvert; then the D20 to the Col de Finiels and Le Bleymard.
The eastern leg from St-Jean to **Le Bleymard** is very slow driving: 90 km of narrow mountain roads over the knotted ridges of the Cévennes and the granite mass of **Mont Lozère**. From the **Col de Finiels** and from the **Châlet du**

197

Mont Lozère (4 km north) there are paths to the Finiels summit (5,573 feet), the top of the Lozère. The Col des Tribes (east of Le Bleymard on D901) marks the Mediterranean/Atlantic watershed. From the road up to the pass, a path leads north to the source of the Lot.

Take the D901 and N88 to Mende and Balsièges, then the N106 via the Col de Montmirat to Florac.

Walk Footpath across the massif.

One of the old transhumance trails is now the GR7 path, which crosses the massif from **Le Bleymard** to the **Col de la Croix de Berthel**, via the **Col de Finiels**. The best section is between **L'Hôpital** and **L'Aubaret** (about two hours). Both can be reached by car from Le **Pont de Montvert**. Along the GR7, farm buildings and isolated bell towers (to help travelers caught in a storm) have been restored as part of the Lozère ecomuseum.

<< Protestants were outlawed in 1685. In the Cévennes they took to the hills (*désert*). Passive resistance to conversion became guerila warfare in 1702, and the Protestants became known as camisards, after their white shirts. There is a camisard museum at **Le Mas Soubeyran** (11 km east of St-Jean-du-Gard by D50). **>>**

MASSIF CENTRAL

The château at Toury is said to have a dragon that acts as its guard.

▶ ▷ ▷   Besbre, Vallée de la

Fertile country southeast of Moulins, with a rich concentration of small châteaus. The busy main road town of **Lapalisse** has the most magnificent of them, rebuilt and decorated by a marshal who brought home a taste for Italian Renaissance art from the Italian war. Downstream there are other châteaus to admire: **Chavroches**, **Vieux Chambord**, **Jaligny** and **Toury**, a delicious pinkish château in miniature, with turrets and towers. There is a zoo, amusement park and train ride at **Le Pal**.

▷ ▷ ▷   Besse en Chandesse

With the ski slopes of Super-Besse 7 km away, the picturesque old gray town of Besse is a year-round mountain resort, popular in summer as a base for hiking, fishing and bicycling (bicycles can be hired locally), and is worth visiting anyway for its old houses, town gates and church (a mixture of Romanesque and late Gothic), all built of black lava. The deep, round Lac Pavin (southwest of Besse) is one of the prettiest of Auvergne's volcanic crater lakes, and a popular local beauty spot. The summit of **Puy de Montchal** (4,628 feet) is about half an hour's walk from the lake.

▶ ▷ ▷   Bort-les-Orgues

This small town on the upper Dordogne sits beneath a remarkable cliff of massive pillars of volcanic rock, the Orgues (organ pipes), which are worth inspecting at close quarters. Walk to the foot of the cliff from the road, then drive on up to the plateau above for good views of the valley and the long reservoir above Bort's hydroelectric dam, the first of five on the Dordogne. When full, it makes an island of the picturesque turreted 15th-century Château de Val (guided tours), whose waterside setting seems quite natural. There is a small beach nearby, with boat trips.

▷ ▷ ▷   Bourboule, La

Restful to a fault, La Bourboule is a big spa spanning the young Dordogne a few kilometers downstream from Le Mont-Dore. There are gardens and long hill walks down from the Charlannes plateau, reached by gondola lift. French parents send their asthmatic children to benefit from La Bourboule's waters, rich in arsenic.

Isolation at Conques

▷▷▷   Cère, Vallée de la
The most beautiful part of the Cère is its upper valley at the heart of the Cantal Mountains, from its source at **Le Lioran** to **Aurillac**. The old village of **Vic-sur-Cère** is a good base for driving tours and/or hiking, notably along the peaks from the **Plomb du Cantal** (6,084 feet), reached by cable car from **Super-Lioran**, to the **Col de Curebourse** (3,270 feet) above Vic. On the other side of the valley, the **Puy de la Poche** (4,930 feet) and **Puy Griou** (5,556 feet) are rewarding targets, the latter hard going near the top.

▶▷▷   La Chaise-Dieu
High up in logging country north of Le Puy, La Chaise-Dieu is a base for outdoor sports. More than this, however, it is a magnificent 14th-century abbey church. It is worth paying to enter the choir and see the tomb of Pope Clement VI, beautiful tapestries, a Dance of Death fresco and Gothic cloister. All the great organ's stops are out for the music festival in August and September.

▶▷▷   Clermont-Ferrand
An industrial city at the heart of a thoroughly rural region, Clermont-Ferrand's dark streets are dominated by the black lava cathedral. Less prominent but at least as interesting is nearby Notre-Dame du Port. To the west, in a fine 16th-century house, the Musée du Ranquet boasts a calculator made by the scientist Blaise Pascal, born locally in 1623. There is another town center to the northwest: Montferrand, which merged with Clermont in the 18th century. Many elegant houses on and around the Rue des Cordeliers have been restored.

▶▶▷   Conques
Tucked away in a remote fold of hill country to the south of the Lot, Conques is a small village and a great pilgrimage church. Thanks to the relics of an early Christian martyr in Agen, Saint Foy, the monastery won a mention in the pilgrim's guide of the day, accumulated a rich treasure and built the church in the late 11th century. Its glory is the Last Judgment carving over the main doorway, and the treasure (entrance charge), which includes a 10th-century gold statuette-reliquary.

For a century and a half before the Revolution the Vallée de la Cère was controlled by the Grimaldis of Monaco, who are still viscounts of Carlat (a château, no longer standing, east of Aurillac). They stayed, as do many tourists today, at Vic sur Cère.

Clermont Ferrand is the home of the French rubber industry, started by the Barbier (later Michelin) family in the early 19th century.

Take the cable car from the source of the Dordogne to a point not far below the summit of the Puy de Sancy, at 6,183 feet the high point of the Massif Central. From here you can hike along the hills to the Capucin (4,805 feet) and take a cable car down to Le Mont-Dore. For the very fit, a full circuit of the amphitheater, starting and finishing at Le Mont-Dore, is possible in a day. Take the Capucin ski lift and proceed counter-clockwise via the Puy de Sancy, descending to Le Mont-Dore at a 98-foot waterfall (Grande Cascade).

▷▷▷ Lioran, Le

With nearby **Super-Lioran**, this is the Cantal's main ski resort, in a forest setting near the Col de Cère (4,244 feet): a watershed between the beautiful upper valleys of Cère and Alagnon, which feed the Dordogne and Loire respectively. Both upper and lower resorts are open for business in summer, as is the cable car from Super-Lioran to the **Plomb du Cantal** (6,183 feet). On the other side of the pass, there is no mechanical help for the ascent of conical **Puy Griou** (5,556 feet). Its last stage is more arduous than most Auvergnat climbs (see page 199).

▶▷▷ Lot, Vallée du

The Lot is one of France's best-loved rivers, less touristy than the Dordogne, more welcoming than the wilder Tarn. A number of unspoiled small towns with medieval bridges reflected in the water complement the scenic drive along the middle reach of the river: **St-Come-d'Olt**, **Espalion**, **Estaing** and **Entraygues**, where the Lot is fed by the Truyère, all have great charm. A minor road continues along the right bank to the turnoff for **Conques** (see page 199). The landscape is at its loveliest between Estaing and Entraygues, with steep wooded slopes above the river, swollen by the hydro-electric Golinhac dam below Estaing.

The River Lot

Murol is a small resort village beneath the ruins of a medieval fortress, which was strengthened and embellished during the Renaissance but used as a quarry after the Revolution. Enough remains for an interesting visit.

▶▷▷ Le Mont-Dore

Charming is not the word that springs to mind first, but Le Mont-Dore is less depressing than most spas, thanks to its location at the foot of an amphitheater of mountains. In winter, it is one of the massif's main ski resorts. The odorous baths, housed in a 19th-century temple-like building, are worth visiting, and there is plenty of scope for car tours combining mountains, lakes (with swimming and water sports at **Lac Chambon**), churches (**St-Nectaire**, **Orcival**), châteaus (**Cordés**, north of Orcival, and **Murol**) and cheeses. Besse, Murol and Orcival are alternative bases for exploring the Monts Dore, without the spa factor.

Volcanoes

■ **Unlike most landscapes of volcanic origin in Europe north of Naples, the area to the west of Clermont-Ferrand looks the part. The Monts Dômes, more than 100 abrupt conical peaks, form a chain on a north–south axis. Rising only a few hundred meters from the fertile surrounding landscape, some of the old volcanoes (*puys*) are grassy, others wooded. ...■**

Most of the volcanoes have craters, in some cases as neatly decapitated as boiled eggs. Volcanologists warn that it is much too early to write them off as extinct. As indicated by the many hot springs (Royat, Le Mont-Dore, Vichy, etc.), underground Auvergne is far from tranquil. The spring water at **Chaudes Aigues** (south of St-Flour) is the hottest in Europe.

The Puy de Dôme The highest of the chain has a road spiraling to the summit, a superb viewpoint, albeit cluttered with weather station and tourist paraphernalia. There are also scant remains of a Roman temple. Hikers use the steeper track from the Col de Ceyssat. Immediately to the north, the **Puy de Pariou** and **Petit Puy de Dôme** both have twin craters. They stand inside the boundaries of a military firing range and access (on foot from the Puy de Dôme, or by car and footpath from the Clermont–Pontgibaud road) is at restricted times.

The Monts Dore and the Cantal To the south of the Monts Dômes are fragments of ~~older and~~ much larger mountains: The Cantal volcano probably reached at least 9,840 feet before explosion and glacier erosion. **Puy Griou**, near the Plomb du Cantal, is one of the chimneys at the center of the original crater. On its northern flank beneath the Puy Violent, the village of Salers occupies one of many lava plateaus known as *planèzes*.

All these volcanic massifs are included in a regional natural park, the Parc des Volcans. The main information centers are at **Aurillac**, **Montlosier** (D5 southwest of Clermont-Ferrand), **Volvic**, near Riom (a lava quarry), **Egliseneuve d'Entraigves**, between Besse and Condat, and **Riom ès Montagnes**. The area around **Le Puy** falls outside the boundaries of the park, but is also volcanic in origin (see pages 202 and 205).

Motorists wanting to combine a scenic drive and a short panoramic walk should head for the Pas de Peyrol, east of Salers by D680. From the car park it is less than half an hour's walk to the Puy Mary (5,861 feet) at the end of a crest of peaks commanding a magnificent view of the Cantal Mountains and valleys, like the ruins of a vast natural fortress, ~~20 million years old~~.

The high tops of Cantal can be very bleak, but meadows on the lower slopes are famous for their wild flowers and for butterflies (above: Scarce Copper)

From Louis X1V's time until the 20th century, much of the female population of the Vélay region made lace. Now that machines do the work more cheaply, country village squares are no longer filled with women deftly manipulating their *fuseaux* (spindles). But Le Puy still has a lace-making school (rue du Guesclin, near place St-Laurent), with a small display of old lace and craftswomen to demonstrate and explain techniques. Training for "professional aptitude" takes three years of eight hours' practice a day.

▶ ▶ ▶   Le Puy

Le Puy fills an old crater punctuated by outcrops of volcanic rock, of which the most spiky is the giddy perch for a medieval chapel, St-Michel-d'Aiguille. On the main hill, the lava-cobbled rue des Tables climbs to the cathedral (see page 203) past tourist shops with costumed lacemakers in the doorway. Above looms a huge statue of green-eyed Virgin and Child, made of melted Crimean cannon, with a viewing platform in the crown. On the approach to Le Puy from the north, eyes left for the ruins of the **Château de Polignac**.

▷ ▷ ▷   Riom

Once Clermont's rival, Riom is now threatened by the sprawl of its neighbor. The old lava-built center, ringed by boulevards, is of interest for its Renaissance palaces, the 14th-century statue *Virgin, Child and Goldfinch* in Notre Dame du Marthuret (rue du Commerce) and a regional museum. There are superb fortress ruins at Tournoël, above Volvic, a source of mineral water and lava. Its lava museum has volcanic sound effects.

▷ ▷ ▷   Rodez

The departmental capital of remote Aveyron has recently benefited from a modest revival in its fortunes as disenchanted urbanites have acquired a taste for rustification. The center and ramparts have been restored. The great red cathedral is a mixture of bare fortification and late Gothic and Renaissance ornament.

▷ ▷ ▷   Royat

A Roman spa overlooking Clermont-Ferrand, Royat was the height of Second Empire fashion. Now it is a comfortable suburb with public gardens surrounding the baths, unexceptional hotels, extensive sports facilities and a fortified Romanesque church.

▷ ▷ ▷   St-Guilhem-le-Désert

After a long career in the armed service of Charlemagne, William of Orange retired to found an abbey at the foot of the Causses. He brought a fragment of the Cross, which put St-Guilhem on the medieval pilgrimage map. The holy splinter is still on display in the church.

Romanesque Auvergne

■ **In a region of dour gray villages it may come as a surprise to find that the local version of the Romanesque style is full of color and invention. The builders of these churches, one feels, had fun exploiting the range of local granite, sandstone and lava to create mosaics of geometric and speckled patterns decorating the walls of churches large and small. ...■**

The striking similarities with the spirit of Oriental art probably reflect crusading contacts. Enjoyment of a Romanesque church is never complete without a good look at the back: a fan of chapels in a rhythmic interplay of curves. Inside the church, every capital tells a lively story.

Clermont and surrounding area

Clermont-Ferrand: Notre-Dame du Port. The most perfect example of the local style: colorful stonework, beautiful capitals and a reproduction black Virgin in the crypt.

Chauriat (east of Clermont-Ferrand): look out for colorful stonework and good capitals.

Marsat (near Riom): features include a severe black Virgin in a golden cloak; and a wheel around which 3 km of wax (the distance from Riom) is threaded.

Mozac (on the edge of Riom): the church is no beauty, but the capitals (including Jonah and a group of acrobats) and reliquary are outstanding.

Monts Dore

Orcival: a harmonious gray pilgrimage church, with a 12th-century Virgin, set in a pretty village. Note the good capitals in the choir.

St-Nectaire: prominently set above a small spa, this handsome 12th-century church has outstanding capitals and treasure.

South of Clermont

Brioude: the biggest and most majestic of all, Brioude has colorful stonework even on the floor. Entertaining rustic themes can be made out in the carved capitals. Look for the 14th-century "leprous" wooden Christ.

Issoire: this grand town-center church was done no favors by its 19th-century decorators; but it has a beautiful east end and fine capitals.

Lavaudieu (southeast of Brioude): a 12th-century former abbey church with a cloister, frescoes and octagonal belfry, set in a rough red village.

Le Puy: set on a steep slope and interestingly constructed on several levels, Le Puy's cathedral has a patterned west end and an unusual vault of oblong domes. There are good frescoes and a superb cloister (entrance charge). The earlier 10th- and 11th-century chapel of St-Michel, erected on a spire of rock, has intricate scalloped decoration surrounding the door, apparently inspired by Muslim art.

Clermont-Ferrand's cathedral

203

The waters of Vichy were known to the Romans, but Vichy's boom time was the 19th century, when it acquired most of its exotic architecture. Marshal Pétain lived at the Pavillon Sévigné, now a luxurious hotel, formerly the residence of the celebrated 17th-century correspondent Madame de Sévigné, who came for her rheumatism, found the water foul-tasting and described the cure routine as purgatory.

Stained-glass windows at Vichy

▶▷▷ Salers

Salers is an outwardly well-preserved old village of gray turreted houses, ramparts and gateways on the western flank of the Cantal mountains and at the heart of cheese country. With several good hotels, it is a good base for exploring the Cantal mountains and Monts Dore. The church has a painted sculptural group of the Entombment (late 15th-century).

▷▷▷ Souvigny

Once an important Cluniac abbey, pilgrimage and burial place for the Bourbon dukes, Souvigny is now a peaceful place, with only the great abbey church (Romanesque and Gothic) to remind visitors of its past glory. There is interesting sculpture, inside the church (two splendid ducal tombs) and in the nearby museum, an old church. St-Ménoux (6 km north) also has a beautiful 12th- to 13th-century church.

▶▶▶ Tarn, Gorges See pages 206–207.

▶▷▷ Thiers

Still dedicated to its traditional manufacture of cutlery, Thiers is remarkably old-fashioned in appearance: steep narrow streets lined with cutlery shops and workshops in old timbered houses, on a promontory above the Durolle. On the rue de la Coutellerie near the domed Romanesque church of St-Genès, you can visit traditional workshops, which are gradually losing out to factory mass production, and a good cutlery museum.

▶▷▷ Truyère Gorges

Once a tributary of the Allier, the Truyère now abruptly changes course near the old gray town of **St-Flour**, beneath a long railway bridge (Viaduc de Garabit) built, before his more famous tower, by Eiffel. Here it swells into the largest of a series of narrow reservoirs on its way to join the Lot at Entraygues. No road follows the valley, but the road from **Pierrefort** to the **Barrage de Sarrans** runs through some of the best scenery. The best thing about St-Flour, the highest cathedral town in France, is its setting on a volcanic outcrop, well viewed from the Clermont–Mende road (N9). About 14 km south, the ruins of the **Château d'Alleuze** overlook a finger of the top lake. At **Pont de Tréboul** a submerged 14th-century bridge (superimposed by a modern replacement) re-surfaces when water is low. **Entraygues** has a 13th-century bridge and château overlooking the confluence of the Rivers Lot and Truyère.

▶▷▷ Vichy

The great spa has lost its share of the fizzy water market and most of its cachet as a resort, partly by association with the 1940–44 period of German occupation, which is often referred to simply as Vichy; partly because staying at a spa is now a cheap holiday for those with a sympathetic doctor. In season, *curistes* (people taking a cure) still line up for a drink at the taps in the Parc des Sources, amble in gardens on the banks of the Allier and avail themselves of Vichy's many seasonal entertainments and sports facilities.

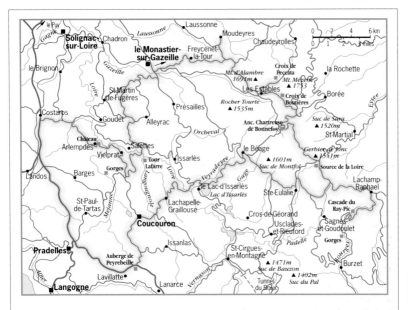

Drive — Mont Mézenc and the source of the Loire

The main appeal of this tour is the beautiful highland scenery around Mont Mézenc (5,750 feet) and the Gerbier de Jonc, a cone of volcanic rock marking the source of the Loire.

Start at Le Monastier. D500/36 to Moudeyres, Les Estables.
Moudeyres has an excellent thatched hotel; Les Estables is a base for cross-country skiing.

D274 to Croix de Peccata; D631/400/ 378 to Gerbier de Jonc (D122/215 to Ray Pic and back (see Walk, below).
The Ray Pic waterfall is 15 minutes' walk from the road by an easy path.

D122 to Le Béage, D16 to Lac d'Issarlès, Coucouron and Auberge de Peyrebeille.

The Lac d'Issarlès, which fills a volcanic crater, has a beach and cafés. Coucouron is a cheese-making village with a Wednesday market. Hoteliers with cash-flow problems may sympathize with Martin and Mary Breysse, who ran the lonely highland inn, Auberge de Peyrebeille, and killed at least 53 guests in 26 years, pocketing their money and burning the bodies in the oven. Finally discovered in 1833, they were guillotined in front of the inn.

N102/88 to Costaros, D49/54 to Arlempdes.
Arlempdes has a simple friendly hotel beneath a medieval fortress high above the Loire.

Return to Le Monastier.

Walk — Mont Mézenc and the Gerbier de Jonc

Marked paths lead to the summit of Mont Mézenc from the road at Croix de Peccata (about half an hour) and Croix de Boutières (slightly longer). The Gerbier de Jonc is a steeper but shorter walk from the roadside, unmarked but obvious.
Alternatively, a round-trip of the Mont Mézenc from Les Estables takes about three hours.

The Grands Causses

■ **Most of the large area between the Upper Lot valley and the Mediterranean coast of Languedoc consists of a high limestone plateau, or *causse*, divided into four by rivers that have cut gorges like great wounds into the land. There are other Causses in France, but these are the serious ones: high, wide, wild, windswept and empty. ...■**

The Larzac is the best known of the Grands Causses, thanks to the outcry provoked by a government plan in the 1970s to expand its military camp at the expense of a few sheep farms. The farmers took their sheep to demonstrate in Paris; angry youth found the military a soft target, and Sauvons Le Larzac fitted nicely on a T-shirt. Suddenly everyone cared about one of the more desolate parts of the country. Worry about Roquefort output may also have influenced opinion. On his election President Mitterrand lost no time canceling the project.

High and wild country: the Causse Méjean

From north to south, the four Causses are: **Sauveterre**, between the Lot and the Tarn; **Méjean**, the highest and wildest, between Tarn and Jonte; the **Causse Noir**, between Jonte and Dourbie; and the **Larzac**, the largest, to the south of the Dourbie. The river gorges can be admired on foot, by boat (in a few places), and by car. Speleomanes can explore potholes equipped with elevators and staircases, artfully lit to reveal delicate translucent curtains of rock and underground lakes.

Chaotic rocks Above ground, chaotic collections of rocks make natural imitations of ruined cities and give a small village like **Le Caylar** the look of a fortified town. **Montpellier-le-Vieux**, on the Causse Noir south of Le Rozier, is an overgrown maze of dolomitic rocks among which it would be easy to get lost without the plan sold on site. Elsewhere, retreating rivers have left bends like natural theaters, or *cirques*: **Navacelles** is the finest example, near the small town of Ganges. Throughout, civilization takes a back seat. Sheep are the most numerous inhabitants and their cheese, the pungent Roquefort, is the main output. Small dry-stone shelters for man and beast dot the landscape like lonely mausoleums.

Access Inhospitable as they are, the Causses are not inaccessible. A toll-free section of the A75 motorway travels across the Massif Central from St-Flour to Montpellier; a good road follows the Tarn Gorges; and the old pilgrimage route across the Causse du Larzac is now a fast main road (N9 from Millau to Montpellier), passing a series of villages with evocative names like **La Cavalerie** and **L'Hospitalet**, built by the Templars and Hospitalers, the area's medieval landlords. **Ste-Eulalie** was the original Templar base, but **La Couvertoirade** (north of Le Caylar, off the main road) is the least modernized, with much of its old ramparts, towers and gates intact. South of Le Caylar the road descends from the Causse in a few hairpins at the **Pas de l'Escalette**, where earlier travelers had to use a staircase in the 984-foot cliff.

Celebrated gorge The most famous river gorge, and the easiest gorge road, is the Tarn between **Ste-Enimie** and **Le Rozier**. There are cliffs of up to 1,640 feet on either side, vividly colored when sunlit; caves in the rock walls, brilliantly clear water and occasional fertile openings in the narrow gorge, with small villages, orchards and riverside châteaus. From **La Malène** there are organized boat trips through a section of the gorge known as **Les Détroits** (the Straits) with beautiful caves, to **Baumes Hautes**. Canoeists can tackle the same section, but should not continue downstream, where a rocky chaos (the Pas du Souci) is a dangerous obstacle. **Le Rozier** is a good base for energetic hikers: There are spectacular cliff paths above the Tarn and Jonte, with exposed sections where ladders have been installed. From **Les Vignes** (below the Pas du Souci) a hairpin road scales the right bank wall and leads to the **Point Sublime**, one of the few easily accessible places where the gorge can be viewed from above.

Other options The other sections of gorge scenery, much less crowded but with slower driving, are the Jonte between **Meyrueis** and **Le Rozier**; and the Dourbie, where two sections of tight gorges are interrupted by a more open valley around the village of **St-Jean-de-Bruel**, a cheerful resort among orchards.

Potholes The Causses' potholes are the grandest in France, although lacking the extra dimension of prehistoric art. The most spectacular are **Aven Armand**, north of the Jonte near Meyrueis, with its "virgin forest" of stalagmites; and the **Grotte des Demoiselles** near Ganges.

Other places to visit
Grotte de Dargilan (near Meyrueis), **Grotte de Clamouse** (near St-Guilhem-le-Désert): stalagmites and stalactites, almost as good as Aven Armand and less crowded.
Hyelzas (4 km west of Aven Armand): restored traditional Causse farm.
La Jasse (beside the N9, between Millau and La Cavalerie): Larzac ecomuseum, a splendid all-round presentation of the history and ecology of the Causse du Larzac.
Roquefort-sur-Soulzon: where the cheese comes from; caves open to visitors.
Sauveterre (north of Ste-Enimie): small village with typical old Causse houses.

When it comes to blue-veined cheese made from the untreated milk of Lacaune ewes, there is Roquefort and Roquefort. These days most of it is made mechanically in southern France and Corsica. But a small amount is produced in the traditional manner at Roquefort-sur-Soulzon, south of Millau, using a natural mold from huge decomposed loaves of two-month-old bread. The cheeses are stored for many months in cold, damp natural caves beneath the village before being wrapped in tin foil and stamped with their red sheep insignia. The caves are open to visitors.

The Cirque de Navacelles, where the course of ancient rivers can still be seen in the land

THE ALPS/RHONE VALLEY

From Lake Geneva to the Mediterranean, the Alpine chain is dominated by the pinnacles and glaciers at the shoulders of Mont Blanc (15,767 feet), a pilgrimage for mountaineers from all over the world. The Alps have their place in the history books, but are primarily a region for sport and leisure in a context of natural beauty. In two uninhabited national parks (**Vanoise** and **Ecrins**) eagle, ibex and gentian enjoy protection and hikers have to make do with simple refuges. The Queyras and Vercors regional parks have been set up to foster traditional crafts and ecosensitive tourism.

French acquisitions The southern province of Dauphiné was sold to France in 1349 and traditionally ruled by the heir to the throne, or dauphin. Grenoble became its capital and remains the metropolis of the French Alps, a dynamic industrial and university city. **Savoie** was a transalpine independent duchy with capitals on either side of the chain at **Chambéry** and **Turin**. In 1860 Chambéry's half voted to join France.

THE ALPS AND THE RHONE VALLEY

Savoie More accessible than Dauphiné, Savoie is greener in summer and whiter in winter, and more developed for tourism. There are old spas and lakeside resorts with casinos and windsurfing schools; prewar resorts grafted on to old chalet villages among woods and pastures; and high-altitude modern resorts planned for convenient skiing, cheap self-catering and never mind the aesthetics.

Face-lifts The current effort is to improve the looks of the new resorts and broaden their summer appeal. Climbing and hiking, golf, riding, mountain biking, tennis, paragliding, rafting and summer skiing are widely available. For the young and hyperactive, the high resorts are great. For cowbells and pretty chalets, look elsewhere.

Cable cars and high roads bring the glories of the Alpine landscape within the reach of the least energetic traveler. Fine weather (never predictable in the mountains) is vital to a good vacation, and the high resorts and road passes open for a short summer season.

The Rhône Valley is a great thoroughfare, much traveled and little visited. Its capital, **Lyon**, is a city of merchants, bankers and gourmets. While others pass through on the way south, gastro-tourists target the Rhône Valley to feast at the tables of Blanc, Bocuse, Chapel and other high priests of gourmandism.

Annecy's lakeside beauty is a mixed blessing...

▶ ▶ ▶ **Annecy, Lac d'**

An old town at the head of a beautiful mountain lake, flanked by elegant villas and smart hotels, Annecy is the French showpiece of lakes-and-mountains beauty. The only complaint may be its popularity: Annecy itself, the most dynamic and prosperous town in Savoie, has industrial and residential suburbs spreading far beyond the old center. And the banks and waters of the lake are approaching saturation with villas and boats. Once seriously polluted, the slow-draining waters are now clear and clean enough for the prized local delicacies, *lavaret* (lake trout) and *omble chevalier* (char).

The heart of town is a delightful canal zone where the Thiou flows from the lake, overlooked by the towers of a vast 16th-century fortress. Strolling around is the main attraction (especially on market day, Friday), but there are a few specific sights: Renaissance frescoes in the church of **St-Maurice**, and two regional **museums** in the château (popular art, furniture) and the Palais de l'Isle (history), a picturesque old prison in midstream. There are extensive gardens beside the lake, with boat trips from the moorings beside the Hôtel de Ville. The best place for swimming and water sports is at the eastern end of the long avenue of planes (**avenue d'Albigny**) near the splendidly restored Imperial Palace hotel.

On the west bank, it is a fine drive up the wooded Semnoz mountain to the **Crête du Chatillon** (5,573 feet) and back to the lake at **Sevrier** via the **Col de Leschaux**, giving good views of the lake and the more interesting mountains climbing steeply from the eastern shore: the cliffs of **Mount Veyrier**, jagged **Dents de Lanfon** and towering crags of **La Tournette** (7,711 feet). The best alternative way to enjoy the scenery is a boat ride from Annecy to **Talloires**, the most fashionable resort on the lake, with prestigious hotels and restaurants in an idyllic leafy setting, sheltered by the 492-foot **Roc de Chère** cliffs, a nature reserve of botanical interest. Facing Talloires across the narrowest part of the lake, the picturesque **Château de Duingt** is not open to visitors.

...bringing admirers from all around

▶ ▷ ▷ Aravis, Massif des

The Aravis is Haute Savoie at its most charming: high mountains, rich pastures, woods, old chalets with flowers on the balcony, creamy Reblochon cheese. The **Cimetière des Glières** and **museum** commemorate the exploits of Resistance forces based on the Glières plateau (to the north) in 1944. **Thones**, an attractive small market town, has a typically Savoyard onion-domed church, good cheese shops and a small local museum; **La Clusaz**, reached along the D909, is one of Haute Savoie's oldest and biggest ski resorts, with traditional chalet-style hotels, lots of sport and good walks from the Beauregard cable car and the **Col des Aravis** (4,913 feet), which commands a famous view of Mont Blanc. From here the return to Annecy, via **Manigod** (D16) and **Col de la Forclaz** (D12, N508, D42), is slower driving through particularly beautiful pastoral scenery with good views over the lake.

▶ ▷ ▷ Assy, Plateau d'

This institutional resort above Le Fayet has a superb view of Mont Blanc. The former tuberculosis clinics are not a cheerful sight, but the modern church of Notre Dame de Toute Grace is worth the long hairpin climb: Its decorators included Lurçat (tapestry behind the altar), Léger (exterior mosaic), Rouault (windows), Chagall and Matisse. If you are bound for Chamonix, take the minor road via **Servoz** and the **Gorges de la Diosaz**, instead of driving back down to the valley.

▷ ▷ ▷ Barcelonnette and the Ubaye

The 13th-century base of the count of Barcelona is a rough mountain town, visibly old if not irresistibly charming, beneath modern ski resorts (**Pra Loup** and **Le Sauze**) at the heart of one of the most remote valleys of the French Alps. Until a road was cut through the tight Ubaye gorges around **Le Lauzet** in the late 19th century, the area's best connections were with Italy via the **Col de Larche**: Savoy ceded it to France in 1713.

All routes south to the Maritime and Provençal Alps are tortuous, slow and closed for a long winter: the 60-km road to St-Etienne de Tinée peaks at the Cime de la Bonette, the highest main road in the Alps. The Col de la Cayolle road is even slower and very narrow. The Col d'Allos road is the least arduous. After the pass it follows the Verdon valley south past the small resort of Allos, good for access to the Mercantour National Park.

211

High above Lake Annecy, the Château de Menthon (guided tours) is the birthplace of the 11th-century saint, Bernard, who founded hospices at the high Alpine passes named after him.

Aix-les-Bains, a long-established Alpine spa

From St-Véran drive 6 km to the pilgrimage chapel Notre Dame de Clausis, beneath a splendid theater of frontier peaks. A marked path leads to the border at the Col de St-Véran in about one and three-quarter hours. From here it is about an hour's walk north along the crest to the Col de Chamoussière, skirting the Pic de Caramantran (9,925 feet). Return to the Clausis chapel by the GR58 trail. This walk requires sturdy footwear and good weather.

▶ ▷ ▷ **Bourget, Lac du, and Chambéry**

Like Lake Annecy, the slightly larger and deeper Lac du Bourget is long and thin. Much though it was admired by Romantic poets (notably Lamartine), its shoreline and surrounding mountains—long ridges towering above it on either side—are less varied than Annecy's. Its main town, **Aix-les-Bains**, an ancient spa and one of the grand Alpine resorts of the 19th century, is lively enough (as spas go), with a beach, gardens by the lake, plenty of sports on and off the water and boat trips to **Hautecombe Abbey**, mausoleum of the Savoyard dynasty and famous for its Gregorian chant. Most of the buildings are in neo-Gothic style. The main road around the southern tip of the lake is of no great interest, but the D914 runs high above the west bank through pretty farmland with good views.

Chambéry Now the busy prefecture of Savoie, Chambéry was the capital of the transalpine kingdom of Savoy until it lost its status and its Holy Shroud to Turin in the mid-16th century. Despite the high reputation of its herby vermouth, it hardly demands a visit, but there is a good regional **museum** next to the cathedral and an amusing 19th-century **elephant fountain** at the central crossroads. The Italianate arcades of **rue de Boigne** lead to the ducal castle and late Gothic **Sainte-Chapelle**. On the southeast edge of town, the home of Madame de Warens (**Les Charmettes**), where Rousseau spent six years (1736–42), has been restored as a museum.

▶ ▷ ▷ **Briançon and the Briançonnais**

The highest town in Europe (4,330 feet) plugs a strategic junction of valleys at the heart of the Dauphine Alps. Above the anonymous modern town that sprawls around a tangled road junction, the walled upper town stands splendidly intact, a gaunt citadel built by Vauban for Louis XIV but subsequently much altered and reinforced with outlying forts on the heights above the town and the Col de Montgenèvre.

Alpine crossroads At 6,068 feet, the Col de Montgenèvre is the easiest crossing of the western Alps, busy with armies and travelers throughout history and still kept open all winter. Since the opening of the Fréjus road tunnel the volume of traffic has declined, improving the quality of life at the border village and ski resort of **Montgenèvre**. A more picturesque route to Italy is via the peaceful **Névache Valley** and **Col de l'Echelle** (5,792 feet) to Bardonecchia. There are interesting churches at **Plampinet** (with frescoes) and Névache. Along the Guisane Valley to the west of Briançon, a succession of hamlets make up the ski resort of Serre Chevalier, named after a rounded peak (8,144 feet) accessible by cable car. Ski lifts from downtown Briançon to **Mont Prorel** (8,436 feet) have opened up additional skiing and summer walks, with views of the Durance Valley and, from the summit, the peaks of the Ecrins.

Chalets and sun To the south of Briançon, the remote and famously sunny **Queyras** (now a regional park) has a few small resorts. **St-Véran** is the most interesting, and

Autumn colors meet snow-covered crags near the crafts center of Aiguilles

at 6,560 feet, one of the highest villages in Europe. St-Véran's sundials, fountains and crosses, adorned with the instruments of the Passion, are typical of the region. One house with traditional Queyras interior is preserved as a museum. **Aiguilles** is the other main crafts center. The massive fortress above the village of **Château Queyras** and the fortified town of **Mont Dauphin** (above Guillestre) are both mostly Vauban's work.

High roads Motorists who are neither in a hurry nor hairpin-shy can travel the length of the Alps via the high road: 80 km from **Chamonix** to **Bourg St-Maurice** via the **Mont Blanc Tunnel** and **Col du Petit St-Bernard** (7,177 feet); 120 km to **St-Michel-de-Maurienne** via the **Col de l'Iseran** (9,086 feet); 67 km to **Briançon** via the **Col du Galibier** (8,679 feet) and **Col du Lautaret** (6,750 feet); 53 km to **Guillestre** via the **Col de l'Izoard** (7,741 feet); 51 km to **Jausiers** via the **Col de Vars** (6,924 feet); and 133 km to **Nice** via the **Cime de la Bonette** (9,191 feet), from which point it is downhill all the way to the sea. All the high passes close for the winter until the snow and ice has thawed in Spring.

Chamonix has the most spectacular ski lifts in the Alps. The most exciting trip is over the Mont Blanc massif to La Palud in Italy via the Aiguille du Midi and six stages of cable car and telecabin (take passport, and return by bus through the tunnel). On the oppposite side of the valley, the Brévent and Flégère cable cars give the best views of Mont Blanc and the snaking Mer de Glacé glacier respectively.

▶ ▶ ▶   Chamonix

Chamonix likes to add Mont Blanc to its name, and throws in "world capital of Alpinism and skiing" for good measure. If it added that the grandeur of its setting is unrivaled in Europe, no one would argue. The white dome of the highest alp (15,767 feet) officially occupies St-Gervais communal territory, but it was at Chamonix that the pioneers of Alpinism looked for a way to cross the chaotic mass of glaciers descending almost to the valley floor: The Glacier des Bossons drops 11,808 vertical feet at a gradient of almost 45 degrees.

Old and new A colorful, often overcrowded and traffic-plagued town of 10,000 inhabitants, Chamonix is a mixture of modern apartment buildings, old-fashioned villas and bulky hotels. Clientele and population are remarkably diverse: old people, rugged mountaineers and sporty vacationers who come for the climbing, skiing, hang gliding, golf and bar crawls. Near the central statue of Mont Blanc's 18th-century conquerors, Balmat and de Saussure, the **Musée Alpin** illustrates the history of the valley and Mont Blanc.

Chamonix now sprawls over the central section of the 15-km valley, where heavy traffic using the road tunnel through Mont Blanc to Italy is an added scourge. The belching procession of 1,000 huge trucks a day rarely lets up, and after a few days of fine weather the pollution haze on the valley floor is worthy of a city center. Above Chamonix the valley is more peaceful. **Argentière**, skiing focus of the valley, is the main resort, but for peace and quiet the best bases are the hamlet of **Le Lavancher** (superb views of the Chamonix aiguilles, and good walks) and the village of **Le Tour**.

Long walk The celebrated Tour du Mont Blanc (GRTMB) walk, via Italy, Switzerland and France, takes more than 10 days to complete. It can be cut in half by taking the cable cars or bus between **La Palud** and **Chamonix**, or joined briefly from any resort along the circuit. The best combination of easy walking and spectacular views is the south-facing balcony walk between **Planpraz** and **La Flégère**, both accessible by ski lift from Chamonix. It takes about two hours, and is nowhere arduous, although sturdy shoes are needed.

Mountaineering

■   Among early mountaineering exploits, one of the most impressive was the conquest of table-topped Mont Aiguille in 1492 by royal command. Curiosity about reported sightings of angels on the summit provoked this expedition, and it was the Enlightenment's spirit of scientific inquiry that gave further impetus to high Alpine exploration. ...■

Interest centered on Mont Blanc, visible from Geneva and increasingly well-known for its glaciers. In August 1786, 25 years after Geneva scientist Horace de Saussure offered a reward to the first man up Mont Blanc, the climb was achieved by a local doctor and guide, **Paccard** and **Balmat**. De Saussure went up with 18 guides and no ropes in 1787. On his return a **Colonel Beaufoy** set off immediately for the summit. This man "was almost the first of the mountaineering race," wrote the English Alpinist **Edward Whymper**: He climbed to amuse himself.

New explorers Colonel Beaufoy's idea of fun did not catch on until the late 19th century, when the railway brought a new generation of explorers to the Alps. In 1864 and '65, Whymper climbed the Aiguille Verte and the Grandes Jorasses in the Mont Blanc massif, the highest peak in the southern Alps (the Ecrins) and, in an expedition that killed four of his team, the Matterhorn in Switzerland.

Chamonix With its guides and scores of rocky pinnacles, Chamonix was the mountaineers' headquarters. Hotels in the village had telescopes through which anxious friends watched progress and, at the wave of a hat from on high, cracked a bottle of champagne. A smart advertiser set up a champagne billboard on the summit, but underestimated the power of the elements, as did the aging **Dr. Janssen** of Meudon, who was carried up Mont Blanc in a litter and devoted years to building an

observatory on top. Completed in 1893, it registered a low temperature of –43° C before sliding off toward the valley as part of a glacier.

New tests Climbers have since continued to seek ever greater challenges—most recently, climbing without ropes or nails driven into the rock. At the same time, competitive climbing on indoor walls has become a TV sport. Traditionalists scoff, but dedicated climbers need the sponsorship celebrity brings. Many mountain resorts now have these artificial climbing walls for practice.

Mont Blanc, Europe's highest peak

<< Chamonards formed the first company of mountain guides in 1832. >>

The famous green and less potent yellow Chartreuse liqueurs, based on a secret herbal elixir whose recipe was imparted to the monks in 1605, are no longer produced at La Grande Chartreuse but at the small town of Voiron (northwest of Grenoble), where the vast cellars are open to visitors. All but the recipe is revealed, and free tasting is offered.

▷▷▷ Chartreuse, Massif de la

Climbing abruptly from the Isère between **Chambéry** and **Grenoble**, the wettest massif in the Alps is thickly forested, at its most beautiful in autumn. Roads are narrow and the main resort, **St-Pierre-de-Chartreuse**, is small. A road from the Col de la Porte leads to open pastures near the top of the **Charmant Som**, a good viewpoint over the remote niche of **La Grande Chartreuse**, founded by St. Bruno in 1084. The present 17th-century buildings, inhabited by a few dozen monks, are not open to visitors and women are not supposed to enter monastic land; but there is an interesting museum at the entrance (**La Correrie**). The monks built the road along the gorge of the Guiers Mort from **St-Pierre** to **St-Laurent du Pont**.

▷▷▷ Die

An ancient walled town beside the Drôme at the foot of the southern flank of the Vercors massif, Die has a few fragments of its Roman buildings: a triumphal arch (Porte St-Marcel) at the southern edge of town and Roman columns in the cathedral porch. The local sparkling wine (Clairette de Die) is one of the best champagne substitutes.

▶▷▷ Evian

A major supplier of mineral water, Evian was transformed from old walled village to grand spa resort after Baron de Blonay gave his lakeside château and park to the town in 1865. Gardens, leafy promenade, domed casino and baths took their place; big hotels have followed as Evian has grown into a major conference center. There is plenty to do: boat trips on the lake, exhibitions and a full range of sports.

▶▷▷ Grenoble

A go-ahead, high-rise, modern university city, Grenoble fills a broad gap in the mountains, with the Vercors and Chartreuse massifs to west and north, and the higher peaks of the Belledonne to the east. The center of life is the pedestrian area around the places Grenette and St-André on the left bank of the Isère. A gondola lift spans the river to the rock-top **Fort de la Bastille**, a good viewpoint with a vintage car museum. Paths lead down to the Musée Dauphinois (regional history and crafts) and the church of St-Laurent. The relocated Musée de Grenoble has an outstanding modern art collection.

▶▷▷ Léman, Lac (Lake Geneva)

The giant of the Alpine lakes is a 70-km-long bulge in the course of the Rhône, which enters in the east near Montreux and exits via Geneva. From the frontier near Geneva a minor road follows the shore of the narrow part of the lake (Petit Lac) to **Yvoire**, a picturesque medieval village. **Excenevex** has the best beach on the lake. **Thonon** is the main town of the French bank and Evian's great rival as resort and spring, with a more everyday lifestyle. Surrounded by its vineyards to the east of town, the splendid **Château de Ripaille** was the retreat of Amadée VIII, first duke of Savoy, who was pulled out of retirement to be anti-pope (Felix V) during the Great Schism. Between Evian and the Swiss border at **St-Gingolph**, mountains climb steeply from the lake's deepest waters. For a bird's-eye view of the lake, take the cable car from **Thollon** (12 km from Evian by the D24) to the **Pic de Memise** (5,501 feet). Thonon and Evian are the best places for boat trips.

▶ ▷ ▷   Lyon

France's second city, famous for its trade fairs and bankers in the Renaissance and its silk and textile industries ever since, spreads over the confluence of Saône and Rhône. On the narrow peninsula between the two rivers, the vast place Bellecour and the place des Terreaux are the twin poles of civic life. Between them, the rue de la République is the city's main shopping axis. There are excellent museums nearby: Musée des Beaux-Arts on the place des Terreaux; Musée des Arts Décoratifs and Musée Historique des Tissus to the south of place Bellecour. The restored old quarter on the right bank of the Saône is now the focus of Lyonnais chic: Renaissance palaces (rue St-Jean and rue du Boeuf), designer shops and restaurants, lively *bouchons* (bistros). Near the unlovely Fourvière basilica there are excavations of Roman Lugdunum and a good Gallo-Roman museum.

217

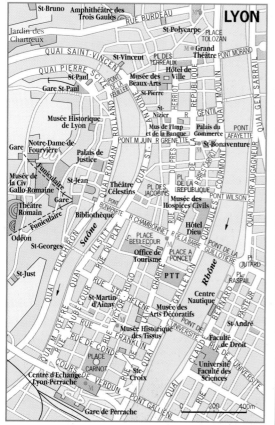

Fourvière basilica, Lyon

Mont Aiguille

▶ ▷ ▷ La Maurienne

The Arc valley is the southernmost of Savoie's great thoroughfares. The main valley, from the dreary border town of **Modane** to the confluence of Arc and Isère near **Chambéry**, is dull, dark country, punctuated with power stations and factories. St-Jean-de-Maurienne (see page 219) is worth a stop for the cathedral, with beautiful 15th-century choir stalls and an alabaster reliquary for three of the Baptist's fingers.

The most developed of the few resorts above the valley is **Valloire**, on the road to the Galibier pass, well placed for an overnight stop. It has an ornate Baroque church and has not lost all its village charm.

Above Modane, the upper Arc valley (**Haute Maurienne**) is of greater interest. Apart from **Lanslebourg**, at the foot of the Mont Cenis pass, the villages have charm and a wealth of art in their churches. The best are at **Avrieux**, **Termignon**, **Lanslevillard** and **Bessans**, where the carving tradition is maintained. **Termignon** is the main gateway to the high mountains of the Vanoise. **Bonneval**, the last village before the long climb to the lofty Iseran pass (summer skiing), is a showpiece unspoiled mountain village in a severe setting, with a few simple hotels.

A typical Maurienne chalet

For many great armies and Grand Tourists on their way to Rome, the passage of Mont Cenis was the centerpiece of the journey. Local guides (known as *marrons*) loaded winter travelers into sleighlike carriages that they guided downhill at high speed, with frequent capsizes. Napoleon had the sweeping hairpin road built, and for a brief period, before the opening of the Fréjus tunnel in 1872, there was a railway over the pass. A reservoir now fills much of the broad basin between the pass and the Italian border.

▷ ▷ ▷ Mont Aiguille

A table-topped tower on the southern flank of the Vercors, Mont Aiguille (6,842 feet) is not remotely like a needle. Its previous name, Mont Inaccessible, had to go once an intrepid team had scaled the cliffs in 1492 by order of Charles VIII, to check for a colony of angels. All they encountered were flowers, birds and chamois. It is well seen from the N75 south of Grenoble.

▷ ▷ ▷ Morzine

A large, traditional year-round resort at the heart of the Chablais between Mont Blanc and Lake Geneva, Morzine fills a complicated junction of narrow valleys and suffers from traffic. It does, however, have delightful surroundings, dotted with chalets and mountain restaurants—good walking country with or without the help of the various ski lifts above Morzine and its smaller neighbor, **Les Gets**. A hairpin road or cable car lead to the cliff-top modern resort of **Avoriaz**, the well-chosen site for a science-fiction film festival every January.

Drive The Croix de Fer and Glandon passes

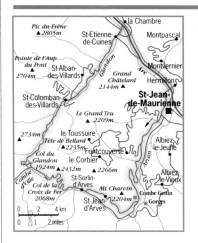

into a beautiful landscape of open high pastures above the modest mountain resort of **St-Sorlin d'Arves**.

D926 as far as Col de la Croix de Fer. D927 to Col du Glandon and La Chambre.
The route switchbacks over the **Croix de Fer** (6,783 feet) and **Glandon** (6,311 feet) passes, close neighbors with differing views. To the south of the Croix de Fer, the spiky **Aiguilles d'Arves** (on the left) and the glaciated **Grandes Rousses** massif together frame the more distant **Meije**.

Start at St-Jean-de-Maurienne.
This splendidly varied 54 km of mountain road presents few map-reading difficulties but demands full concentration from the driver at all times, climbing steeply via tunnels and hairpins from the Maurienne up the Arvan valley before emerging

The **Col du Glandon** gives a good view north to Mont Blanc. The descent to **La Chambre** is also narrow, mostly tortuous and in places steep, requiring careful attention to the road.

Take the N6 for the return journey to St-Jean.

Drive Over the mountain from Morzine

Start at Morzine. D354 to Samoëns.
From Morzine it is a beautiful drive over the mountain to **Samoëns** (woods and orchards) via the **Col de Joux Plane**, a popular picnic spot with a view of Mont Blanc. At Samoëns, an old village once famous for its stone masons, a 550-year-old lime tree shades the central square. There are botanical gardens and summer and winter sports facilities, including river rafting and skiing.

D907 to Sixt-Fer-à-Cheval (for excursions to Cirque du Fer à Cheval and Cascade du Rouget).
At **Sixt**, 13th- to 17th-century former abbey buildings surround another fine lime tree. East of Sixt the road ends beneath a magnificent horseshoe of cliffs and waterfalls (**Fer à Cheval**). To the south, the narrow D29 climbs to the **Cascade**

du Rouget; hikers can continue uphill to more waterfalls.

D907 back to Samoëns and Taninges; D902 to Les Gets and Morzine.
The return from Samoëns to Morzine passes the small resort of **Les Gets**, with ski lifts to **Mont Chéry** (5,999 feet), a superb viewpoint.

Skiers congregate on the slopes of the Alpe d'Huez

A two-stage telecabin climbs from La Grave to the Col des Ruillans (10,496 feet) for a close-up view of the Meije and a distant one of Mont Blanc. The surroundings are a glacier: not for walkers. From the mid-station it is about an hour's walk up to the picturesque old Evariste Chancel refuge/restaurant, via the Puy Vachier lake, rich in trout. A well-marked path leads down through woods to the river below the village. Stick to the path (cliff danger to the left). The descent from Chancel to La Grave takes about an hour and a half.

▷▷▷ L'Oisans

Facing each other across the dark Romanche valley, L'**Alpe d'Huez** and **Les Deux Alpes** are the big ugly sisters of Dauphiné skiing, with high open snowfields in easy reach of Grenoble. In summer both offer plenty of sport, including glacier skiing. L'Alpe d'Huez is reached by a famous hairpin climb (a punishing finale to one stage of the Tour de France) from the small town of **Bourg d'Oisans**. A summer road continues over the Col de Sarenne to the picturesque old villages of **Clavans** and **Besse**. The narrow Vénéon valley road leads to the heart of the **Ecrins massif**, the highest mountains in the southern Alps and a famous climbing area. At the end of the dark road, **La Bérarde** is an austere village, mainly of interest to climbers. In winter the road is closed beyond **St-Christophe** and its population dwindles to one.

Beside river and main road to the west of the Lautaret pass, the rough old village of **La Grave** and its Romanesque church are dominated by the mighty pillars and hanging glaciers of the **Meije** (13,064 feet), which is best admired from the road up to **Le Chazelet**, a delightfully rustic village. La Grave has simple hotels, a good cheese shop and a tall, wild ski area with gentle glacier slopes open for summer skiing.

▷▷▷ Serre Ponçon, Lac de

When full, the V-shaped reservoir at the confluence of the Durance and Ubaye Rivers is popular for water sports, especially windsurfing, for which the prevailing winds are excellent. **Savines-le-Lac** is the main lakeside resort, a modern and characterless place. The old town of **Embrun** makes a more appealing base, with simple hotels and an Italianate 12th-century cathedral, where marble lions support the columns of the main doorway. The tourist office is housed in a chapel with 15th-century murals. A special geological feature of the area is the **Demoiselle Coiffée**—a pillar of earth saved from erosion by the boulder on top. The best examples are beside the road climbing steeply from **Rebollon** (on the Sisteron road) to **Mont Colombis**.

The Rhône Valley

■ **The Rhône Valley remains what it has always been: a north–south thoroughfare for travelers and traders. Motorway and railway follow the broad river past power stations, cement factories, unlovely towns and vineyards that produce muscular red and white wines. The motorway plunges through the middle of Lyon—a hazardous crossing in view of the Lyonnais' customary lunacy at the wheel. ...■**

Lyon (see also page 217) has had a long history of success, since its foundation in 43 BC and its subsequent elevation to the status of capital in Roman-occupied Gaul. Its strategic position on the banks of the Saône and Rhône rivers, on the route between Paris and the Mediterranean, has made this a prosperous city, and the focus of busy development.

221

There are plenty of aesthetic attractions for visitors— mainly due to the commercial and industrial (silk and textiles) successes of the past: Wealthy merchants and bankers of the 16th century built tall, elegant houses that still stand, some having been extended upward with an extra floor.

To the south of Lyon the mountains of the Vercors and the eastern wall of the Massif Central enclose the valley before it opens out beyond **Montélimar**, city of nougat and gateway to the land of almonds and honey, **Provence**.

Valley cuisine Food is the main reason to visit the Rhône Valley, rather than pass swiftly through it. The most famous landmarks on a gastronomic itinerary are **Paul Bocuse** at Collonges, a northern suburb of Lyon; **Pyramide** at Vienne; and **Pic** at Valence. These are not the only outstanding restaurants in the region, and many would say they are no longer the best. But they are generally regarded as holy places in the modern history of French cooking.

Valley sights Sightseeing interest is contrastingly modest: an outstanding vintage car/motorbike/bus/ bicycle museum (Musée de l'Automobile) at **Roche-taillée sur Saône**, north of Lyon; a Roman theater and well-preserved temple, and two interesting medieval churches (the cathedral and St-André-le-Bas) at **Vienne**; a restored Romanesque cathedral at **Valence**, where the museum has a fine collection of Roman drawings by Hubert Robert, leading exponent of this favorite 18th-century genre; and a few well-sited fortress ruins, notably **Crussol**, near Valence.

East of Lyon, on the way to or from the Alps, the film-set walled village of **Pérouges** (on a hill outside Meximieux) has been scrupulously restored and preserved, and its old traditions of craftsmanship have been revived, albeit for tourists.

N 7
MONTELIMAR
NOUGAT
LE BOUQUET
Z.I. Nord du Meyrol BP 71
26202 MONTELIMAR CEDE

Pont en Royans, where rivers converge

La Vallouise see panels.

▶ ▶ ▷   La Vanoise

The oldest French national park, founded in 1963, is a wilderness of empty high valleys, glaciers and rocky peaks culminating at the 12,644-foot **Grande Casse**, and bordering the older Italian Gran Paradiso National Park. The peripheral area has seen ski resort development on a scale unrivaled elsewhere in the Alps. **Val d'Isère, Tignes, Les Arcs, La Plagne, Courchevel, Méribel** and **Val Thorens** are the big resorts. More charming alternatives are the old villages of **Pralognan, Champagny** and **Peisey-Nancroix** on the Tarentaise side of the park; **Bonneval, Termignon** and **Aussois** on the Maurienne side. The old village of Champagny en Vanoise is a center of traditional Beaufort cheese, the best of hard French Alpine cheeses, produced throughout Savoie. Its quality depends on the high pastures and flowers. Winter Beaufort, produced from cows fed on hay, is a quite different, soapy thing.

Hiking trails cross the park and refuges offer simple accommodation. At the heart of the park, the **Vallon de la Leisse** is rich in wildlife. The parking lot north of Termignon is the closest access point.

▶ ▷ ▷   Vercors

To the south and west of Grenoble, the unbroken walls of the Vercors rise abruptly to peaks of over 6,560 feet. Behind lies a tranquil, thickly forested highland region. Its most striking features are the limestone gorges of rivers that converge at **Pont en Royans** before feeding the Isère. **Villard de Lans** is the largest of the modest resorts, a good base for impressive drives—along the dark Gorges de la Bourne and Grands Goulets (very narrow) and the St-Jean-en-Royans to Vassieux road (D76). The Vercors was a Resistance base until 1944, when German forces launched an aerial assault on the region and the villages of **Vassieux, La Chapelle** and **St-Nizier** were razed. Vassieux has a Resistance museum.

■ In 1874 a visiting lawyer recorded his impressions of Bonneval-sur-Arc, at the head of the Haute Maurienne: "low gray houses, half buried and huddled tightly together for warmth. In winter the inhabitants live in the underground stables warmed by their animals. Wood being rare and coal too expensive, the usual fuel is sun-dried dung. Snow covers the ground for six or seven months a year, often cutting communications and trapping the villagers like marmots in their burrows." ...■

Although modernized, Bonneval has changed remarkably little externally. In the absence of local forest, the houses are built almost entirely of stone, wood being reserved for the balconies. The Bonnevalains still dry dung in the sun as a fuel.

Sun and shelter Alpine architecture is adapted to the hardships of mountain life. Warmth, exposure to the sun and winter storage space for animals, grain and the staple ingredients of the Alpine diet—long-life cheeses, hams and big disks of dark bread—are the priorities.

In some places villages are widely spread across the steep sunny slope (*adret*) of a valley. **St-Véran**, in the Queyras, is a fine example. Elsewhere, as at **Bonneval**, where the slopes are too steep, the houses are clustered around the church on the valley floor at a safe distance from regular avalanche paths.

Wooden castles Except at high altitudes, wood is generally plentiful in the Alps, and widely used in the construction of the chalet (the word is a diminutive of château). In the northern Alps a few old chalets with wooden roofs and chimneys survive. More often, chalet roofs are rough stone tiles (*lauzes*), gently pitched to support a thick insulating blanket of snow for the winter. In the Vercors steeper roofs are the custom, and the end walls are traditionally stepped to facilitate access to the roof.

Most chalets are equippped with large, sheltered balconies exposed to the sun, for storing firewood and putting things out to dry. Grain is stored either under the eaves or in separate buildings, raised on stone stilts to prevent the rats from getting in.

Alpine architecture at Bonneval

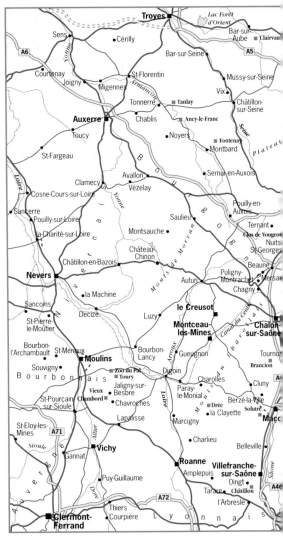

This is the warm heartland of gastronomic France, a welcoming and colorful landscape of dazzling mustard fields, rich pastures and golden villages. There are snails (France's finest) and smelly cheeses, best beef from the gleaming white Charolais herds, and the sumptuous wines of the Côte d'Or. The best wine tourism is at Beaune, headquarters of the industry. Great pageantry surrounds the climax of the wine calendar in November, a famous harvest festival and wine auction at Beaune.

The fancy dress and the noble brotherhoods of *vignerons* (wine producers) recall the golden age of Burgundy, when its 14th- and 15th-century Valois dukes lived in splendor appropriate to the imperial status they craved. In the Hundred Years' War they skillfully switched allegiance between French and English camps. Their real power base was in the Low Countries. Only

BURGUNDY AND THE JURA

BURGUNDY AND THE JURA

Map labels:

Vignory · Contrexéville · **Épinal** · Gérardmer · Munster
Chaumont · Darney · Remiremont · *1362m* Hohneck
Nogent · Bourbonne-les-Bains · Plombières-les-Bains · *1424m* le Grand Ballon
Montigny-le-Roi · le Thillot · Thann
Langres · Luxeuil-les-Bains · **Ballon d'Alsace**
Lure · Ronchamp
A31 · Champlitte · Vesoul · **Belfort**
-sur-ille · Héricourt · Delle
Gray · **Montbéliard** · Audincourt
Dijon · Pesmes · **A36** · Pont-de-Roide
Auxonne · Baume-les-Dames · *Doubs* · Maîche
Cîteaux · Ornans · **Besançon** · Cirque de Consolation
Dole · Arc-et-Senans · Saut de Doubs · Morteau
Seurre · Salins-les-Bains · **Montbenoît**
Arbois · Reculée des Planches · Pontarlier · Cluse de Pontalier
Poligny
Baumes-les-Messieurs · Champagnole · Malbuisson · **CH**
Lons-le-Saunier · Perte de l'Ain · Mouthe
Louhans · Cirque de Baume · Doucier · Gorges de la Langouette
Cuisery · Cascades du Hérisson
Morez · les Rousses · *Lac Léman*
St-Amour · Divonne-les-Bains · Evian-les-Bains
St-Claude · Yvoire · Thonon-les-Bains
A40 · Dyonnax · *Mont Colomby de Gex 1689m* · Gex · *Chablais*
Bourg-en-Bresse · Annemasse · Morzine
átillon-Chalaronne · Nantua · Bonneville · Cluses
Pont-d'Ain · Bellegarde · **A40** · St-Julien-en-Genevois · la Roche-sur-Foron · Flaine · Argentière
Hauteville-Lompnès · Seyssel · Chamonix
rouges · Rumilly · **A41** · **Annecy**
A42 · *Mont Blanc 4807m* · **I**
YON · **Aix-les-Bains** · *Rhône*

Rivers: *Marne*, *Meuse*, *Moselle*, *Saône*, *Langres*, *Canal de la Marne à la Saône*, *Ognon*, *Doubs*, *Saône*, *Ain*

Scale: 0 — 20 — 40 — 60 km · 0 — 10 — 20 — 30 miles

when the English were finally expelled could the French crown turn its attention to the problem of Burgundy. The struggle between the valiant knight Duke Charles the Bold and the arch manipulator King Louis IX can be seen as the clash of two eras. Charles went down fighting in 1477 and France took control. In an earlier age (the 10th to 12th centuries), Burgundy saw the foundation of two monastic orders: first at Cluny, later at Cîteaux near Dijon, where Bernard of Clairvaux led the reaction to Cluniac decadence. Burgundy has fine Romanesque churches and abbeys in unadorned Cistercian style.

The old county of Burgundy, Franche Comté, is quite different—a remote region of forests, mountains (the Jura) and notoriously unruly inhabitants. The Jura offers its own unusual wines and an escape to the simple life.

Louis Pasteur's house in Arbois

Louis Pasteur (1822–95) was born at Dole and five years later moved with his family to Arbois. Pasteur discovered the causes of fermentation and developed the heat treatment of milk known as pasteurization; his work opened a new era of preventive and curative medicine.

The salt springs in Lons-le-Saunier and Salins-les-Bains have been exploited since prehistoric times. At Salins, a handsome old town hemmed in between hills beside the fast-flowing Furieuse River, the salt mine is still operational and open to visitors. In underground galleries salty brine is pumped from a depth of 820 feet. The brine is then reduced to salt in large cauldrons over a coal fire. These days the salt waters of Salins are used only for medicinal purposes (whence Salins les Bains).

▷▷▷ Ain, Vallée de l'

The much-dammed River Ain feeds hydroelectric plants as it descends through rapids, gorges and reservoirs on the 190-km journey from its source near Champagnole to the Rhône. In and around the upper valley, watery beauty spots include the Gorges de la Langouette and the Perte de l'Ain, where the river disappears into a rocky cleft. But the outstanding attraction (except during a drought) is the Cascades du Hérisson, a series of magnificent waterfalls reached by D326 (and subsequently on foot) from Doucier. There is fishing and boating on the Lac de Chalain, east of Lons-le-Saunier, and a number of water sports centers on the long stretches of reservoir lower down the Ain.

▶▷▷ Ancy-le-Franc, Château de

A fine Renaissance château, still in the hands of its original owners, the family of Clermont-Tonnerre, Ancy-le-Franc was designed in the mid-16th century in a new classical style. The sobriety of the exterior is quite different from the exuberant ornamentation of earlier Loire châteaus, and contrasts with the more complex design of the inner court. Inside (guided tours), much of the furniture and decoration is original.

▷▷▷ Arbois

The home of Louis Pasteur is an attractive honey-colored small town beside the Cuisance, close to some of the best Jura scenery. Arbois produces interesting, little-known wine, including one of the best of all rosés, much appreciated by Henri IV, and the exceptionally strong and expensive *vin jaune* (from Château-Chalon and Arbois), which is not bottled for years and keeps for up to a century. *Poularde au vin jaune* is a ubiquitous local specialty. *Vin de Paille* is made from overripe grapes traditionally dried on straw. There is a small wine museum near the arcaded central square, and the main production house, Henri Maire, opens its doors to visitors and offers tastings (not of *vin jaune*!). Pasteur's house is beside the river on the way out of town toward Dole.

▶▷▷ Arc-et-Senans

Although incomplete, the monumental complex of buildings (Sallines Royales) erected for the royal saltworks near Salins is a rare and fascinating survival of late 18th-century industrial architecture by the visionary Claude Nicolas Ledoux (1736–1806). Eleven buildings of the ambitious project for an entire Utopian town, built on a concentric plan, form a semicircle around the director's house, with a handsome colonnaded portico. It is flanked by the main salt evaporation halls, where salt was produced until the works were abandoned in the late 19th century. The buildings are now used for various futuristic exhibitions and a presentation of Ledoux's work and ideas.

▶▶▷ Autun

Autun has interesting survivals from antiquity, including two town gateways and fragments of the largest Roman theater in Gaul. But its great treasure is the 12th-century cathedral of St Lazare, with outstanding carved tympanum and a wealth of lively carving on the capitals inside. The nearby Musée Rolin has a rich collection of Gallo-Roman and Gothic statuary (a lovely polychrome Virgin), and the 15th-century Moulins Master's beautiful painting of the Nativity.

▶▷▷ Auxerre

An old town of cobbled streets and timbered houses, Auxerre makes a good first Burgundian stop for motorway travelers on the way south from Paris. The most central of the three churches turning their backs to the river is the Gothic cathedral of St-Etienne. Its elaborate lopsided facade was robbed of much of its sculptural decoration during the Wars of Religion. There are beautiful 13th-century windows inside, and 11th-century frescoes in the crypt. The crypt of the former abbey of St-Germain is still older and has frescoes from the mid-9th century, depicting scenes from the life of the saint. The main square (place Leclerc) has a Renaissance gateway with 17th-century astronomical clock.

▶▷▷ Avallon

Old Avallon, a well-preserved walled town, is a good place to stretch the legs at the end of a day at the wheel and has hotels and restaurants for most pockets in town and nearby. Inside the ramparts, all is convincingly old and cobbled. A 15th-century watchtower spans the main street, the old church of St-Lazare had good carvings on the facade doorway and there are gardens outside the walls, looking out over rolling Burgundian countryside and the leafy Cousin valley, which has good secluded hotels.

France's three greatest rivers, the Loire, Seine and Rhône, have added to Burgundy's navigable rivers to create a 1,200-km network of waterways, now little used for commercial traffic (except for the Canal du Centre between Digoin and Chalons) and ideal for slow-moving houseboat vacations. The best choices are the Canal du Bourgogne (at its best in the Auxois, between Tonnerre and Vénarey) and the Canal du Nivernais, which crosses wonderfully peaceful countryside between Decize and Cravant (south of Auxerre). Two of the main suppliers of rentals are Bâteaux de Bourgogne at Auxerre (tel: 86 52 18 99) and Burgundy Cruisers at Cravant (86 81 54 55). Both offer bicycle rentals.

Gateway to the former abbey of St-Germain in Auxerre

The Burgundy Vineyards

■ **The hills of Burgundy produce the world's greatest white wine (Montrachet), the most expensive red (Romanée Conti) and also everday Beaujolais by the unpretentious boatload. About four-fifths of burgundy is red. ...■**

The wines The greatest vineyards form a long narrow strip (only 4,000 hectares in total) along a southeast facing slope extending south from Dijon and past Beaune. This is the Côte d'Or, of which there are two halves. Between Nuits St-Georges and Dijon, the Côte de Nuits vineyards (including Gevrey Chambertin, Vosne Romanée and Vougeot) produce red wine. The southern half is the Côte de Beaune, which makes red and white. Villages include Aloxe Corton, Pommard, Meursault and the two Montrachets (Chassagne and Puligny).

Golden-green wines of a different style, but scarcely less prestigious, are produced at Chablis near Auxerre. Geographically and in the taste of its wines, Chablis is closer to Champagne than the Côte d'Or.

The output of the small Côte Chalonnaise, a few miles south of the Côte d'Or, is no match for the Grands Crus (see page 229) to the north but is fine wine by any other criterion. Mercurey and Rully are the best-known appellations. South of Tournus, a large area of the Mâconnais and Beaujolais produces excellent everyday wines, mostly white in the Mâconnais, almost all red in Beaujolais. In northwestern Burgundy, Pouilly-sur-Loire's white wines have more in common with those of its neighbour Sancerre than any burgundy. Pouilly Fumé is its best wine, not to be confused with Pouilly Fuissé, pride of the Mâconnais.

The grapes In Burgundy proper, the Chardonnay grape is used throughout for white wine, Pinot Noir for red. Pouilly Fumé is made from the Sauvignon grape, Pouilly-sur-Loire from the Chasselas. In the Beaujolais the Gamay thrives on sandy ground, giving light and fruity wine that is drunk young—often within weeks of the harvest (*beaujolais nouveau*).

Vineyards and tasting Many of the finest vineyards belonged to the church, whose estates were broken up after the Revolution. The high price of the best wines is another reason for fragmentation: Prime vineyards cost as much as 5 million francs a hectare and change hands in tiny lots. The 50-hectare vineyard of Clos de Vougeot is split between 60 growers, who produce wines of different character and quality all called Clos de Vougeot. Many of the big *négotiants* (wholesale merchants, such as Calvet, Bouchard, Drouhin) are based at Beaune. A few welcome visitors and offer tastings but many charge a fee, and there is pressure to buy. Much the best alternative is to pay to visit the Marché Aux Vins in Beaune, a cooperative where a fine selection of bottles stands open at your disposal, in tasting order—from

There are few impressive vineyard châteaus to rival those in the Médoc, and the villages themselves lack the charm of the Alsace wine route. Clos de Vougeot is one of the few exceptions to the no-châteaus rule. Originally a Cistercian property, it is now the headquarters of the proud Confrérie des Chevaliers du Tastevin, who hold banquets and initiation ceremonies there. The interior (guided tours) has vaulted cellars and old wine presses.

Vins de la Côte de BUXY

white to beaujolais to the big reds of the Côte d'Or—with only discreet supervision and a generous time limit to make sure you don't overindulge. A *tastevin* (wine taster) and spittoons are provided. Tasting at the 16th-century Château de Meursault is organized similarly. Beaujolais is higher and steeper hill country than Burgundy, almost mountainous in places. Driving is slow but pretty, and many villages have great charm, with tastings at wine growers' cooperatives. The best area to explore is southwest of Villefranche, but this is not Grand Cru country. There are lovely ruins at Châtillon and Oingt, 9th-century murals and capitals in the church at Ternand.

Classification Burgundy production and labeling are strictly controlled and classified. On the Côte d'Or the best vineyards (called *climats*) are designated Grands Crus (32, including Richebourg, Romanée Conti, Chambertin and Montrachet). Next comes a larger number of Premiers Crus; then vineyards entitled to use the communal name (Gevrey Chambertin, Beaune, and so on); finally plain Bourgogne. Chablis also has Grands Crus and Premiers Crus; followed by Chablis and Petit Chablis. In the Mâconnais, Pouilly-Fuissé and St-Véran are the best appellations. Mâcon plus the name of a village (Mâcon-Viré, for example) indicates a better wine than Mâcon Villages, which is better than plain Mâcon. Beaujolais also has a superior subsection of Beaujolais-Villages and ten Grands Crus, of which Moulin à Vent is usually rated the best. Unlike most Beaujolais wines, it keeps.

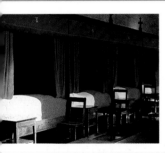

■ **If half a day en route is all you can afford for the region, devote it to Beaune, capital of burgundy with a small *b* (the wine), at the heart of the area's most prestigious vineyards. Ducal capital until the 14th century, it remains a medium-size town with its old walls and town gates intact. Its position at a motorway junction two and a half hours south of Paris is ideal for a break in the journey. ...■**

230

Hôtel Dieu On the main square in the heart of the old town, the market hall houses the tourist office. Across the street is the Hôtel Dieu, an outwardly unspectacular charitable hospital founded in 1443 by Nicolas Rolin, chancellor of Burgundy and great art patron. A unique survival, the Hôtel Dieu functioned as a hospital until 1971 and is now an old people's home, staffed by nuns and funded by the famous annual auction of the produce of its many Côte de Beaune vineyards. The auction sets the annual price level for burgundy and is the centerpiece of the *Trois Glorieuses*, a three-day wine festival in late November. The other two events are banquets at Clos de Vougeot and Meursault.

From the entrance portico, you can glimpse the brilliantly colorful tiled

Beaune lies in the very heart of Burgundy's most celebrated vineyards

roof of the Hôtel Dieu's beautiful courtyard, but it is well worth taking the guided tour to see the old pharmacy, the kitchens (still in use) and the vaulted 230-foot ward, which remains in its original disposition: beds (with room for two in each) in the nave, curtained off from the choir and altar except for services. The original altarpiece, Van der Weyden's magnificent polyptych of the Last Judgment is now displayed in a separate museum section, with tapestries also from the main ward.

Before you leave The 12th- to 13th-century church of Notre Dame has beautiful tapestries of the life of the Virgin (not on show in winter). There is an excellent wine museum near the church, good wine and food shops on the pedestrian streets near the market square, and an unmissable wine-tasting opportunity at the Marché Aux Vins, opposite the Hôtel Dieu (see pages 228–229).

Medieval Monasteries

■ **In 910, 12 monks left the abbey of Baume les Messiers and founded a new community at Cluny, not far from Mâcon. Under abbots answerable only to Rome, Cluny's influence spread rapidly, and hundreds of dependent houses were founded throughout Europe. ...■**

The abbey of Cluny The mother abbey's 581-foot-long third church, built between 1080 and 1130 at the height of Cluniac power, was the largest and most splendid church in Christendom, unsurpassed by any Gothic cathedral. If the heavenly host could be content with earthly habitation, declared one impressed visitor, this would be the ambulatory of angels. Cluny later fell into decline under absentee abbots and was systematically dismantled after the

Cistercian austerity Cluniac churches were erected to glorify God; the more splendid, the better. In 1098 a new abbey was founded at Cîteaux near Dijon, in a spirit of reaction to the excesses of Cluniac life and art. A 21-year-old local nobleman, known to history as St. Bernard of Clairvaux, went to Cîteaux in 1112 and later founded an abbey at Clairvaux (now a prison, near Bar-sur-Aube). Preaching a return to the frugal spirit of the Benedictine rule,

Revolution, when the Cluniac order was suppressed. A single tower of the transept remains standing to give an idea of its scale and style. A grain store also survives, and houses a collection of capitals from the church. Of many examples of Cluniac architecture in Burgundy (especially in the Brionnais), **Paray-le-Monial**'s church, contemporary with Cluny, is almost a replica of the lost original on reduced scale. A chapel at **Berzé-la-Ville** (between Mâcon and Cluny) has a series of early frescoes, probably by the artists employed at Cluny itself.

Top: Berzé-la-Ville; above: Cluny

Bernard condemned ornamental figurative carving and the waste of money lavished on vast churches; for him, even bell towers were superfluous in an abbey. Life under the Cistercian rule was austere in the extreme, and the architectural style of the monasteries is one of unadorned simplicity. There is no better example than **Fontenay,** near Montbard (see page 233). Cîteaux was suppressed in 1790 but revived in 1898 and rebuilt as the headquarters of the Trappist order.

Besançon, seen from the citadel

King of chickens, chicken of kings: the *poulet de Bresse* is to the battery-reared oven-ready bird what a Grand Cru burgundy is to table wine. Bresse is in fact a poultry appellation, with limited output and strict production rules. The birds are sold with a seal, a numbered ring and a certificate of origin. In their early months they enjoy the freedom of the farmyard before spending two weeks in a finishing room, where they are fed a mixture of creamy milk and wheat. The result is peerless white meat, firm but succulent, with no fat.

▶▷▷ Besançon

The capital of Franche-Comté, Besançon is a place for sightseeing on a wet day. It is a dignified, if somewhat gloomy, city, with fine facades along the Grande Rue and a Roman triumphal arch next to the cathedral. The latter is a building of many periods: Its contents include a Roman altar, a 19th-century astronomical clock, the 16th-century tomb of diplomat and art patron Ferry Carondelet, and a painting of the Virgin and Child commissioned by him from Fra Bartolommeo (1512). The Musée des Beaux Arts has tapestries, ceramics, clocks and paintings, including works by Titian, David, Géricault, Renoir, Bonnard and many local Courbets. The citadel encloses a zoo and several museums.

▷▷▷ Bresse

From the Saône to the Ain at the foot of the Jura, the Bresse plain is rapidly crossed now that there is uninterrupted motorway from Mâcon to Geneva. Travelers who prefer the slow road can admire the area's handsome old barns and farmhouses, their roofs almost reaching the ground. Its busy market town, Bourg-en-Bresse, is great fun on market day (Wednesday and Saturday morning). The main sightseeing attraction is the church at Brou (see below).

▶▶▷ Brou

A suburb of Bourg-en-Bresse, Brou contains some rare treasures of late Gothic art in the 16th-century monastery church, behind which lies a story. Margaret of Bourbon vowed to upgrade the priory if her husband (count of Bresse) recovered from a hunting accident. He did, but she died soon afterwards. When their son Philibert died young in 1504, his young widow, Margaret of Austria, took it upon herself to fulfill the promise. The choir contains the three beautiful marble tombs of Philibert and both Margarets, painted windows, and carved wood and stonework, all of breathtaking quality. The adjacent monastery is now a regional museum.

▶▷▷ Châtillon-sur-Seine

The treasure in the museum of this peaceful little town is a huge 6th-century BC bronze vase, decorated with a relief frieze of warriors in horse-drawn chariots. It was found with jewelry in a princess's tomb at Vix, 7 km north of Châtillon.

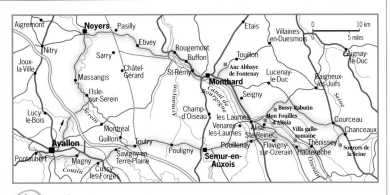

Drive **The Auxois**

Start at Avallon. Take the D86 to Noyers.
Noyers is a delightful old village: Admire its town gates, timbered houses and towers from the old fortfications.

D956 takes you to Rougemont.
Montbard near Rougemont was the home of the 18th-century natural historian, the comte de Buffon. The forge he founded between Rougemont and the hamlet of Buffon has been restored.

A detour on D905/D32 takes you to the Abbaye de Fontenay.
This is the outstanding surviving example of Cistercian simplicity and peace.

Back to D905 and on to Venarey-les-Laumes and Alise-Ste-Reine.

Timbered house at Noyers

Alise-Ste-Reine has a museum with finds from a Gallo-Roman town on the slopes of Mont Auxois, thought to be Alesia, site of the Gauls' heroic last stand against Rome in 52 BC.

D954 to Bussy-Rabutin.
The Château de Bussy-Rabutin (guided tours) has an entertaining collection of portraits of warriors and royal mistresses.

Take D19/D6 to Courceau, N71 to Chanceaux and D103C to St-Germain-Source-Seine.
The river issues from a cave 2 km south of St Germain. A Roman temple once stood nearby.

Take D10 to Thénissey and Hauteroche, then D9 to Flavigny-sur-Ozerain.
Flavigny-sur-Ozerain is a walled village of tumbledown charm, known for its aniseed sweets (*dragées*).

Continue to Semur-en-Auxois.
Admirably set on a rocky spur almost encircled by the Armançon, the old town of Semur-en-Auxois still bristles with towers. There is swimming and water sports at the Lac de Pont (4 km south by D103B).

Take the D954 to Cussy-les-Forges, N6 to Magny, D427 to Pontaubert and D957 back to Avallon.
The route follows the pretty Cousin valley, skirting Avallon.

Bourgogne aligoté (local white wine made from the inferior *aligoté* grape) mixed with Dijonnais crème de cassis is a traditional regional aperitif, now named after Canon Kir, mayor of Dijon during the 1940s. Kir served the drink at all public functions in a bid to boost flagging sales of cassis. In what many kirophiles would consider an excess of promotional zeal, the canon's recipe was one-third cassis to two-thirds wine; one-fifth to four-fifths is a more palatable mixture. *Kir royal* substitutes champagne for the aligoté.

▶ ▷ ▷ Dijon

The first Valois duke, Philip the Bold, made Burgundy a great independent power at the heart of Europe by marrying the heiress of Flanders. Dijon became his capital and here, with the help of Flemish artists, Philip and his successors built themselves a magnificent palace and an equally lavish necropolis, the Chartreuse de Champmol. Both have been transformed and now only hint at their original splendor. Dijon still has a core of medieval streets, but it is primarily a busy industrial city, great for gourmets (as you would expect of the Burgundian capital, famous for its mustard and *crème de cassis* (blackcurrant liqueur) but short of charm.

The **Palais des Ducs** overlooks the semicircular colonnade of the elegant 17th-century place de la Libération, at the end of Dijon's main shopping axis, the rue de la Liberté. As well as the town hall, the palace houses the Musée des Beaux Arts, with medieval kitchens and an outstanding collection of sculpture, of which the highlights are two masterpieces of 14th- to 15th-century Burgundian-Flemish art and the tombs of Philip the Bold and John the Fearless (with consort) in the vast Salle des Gardes. Two beautiful altarpieces in the same room also came from **Champmol,** now a mental hospital on the western edge of the city (toward the A38 motorway). Most of its original buildings and works of art have been destroyed or removed, but it retains the Puits de Moïse (Moses' Well), a magnificent group of six statues of prophets (Moses is the one with horns) by 15th-century sculptor Claus Sluter, who also carved the statues of Philip the Bold and Margaret of Flanders inside the chapel doorway.

Dijon's churches are of minor interest. The cathedral has a round 10th-century crypt, St-Michel a good Renaissance facade. Notre-Dame's Gothic facade has rows of grimacing monsters and a 14th-century Jacquemart (mechanical clock with figures hammering the chimes). The most interesting old streets in the medieval zone behind the palace are rue des Forges (where the 15th-century Hôtel Chambellan is the tourist office), rue Verrerie and rue de la Chouette.

The Palais des Ducs in Dijon

▷▷▷ Divonne-les-Bains

An old Roman spa between Lake Geneva and the steep mountain wall of the Jura, Divonne communicates most easily with Switzerland. Fat cats come from Geneva and Lausanne for a first-rate dinner and gambling at the casino. Organizers of conferences and corporate entertainment also like Divonne: It is no distance from Geneva's airport and has the required palatial hotels and extensive sports and health facilities, including golf, water sports on a small artificial lake, and spring water deemed beneficial for a variety of ailments, including stress and hypochondria. Charming, it is not.

▶▷▷ Doubs, Vallée du

From its source in a forest cave near the village of Mouthe, the River Doubs charts an indecisive course, flowing five times as far as a crow would fly on its way towards the Saône. The most beautiful stretch of the valley is where the river defines the Franco-Swiss border between the Saut du Doubs (a splendid 98-foot waterfall near Morteau) and the village of Goumois: impressive limestone gorges and good canoeing and trout fishing. In the upper valley, Malbuisson is a peaceful lakeside resort, also popular with fishermen. Between Pontarlier and Morteau, **Montbenoît**'s abbey church has a richly decorated 16th-century choir with beautiful carved stalls.

▷▷▷ Lons-le-Saunier

An old Roman salt town, Lons-le-Saunier is now the moderately busy prefecture of the Jura. Its best aspect is the arcaded rue du Commerce; Rouget de Lisle, composer of the "Marseillaise," was born at No. 24 in 1760. The town clock plays a few notes of the tune on the hour.

▷▷▷ Moulins

The capital of the dukes of Bourbon, big players in the politics of medieval and Renaissance France, Moulins is now a quiet market town off the beaten tourist trail. The cathedral has good windows in the 15th-century choir and, in the sacristy, a triptych of the Virgin in Glory (1500), with donor portraits of the duke and duchess of Bourbon, by the artist known to art history as the Moulins Master. Mechanical figures hammer the chimes on the 15th-century Jacquemart clock tower.

In the vineyard hills between Lons-le-Saunier and Arbois, erosion has carved a series of splendid valleys (*reculées*) ending in abrupt theaters (*cirques*) of cliffs with caves, resurgent streams, stalactites and underground lakes. The Cirque de Baume heads a valley occupied by the ancient abbey of Baume les Messieurs. There is a good viewing place that looks over the valley from the D471 east of Lons-le-Saunier. A similar cliff-top belvedere overlooks the Reculée des Planches and Cirque du Fer à Cheval beside the D469 Arbois–Champagnole road.

235

Lons-le-Saunier

Nevers cathedral

In Parisian café society Courbet posed as a rough peasant, embraced revolutionary politics and professed an anti-everything philosophy of art, conveniently known as Realism. Returning often to Ornans, he painted local landscapes, hunting and village scenes, including the still disturbing *Burial at Ornans* (1850; Louvre), executed on a grand scale. His favorite subject, however, was himself. After a spell in jail for helping to pull down Napoleon's column at place Vendôme in 1871, Courbet spent his last years in Swiss exile.

▷▷▷ Nantua

An old stagecoach post on the way to Switzerland, filling a gap between steep mountainsides, Nantua remained a bottleneck on the way to the Alps until recently relieved by an impressive elevated stretch of motorway. It is now a quiet place, hardly a resort despite the charm of boating on its small lake.

▶▷▷ Nevers

A gray town at the confluence of the Nièvre and Loire, Nevers has been famous for its spun glass and faience porcelain since the 16th century, when Lodovico Gonzaga of Mantua, duke of Nivernais, imported specialist artists from Italy. The industry survives, and there are good faience and glass collections in the town museum. Other buildings of interest include the cathedral, with Romanesque and Gothic apses at west and east end; the turreted 15th- to 16th-century ducal palace (now the law courts); the Porte du Croux, a splendid old town gate near the station; and St-Etienne, a harmonious 11th-century church to the east of the center. The tomb of Bernadette Subirous, visionary of Lourdes, is displayed at the convent of St-Gildard, north of the station near the Fourchambault road.

▷▷▷ Ornans

In this small Jura town between Besançon and Pontarlier, old ramshackle houses prettily overhang the waters of the River Loue against a backdrop of wooded escarpments that will be instantly recognizable to those familiar with the work of Ornans's favorite son, painter Gustave Courbet (1819–77). There is a good Courbet museum on the left bank near the bridge.

▷▷▷ Les Rousses

On a high (3,608-foot) plateau at the foot of the summit ridge of the Jura Mountains, Les Rousses is a busy summer and winter resort, with water sports on its lake, walking and riding in the forest. In winter there are long cross-country ski trails and the Jura's best downhill skiing (lifts up to 5,510 feet). Local cheese and butter is made at the dairy, which you can visit. There is more skiing at the Col de la Faucille (4,264 feet) 18 km up the N5 toward Switzerland. Mont Blanc, 80 km away, is visible on a clear day.

▷▷▷ Saulieu and the Morvan

Saulieu is what the French call an *étape gastronomique*: a punctuation mark on an ancient thoroughfare with a long-established reputation for good restaurants ideal for an overnight of overindulgence. Saulieu still lives up to its reputation. The town can also boast beautiful carved capitals in the 12th-century basilica (St-Andoche), and a bronze statue of a bull. This is the acclaimed masterpiece of the sculptor Pompon, born at Saulieu in 1855.

To the west of Saulieu, the Morvan Hills stretch north to Avallon and south to Autun. The Morvan is Burgundy's wilderness, with fast-flowing rivers for canoeists and fishermen, reservoirs for water sports and hydroelectric power, rocky escarpments for climbers, and forests for walkers. However, its peaks scarcely soar, and the views from its finest belvedere—Mont Beuvray (2,693 feet) near Autun—do not take the breath away. For this sort of vacation, there are better regions—the Massif Central, for example. Château Chinon is the main accommodations center.

▶▷▷ Sens

Northern gateway to Burgundy, Sens is a moderately attractive country town with the first pure Gothic cathedral to be built in France, begun in the mid-12th century. Sculptures around the main doorway, much damaged in the Revolution, include a statue of St. Stephen, to whom the cathedral is dedicated. The interior has fine medieval and Renaissance stained glass; the oldest windows are on the north side of the choir, and include a depiction of the murder of Archbishop Thomas à Becket of Canterbury, who had spent six years at nearby Pontigny hiding from the ill-disposed English king, Henry II. The treasury is unusually rich in vestments, tapestries and miscellaneous religious objets d'art.

▷▷▷ Solutré

The great rock of Solutré hangs over the best vineyards in the Mâconnais (Pouilly and Fuissé) like an unfurling wave. The foot of the cliff has been excavated to reveal the bones of 100,000 horses from the period ~~15,000~~ to ~~12,000~~ BC, now known as the Solutrean age. A few human skeletons and artifacts ~~from earlier and later periods~~ have also been found. There is a small museum on site, but the most interesting finds are in the museum at Mâcon.

Place of ritual sacrifice or prehistoric knacker's yard? The usual explanation for the hapless horses of Solutré is that the local inhabitants cornered wild horses on top of the rock and scared them with fire into jumping off the cliff. Down below, the dead animals were cooked and eaten, and their bones discarded. An early example of *boucherie chevaline*.

The riverside at Sens

Drive The Charollais and the Brionnais

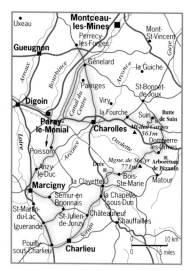

This is a tour of Burgundy at its most picturesque: pastures dappled with white Charollais (often incorrectly spelled Charolais) cattle; golden churches (keys usually from the *patronne* at the café next door); beret-clad locals with baguettes under their arms, pedaling rusty bicycles.

Start at Paray-le-Monial.
Paray-le-Monial's 12th-century basilica of Sacré Coeur is no humble village church but a majestic example of Cluniac Romanesque, a smaller version of the demolished abbey church at Cluny itself.

Take D34, then D10 to Marcigny. Continue on D989 to Semur-en-Brionnais and D9 to St-Julien-de-Jonzy and Iguerande.
The tour continues via a series of smaller churches in more rustic surroundings, with octagonal towers and richly carved doorways and capitals: Anzy-le-Duc, Semur-en-Brionnais, St-Julien-de-Jonzy and Iguerande.

Take the D482 to Pouilly-sous-Charlieu, then D487 as far as Charlieu.
Charlieu is a busy little market town with fragments of an old abbey. There are guided tours of the ruins, but the best part is the 12th-century carved doorway of the porch, visible from outside.

The route continues along the D987 to La Clayette and D193 as far as Drée.
La Clayette and Drée have châteaus to admire from outside, but not to visit.

Take D325/D41 to Dompierre-les-Ormes and continue via D41 and D379 to Butte de Suin.
The route meanders through the wooded hills and farmlands of the Charollais region, passing Pézanin arboretum, with hundreds of exotic species (near Dompierre-les-Ormes) and offering a choice of panoramic picnic spots – the Montagne de St-Cyr near Montmelard (2,529 feet) or the Butte de Suin (1,945 feet).

D17 and N79 take you back to Paray-le-Monial via Charolles.
Charolles has given its name to the finest provider of steak to French tables. Apart from this, unless your visit coincides with the weekly cattle market, the town is of little interest.

Farther on along this route, Perrecy-les-Forges has an old priory with some beautiful carvings in the porch.

▶▷▷ Tanlay

A gracious moated Renaissance château near Tonnerre, Tanlay has elegant round towers, bell-shaped domes, and swans in the moat. The interior (guided tours) is equally splendid, with period furniture, fine sculpted chimneypieces and a long trompe l'oeil gallery.

▷▷▷ Ternant

This humble village church, in the middle of nowhere between the Loire and the Morvan, contains two beautiful wooden triptychs donated in 1435 by Duke Philip the Good's chamberlain, Philippe de Ternant, who is portrayed in both works.

Tanlay's Renaissance château

▶▶▷ Tournus

Tournus is a quiet town sandwiched between the motorway and the Saône, and dominated by the towers of St-Philibert, one of the oldest and finest of France's great Romanesque churches. In the cobbled center, old houses and former abbey buildings cluster beneath the martial walls and towers of the 11th- to 12th-century church. Inside, massive unadorned pillars of salmon-colored stone support a series of transverse barrel vaults. Oldest of all is the crypt with several Roman columns and 12th-century frescoes. From Tournus, the D14 west takes you to **Brancion** (15 km), a picturesque semi-ruined fortified village.

▶▷▷ Vézelay

The single street of a picturesque old village, usually overrun with tourists, climbs a steep hill toward a great pilgrimage church. By laying false claim to the relics of Mary Magdalen, the abbey at Vézelay became a popular stop on the pilgrimage to Santiago de Compostela. St. Bernard of Clairvaux launched the Second Crusade there in 1146. The present church, rescued from dilapidation by the much-maligned Viollet-le-Duc in 1840, dates mostly from the 12th century. Its most striking features are the colorful alternation of chocolate and golden stone in the arches and bands of the vault; and the beautiful relief carving over the doorway leading from narthex to nave and on the capitals along the nave. A detailed guide to the capitals is available on the spot.

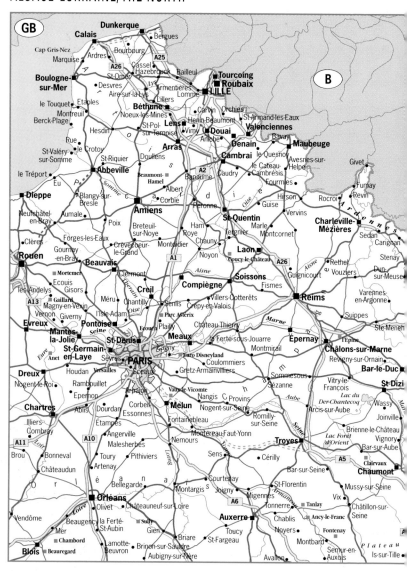

The north prospered in the Middle Ages, and the profits of the great trading towns were channeled into Gothic buildings of unequaled splendor in Amiens, Laon or Reims. There is fine building from other periods too, as in the Renaissance squares of Arras and Charleville. While the Loire may be the natural habitat of the *château-de-luxe*, this border country is studded with fortress-châteaus of all ages, from fearsome feudal ruins like Coucy to the star-shaped strongholds of Louis XIV and the indestructible remains of Hitler's Atlantic Wall.

The countryside too is worth exploring, especially where the bare and spacious plateaus give way to the lush valleys of slow-moving rivers like the Somme. With its superb sandy beaches and high cliffs alternating with

ALSACE - LORRAINE AND THE NORTH

NL

D

L

0   20   40   60   80   100 km
0 10   20   30   40   50 60 miles

nédy • Longwy
Fermont • Longuyon Aumetz
ire • Etain
dun **A4** • Jarny
Ars • **Metz**
Pont-à-Mousson
l o r r a i n e
Dieulouard
ommercy Pompey • **Nancy**
y-en Toul
ois • Vaucouleurs
château
Liffol-le-Grand
• Vittel • Contrexéville
Montigny-le-Roi
Bourbonne-les-Bains
Champlitte Vesoul

• Uckange
• Hagondange
Creutzwald • • Forbach
Preyming • Merlebach Sarreguemines
Nied
• Sarre-Union • Morhange
Château-Salins
Sarrebourg
Canal de la Marne au Rhin
• St-Nicholas-de-Port
Neuves-Maisons Lunéville
Baccarat
A31
Charmes • Mirecourt
Rambervillers
St-Dié
Epinal Bruyères Gérardmer
Darney • Remiremont
Plombières-les-Bains le Thillot
Luxeuil-les-Bains Thann
Lure Ronchamp
Belfort Altkirch St-Louis
Héricourt Delle
Montbéliard • Audincourt

• Wissembourg
Bitche Reichshoffen • Lembach
Bouxwiller Seltz
A4 Haguenau • Brumath
Saverne
Marmoutier
STRASBOURG
Molsheim • Obernai
Mont Ste-Odile • Barr
Haut-Koenigsbourg
• Sélestat
Ste-Marie-aux-Mines • Ribeauvillé
Colmar
Munster Neuf-Brisach
Hohneck 1362m
Grand Ballon 1424m Rouffach
Cernay • Ensisheim
Ballon d'Alsace
A36 **Mulhouse**

Thionville

D

Meuse

Moselle

Meurthe

Rhin

Saône

CH

241

great sweeps of sand dunes, the Channel coast is one of France's finest. Its ports, Calais, Boulogne and Dunkerque, are among the country's busiest. The chalk hills and escarpments of champagne country around Reims and Epernay lead to Lorraine, with heavy industry to the north and its elegant capital, Nancy, to the south. The wooded Vosges Mountains guard the way to the Rhine Valley and Alsace. Indisputably French, this easternmost province has a Germanic flavor expressed in its dialect, its food and wine, and above all in the utter charm of its half-timbered and flower-bedecked towns and villages, from dynamic Strasbourg, one of the capitals of the new Europe, to the humblest wine village along the Route des Vins (Wine Road).

Legend has it that France's patron saint of beer, Arnoldus, provided a miraculous draft of the foaming liquid for the pallbearers at his funeral. Arnoldus was bishop of Metz in Lorraine, and while his province still brews beers of reputation, it is neighboring Alsace that has acquired international fame with Germanic-sounding and tasting brands like Kronenbourg. In the industrial north, as well as lagers the many breweries also make top-fermented alelike beers in Belgian style, as well as a curious "red" beer.

Market produce on sale in Arras

▶▶▷ Amiens

Much battered in two world wars and extensively modernized since, the ancient capital of Picardy on the banks of the Somme boasts one of France's most glorious Gothic cathedrals.

The sheer size of the great **cathedral** is impressive enough (367 feet to the tip of the spire), but it is the array of sculpture adorning the glorious west front that first captures the visitor's attention. This Bible story in stone focuses on the famous statue of Christ known as *Le Beau Dieu*. The serene simplicity of the interior is enhanced by the almost incredible richness of the choir stalls, carved imaginatively in oak by master carpenters of the early 16th century.

The city's other attractions include the **Musée de Picardie** with archaeological finds and paintings, the local history museum in the 17th-century **Hôtel de Berny**, and a center and theme park devoted to the author **Jules Verne**. In the floodplain of the Somme are Amiens's watery **Hortillonnages**, a strange area of market gardens threaded by innumerable little channels and in part accessible only by boat.

▶▷▷ Ardennes, les

These densely wooded uplands, most of them on Belgian territory, are the abode of deer and wild boar, a paradise for hunters and walkers. They form a high plateau penetrated by the deep valley of the meandering Meuse, best experienced by boat or when viewed from the numerous crags along its course.

Industry found an early foothold along the banks of the river; engineering works and quarries are today complemented by a brace of nuclear power stations at Chooz. There are fine fortresses at **Rocroi** as well as at **Sedan**, and Charleville-Mezières boasts one of France's most splendid Renaissance squares, the **place Ducale**.

▶▶▷ Arras

Renowned for its tapestries in the late Middle Ages, Arras spent its accumulated wealth on its 16th-century **town hall** and on adorning its two squares, the **Grand' Place** and the **place des Héros**, with the dignified town houses we see today. Flemish gables, harmonious brick and stonework, and continuous arcades combine to form one of the finest urban compositions in northern Europe. Beneath it all run the extensive cellars that sheltered the citizens of Arras during the devastating bombardments of World War I.

Gothic Churches of the North

■ **Born in the Ile-de-France, the Gothic style flourished in the prosperous towns and cities of the north. Its liberating effect can be seen not only in world-famous cathedrals like Laon, Reims and Amiens, but across the whole region, in great abbey churches like St-Riquier and urban basilicas like St-Omer and St-Quentin. There are less well-known cathedrals at Soissons and Noyon, both masterpieces in their own right, though the latter is upstaged by the majestic facade of the great monastery church of St-Jean-des-Vignes. ...■**

The achievement of the Gothic architects is matched by that of the sculptors and craftsmen who collaborated with them. Fine-grained local limestone often lent itself to masterly carving, as in the sculpted figures adorning the west front at Amiens. At Amiens, too, similar virtuosity is evident in the wood carving of the splendid choir stalls.

Emergence of Gothic The style underwent constant development as the great master-masons sought to exploit its technical and symbolic possibilities. At 12th-century Laon, we see it still in an early stage of evolution; the cathedral has the many towers typical of earlier churches, and its minimally pointed arches seem to hark back to their rounded Romanesque predecessors, while the deeply modeled west front, with its bold projections, openings and deep shadows, has an extraordinary plastic quality.

Flowering and flamboyance In the 13th century the style reached its zenith; at Amiens, the use of flying buttresses enables the masonry of the walls to be reduced to an absolute minimum, making way for the great windows through which the daylight streams into the soaring spaces of the interior.

By the time Abbeville's St-Vulfran was built in the 15th century, decoration had become more important than structure; in this final, Flamboyant phase, window tracery writhes, flamelike, and the west front carries an extraordinary overload of ornament.

Occasionally a cooler influence is felt from across the Channel, as in the tall, soberly decorated tower of St-Omer's Notre-Dame, an echo of English Perpendicular.

Reims cathedral

▶ ▷ ▷ Ballon de Gruebwiller

At 4,671 feet, this (also called the Grand Ballon) is the highest of the *ballons*, the bare, rounded mountaintops rising impressively from the tree-clad slopes of the southern Vosges. No one should shirk the short walk up from the parking lot to the summit: at your feet the Alsace plain; beyond, the Rhine, the wooded heights of the Black Forest; to the south the Jura and the distant Alps.

▷ ▷ ▷ Belfort

Connoisseurs of station names on the Paris Métro will remember Denfert-Rochereau, named after a hero of the Franco-Prussian War. Besieged in Belfort's citadel by superior force, this doughty colonel and his men withstood the German assault for 103 days, only giving up after the armistice. Their heroism is commemorated by the **Belfort Lion**, a great beast in red sandstone guarding the way up to the citadel and overlooking the workaday town on the banks of the Savoureuse far below.

▶ ▷ ▷ Bergues

Sitting serenely behind its protective walls and elaborate moats, this is one of the prettiest little places in French Flanders. Built in yellow brick, it has resisted many an attacking army.

▶ ▷ ▷ Boulogne

With its old core, the **Vieille Ville**, still surrounded by medieval ramparts and dominated by its idiosyncratic 19th-century cathedral, Boulogne beats its rivals Calais and Dunkerque for character. Nausicaä, France's largest aquarium, is (despite its off-putting name) another good reason to visit. Its harbor lands more fish than anywhere else in France—though UK visitors have dwindled along with the ferry services. To the north of Boulogne stretch the cliffs and beaches of the **Côte d'Opale** (Opal Coast), culminating in the mighty headland of **Cap Gris Nez**.

▷ ▷ ▷ Calais

Wrecked during World War II and unstylishly rebuilt afterward, France's busiest passenger port owes everything to its location a mere 38 km from the English coast, whose chalk cliffs are clearly visible on a fine day. Calais's links with the far side of the Channel go back a long way; the English siege of 1346–47 is commemorated by Rodin's bronze of the **Burghers of Calais**, set up at the foot of the tall town-hall tower. This celebrated and moving sculpture shows the fathers offering themselves as hostages to the ruthless English king. Nearby, an old German bunker has been converted into a **War Museum**.

▷ ▷ ▷ Cambrai

Famed since medieval times for its fine linen known in English as cambric, Cambrai suffered terribly during the German retreat of 1918. An industrial town, it is also the center of a rich agricultural area and is famous for its tripe and sausages as well as for the minty tidbits called *bêtises* (silly things).

Old Boulogne

▶▶▷ **Cassel**

The flat farmlands of French Flanders are relieved by a number of isolated knolls, the Monts de Flandres. On the highest of these (577 feet) perches this exquisite little Flemish town, its elongated and cobbled **Grande Place** lined with fine old buildings, among them the 16th-century **Hôtel de la Noble Cour**, now the local museum. From the summit of the knoll with its 18th-century windmill there are terrific views toward the far-off Channel and into Belgium.

▶▷▷ **Colmar**

Large numbers of visitors come to Colmar to savor the special character of Alsace. High-gabled timber-framed houses front the old streets and squares of the perfectly preserved town center; outstanding are the galleried **Ancienne Douane** (Old Customs House) and the **Maison Pfister**, adorned with frescoes and medallions. The Krutenau district, Colmar's "Little Venice," is particularly picturesque.

But Colmar's greatest treasure is kept indoors, in the tranquillity of the chapel in the **Musée d'Unterlinden**. Here, in all its terrifying intensity, is the *Issenheim Altarpiece*, the masterwork of Matthias Grünewald. The folding panels of the altarpiece were painted around 1515 for the prior of the monastery of St. Anthony at nearby Issenheim. Its visionary evocation of suffering in the *Redemption of Christ* still has the power to move the most casual observer; seldom has the agony of the dying Savior been more forcefully portrayed.

The impact of the altarpiece is such that it is best left to the end of your visit to the museum, which has much else to offer. Apart from the 24 panels of the *Passion* by Grünewald's near-contemporary, Martin Schongauer, there are local collections and an array of modern French paintings (by Braque, Picasso, and Léger, among others). Schongauer's work can be seen again in the **Dominican Church**, where his *Virgin in the Rose Bower* has pride of place.

Alsace is one of France's gastronomic provinces, serving Germanic food with a French accent, like the hearty plates of *choucroute* (sauerkraut) garnished with Strasbourg sausages or pork chops. From Strasbourg too comes foie gras, goose liver eaten au naturel or as pâté. Pork plays a big role, but so do delicately flavored poultry and trout (from the Vosge) and eel. Munster cheese is renowned, as is *kougelhopf* cake.

Colmar's glistening streets at night

Drive **Route des Crêtes**

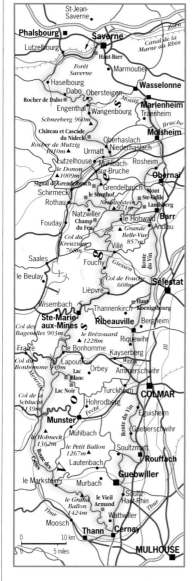

From rugged sandstone heights in the north to the gently rounded forms of the ballons in the south, this superb walking country extends for 170 km between the German border and the Belfort Gap. The Route des Crêtes was built in World War I to serve the French front line; it now forms a magnificent drive.

Start at Saverne. Take the D132 southwest and turn left onto D98 at Lutzelbourg. At Haselbourg follow the D45, and at the little resort of Obersteigen turn right onto the D218.
This part of the Vosges has romantic landscapes of woods, pretty valleys and castle ruins commanding fine views.

Just beyond Niederhaslach with its great Gothic church, turn right onto the N420 along the picturesque valley of the Bruche. At Lutzelhouse you can either head south via Muhlbach up to the panoramic overlook at the Signal de Grendelbruch or continue along the valley past Schirmeck to Rothau and turn left up the D130 toward Le Struthof. The approach road to **Le Struthof** was built by the forced laborers of the Nazi concentration camp, chilling remains of which are still standing here.

The alternative routes rejoin near the Neuntelstein overlook. Head east on D130 and D426 toward Mont-Ste-Odile.
Vistors crowd the mountaintop convent dedicated to **St. Odile**, above all on her feast day (December 13). Alsace's patron saint lived in the 8th century; the imposing masonry of the great defensive earthwork known as the **Mur Païen** (Pagan Wall) harks back to much earlier times, when Gaul was ruled by the mysterious Celts.

Return westward via D109. Turn left onto D426 toward the little upland

Rising gently eastward from the Lorraine plateau, then dropping abruptly through the vineyards to the broad plain of the Rhine, the wooded Vosges Mountains are among France's most attractive uplands.

resort of Le Hohwald, then go
southwest on D425, turning right
after the Col du Kreuzweg to the
Champ du Feu.

From the **Champ du Feu**
observation tower there are
staggering views which can extend
as far as the Black Forest or even
as far as the Swiss Alps on a clear
day.

*Return to D425 and continue south
to Villé, then to Fouchy and the
pretty Col de Fouchy. Down in the
valley again at Lièpvre, turn right
toward the small industrial
settlement of Ste-Marie-aux-Mines.
At the Col des Bagenelles, follow
signs to Le Bonhomme, where you
turn right to travel toward the Col du
Bonhomme.*

The **Col du Bonhomme**, traversed
by one of the main routes linking
Alsace with Lorraine, marks the
northern end of the Route des
Crêtes.

*The route winds along for 83 km
from here as far as Thann in the
south.*

Splendid forests alternate with high
pastures, while deep below are
attractive lakes. All along the route
are spectacular overlooks, the most
celebrated being that of the **Grand
Ballon** (4,671 feet). A somber
reminder that the ridgeline was
bitterly contested by the opposing
armies is the National Memorial at
Vieil-Armand. The route descends
sinuously to Cernay and then 6 km
west to Thann.

 **Route du Vin**

This second tourist route of Alsace,
some 180 km long between Thann
in the south and Marlenheim in the
north, is well signposted. Its winding
course is best taken at a leisurely
pace, with ample time for tasting—
details available locally or from Vin
d'Alsace, place de la Gare, in
Colmar.

*From Thann, follow the route via
Eguisheim, past Colmar to
Kaysersberg.*
The vines grow in a narrow
north–south band along the foothills
of the Vosges. Here are immaculate
villages, whose cobbled streets and
squares and high-gabled timber
houses epitomize Alsace. Many, like
three-towered **Eguisheim** or
triangular **Turckheim** have all the
airs of miniature towns. The favorite
town is probably **Riquewihr**, almost

unbearably crowded on occasion.
Kaysersberg, with its fortified
bridge, was the birthplace of ~~the
great humanitarian~~ Albert
Schweitzer.

*Continue north past Sélestat and
Obernai to Marlenheim.*
Castles abound in this frontier
province, most of them in romantic
ruin. One exception is **Haut-
Koenigsbourg**, its formidable
silhouette rising imperiously over the
forested slopes above Sélestat. It
was reconstructed for Kaiser
Wilhelm II in the early years of this
century, when Alsace was ruled
from Berlin. Disillusioned by the
course of the Great War, the
emperor left a brief but telling
comment here on his last visit in
1918, an inscription reading: "I did
not want this."

One of the emblems of Alsace is the stork's nest atop a chimney stack or steeple. Weighing up to half a ton, these form annually refurbished residences, occupied each summer. Courtship is noisy, with much flapping of wings and clattering of bills. Eggs can number up to half a dozen. Sadly, the stork population has declined dramatically in recent years, though efforts are now being made to augment their numbers by breeding them in captivity.

Long settled by German speakers, Alsace was assimilated into France as Louis XIV pushed eastward to the "natural" frontier along the Rhine. While accepting French rule, the population felt uneasy with Paris's centralizing tendencies, and not everyone regretted being reabsorbed into German rule after the Franco-Prussian War of 1870–71. Re-annexation by Nazi Germany in 1940 was a less happy experience. Today's Alsatians are content to live in a Europe where Germany and France are partners and where their own identity can flourish.

▶▷▷ Coucy-le-Château

In the Middle Ages this ridge-top castle was one of the greatest strongholds in the land. Toward the end of World War I, the retreating Germans added to the depredations of the centuries by blowing up the massive keep. But enough remains of walls, towers and massive gateways to enclose completely the modern village of Coucy and to leave an unforgettable memory of medieval might. The usual approach winds up from the south to the Porte de Soissons; inside the gateway is a little museum with a scale model of the castle as it was.

▷▷▷ Douai

War-damaged in 1914–18 and again in 1940, Douai nevertheless retains a good number of 18th-century houses as well as its 210-foot Gothic **Beffroi** (Bell Tower), one of the finest in the north. In the 17th century, the town became a refuge for English Roman Catholics. Driven out by the anti-religious fervor of the Revolution, their descendants returned to England, where they founded Downside Abbey and, later, its famous school. Douai is the administrative center for France's great northern coalfield; at nearby Lewarde, in an old mine, is the **Centre Historique Minier**, which gives a good picture of mining life.

▶▷▷ L'Epine

Pilgrimages have taken place here ever since shepherds saw a statue of the Virgin Mary in the middle of a burning thorn (*épine*) bush. The great late Gothic church erected to commemorate the miraculous apparition easily dominates the humble half-timbered houses of the village huddling at its foot. Its grandeur is relieved by its many gargoyles.

▶▷▷ Langres

The **Plateau de Langres** is a vast rolling upland straddling the headwaters of three of France's great rivers: the Marne, the Meuse, and the Seine. Perched on one of its limestone promontories is the ancient town of Langres itself, still intact within its well-preserved walls. The most rewarding walk leads around the ramparts, passing towers and gateways and offering fine views over the valley of the Marne. Within the town are many splendid old houses, some of them of Renaissance date. In one such mansion is the **Musée du Breuil-de-St-Germain**, with a room devoted to the great encyclopedist Denis Diderot, born here in 1713.

▶▶▷ Laon

It is 1,000 years since Laon was France's capital, but this walled, gated city still dominates the flatlands all around from its spectacular ridge-top site. The glorious Gothic **cathedral**, begun in the late 12th century, rises grandly over the rooftops. With deeply inset porches and windows, the west front is a triumph of early Gothic drama and ebullience, while the interior has a monumental simplicity and dignity. The figures of oxen high up in the towers commemorate the beasts that hauled the heavy stone from quarry to cathedral building site.

▶▷▷ Lille

Lille is the undisputed capital of the north, the focus of a sprawling industrial conurbation of more than a million inhabitants. While much of this sprawl lacks allure, the city's pedestrianized center is full of style and vigor, a fascinating mix of French and Flemish influence, though the huge **Citadel** is entirely French, built by Louis XIV's military engineer Vauban. The big **Musée des Beaux Arts** has much to offer, from Flemish and Dutch masters through to Impressionists. The displays in General de Gaulle's birthplace, the **Maison natale du Général de Gaulle**, include the great man's christening robe and also the car in which he narrowly escaped assassination in 1962.

▷▷▷ Lunéville

In the early 18th century, the Duke of Lorraine built a château here to rival Versailles. His palace still stands, somewhat the worse for wear, but still mightily impressive in terms of sheer size.

▶▷▷ Marmoutier

Just to the south of Saverne stands the splendid church of Marmoutier. Built in red Vosges sandstone, beginning in the 11th century, it has a complex and commanding west front that forms one of the finest examples of Romanesque architecture in Alsace.

▶▷▷ Metz

Strategically located not far from France's eastern frontier, Metz has been a fortress city for most of its long existence. Between 1871 and 1918 it belonged to Germany, and buildings dating from this period, like the huge **railway station,** have a distinctly Germanic air. But the cathedral is characteristically French, with a lofty interior and sumptuous stained glass, including modern work by Marc Chagall. Metz's riverside is worth seeking out, not least for the formidable gateway known as the **Porte des Allemands.**

Laon, once the capital of France

Little is known of the life of painter Georges de la Tour, born at Vic-sur-Seille near Lunéville in 1593. It appears that he pursued his career as court painter to both the duke of Lorraine and King Louis XIII with a worldly and ruthless determination, certainly not reflected in his pictures, which have a mystical stillness and tranquillity never since equaled. He is the master of nocturnal interiors peopled by serene figures whose calm features are lit by the concealed flame of a single candle. Few works survive, but examples can be seen in the Musée Historique Lorraine at Nancy.

249

Lorraine is world-famous for its water—few can fail to recognize the name Vittel—and any number of spas have grown up in the south of the province. As well as Vittel and its neighbor Contrexville (both with bottling plants open to the public), there are several places (Plombières, Luxeuil, Bourbonne, for instance) tapping the waters springing from the fringe of the Vosges Mountains. Pretty surroundings, parks and gardens, elegant old-fashioned spa architecture and a general atmosphere of leisure and pleasure make these little resorts as attractive to the casual visitor as to those in search of a cure.

▷▷▷ Meuse

Some 900 km long from its source near Bourbonne-les-Bains to its mouth in the North Sea, the Meuse is part of the extensive system of canalized waterways linking France to her neighbors to the northeast. For nearly 160 km between Neufchâteau and Stenay, it flows in a trenchlike valley marked to the east by the high limestone hills of the Côtes de Meuse. Fortress-cities like Verdun guard this section of the river, and some of France's most fateful battles have been fought along its banks, at Sedan in 1871 and again in 1940, and above all at Verdun (see page 259).

▷▷▷ Moselle

A river of contrasts, the Moselle starts its life as a mountain stream high in the Vosges near the Col de Bussay. The most attractive part of its course is between here and Epinal, where it flows through rich farmlands. From Neuves-Maisons near Nancy, however, it becomes one of Europe's great industrial waterways, particulary around Thionville, France's "Pays de Fer" ("Land of Iron").

▶▶▷ Mulhouse

The industrial town of Mulhouse attracts visitors less for its townscape (though it does have a splendid 16th-century town hall) than for its array of outstanding museums. The **Musée de l'Automobile** has an extraordinary collection of vehicles, French and foreign. The **Musée du Chemin-de-Fer** is the national collection of railwayana, featuring the French steam locomotives of yesteryear, perhaps the most beautiful machines of their kind ever made. The **Musée de l'Impression-sur-Etoffes** has brilliant explanations of the various processes of printing on cotton, complemented by an unsurpassed display of fine fabrics. **Electropolis** is a recent attraction devoted to the story of electricity. At the open-air **Ecomusée d'Alsace**, off the D430 to the north, dozens of traditional buildings have been reconstructed to show examples of the domestic life and crafts of past generations.

▷▷▷ Munster

This little resort in the vine-clad and wooded valley of the Fecht in the southern Vosges is famous for the pungent and semisoft Munster cheese. Nearby is the **Petit Ballon**, 4,156 feet high and one of the province's most spectacular viewpoints.

■ **Capital city of the duchy of Lorraine before becoming part of the kingdom of France on the death of its last duke, Stanislas, Nancy prides itself on its classical townscape, product of the urban planning of its enlightened rulers. ...■**

Elegance and harmony Stanislas had been king of Poland. When he was deposed in 1736, his son-in-law, Louis XV, managed to engineer him the dukedom of Lorraine. Full of architectural enthusiasm, Stanislas set about linking the rectilinear "New Town" laid out by his predecessor, Duke Leopold, to the old town around the Ducal Palace. Together with his architect, Héré, he planned an urban composition of unsurpassed elegance and harmony, the place Royale (now **place Stanislas**).

Flanked by lesser buildings in the same richly ornate but dignified style, the monumental **Hôtel de Ville** dominates the square, facing north toward an **Arc de Triomphe**. The exits from the square are guarded by gilded ironwork grilles of the utmost sumptuousness. The best view of the whole ensemble is from the Hôtel de Ville's upper floor, reached by a splendid staircase, also the work of Héré.

Museums and galleries Beyond the Arc de Triomphe extends the lengthy place de la Carrière, lined by fine 18th-century town houses and terminated by the colonnaded Palais du Gouvernement. Beyond is the austere Ducal Palace containing the **Musée Historique Lorraine**, with much material on the history of Lorraine and its capital as well as engravings by local artist Jacques Callot depicting the horrors of war. In contrast is the mood of peacefulness in the luminous interiors by the painter Georges de la Tour (see page 249).

Nancy's other museums include the **Musée des Beaux-Arts** with collections of European art from medieval to modern times, and the not-to-be-missed **Musée de l'Ecole**

<< Emile Gallé had established his glass workshop in Nancy in the early 1870s. He excelled in making exquisitely beautiful vases in translucent cameo glass, inspired by English glassware and by the motifs and techniques of Japanese art. The Daum brothers, Jean and Antonin, developed complex techniques for giving glass ever-greater subtleties of color and texture. Gallé was also a designer of extravagant furniture, like the extraordinary bed inlaid with a huge mother-of-pearl moth that can be seen on display in the Musée de l'Ecole de Nancy. >>

de Nancy. The city was France's most important center of Art Nouveau outside Paris, and the fascinating collections of this museum, housed in an elegant residence of the period, make this one of the best places to experience the heady luxuriance of the decorative arts of the turn of the century.

Nancy's Baroque architecture

251

Le Quesnoy's ingenious design failed to protect its German defenders from the New Zealand Rifle Brigade in 1918; they employed medieval siege tactics and scaled its walls with ladders.

▷▷▷ Neuf Brisach

In 1697, the French were forced to withdraw from Alt (Old) Breisach, one of the chain of strongholds they had built on the east bank of the Rhine. The fortress-town of Neuf (New) Brisach was its replacement. Sited among the flat farmlands of the west bank of the frontier river, it is a perfectly preserved example of the genius of Louis XIV's military engineer Vauban.

▶▷▷ Obernai

Among the vineyards at the foot of the ~~sacred~~ mountain of Mont-Ste-Odile, Obernai is the epitome of an Alsace wine village, with crumbling walls and ancient, narrow streets lined with timber-framed houses. In the place du Marché stand the 15th-century **town hall** and the 16th-century **Corn Hall**, overlooked by the tall **Tour de la Chapelle**. A statue of St. Odile graces the fountain in the center of the square, and not far away stands the pretty **Puits aus Sis-Sceaux**, a little Renaissance well whose six buckets hang in pairs.

▶▷▷ Le Quesnoy

Still intact after more than three centuries, the extensive moats and bastions of this quiet little fortress-city are a masterpiece of Baroque military engineering and a potent reminder of the vulnerability of France's northern frontier.

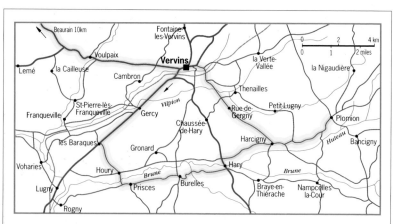

Drive La Thiérache

This lush green frontier countryside with its rich pastures and cider orchards was always vulnerable to the ravages of invading armies. The harrassed locals' response was to fortify their parish churches, many of which still stand.

A drive through La Thiérache can be centered on the town of Vervins.

From here a number of fortress churches are within easy reach: brick-built **Burelles**, twin-towered **Plomion**, 12th-century **Prisces** with its massive tower, lonely **Beaurain** on its isolated eminence. The churches' interiors were adapted to withstand a siege, with a well, a bread oven, and upper floors to house the villagers.

■ **World famous for its great Gothic cathedral, Reims owes its name to St. Rémi, the saint who, in the year 498, baptized the heathen Clovis, king of the Franks. Later, Reims became France's coronation city, with 25 rulers crowned here. ...■**

Treasures of Reims The cathedral was begun in 1211, and all but ruined by the bombardments of World War I. Expertly restored, it has an inspiring west front with an array of splendid statuary. High above the great rose window is the Gallery of Kings, 56 solemn figures with Clovis at their center; down below, in the left porch, the Smiling Angel strikes a lighter note. Inside, the stained glass is among the finest in France.

Adjoining the cathedral is the old Bishops Palace, the **Palais du Tau**, housing the Cathedral Treasury as well as a number of statues removed from their exposed position in the open. Not far away is the **Basilica of St-Rémi**, whose monastic buildings are a storehouse of medieval art, arms and armor.

Champagne The chalky rock on which Reims stands is as hollow as a Swiss cheese, with mile upon mile of caves providing ideal conditions for the production and storage of the region's most renowned product. The process by which champagne acquires its sparkle was invented, almost accidentally, by a 17th-century monk, Dom Pérignon. The caves (premises with famous names such as Veuve-Clicquot, Piper-Heidsieck, Pommery, Taittinger and Moët et Chandon) can be visited and a discreet *dégustation* (tasting) enjoyed.

On the flanks of the Montagne de Reims just to the south of the city, vines give way to woods of beech, oak and chestnut, a regional park harboring deer and wild boar. The vines spread out along the valley of the Marne to either side of Epernay, and south of the town are the slopes known as the Côte des Blancs. A sojourn hereabouts may convince you of the justification for the staunch refusal by the French to let any other beverage be marketed under the name of champagne. Overpossessive? Perhaps, but you are likely to come away convinced that no other sparkling wine, however carefully produced and labeled, can ever match the refinement of the product of France's northernmost vineyard.

Reims's Musée St-Denis, in the Abbaye St-Denis, has fine tapestries, paintings and sculpture (below: Rodin's Lover)

253

The Bibliothèque Humaniste in medieval Sélestat

▶▶▷ Ronchamp

High up on its hilltop, the pilgrimage chapel of Notre-Dame-du-Haut is one of the most atmospheric of modern churches. Designed by Le Corbusier, it is as much a sculpture as a building, with a billowing roof covering the mysterious interior, which is lit by stained-glass windows deeply set into the massive concrete walls.

▶▷▷ St-Omer

Now bypassed by the A26 motorway, this small town was once the first stop for visitors heading inland from Calais. It is a dignified place with fine old 17th- and 18th-century houses. The imposing **Basilica of Notre-Dame** has a tall tower in English Perpendicular style and an interior that is a veritable museum of ecclesiastical art. The **Hôtel Sandelin** has collections of local ceramics and delftware, together with the extraordinary gilt and enamel pedestal for a medieval crucifix known as the Pied de Croix de St-Bertin.

▶▷▷   St-Riquier

The village is dominated by its great abbey church, founded by the Benedictines in the 7th century. The present building dates mostly from the 15th and 16th centuries; built in pale local limestone in Flamboyant Gothic style, it has the scale and presence of a cathedral, with a massive tower and a calm interior of great dignity.

▷▷▷   Sélestat

The cramped network of medieval streets is contained within Sélestat's ring of long-since demolished walls. It has two good churches, Gothic St-Georges and 12th-century Ste-Foy; the latter, with its three towers, is one of the finest Romanesque buildings in the province. The **Bibliothèque Humaniste** contains collections of books and manuscripts dating back to the 7th century.

▶▷▷   Somme

Despite witnessing some of the bloodiest battles of World War I, the Somme flows peacefully and languidly through a lush valley set among open chalklands. It reaches the sea at the wide Baie de la Somme, an attractive estuary well endowed with crustaceans and other forms of marine life, much of which is consumed by visitors to the little port-resorts of **Le Crotoy** (to the north) and **St-Valéry** (to the south). Vintage trains run from Le Crotoy via St-Valéry to the sandy beaches of Cayeux-sur-Mer.

▶▶▶   Strasbourg

Seat of the Council of Europe and the European Parliament, Strasbourg is the jewel in the crown of Alsace. Sited between the branches of the River Ill just west of the Rhine, the ancient city center is dominated by the single soaring spire of the superb medieval **cathedral**, a building particularly rich in sculptural decoration. Inside, a three-tiered triumph of Gothic carving known as the Angel Pillar depicts the drama of the Last Judgment, while close by is a 19th-century astronomical clock, a favorite with the crowds who gather to enjoy its midday performance.

Strasbourg is well endowed with museums. The **Musée de l'Oeuvre Notre-Dame** has original sculpture from the cathedral. Three museums (Beaux-Arts, Archéologique, Arts Décoratifs) are grouped in the **Château des Rohan**; the ceramics collection is one of the best in France. The **Musée Historique** (Strasbourg history) is in the Grande Boucherie of 1586, while the **Musée Alsacien** (folk culture) is spread over three 16th- and 17th-century dwellings, and the **Musée d'Art Moderne** (modern European painting and sculpture from Impressionism onward) is in the 14th-century Old Customs House.

At the west end of the "island" formed by the arms of the Ill is **La Petite France**, with winding streets, half-timbered houses and covered bridges, best observed from the **Barrage Vauban** with its viewing terrace.

A symbol of the aspirations that rose from the ruins of two world wars, Strasbourg's Palais de l'Europe houses the Council of Europe and the European Parliament. Other institutions, like the European Court of Human Rights and the European Science Foundation, have found Strasbourg's location on the border between western and central Europe a congenial place to be.

255

Buildings in the cathedral square, Strasbourg

Battlefields of the North

■ **Many of the most dramatic struggles in the course of French history have taken place in this region whose gently rolling countryside offers few natural barriers to invasion from the northeast. ...■**

Early days The English—called *les goddons* (= God damn!) for their peculiar habit of continuous swearing—were the perennial enemy, and some of the decisive battles of the Middle Ages were fought here, such as **Crécy** and **Agincourt** (Azincourt in French). Later, French anxiety about the exposed frontier fueled successful attempts to push the kingdom's border northeastward, cementing it in place with chains of fortresses and fortified towns. Many of them designed by Louis XIV's ingenious military engineer, Sebastien Le Prestre de Vauban, these Baroque strongholds were the ultimate deterrent of their day, with few financial constraints inhibiting the lavish layout of places like **Le Quesnoy** or the Citadel at **Lille**.

The war to end wars The outcome of the Franco-Prussian War of 1870–71 was decided by Napoleon III's humiliating defeat at Sedan. His successors labored for decades to create an impregnable chain of huge forts along the Meuse. But in 1914, in the opening weeks of World War I, the river was crossed again as the German armies marched southwestward. Stalemate followed the successful French counterattack on the Marne, and for four long years the opposing armies attempted to bleed each other white in a series of lumbering and indecisive offensives. The scenes of the greatest devastation, both of landscape and of human life, took place along the Somme (where the British attack in 1916 cost 600,000 casualties before grinding to a halt), in the soggy fields of Flanders, and at Verdun, where relentless German pressure was countered by equally determined French resistance.

Afterward, memorials arose all over the now silent battlefields to commemorate the unprecedented slaughter. The cemeteries of the British War Graves Commission, much of their classical architecture designed by the great Edwin Lutyens, have a serene, timeless air. They are thickest on the ground in the windswept fields north of the Somme around the rebuilt town of **Albert**, from which a marked Circuit de Souvenir guides the visitor around the killing grounds. A stretch of trenches has been preserved at the Newfoundlanders' memorial at **Beaumont-Hamel**. Farther north, at **Vimy Ridge**, dramatically visible from the A26 motorway, the Canadian Memorial towers over the hilltop. Here, the land has been given in perpetuity to the Canadian nation, a tribute to the 60,000 sacrificed in its capture. The clash of arms in the titanic struggle that raged for eighteen months around **Verdun** finds no echo today in the eerie forest now covering the land deeply plowed by shellfire. Here are some of the most poignant memorials of the war, like the white-towered **Ossuary** of Douaumont, as well as the **Memorial Museum** at nearby Fleury.

World War II Haunted by memories of the carnage, inter-war French governments sought to protect the nation from a recurrence by building a 20th-century equivalent of Louis XIV's frontier fortresses along the Franco-German border. As in the time of Vauban, no expense was spared, but when the test came in 1940, the ultra-modern defenses of the Maginot Line were simply outflanked by the Wehrmacht's blitzkrieg through the "impenetrable" Ardennes to the coast. Remains of this costly deterrent that failed to deter can be seen at **Fermont** near Longwy or at **Lembach** in Alsace.

Fighting in the north, both in the spring of 1940 and in the Liberation of 1944, was brief when compared with the long, drawn-out battles of 1914–18. The epic of **Dunkerque** is recalled by exhibits in the town's Musée des Beaux-Arts, the fate of Calais during the war and occupation by a museum housed in a German bunker. The most tangible remains from World War II are the formidable concrete coastal defenses built to repel the Allied invasion that the Wehrmacht had convinced itself would be launched against the beaches of the Pas de Calais rather than in Normandy. One of the blockhouses of this Atlantic Wall at **Audinghen** on the cliffs between Calais and Boulogne has been converted into a private museum. Germanic mastery of reinforced concrete is demonstrated again in what is supposedly the biggest such structure ever built, the bunker rising ominously over the treetops at **Eperleques** near St-Omer. It was constructed by forced labor, and was built to serve as one of the launching ramps for the V2 rocket bombardment of London, but was put out of action by air attack.

The town center, Toul

Le Touquet airfield, now only used by the private planes of the prosperous, was busy in the 1950s with the bulky Bristol Freighters of Silver City Airways, whose pioneering attempts to fly travelers' cars across the Channel eventually came to nothing.

▶ ▷ ▷   Thann

This little industrial town, southern terminus for both the Route des Crêtes and the Route du Vin (see pages 246–247), is overlooked by the ruins of its medieval castle, the Engelsbourg. The demolition of the fortress in 1673 left a massive cylindrical chunk of the keep lying on its side. Seen from a distance, it resembles a huge eye staring down the valley—hence the local name, *L'Oeil de la Sourcière* (Witch's Eye). Thann's imposing Gothic church is called "the Cathedral" by locals; beneath its tall spire it has an ornately sculpted porch, while inside, the carving of the choir stalls is equally lively. *The Madonna of the Vineyards* is the name given to the church's painted wooden statue of the Virgin and Child, a reminder of the Rangen wine produced here.

▷ ▷ ▷   Toul

Long a fortress city, Toul possessed a strategic importance that was suddenly reinforced when Alsace-Lorraine was lost following the Franco-Prussian War of 1870–71. Huge sunken forts like the one open to the public at nearby **Villey-le-Sec** were hurriedly built to protect France's shrunken eastern frontier. But the star-shaped moats and bastions that still ring the old center are much older, as is the Porte de Metz, a creation of Louis XIV's engineer, Vauban. Toul's **cathedral** has an ornate west front and pretty cloisters, the latter a feature too of the town's other principal church, St-Gengoult.

▶ ▷ ▷   Le Touquet

Known as Paris-Plage (Paris Beach) when first laid out in the 19th century, this seaside resort with its 12-km sandy beach soon became popular with wealthy visitors from the far side of the English Channel, and its chic shops, Club Nautique, and many other sports and leisure facilities still attract the would-be smart set. Behind the main part of the town, its roads laid out grid-fashion, are villas set among the pine trees of a planted forest.

Past glories are characteristic too of enchanting little **Montreuil**, a short way inland up the pretty valley of the Canche. Its population may only be a fraction of what it was in the Middle Ages, but its citadel and ramparts still stand, a fascinating mixture of medieval and Renaissance defense works.

▶ ▶ ▷ Troyes

The ancient capital of the province of Champagne, Troyes has a wealth of half-timbered houses and medieval streets and passageways. A stroll around the old center evokes the atmosphere of medieval times when merchants congregated from all over Europe to attend the great fairs held here. Beyond the elegant Gothic facade of the Basilica of St-Urbain stands the **cathedral,** its interior bathed in the light streaming in through the magnificent stained glass.

Troyes has almost as many museums as churches, all of them housed in venerable buildings and dealing with a range of subjects (tools and implements, local history, hosiery). Outstanding among them is the **Museé d'Art Moderne,** whose modern art includes work by Fauve masters Vlaminck, Van Dongen and Derain.

▶ ▶ ▷ Verdun

The name of Verdun seems fated to be forever associated with the attempt by the German High Command to decide the course of World War I by "bleeding France to death." A tour of the battlefield extending along the Meuse to either side of the city is a powerful reminder of the futility of war. The most evocative monuments are on the right bank, among the new-grown forest blanketing the scenes of devastation (though even the coarsest weeds refuse to grow in places). There are great fortifications like **Fort de Vaux** or **Fort Douaumont,** captured almost accidentally in February 1916 by a German platoon in the early stages of the 18-month battle. Nearby is the **Ossuary** with its tall white Tower of the Dead rising over the countless graves. The course of the struggle is compellingly re-created in the **Mémorial-Musée de la Bataille de Verdun,** built on the the the site of the village of Fleury.

▶ ▶ ▷ Wissembourg

In a pretty position on the banks of the River Lauter, this is one of the most charming little places in Alsace, with old houses, ancient ramparts and a big Gothic church in red sandstone. Wissembourg makes a good base from which to explore northern Alsace. Nearby are some of the province's most delightful villages, Oberseebach, Hoffen, and rustic perfection itself, **Hunspach.** To the west is the rugged, wooded country of the northern Vosges, with ruined medieval castles like **Fleckenstein** and **Falkenstein** glowering from their crags. A later age contributed one of the key strongholds of the Maginot Line, the fort near Lembach known as the **Ouvrage du Four à Chaux** .

The white wines of Alsace are some of France's most distinctive. Unlike their mild-mannered cousins from across the German border, they have a dryness and power which makes them ideal companions for the hearty food of the region. And unlike other French wines, they are generally identified by type of grape (everyday Sylvaner, fruity Gewürztraminer, robust Riesling) rather than by locality.

259

CONVERSION CHARTS

FROM	TO	MULTIPLY BY
Inches	Centimeters	2.54
Centimeters	Inches	0.3937
Feet	Meters	0.3048
Meters	Feet	3.2810
Yards	Meters	0.9144
Meters	Yards	1.0940
Miles	Kilometers	1.6090
Kilometers	Miles	0.6214
Acres	Hectares	0.4047
Hectares	Acres	2.4710
U.S. Gallons	Liters	3.7854
Liters	U.S. Gallons	0.2642
Ounces	Grams	28.35
Grams	Ounces	0.0353
Pounds	Grams	453.6
Grams	Pounds	0.0022
Pounds	Kilograms	0.4536
Kilograms	Pounds	2.205
U.S. Tons	Tonnes	0.9072
Tonnes	U.S. Tons	1.1023

MEN'S SUITS

U.K.	36	38	40	42	44	46	48
Rest of Europe	46	48	50	52	54	56	58
U.S.	36	38	40	42	44	46	48

DRESS SIZES

U.K.	8	10	12	14	16	18
France	36	38	40	42	44	46
Italy	38	40	42	44	46	48
Rest of Europe	34	36	38	40	42	44
U.S.	6	8	10	12	14	16

MEN'S SHIRTS

U.K.	14	14.5	15	15.5	16	16.5	17
Rest of Europe	36	37	38	39/40	41	42	43
U.S.	14	14.5	15	15.5	16	16.5	17

MEN'S SHOES

U.K.	7	7.5	8.5	9.5	10.5	11
Rest of Europe	41	42	43	44	45	46
U.S.	8	8.5	9.5	10.5	11.5	12

WOMEN'S SHOES

U.K.	4.5	5	5.5	6	6.5	7
Rest of Europe	38	38	39	39	40	41
U.S.	6	6.5	7	7.5	8	8.5

Arriving

U.S. citizens need a valid passport to enter France for stays of up to 90 days. First-timers should apply in person five weeks before departure to one of the 13 U.S. Passport Agency offices. Also, local county courthouses, many state and probate courts, and some post offices accept applications. Necessary documents are: (1) a completed passport application (Form DSP-11); (2) proof of citizenship (certified birth certificate issued by the Hall of Records of your state of birth, or naturalization papers); (3) proof of identity (valid driver's license or state, military, or student ID card with your photograph and signature); (4) two recent, identical, two-square-inch photographs (black-and-white or color head shot with white or off-white background); and (5) $65 for a 10-year passport (those under 18 pay $40 for a five-year passport). Check, money order, or cash (exact change) are accepted. Passports are sent in 10 to 15 business days.

You may renew in person or by mail. Send a complete Form DSP-82; two recent, identical passport photographs; your current passport (if it's less than 12 years old and issued after your 16th birthday); and a check or money order for $55.

Air The national airline is Air France, which operates worldwide. France's largest airport by far is Roissy Charles de Gaulle in Paris, to which most international carriers fly. Other airports used for direct scheduled international flights include: Bordeaux, Lyon, Marseille, Nantes, Nice, Strasbourg, and Toulouse. Several smaller airlines use other regional airports (Brest, Rennes, etc.) for international flights, while the domestic airline Air Inter (an offshoot of Air France) links a further 30 or so destinations in France with international services.

Bicycling

Ride on the right-hand side of the road unless there are bicycle paths.

Bicycles can be hired from bicycle shops (obtain local information from tourist offices) and also from French Railways (SNCF). Two hundred railway stations offer Train + Vélo

service; travelers can pick up their bicycle from one station and return it to another. If you want to take your bicycle on a train you must register it, but as it will not necessarily travel with you, try to send it a few days in advance. For short journeys it can travel in the luggage van; this service is free. The leaflet *Guide du train et du vélo* lists participating stations and prices.

More information can be obtained from Fédération Française de Cyclisme, Bâtiment Jean Monnet, 5 rue de Rome, 95561 Rosny-sous-Bois (tel: 49 35 69 00).

Camping

There are over 11,000 campsites throughout France. They have to be registered and are then graded (by the Fédération Française de Camping et Caravanning, 78 rue de Rivoli, 75004 Paris) from one to four stars, depending on the facilities provided. A four-star site has communal indoor recreation areas, hot water, washing machines and lock-up for valuables; one-star sites are more crowded and sometimes have only cold water. Local farmers often rent their fields to campers— *camping à la ferme*—with basic or nonexistent facilities.

A camping *carnet* (book of tickets) is useful; some sites won't let you in without one, and they include some third-party insurance cover. Carnets are obtainable by members from motoring organizations and affiliated trailer and bicycling clubs. One carnet covers up to 12 people.

The Camping Traveler in France, published by the French Government Tourist Office (FGTO), has up-to-date information.

Children

The French tourist industry shows a keen interest in children and several cities provide amusement parks and museums designed to attract them. The **EuroDisney** resort (32 km east of Paris) offers not only a theme park but also hotels, a campsite and a golf course (for parents). **Parc Astérix**, (38 km north of Paris) is already a established as a popular attraction. A new theme park, France Miniature (scale models), has just opened southwest of Paris.

Many large towns have museums, often with hands-on exhibitions, parks (sometimes with puppet shows), circuses, water parks (*parcs et centres aquatiques*) and zoos. In Paris, **Les Musées en Herbe** (Halle-St-Pierre and Jardin d'Acclimation) and **Cité des Sciences**, with its Argonaut and Inventorium, will appeal.

Most hotels reduce the price of accommodations for children, particularly when staying in their parents' room. Some provide a baby-sitting service.

A good children's introduction to France is the Usborne *First Book of France*, obtainable from the publishers (83 Saffron Hill, London EC1N 8RT).

Climate

The south of France, including the Mediterranean coast, has hot, dry summers and warm, wet winters. Showers are short and sharp, often in the middle of the day. Summer winds are cooling and gentle, but the colder and fiercer mistral, which comes from the north, can swirl around for days.

Northwest France is affected by the

Sabots on sale in Chinon

Atlantic; it's often rainy, yet with mild winters and rather cool summers. The southwest area of Aquitaine, including the Dordogne, has hot summers.

Eastern France has a more Continental climate with hot summers and cold winters. In the mountains, altitude is an important factor. While the Vosges are hot in summer, the Massif Central is stormy and the southern massif very dry. In contrast, the Cévennes get a lot of rain and the northern massif can become very hot. As for Paris, late April to early May is probably the best time for a visit—neither too hot, too wet nor too crowded. In July and August, many good restaurants close, and the city can be stifling.

Weather Chart Conversion
25.4 mm = 1 in
0°C = 32°F, 15°C = 59°F,
30°C =86°F

Crime

Vacationers are often more careless abroad than at home. They leave tents open, luggage visible in cars and personal property unattended on beaches, making life easy for opportunist thieves. Pickpockets travel on public transportation and visit fairs and other busy places. If your money or belongings are stolen, contact the police immediately (tel: 17). You'll also need to report the theft in person and sign a statement at the local police station—ask at your hotel where the nearest *gendarmerie* is.

Customs Regulations

You may bring home up to $400 of foreign goods duty-free, provided you've been out of the country for at least 48 hours and you haven't made an international trip in the past 30 days. Each member of the family, regardless of age, is entitled to the same exemption; exemptions may be pooled. For the next $1,000 of goods, a flat 10 per cent rate is assessed; above $1,400, duties vary with merchandise. Travelers 21 or older are allowed one liter of alcohol, 100 cigars (non-Cuban), and 200 cigarettes, and one bottle of perfume

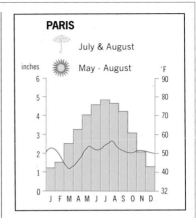

PARIS

☂ July & August

☀ May · August

inches / °F

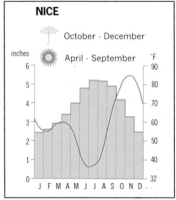

NICE

☂ October · December

☀ April · September

inches / °F

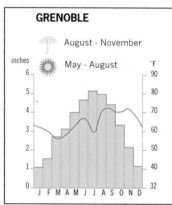

GRENOBLE

☂ August · November

☀ May · August

inches / °F

trademarked in the United States. Antiques and works of art over 100 years old are duty-free. Exceed these limits, and you'll be taxed at the port of entry and additionally in your home state. Gifts under $50 may be mailed duty-free to stateside friends or relatives, with a limit of one package per day per addressee. Perfumes over $5, tobacco, and liquor are prohibited. For "Know Before You Go," a free brochure detailing what you may and may not bring back to this country, contact the U.S. Customs Service (1301 Constitution Ave., Washington, DC 20029, tel. 202/927–6724).

Disabled Travelers

Facilities for the disabled have improved greatly over the past few years, and now many hotels and public buildings, airports and the railway system (SNCF) have been modified to provide help.

A two-volumed publication covering Paris and the provinces, *Touristes Quand Même* (*Travel Just the Same* in English), lists facilities for wheelchair-bound, blind or deaf visitors to museums, major sights, shops, parks, places of worship, theaters, etc. Available from the publishers, CNFLRH, 38 boulevard Raspail, F-75007 Paris (tel: 45 48 90 13). *Europe for the Handicapped Traveler* is available from Mobility International (see addresses below).

Useful addresses

Mobility International, Box 10767, Eugene, Oregon OR 97440 (tel: 503/343 1284).
SATH (Society for the Advancement of Travel for the Handicapped), 347 Fifth Avenue, Suite 610, New York NY 10016 (tel: 212/447 7284).

Driving

Accident Contact the police immediately (tel: 17—this calls the ambulance too), particularly if someone is injured. All parties involved must complete and sign an accident statement form (*constat à l'amiable*) and exchange insurance details. Try to persuade witnesses to stay in order to make statements.

Age You must be at least 18 years of age to drive in France.

Breakdown If your car breaks down, try to move it to the side of the road, and flash your hazard warning lights. If the fault is electrical or the car is on a bend or on a hill, place a red warning triangle on the road 100 feet behind your car (330 feet on motorways). Emergency phones (*postes d'appel d'urgence*), linked to a local police station, are situated at 4-km intervals on main roads and every 2 km on motorways.

Children Children aged 10 and under must sit in the backseat of the car, belted up. If, however, a specially approved fitted seat facing backward is fixed in the front of the car, a baby may use it.

Documents You must bring with you a full valid national driving license, the vehicle's original registration

Costumes and gifts on display in a central Strasbourg shop

document and insurance certificate. If you've borrowed the car, you'll need a letter of authorization from the owner. You'll also need a nationality plate or sticker. You are allowed to bring any vehicle into France for up to six months in a year without customs documents.

Drink It is not forbidden to drive after imbibing alcohol—the limit is 80 mg alcohol per 100 ml blood—but it is much wiser not to drink at all. The penalties are high, and the French police carry out random breath testing. Any driver found to be above the legal limit can be fined on the spot, and visitors may be banned from driving in France.

Fines Drivers can be fined on the spot, although for some infringements the police may accept vouchers from drivers with insurance coverage. If motorists consider themselves innocent, they can pay a deposit *(amende forfaitaire)*, and the police will issue a receipt.

Fuel Leaded gas *(essence super)* is now only sold in one grade (98 octane), while unleaded is sold in two: 95 octane *(essence sans plomb)* and 98 octane *(super sans plomb)*. The minimum amount of gas you can buy is five liters. Diesel *(gazole)* is much cheaper and readily available. A list of cheap stations is available from FGTO.

Garages There is no shortage of garages in France: On motorways they are placed about every 24 km. In some areas of the country, such as the Dordogne, they may be shut on Sundays. You can often pay for gas with a credit card. Garages displaying the *Bison Futé* (wily buffalo) sign give away a free road map of France produced by the French Ministry of Transport. The map shows less congested routes and information centers and lists restaurants, garages and hotels.

Useful phrases include *faîtes le plein* (fill it up) and *vérifiez l'huile, s'il vous plaît* (check the oil, please).

Insurance Fully comprehensive insurance, which will cover you for

some of the expenses incurred after a breakdown or an accident, is advisable; motorists can easily extend their national coverage to go abroad. The best policies provide you with accommodations while your car is being repaired, or replace your vehicle if it's totalled. Policies are likely to cover spare parts and labor charges up to a certain amount.

Lights If another driver flashes his headlights at you, this means that he has priority and you should give way.

Renting a car Most major car-rental companies are represented in France, and visitors are advised to make a reservation in advance. Usually, you must be over 21 (25 in some cases) to rent a car, and restrictions may apply to drivers over 60. Your current driver's license is usually acceptable, but some require an International Driver's Permit, available through an Automobile Club (AAA or CAA) office. For reservations call:
Avis (tel. 800/331–1212);
Budget (tel. 800/527–0700);
Dollar (tel. 800/800–4000);
Hertz (tel. 800/654–3131);
National (tel. 800/328–4567).

Road signs Driving is on the right *(serrez à droite)*. In built-up areas, give way to traffic coming from the right *(priorité à droite)*. The exception is in traffic circles, where signs such as *Vous n'avez pas la priorité* (you do not have priority) or *Cédez le passage* (give way) means you give way to cars already in the circle; where no such sign exists, traffic entering the circle has priority.

Outside built-up areas, traffic on main roads has precedence over traffic from side roads.
toutes directions route for through traffic
sens interdit no entry
sens unique one-way street
déviation diversion
passage protégé main roads having priority
rappel restriction continues (lower speed limit, for example)

Seat belts It is obligatory to wear these, in the back too, if they are

Setting the world to rights: women in traditional Breton dress

fitted. If you are stopped by the police for not wearing them, you can be fined on the spot.

Speed limits In dry weather a higher speed limit applies than in wet weather; wet weather maximum speeds are given in parentheses. On motorways with tolls *(autoroutes à péage)*, the maximum speed is 130 kph (110 kph); on dual carriageways and motorways without tolls, 110 kph (100 kph); other roads, 90 kph (80 kph); in built-up areas, 50 kph under all conditions.

On motorways there is a minimum speed limit of 80 kph in the outside (passing) lane during daylight on flat roads with good visibility. For a year after passing their test, drivers may not exceed 90 kph.

Toll roads Most motorways in France impose tolls and the cost per km varies widely.

Electricity
In France, the supply is 220 volts and the frequency is 50 Hertz (Hz), including electricity on graded campsites. The most commonly used plugs have two round pins, so visitors from countries with flat-pin plugs must take travel adaptors for such gadgets as hairdryers and shavers. The higher frequency (60 Hz) used in Canada and the U.S. may make some appliances run too fast, so you need a transformer too.

Embassies and Consulates
Only in extreme circumstances do you contact your embassy. It is the consul who issues emergency passports, contacts relatives and advises how to transfer funds.
U.S. Embassy: 2 avenue Gabriel, 75382 Paris Cedex 08 (tel: [1] 42 96 12 02). There are consuls-general in Bordeaux, Strasbourg and Marseille.

Emergency Phone Numbers
Police and ambulance—17
Fire *(Pompiers)*—18
Emergency medical aid is available through SAMU *(Service d'aide médicale d'urgence)*; local numbers are on the first page of local phone directories *(l'annuaire)*.

Health
No vaccinations are required for visitors from the U.S. The cost of urgent medical treatment, after an accident, for example, will be covered by normal vacation insurance, but a non-urgent visit to a doctor may not be.

If you need to buy prescription drugs, have your doctor write a prescription using the drug's generic name; brand names vary from country to country.

To find a doctor, ask at your hotel or campsite, or inquire at a local pharmacy. For such minor problems, you can go to a pharmacy (see Pharmacies).

The International Association for Medical Assistance to Travelers (in the U.S.: 417 Center St., Lewiston, NY 14092, tel. 716/754–4883) offers a free worldwide list of approved physicians and clinics whose training meets British and American standards.

U.S. residents should take out a personal health insurance policy before traveling to France.

Hitchhiking
It is forbidden to hitchhike on motorways but permitted on other roads.

Insurance
If you go on a package vacation, the tour operator will offer an insurance policy, but you are under no obligation to buy it, although you may have to buy equivalent coverage from another insurer.

A vacation insurance policy should cover (at least) medical expenses; loss of luggage and money; cancellation or curtailment of your vacation; delayed departure and delayed baggage.

Language

Two separate Romance languages evolved within France: in the north, the *langue d'oïl* , and in the south, the *langue d'oc*, or Occitanian, which included dialects spoken in Limousin, Auvergne and Gascony, as well as in Provence. Today, many Provençal words survive and the **Institute of Occitanian Studies** strives to promote the language, in which some vowel sounds differ from the French and the last syllable is often pronounced.

Roman influence was felt less in Brittany, which had been invaded by Celts driven out of Britain by the Saxons hundreds of years earlier. The Breton language, closely related to Welsh, is spoken in the west, and there is a strong movement to promote it.

In the south, the Pyrenees divide two groups of people from their more politically active counterparts in Spain, with whom they would like to form a separatist nation. In the west are about 50,000 Basques; in the east are the Catalans. Both groups speak their own languages: Basque is unlike any other, while Catalan is similar to Provençal. In Alsace, which for so many years bounced between Germany and France, the local language is more akin to High German.

Meanwhile, the **Académie Française** works hard to preserve the purity of the French language; but speech changes faster than the written word and, to their annoyance, many words of English and American derivation (*le parking*, *le weekend*) are now firmly part of the language.

Basic phrases

yes oui
no non
thank you merci
please s'il vous plaît
hello bonjour
good evening bonsoir

goodnight bonne nuit
goodbye au revoir
can you show me the way to...? pouvez-vous m'indiquer la direction de...?
where is...? où se trouve...?
I would like/we would like...je voudrais/on voudrait
how many/much? combien?
this one ceci
that one cela
that's enough ça suffit
left à gauche
right à droite
near près
straight on tout droit
opposite en face de
what time? à quelle heure?

Numbers

one un/une
two deux
three trois
four quatre
five cinq
six six
seven sept
eight huit
nine neuf
ten dix
first premier/première
second seconde/deuxième
third troisième
fourth quatrième
fifth cinqième

Days of the week

Monday lundi
Tuesday mardi
Wednesday mercredi
Thursday jeudi
Friday vendredi
Saturday samedi
Sunday dimanche

Haras du Pin stud, Normandy

Maps

For planning a vacation in France, and when you get there, good maps are essential. Two useful country maps to have are the Michelin Route Planning Map 911 and the AA Road Map France.

Once you have arrived in France, you need maps on a larger scale (1:200,000).
The IGN (*Institut Géographique National*) publishes a series of large-scale maps of long-distance footpaths (*Grandes Randonnés*). The largest scale maps are the blue ones (*Série Bleue*—1: 25,000).

Local information offices or tourist offices may supply visitors with free town plans.

Media

English-language newspapers are on sale in most towns, but the farther south you go, the more likely they are to be a day or two late. *Le Monde* is the most distinguished French newspaper; *Le Figaro* is the longest established; and several newsmagazines, published on Thursdays, cover a broad range of emphasis and bias.

Almost any type of music can be found on the crowded French airwaves; for news, tune in to France Infos (105.5 MHz).

The BBC World Service broadcasts in English on medium wave 648 KHz. For entertainment in Paris, get a free copy of the monthly *Paris Sélection* magazine from the local tourist office.

Money Matters

The French franc (FF) is made up of 100 centimes. There are coins of 5, 10, 20 and 50 centimes and 1, 2, 10 and 50 francs. Banknotes are denominated in 20, 50, 100, 200 and 500 francs.

To change foreign currency into francs, find a bank displaying a *Change* sign or a foreign exchange bureau; avoid changing money at hotels, as the rate is poor.
Major credit cards—Eurocard (Access/ Mastercard) and Carte Bleue (Visa/Barclaycard) and charge cards (Diners club and American Express)—are widely accepted in larger hotels and restaurants and many shops. Garages, hypermarkets and smaller establishments may not accept them.

Museums

National museums usually charge an entrance fee but allow free entry to anyone under 18, and half-price entry for those aged between 18 and 25 or over 60. Everyone is entitled to half-price entry on Sundays. Municipal museums offer free entry to their permanent collections every day to children under seven and people over 60, and to everyone on Sundays.

National Holidays

Most shops and banks are shut on the days listed below. If any falls on a Sunday, the holiday is taken on the Monday.
New Year's Day—January 1
Easter Monday
Labor Day—May 1
VE Day—May 8
Ascension Day
Whitsun (Monday)
Bastille Day—July 14
Assumption Day—August 15
All Saints' Day—November 1
Armistice Day—November 11
Christmas Day—December 25

Opening Hours

Banks Hours vary, but banks are generally open 9–noon and 2–4. They are closed on Sundays and either Monday or Saturday. Banks close early the day before a public holiday.

Museums National museums are closed on Tuesdays—except Versailles, the Trianon Palace and the Musée d'Orsay, which are closed on

Mondays. Municipal museums are closed on Mondays. Most museums close on Easter Sunday and Monday, Christmas Day and public holidays. Opening hours may be longer in summer.

Shops Hours vary depending on the type of shop, location and season. For example, lunchtime in the heat of summer in the south of France may extend to 4 PM, but then the shops will stay open later in the evening.

Food shops are open Tuesday to Friday 7 or 8–6:30 or 7:30. Most close all day Monday but some may open on Monday afternoon. On Saturday and Sunday they may open mornings only. Smaller shops may close at lunchtime (noon–2). Bakers are open on Sunday mornings. Supermarkets and hypermarkets open from about 9 until 9 or 10. They are closed on Sunday and some hypermarkets also close on Monday mornings.

Pharmacies

Easily recognized by the illuminated green cross, pharmacies are mostly privately owned, and they're run by highly trained staff who can give first aid and advice about ailments. They are not allowed to dispense prescriptions from a foreign doctor. Pharmacies are usually open six days a week, and on Sundays at least one pharmacy in a town is open (*pharmacie de garde*). Its name and address will be displayed outside other shops, announced in the local paper and available from the local *gendarmerie*.

Places of Worship

Every town and village has a Catholic church offering Sunday masses: Look on notice boards to find what time services start—priests often officiate in more than one village. Protestant churches exist in most large towns, particularly in Paris and the Dordogne, which was once a Huguenot area. Jews, Buddhists and members of nonconformist churches may have more difficulty finding out whether there is a place of worship in the town—it's best to ask at the tourist office. Muslims are well-catered to throughout France because of the large North African population.

Tourist offices and town halls can give information on religious services.

Post Office

Open: 8–5, 6 or 7 weekdays, 8–noon Saturday. Small offices close for lunch weekdays.

Recognized by the letters PTT, French post offices deal with mail and telecommunications. You can buy stamps (*timbres de poste*), phone cards (*télécartes*) and cash mail orders, and send telexes. You can also collect letters (showing your passport as proof of identity), which you should have addressed to yourself, c/o Poste Restante, Poste Centrale, followed by number of the department and the name of the town.

Letter boxes are mustard yellow and often fixed on walls. For posting abroad, use the slot marked *départements étrangers*.

Public Transportation

Air A comprehensive and frequent air network links major French cities with one another. Two French

Detail from a fountain in Evreux, Normandy

airlines, Air Inter, part of the Air France group, and TAT, a private airline, fly to a total of 44 airports. Almost all of Air Inter's 30 routes go to Paris; only about half of TAT's 26 routes do. Both airlines operate a complicated ticket system offering red flights (full-price tickets) and blue and white flights (discounts for certain categories of passengers).

Road Local buses serving towns and villages often run once in the morning and once in the afternoon (to take people to market, say, and then home again)—but not necessarily every day. Buses running between towns are cheaper and slightly slower than trains, but long-distance buses do not operate widely in France.

Tickets are bought on the bus and must be canceled (*composter*). If you are in a group or making several journeys, it's worth buying a book of tickets (*carnet*).

Rail French Railways or SNCF (*Société Nationale de Chemins de Fer*) operates a 35,000-km network throughout France. The flagship of the rolling stock is the fleet of high-

speed **TGV** trains (*trains à grande vitesse*), which hold the world train speed record (515.3 kph); normal passenger services operate at about 300 kph. There are now three routes, and the system is steadily expanding, despite environmental concerns. The Atlantique route goes west to Lorient in Brittany and southwest to Toulouse, and the Sud-Est heads for Nice and other Mediterranean resorts via Dijon and the new Nord line links Paris with Lille, Calais and ultimately the UK via the Channel Tunnel. All routes start in Paris, stopping at the new station at Massy. For travel on these trains, a reservation fee is payable, varying according to the time of day and distance. This ticket, as well as the travel ticket, must be validated (stamped with the date) at machines on the platform before boarding the train.

Euro City trains are fast, comfortable, international trains that go to over 200 towns, including 14 European capitals. They are slower than the TGVs but also require a reservation fee. Within France the *rapide* and *express* trains (first and second class) stop more often, and there are even slower local trains. The RER (*Réseau Express Régional*) rail service runs on suburban routes around Paris.

For longer distances, you may decide to travel at night. Many trains have couchettes holding up to six people, both sexes, second class (four people, first class), with washing facilities at the end of the carriage. Two- or three-bed sleepers are more comfortable, with their own washbasins, but first-class sleepers can cost nearly five times as much as a couchette.

Tickets: SNCF divides each day into three sections: red (the most costly time to travel), white, or blue (the cheapest). Travel costs most at weekends, especially from noon on Fridays and on Saturday mornings, while weekdays, from noon on Monday to noon on Friday, are the cheapest times to travel.

A *billet séjour* gives a 25 percent reduction for any return or round trip of 1,000 km or more; each journey

The 15th-century Hôtel Dieu in Beaune, founded as a hospital

must be at least 200 km and start in a blue period.

Paris For traveling on the *Métro* (subway) it's cheapest to buy a book (*carnet*) of 10 tickets; one ticket can be used for journeys of any length. Tickets from the same carnet can be used on buses, but here, the longer your journey, the more tickets you must use. (Tickets are available from some tobacconists, bus terminals or Métros).

A tourist ticket called *Paris Visite* is valid for three or five days and allows unlimited train and bus travel. *Carte jaune* also gives unlimited travel on transport in Paris. This is valid for a week, Monday to Sunday, and can be purchased only up to Wednesday of that week; you need a photo. (Tickets available in Paris from Métro, RER and SNCF stations and the Paris Tourist Office.)

Senior Citizens

National and municipal museums offer half-price tickets to people age 60 or over.

Student and Youth Travel

Three types of reasonably priced cards are available to young people under 26, giving discounts on accommodations, meals and travel as well as to cultural and sporting events. *La Carte Jeune* (Youth Card) is on sale in France at post offices, savings banks, youth hostels and AJF offices (see below) if you have been in France for six months or more.
The International Student Card entitles you to the facilities mentioned above as well as giving museum entry at a discount and beds in university residences. You must provide a photo and identity card. The International Youth Card is issued by FIYTO (Federation of Young Travelers' Organizations) and is for non-students under 26. Buy it in France from OTU Voyages, 6–8 rue Jean Calvin, 75005 Paris; it is valid in 60 countries.

Accommodations

France has 200 youth hostels. Members of national associations can stay at French

Marker flags for oysters, the Atlantic coast's special delicacy

hostels on provision of a membership card with photo. Write to Fédération Unie des Auberges de Jeunesse, 27 rue Pajol, 75018 Paris, for a list of hostels. Youth Card holders are also regarded as members. Over 60 International Accommodation Centers, providing 11,000 beds, give another cheap alternative; they also offer sports and sightseeing programs. They go by different names in different areas of France: FIAP and CISP in Paris and CRID in Dijon. All the centers belong to an organization called UCRIF, and a list of them is available, free, from the FGTO or La Maison de l'UCRIF, 72 rue Rambuteau, 75001 Paris. (tel: [1] 40 26 57 64).

Other places where young people can stay are called *centres de séjour* and *résidences des jeunes*. Accommodation information is available from AJF (Accueil des Jeunes de France), 119 rue St-Martin, Paris 4, and from the Paris Tourist Office at 127 Avenue des Champs-Elysées, 75008 Paris.

Travel Travelers under 26 can buy an Inter-Rail pass, valid for one month and giving free train travel in 24 European countries and a 30 percent to 50 percent discount in the country of purchase. A Eurail Youth Pass offers similar reductions and is available for non-Europeans.

TRAVEL FACTS

Telephones

The coins that pay phones accept are one, five and 10 francs. But some phones accept only *jetons* worth .50FF: small metal discs sold at bars, tobacconists and post offices. You can receive a call in a phone booth if a blue bell sign is shown.

Many booths accept phone cards (*télécartes*): buy them from post offices, tobacconists and railway stations.

National and International Dialing

Every French phone number has eight digits, and the country is not divided into area codes for phone calls; only Paris is different from the rest of the country. If you're phoning Paris from the provinces, dial 161 before the eight digits; to dial the provinces from Paris, dial 16 first.

If you're phoning France from abroad, dial the international code, then 33 (for the provinces), then the eight digits; for Paris, dial 331.

To dial the U.S. from France, dial 19, then 1. Then dial the area code

Honfleur harbour

(omitting the first 0), followed by the number.

Time

France is six hours ahead of the eastern U.S., nine hours ahead of the western U.S.

Toilets

Men are *Messieurs*; women are *Dames*. Public toilets vary from the older, smelly ones with footrests and a hole, to the self-flushing variety. Many have attendants who may sell you paper, but it's always a good idea to take your own.

Tourist Offices

There are over 5,000 tourist offices, in France, called either *Offices de Tourisme* or *Syndicats d'Initatives*. Larger towns have tourist offices called *Acceuil de France*.

The French Government Tourist Office (FGTO) publishes a great deal of literature in English, available from the following address: **United States**: FGTO, 610 Fifth Avenue, Suite 222, New York, NY 10020-2452 (tel: [212] 757 1125).

Groups If you care to balloon over the Loire Valley, sip wine with a countess in Burgundy, or just hop aboard a whistle-stop tour of the country's most famous highlights, then you may want to consider a package tour. Creative itineraries abound, offering access to places you may not be able to get to on your own, as well as the more traditional spots. They also tend to save you money on airfare and hotels. If group outings are not your style, check into independent packages; somewhat more expensive than package tours, they are also more flexible.

When considering a tour, be sure to find out exactly what expenses are included (particularly tips, fares, side trips, additional meals, and entertainment); governmental ratings of all hotels on the itinerary and the facilities they offer; cancellation policies for both you and the tour operator; and, if you are traveling alone, the price of the single supplement. Most tour operators

Caen cathedral

request that bookings be made through a travel agent (there is no additional charge for doing so). There follows a sampling of the many tour options that are available. Contact your travel agent or the French Government Tourist Office for additional resources.

General-Interest Tours
American Express Vacations (110 E. Broward Blvd., Ft. Lauderdale, FL 33301, tel. 800/241–1700) is a veritable supermarket of tours; you name it—they've either got it packaged or they'll customize a package for you.
Globus and Cosmos Tourama (5301 S. Federal Circle, Littleton, CO 80123, tel. 303/797–2800 or 800/221–0090) offers the hectic but comprehensive 15-day "La France".
Jet Vacations (1775 Broadway, Suite 2405, New York, NY 10019, tel. 212/247–0999 or 800/JET–0999) features freewheeling driving itineraries through all regions of France.
Trafalgar Tours (11 E. 26th St., New York, NY 10010, tel. 212/689–8977 or 800/854–0103) offers a moderately priced, two-week "Best of France" program.
Olson-Travelworld (970 W. 190th St., Suite 425, Torrance, CA 90502, tel. 800/421–5785 or 310/354–2600) has 15- and 21-day "French

Masterpieces" and "Treasures of France" tours.
Maupintour (1515 St. Andrews Dr., Lawrence, KA 66047, tel. 800/255–4266 or 913/843–1211) has 13-day "France Highlights" and "Southern France/Provence and the Riviera" tours.

Special-Interest Tours
Wine/Cuisine Travel Concepts (62 Commonwealth Ave., Suite 3, Boston, MA 02116, tel. 617/266–8450) serves up such specialties as "Champagne and Cuisine with Mrs. Charles Heidsieck" (of Heidsieck Champagne fame), "Burgundy: History of Wine & Cuisine with Countess De Loisy."

Art/Architecture Past Times Arts and Archeological Tours (800 Larch La., Sacramento, CA 95864–5042, tel. 916/485–8140) escorts the curious through the strange world of prehistoric cave art in southern France. Its "Paris Art Museums and Historic Neighborhoods" is a tour that tells as well as it shows.

Ballooning Buddy Bombard's European Balloon Adventures (855 Donald Ross Rd., Juno Beach, Fl 33408, tel. 407/775–0039 or 800/862–8537) takes groups of 18 or less into the gentle breezes above Burgundy and the Loire Valley during its three- to six-night tours, and offers fine dining on the ground.

Hotels and guest houses

The French Government Tourist Office (FGTO) publishes lists of approved hotels, which are rated on a scale from one-star to four-star. Some local tourist offices (those with an Accueil de France service) can help with last-minute hotel bookings.

Although it is possible to stay throughout the country in hotels belonging to perfectly reputable hotel chains (including Frantel, Ibis, Mercure, Novotel and Sofitel), which provide a formula of convenient and often high-standard bases for business or passing-through travelers, it is generally the traditional French hotel that offers the chance of combining picturesque charm and ambience with a memorable gastronomic experience. Many of the simpler (one- and two-star) family-run hotels, mainly in rural areas, belong to the Logis de France marketing organization and can be recognized by a distinctive yellow fireplace logo. Following inspections, they are classified with one, two or three "chimneys." A guide to the 5,000 or so Logis hotels is available from the FGTO, bookshops, or La Fédération Nationale des Logis de France, 25 rue Jean Mermosz, 75008 (tel: [1] 43 59 86 67).

At the opposite end of the spectrum, some well-established luxury hotels belong to the Relais et Châteaux organization; their annual brochure is available from the FGTO.

Staying in a château can be a more personal experience, and not necessarily an inordinately expensive one. The association Château Accueil covers 75 privately owned castles, mansions and historic buildings that offer house-guest accommodations, either on a bed-and-breakfast basis or with an evening meal (taken en famille).

More modest guest-house accommodation is available in over 2,000 country houses, farms and even châteaus, through the organization Gîtes Chambres d'Hôte/Gîtes Tables d'Hôte, identified by the yellow and green Gîtes de France logo, which features a cockerel and a roof, together with a Chambres d'Hôtes sign. Information is available from: Fédération National des Gîtes Ruraux, 35 rue Godot de Mauroy, 75009 Paris (tel: [1] 47 42 20 20).

Some establishments place the emphasis on their restaurant and offer bedrooms as an ancillary service. The list of recommended hotels that follows gives a selection of places where the standard of cooking is above average in its category. Restaurants are listed separately for Paris and other cities where you are more likely to stay in a hotel without one.

Self-catering

France is extremely well endowed with self-catering vacation accommodation of all kinds, largely as a result of the very high level of second-home ownership. The Gîtes de France organization offers thousands of simple rural properties all over the country; many are converted farm buildings, and may be remote. All are inspected and graded into three categories (tel: [1] 47 23 77 30).

PARIS

Accommodations

Expensive

L'Abbaye St-Germain, 10 rue Cassette, 75006 Paris (tel: [1] 45 44 38 11). Fine 17th-century town house with charming courtyard and sophisticated decor. Airy, open-plan bar/salon area. No restaurant.

Le Crillon, 10 place de la Concorde, 75008 Paris (tel: [1] 44 71 15 00). One of the world's great hotels, classical and elegant throughout, with the most lavishly decorated restaurant in Paris (lunch menus are good value for the quality of the surroundings).

L'Hôtel, 13 rue des Beaux-Arts, 75006 Paris (tel: [1] 43 25 27 22). Truly idiosyncratic, sophisticated Left Bank hotel, frequented now, as always, by the famous. You can chose Oscar Wilde's or Mistinguett's bedroom; all are individually decorated, some very eccentrically. Piano bar; popular small restaurant.

Le Pavillon de la Reine, 28 place des Vosges, 75003 Paris (tel: [1] 42 77 96 40). On Paris's most beautiful old square, a comfortable hotel with garden and courtyard. Parking. No restaurant.

Moderate

Les Deux Iles, 59 rue St-Louis-en-l'Ile, 75004 Paris (tel: [1] 43 26 13 35). Beautiful 18th-century town house on the island, charmingly furnished. Cosy bar and elegant little sitting room. No restaurant.

Des Grands Hommes/Panthéon, 17–19 place du Panthéon, 75005 Paris (tel: [1] 46 34 19 60 and [1] 43 54 32 95). Neighboring buildings, hotels since the 18th century, with glassed-in garden, on quiet (at night) square. Smart bedrooms with good bathrooms. No restaurant.

Latitudes St-Germain, 7–11 rue St-Benoît, 75006 Paris (tel: [1] 42 61 53 53). Large, recently converted hotel, set in former printing house in heart of St-Germain; spacious bedrooms in classic style. Piano bar. No restaurant.

Lenox, 9 rue de l'Université, 75007 Paris (tel: [1] 42 96 10 95). In street of antique shops in St-Germain, a stylish and classic little hotel with small bedrooms. Bar, chintzy salon. No restaurant.

Des Marronniers, 21 rue Jacob, 75006 Paris (tel: [1] 43 25 30 60) Popular little hotel with small garden and

HOTELS AND RESTAURANTS

colorful veranda. Small rustic-style bedrooms with some tiny bathrooms. No restaurant.

Budget

Esméralda, 7 rue St-Julien-le-Pauvre, 75005 Paris (tel: [1] 43 54 19 20). Views of Notre-Dame; objets d'art; and an eccentric style in this 16th-century building. No restaurant.

Le Jardin des Plantes, 5 rue Linné, 75005 Paris (tel: [1] 47 07 06 20). Located opposite the botanical gardens, with flower themes in bedrooms. Roof terrace, tearoom (and light meals), bar.

Place des Vosges, 12 rue de Birague, 75004 Paris (tel: [1] 42 72 60 46). Just around the corner from the glorious square, a 17th-century house decorated and furnished in rustic style. No restaurant.

Prima Lepic, 29 rue Lepic, 75018 Paris (tel: [1] 46 06 44 64). Pretty, plant-filled hotel in the heart of bohemian Montmatre.

Restaurants
Expensive

L'Ambroisie, 9 place des Vosges, 75004 Paris (tel: [1] 42 78 51 45). Booked well ahead, small and exclusive, with superb decor and highly talented cooking by Bernard Pacaud.

Grand Vefour, 17 rue de Beaujolais, 75001 Paris (tel: [1] 42 96 56 27). Arguably the most attractive restaurant in Paris, a historic monument under the arcades of the Palais Royal. Formal elegance.

Jöel Robuchon, 59 avenue Raymond Poincaré, 75016 Paris (tel: [1] 47 27 12 27). Palatial new quarters for one of France's greatest

living chefs; a superb art nouveau setting complements the magnificent food.

Moderate

Le Boeuf sur le Toit, 34 rue du Colisée, 75008 Paris (tel: [1] 43 59 83 80). Elegant brasserie with '20s decor, near the Champs-Elysées. Good seafood, choucroute, foie gras.

Le Bourdonnais, 113 avenue de la Bourdonnais, 75007 Paris (tel: [1] 47 05 47 96). A place for serious foodies who appreciate what's on their plate more than the decor (however comfortable, even elegant). Excellent value for memorable standard of cooking.

Brasserie Flo, 7 cour des Petites-Ecuries, 75010 Paris (tel: [1] 47 70 13 59). Jolly and authentic turn-of-the-century brasserie.

La Coupole, 102 boulevard du Montparnasse, 75014 Paris (tel: [1] 43 20 14 20). Famous and noisy brasserie with literary and artistic associations, still atmospheric. Open till 2 AM.

La Ferme St-Simon, 6 rue Saint-Simon, 75007 Paris (tel: [1] 45 48 35 74). Cramped and popular (with writers, editors, politicians), a plush and elegant small restaurant with excellent food.

La Fermette Marbeuf 1900, 5 rue Marbeuf 75008 Paris (tel: [1] 47 23 31 31). Glorious Belle Epoque decor. Good value menu and wine list.

La Guirlande de Julie, 25 place des Vosges, 75003 Paris (tel: [1] 48 87 94 07). Fresh, winter garden decor, with terrace, on beautiful square.

Au Pied de Cochon, 6 rue de Coquillière, 75001 Paris (tel: [1] 42 36 11 75). Pork, pork and more pork. A Parisian institution on the site of the former Halles market, now more popular with tourists than early-morning porters, but still open 24 hours a day and still good.

Le Procope, 13 rue de l'Ancienne-Comédie, 75006 Paris (tel: [1] 43 26 99 20). One of the oldest café/restaurants (1686) in the world, another with literary associations (Racine, Voltaire, Rousseau. . . .). Agence France Presse telex, fax; piano and pianola. Open till 2 AM.

Budget

Brasserie Lutetia, 23 rue de Sèvres, 75006 Paris (tel: [1] 49 54 46 76). Bustling, modern brasserie in the hotel of the same name opposite the Luxembourg gardens. Good-value menu includes wine.

Au Gourmet de l'Isle, 42 rue St-Louis-en-l'Ile, 75004 Paris (tel: [1] 43 26 79 27). Traditional, hearty fare (andouillettes, tête de veau) with bistro atmosphere.

Le Petit Mabillon, 6 rue Mabillon, 75006 Paris (tel: [1] 43 54 08 41). Picturesque old bistro, with terrace. Simple dishes of the day.

Thoumieux, 79 rue St-Dominique, 75007 Paris (tel: [1] 47 05 49 75). Country cooking and provincial style in bustling bistro.

NORMANDY

Accommodations
Expensive

Château d'Audrieu, Audrieu, 14250 Calvados (tel: 31 80 21 52). Fine 18th-century château, in large grounds with swimming pool. Excellent and inventive cooking and an extensive wine list

Manoir d'Hastings, 18 avenue de la Côte-de-Nacre, Bénouville, 14970 Calvados (tel: 31 44 62 43). Renowned restaurant, now with rooms (though that should not suggest meager comforts; merely that the bedrooms, in a rather dull modern building in the garden, came after the restaurant). Glorious breakfasts, and a particularly fine tarte chaude normande.

Pullman Grand Hôtel, Cabourg, 14390 Calvados (tel: 31 91 01 79). Enviable position right on the beach, with terrace, tea dancing in summer and lots of bustle. Some bedrooms are enormous.

Moderate
Auberge de l'Abbaye, Le Bec-Hellouin, 27800 Eure (tel: 32 44 86 02). Exceptionally charming Norman village house. Resolutely Norman cooking—veal, apple tart, cheese, and cream with everything.
Auberge du Vieux Puits, 6 rue Notre-Dame-du-Pré, Pont-Audemer, 27500 Eure (tel: 32 41 01 48). Splendid, timbered, 17th-century former tannery. The focal point is the restaurant—all gleaming copper, polished wood and flowers.
Le Dauphin, place de la Halle, L'Aigle, 61300 Orne (tel: 33 24 43 12). Old post house, renovated with care, in traditional style. There's a fine collection of Calvados on offer, in the restaurant and in a little shop.
France et Fuchsias, St-Vaast-La-Hougue, 50550 Manche (tel: 33 54 42 26). Well-run, simple town hotel with an excellent restaurant popular with the yachting fraternity from the nearby marina.
Hostellerie Lechat, place Ste-Catherine, Honfleur, 14600 Calvados (tel: 31 89 23 85). Right in the bustling heart of town, with terrace looking out over the church.
Le Lion d'Or, 71 rue St-Jean, Bayeux, 14400 Calvados (tel: 31 92 06 90). Still the best-known hotel in town, with bedrooms around a flowery courtyard, and a busy restaurant. You may not hear much French, though.
Le Manoir du Lys, route de Juvigny, Bagnoles-de-l'Orne, 61140 Orne (tel: 33 37 80 69). A 19th-century hunting lodge in spacious grounds (with tennis). Very comfortable; good cooking.
Relais des Gourmets, 15 rue de Geôle, Caen, 14300 Calvados (tel: 31 86 06 01). High standard of comfort behind a dull exterior, just

by the grounds of the château (and museums). Very attractive restaurant.
Saint Pierre, Grande-Rue, Le Mont-St-Michel, 50116 Manche (tel: 33 60 14 03). Rampart building on the way up to the great abbey church (you'll need to leave your car way below). Well-modernized bedrooms; bustling restaurant.
La Verte Campagne, Hameau Chevalier, Trelly, 50660 Manche (tel: 33 47 65 33). This old farmhouse is profoundly peaceful, and the dining and sitting rooms (with log fires) are cosy.

Budget
Les Isles, 9 boulevard Maritime, Barneville-Carteret, 50270 Manche (tel: 33 04 90 76). Solid family seaside establishment, with straightforward cooking.
La Rançonnière, Crépon, 14480 Creuilly (tel: 31 22 21 73). Between Bayeux (12 km) and landing beaches, this is a real and very old farm. Simple country fare is served in a barnlike dining hall.

BRITTANY

Accommodations
Expensive
Château de Coätguelen, Pléhédel, 22290 Côtes-d'Amor (tel: 96 22 31 24). Stylish 19th-century château 9 km from the port of Paimpol, set in extensive grounds.
Château de Locguénolé, route de Port-Louis, Hennebont, 56700 Morbihan (tel: 97 76 29 04). Another 19th-century château, rather formal in parts, with a renowned restaurant. Large wooded grounds.
Manoir de Lan-Kerellec, Trébeurden, 22560 Côtes-d'Amor (tel: 96 23 50 09). Sophisticated and elegant little manor house in leafy residential area with path down to the beach.
De la Plage, Ste-Anne-La-Palud, 29127 Finistère (tel: 98 92 50 12). Isolated at the edge of an enormous

expanse of sandy beach. High standard of cooking, with a well-chosen wine list.

Moderate
D'Avaugour, 1 place Champ, Dinan, 22100 Côtes-d'Amor (tel: 96 39 07 49). Solid old town house with rampart gardens and an airy restaurant. Bedrooms comfortable, if a little dull.
Le Bretagne, 13 rue St-Michel, Questembert, 56230 Morbihan (tel: 97 26 11 12). If you're tired of seafood platters, this is the place for a gastronomic pilgrimage. Georges Paineau is one of France's foremost chefs. A few elegant little bedrooms.
Central, 6 Grande-Rue, Saint-Malo, 35400 Ille-et-Vilaine (tel: 99 40 87 70). In the old town (intra-muros). Comfortable little bedrooms; popular restaurant (La Frégate).
Le Goyen, place J Simon, Audierne, 29770 Finistère (tel: 98 70 08 88). Solid, port-side hotel, impeccably run. Adolphe Bosser, the owner, is one of the best chefs in Brittany.
Kastel-Moor and Ker-Moor, avenue de la Plage, Bénodet, 29950 Finistère (tel: 98 57 05 01 and 98 57 04 48). Twin hotels sharing large garden, with swimming pool and tennis, just across the road from the resort beach.
Manoir de Moëllien, Locronan, 29550 Finistère (tel: 98 92 50 40). Austere old stone manor, in isolated

277

Pottery from Gien

setting 2.5 km northwest of Locronan. Ten ground-floor bedrooms with french windows.

Le Roof, Presqu'île de Conleau, Vannes, 56000 Morbihan (tel: 97 63 47 47). Fine situation by a small beach on Morbihan Gulf. Part of Best Western group.

Budget

Chez Pierre, Raguenès Plage, 29139 Névez (tel: 98 06 81 06). Delightful family hotel in a rural setting close to the beach. New annex across the garden has duplex rooms. Children can eat early and are well catered for.

Du Port, Port-Manech, 29920 Névez (tel: 98 06 82 17). Neat and compact hotel up a short hill from the port and beach of this bustling little resort.

Thalamot, Le Chemin-Creux, Beg-Meil, 29170 Fouesnant (tel: 98 94 97 38). Straightforward little establishment, near beach and harbor.

LOIRE

Accommodations
Expensive

Château d'Artigny, Montbazon, 37250 Indre-et-Loire (tel: 47 26 24 24). Arguably one of the finest château hotels in France (1919; loaded with marble, gilt, frescoes). Comfort and facilities cannot be faulted, provided you like the style.

Domaine des Hauts de Loire, Onzain, 41150 Loir-et-Cher (tel: 54 20 72 57). Sober and elegant 18th-century mansion, with very large and beautiful bedrooms and apartments.

Grand Hôtel du Lion d'Or, 69 rue G. Clemenceau, Romorantin, 41200 Loir-et-Cher (tel: 54 76 00 28). Didier Clement is one of France's finest chefs. If you're fearful of over-indulgence, you can opt for half portions. Old coaching inn around courtyard.

Moderate

d'Angleterre, 1 place des Quatre Piliers, Bourges, 18000 Cher (tel: 48 24 68 51). Very central, traditional old hotel near Palais Jacques Coeur.

Jeanne de Laval, 54 rte Nationale, Les Rosiers-sur-Loire, 49350 Maine-et-Loire (tel: 41 51 80 17). One of the best-known eating establishments in the Loire. Its reputation was created by the current owner's father some 50 years ago. Bedrooms are more simple.

Le Bon Laboureur et Château, Chenonceaux, 37150 Indre-et-Loire (tel: 47 23 90 02). An attractive and peaceful establishment, with bedrooms in annexes or around the flowery courtyard.

La Caillère, 36 route des Montils, Candé-sur-Beuvron, 41120 Loir-et-Cher (tel: 54 44 03 08). Small country house, with the emphasis on the restaurant—one of the best in the area.

Gargantua, 73 rue Haute-St-Maurice, Chinon, 37500 Indre-et-Loire (tel: 47 93 04 71). Restaurant with rooms in beautiful 15th-century town mansion in old town.

Grand St-Michel, Chambord, 41250 Loir-et-Cher (tel: 54 20 31 31). The position is everything—isolated at the edge of a forest clearing opposite the great château. The hotel is comfortable but rather unexciting.

Budget

Annexe Le Bussy, Montsoreau, 49730 Maine-et-Loire (tel: 41 51 71 76). Fine views of the powerful white château; rustic-style bedrooms.

Le Cheval Blanc, Ste-Montaine, Aubigny-sur-Nère, 18700 Cher (tel: 48 58 06 92). Traditional and peaceful little Solognote hotel, 9 km west of the attractive village of Aubigny.

Aux Naulets d'Anjou, 18 rue Croix-de-Mission, Gennes, 49350 Maine-et-Loire (tel: 41 51 81 88). Modern house in residential area, with garden. Owners run art, crafts and music courses.

Le Pont d'Ouchet, 50 Grande-Rue, Onzain, 41150 Loir-et-Cher (tel: 54 20 70 33). Basic, central restaurant with rooms, offering good food and very good value. Some family-size bedrooms.

Splendid, 139 rue du Dr Gaudrez, Montreuil-Bellay, 49260 Maine-et-Loire (tel: 41 53 10 00). Small and pretty bedrooms, some with château views; annex Le Relais du Bellay has swimming pool and garden.

ATLANTIC COAST

Accommodations
Expensive

Château Cordeillan-Bages, Route des Châteaux, Pauillac, 33250 Gironde (tel: 56 59 24 24). Paradise for oenophiles among the

Taking the air, Honfleur

world's finest vineyards.
Charming, light bedrooms.
Hôtel du Chantaco, Golf de
Chantaco, Saint-Jean-de-
Luz, 64500 Pyrénées-
Atlantiques (tel: 59 26 14
76). Basque-style house,
with gardens looking over
the famous golf course.
Hôtel du Palais, 1 avenue de
l'Impératrice, Biarritz, 64200
Pyrénées-Atlantiques (tel:
59 41 64 00). Empress
Eugénie's villa, high above
the sea, furnished in
appropriate style. The
cooking does justice to its
surroundings.

Moderate
Au Bon Coin du Lac, 34
avenue du Lac, Mimizan,
40200 Landes (tel: 58 09 01
55). Elegant restaurant-with-
rooms in lakeshore gardens.
Shady courtyard setting for
memorable food.
**France-Angleterre et
Champlain**, 20 rue
Rambaud, La Rochelle,
17000 Charente-Maritime
(tel: 46 41 34 66). Fine old
town house, in heart of old
town (noisy in the
morning, quiet at night);
pretty garden. No
restaurant.
Plaisance, place du Clocher,
Saint-Emilion, 33330
Gironde (tel: 57 24 72 32).
Renovated old building by
the bell tower. Competent
cooking and has a large
wine list.

Budget
Central, 8 rue Maison
Suisse, Biarritz, 64200
Pyrénées-Atlantiques (tel:
59 22 02 06). Quietly
situated, simple and well
kept. No restaurant.
Logis de la Couperie, La
Roche-sur-Yon, 85000
Vendée (tel: 51 37 21 19).
Romantic, personally run
hotel in large 19th-century
country house with extensive
grounds. Peaceful and
elegantly furnished. No
restaurant.
Au Marais, 46–8 quai L.
Tardy, Coulon, 79510 Deux-
Sèvres (tel: 49 35 90 43).
Riverside inn, well placed
for canal boat trips. Good
regional cooking; peaceful
rooms in an annex.

Restaurants
Expensive
Le Chapon Fin, 5 rue
Montesquieu, Bordeaux,
33000 Gironde (tel: 56 79 10
10). A Bordeaux institution,
with extravagant decor.
Weekday lunch menus offer
outstanding value.

Moderate
Le Vieux Bordeaux, 27 rue
Buhan, Bordeaux, 33000
Gironde (tel: 56 52 94 36).
One of the best of
Bordeaux's restaurants.

Budget
L'Assiette Saint Jean, 18 rue
St Jean-du-Pérot, La
Rochelle, 17000 Charentes-
Maritimes (tel: 46 41 75 75).
Small, rustic restaurant offer-
ing local seafood recipes.

DORDOGNE

Accommodations
Expensive
Des Beaux-Arts, 1 place du
Pont-Neuf, Toulouse, 31000
Haute-Garonne (tel: 61 23 40
50). Recently renovated
small hotel, with a
neighboring brasserie open
till the small hours.
L'Esplanade, Domme, 24250
Dordogne (tel: 53 28 31 41).
Very traditional old hotel at
edge of tourist village.
Grand Ecuyer, rue Voltaire,
Cordes, 81170 Tarn (tel: 63
56 01 03). Wonderful
medieval mansion,
sumptuously restored, with
renowned patron/chef.
Le Vieux Logis, Trémolat,
24510 Dordogne (tel: 53 22
80 06). Very peaceful old
buildings set in immaculate
gardens (with helipad).

Moderate
Auberge du Noyer, Le
Reclaud de Bouny Bas, Le
Bugue, 24260 Dordogne (tel:

53 07 11 73). Splendid converted farmhouse and out-
buildings. Large bedrooms.
Auberge du Sombral, St-
Cirque-Lapopie, 46330 Lot
(tel: 65 31 26 08). Very old
house, beautifully restored,
in high medieval village.
Simple country style with
cooking to match.
De Bordeaux, 38 place
Gambetta, Bergerac, 24100
Dordogne (tel: 53 57 12 83).
On main square. Terrace for
eating out.
De la Bouriane, place du
Foirail, Gourdon, 46300 Lot
(tel: 65 41 16 37). Simple,
traditional hostelry in small
market town. Above-
average cooking.
Le Centre, place de la
Mairie, Les Eyzies, 24620
Dordogne (tel: 53 06 97 13).
Better value than some of
its competitors in this major
tourist center, with riverside
setting and good cooking.
France, avenue F. de
Maynard, Saint-Céré, 46400
Lot (tel: 65 38 02 16).
Modern, rustic-style hotel
with fine garden. Good-
value menus.
Les Griffons, Le Pont,
Bourdeilles, 24310
Dordogne (tel: 53 03 75 61).
Fine 16th-century house on
the banks of the Dronne,
with popular restaurant.
Jean-Marie Miquel, place du
Faubourg, Najac 12270
Aveyron (tel: 65 29 74 32).
Fine old house in medieval
village; some bedrooms
have excellent views. Good-
value menus.
Laborderie, Tamniès, 24620
Dordogne (tel: 53 29 68 59).
Village-center hotel with
annexes. Traditional
Perigordian cooking.
L'Univers, 2 place de la
République, Villefranche-de-
Rouergue, 12200 Aveyron
(tel: 65 45 15 63). Simple,
central hotel with views
over hills and old town.
Good-value menus.

Budget
Bonnet, Beynac-et-Cazenac,
24220 Dordogne (tel: 53 29
50 01). Very popular family
hotel in heart of picture-
book village; fine terrace.
Au Déjeuner de Sousceyrac,
Sousceyrac, 46190 Lot (tel:

Lavender on display in a Provence shop

65 33 00 56). Simple auberge in remote village, with small bedrooms. Excellent cooking and good value local wines.

France, 3 rue M Dufraisse, Ribérac, 24600 Dordogne (tel: 53 90 00 61). Revitalized old building, with small garden. Good-value menus.

Pagès, route de Payrac, Calès, 46350 Lot (tel: 65 37 95 87). Simple stone hostelry on the Causse de Gramat, with popular and good-value restaurant.

Relais Saint-Jacques, Collonges-la-Rouge, 19500 Corrèze (tel: 55 25 41 02). Attractive auberge in wonderful, red, stone medieval village.

De la Tour, place de l'Eglise, Aubazine, 19190 Corrèze (tel: 55 25 71 17). Central, with good-value menus.

PYRENEES

Accommodations
Expensive
Hostellerie des Sept Molles, Sauveterre-de-Comminges, 31510 Haute-Garonne (tel: 61 88 30 87). In a secluded rural setting 3 km from Sauveterre. Elegant but informal, with large garden.

Les Prés d'Eugénie, Eugénie-les-Bains, 40320 Landes (tel: 58 05 06 07). Michel Guérard's luxury and very expensive restaurant/hotel/health farm. Bedrooms in a Second Empire mansion or in a converted convent.

Pyrénées, 19 place Général de Gaulle, St-Jean-Pied-de-Port, 64220 Pyrénées-Atlantiques (tel: 59 37 01 01). Busy, traditional hostelry in the center of this stop for Santiago-bound pilgrims. Excellent-value restaurant.

Moderate
Arraya, Sare, 64310 Pyrénées-Atlantiques (tel: 59 54 20 46). Glorious old Basque village house, beautifully furnished and maintained, with small garden. Sophisticated atmosphere, good food.

Auberge Atalaya, Llo, 66800 Pyrénées-Orientales (tel: 68 04 70 04). Delightful old converted farmhouse in tiny Cerdagne village.

Des Cèdres, Villeneuve-de-Rivière, Saint-Gaudens, 31800 Haute-Garonne (tel: 61 89 36 00). Former summer house of the marquise de Montespan. Comfortable bedrooms; large grounds. Classic cooking with Gascon specialities.

Errobia, avenue Chantecler, Cambo-les-Bains, 64250 Pyrénées-Atlantiques (tel: 59 29 71 26). Fine old-fashioned Basque house in charming grounds some distance from resort center. No restaurant.

Budget
Auberge du Poids Public, St-Félix-Lauragais, 31540 Haute-Garonne (tel: 61 83 00 20). Old inn in hilltop village. Local reputation for good cooking and wine list.

Brèche de Roland, Gèdre, 65120 Hautes-Pyrénées (tel: 62 92 48 54). Village center, 8.5 km from Gavarnie, in fine walking country. Cheerful, rustic style.

Mir, St-Lary-Soulan, 65170 Hautes-Pyrénées (tel: 62 39 40 03). In heart of resort; owned by a ski champion's family. Simple and good value.

Nivelle, St-Pée-sur-Nivelle, 64310 Pyrénées-Atlantiques (tel: 59 54 10 27). Little Basque auberge. Small, simple bedrooms (plus some in modern annex across field). Good food.

L'Oustal, Unac, 09250 Ariège (tel: 61 64 48 44). Pretty auberge in tiny village (13 km northwest of Ax-les-Thermes) with views. Cooking well above average.

Pic d'Anie, Lescun, 64490 Pyrénées-Atlantiques (tel: 59 34 71 54). Simple old mountain hotel in center of walking village.

PROVENCE AND THE MEDITERRANEAN COAST

Accommodations
Expensive
L'Abbaye de Sainte-Croix, route du Val-de-Cuech, Salon-de-Provence, 13300 Bouches-du-Rhône (tel: 90 56 24 55). Twelfth-century abbey buildings, beautifully converted, in rural setting between Aix and Arles. Beautiful swimming pool, cool and elegant public rooms, very good cooking.

d'Europe, 12 place Crillon, Avignon, 84000 Vaucluse (tel: 90 82 66 92). Just outside the city walls, but near the sights, an elegant 16th-century mansion with formal atmosphere.

La Réserve, boulevard Maréchal Leclerc, Beaulieu-sur-Mer, 06310 Alpes-Maritimes (tel: 93 01 00 01). Scott Fitzgerald, Greta Garbo—the prewar atmosphere of this Italianate palace lingers on.

Moderate
Les Antiques, 15 avenue Pasteur, Saint-Rémy-de-Provence, 13210 Bouches-du-Rhône (tel: 90 92 03 02). Very charming 19th-century mansion near the center. No restaurant.

Auberge de la Madone, Peillon, 06440 Alpes-Maritimes (tel: 93 79 91 17). Astonishing situation, perched high in an isolated medieval village 18 km behind Nice.

Les Arcades, 16 place des Arcades, Biot, 06410 Alpes-Maritimes (tel: 93 65 01 04). Village-center bistro/art gallery, with good local cooking and simple rustic bedrooms.

Arène, place des Langes, Orange 84100 Vaucluse (tel: 90 34 10 95). In the heart of the old town, on a delightful shady square. Your car is parked for you. No restaurant.

D'Arlatan, 26 rue du Sauvage, Arles, 13200 Bouches-du-Rhône (tel: 90 93 56 66). Fine and very old mansion near the place du Forum. Your car is parked for you. No restaurant.

Le Beffroi, rue de l'Evêché, Vaison-la-Romaine, 84110 Vaucluse (tel: 90 36 04 71). Wonderful 16th-century building up a steep hill in the medieval quarter.

Clair Logis, avenue Centrale, St-Jean-Cap-Ferrat, 06230 Alpes-Maritimes (tel: 93 76 04 57). Very simple establishment in large and lush gardens at the heart of the Cap. No restaurant.

D'Entraigues, place de l'Evêché, Uzès, 30700 Gard (tel: 66 22 32 68). Fine old town house; small bedrooms, a few self-catering apartments, and a wonderful restaurant terrace with a view of the Tour Fenestrelle.

Les Florets, route des Dentelles-de-Montmirail, Gigondas, 84190 Vaucluse (tel: 90 65 85 01). At the foot of the rugged Dentelles and near the wine village of Gigondas. Good cooking and wine list (the patron has his own vineyards).

Le Manoir, 8 rue de l'Entrecasteaux, Aix-en-Provence, 13100 Bouches-du-Rhône (tel: 42 26 27 20). Former cloister in quiet situation near center. No restaurant.

Lou Troupelen, chemin des Vendanges, St-Tropez, 83990 Var (tel: 94 97 44 88). Modern, Provençal-style buildings, at the back of town, with garden and views. No restaurant. One of the cheapest St-Tropez hotels.

Mas d'Aigret, Les Baux-de-Provence, 13520 Bouches-du-Rhône (tel: 90 54 33 54). The best value of all the luxury hotels in this extraordinary resort, below the medieval village.

La Table du Comtat, Séguret, 84110 Vaucluse (tel: 90 46 91 49). Attractive old house set in picturesque hillside village, comfortable and sophisticated. Excellent cooking and wine list.

Budget

Les Aurics, route Avignon, Vaison-la-Romaine, 84110 Vaucluse (tel: 90 36 03 15). Old house with simple, rustic decor, 2 km west of town. Swimming pool. No restaurant.

Café Des Arts, 30 boulevard Victor Hugo, Saint-Rémy-de-Provence, 13210 Bouches-du-Rhône (tel: 90 92 08 50). Bistro with rooms on the busy boulevard circling the old town.

Les Géraniums, Le Barroux, 84330 Vaucluse (tel: 90 62 41 08). Impeccable little hotel in hilly hamlet, with terrace and views. Cosy bedrooms and good-value country cooking.

Médiéval, 15 rue Petite Saunerie, Avignon, 84000 Vaucluse (tel: 90 86 11 06). Old building with pretty courtyard; self-catering studios for stays of a week or more.

Le Vieux Fox, Fox Amphoux, 83670 Var (tel: 94 80 71 69). Eleventh-century priory in delightful tiny hilltop village.

Restaurants
Moderate
Don Camillo, 5 rue des Ponchettes, Nice, 06300 Alpes-Maritimes (tel: 93 85 67 95). Small and simple, with some of the best local dishes in the old town (raviolis, cheeses and desserts are particularly good).

La Merenda, 4 rue de la Terrasse, Nice, 06300 Alpes-Maritimes. No telephone. You have to take potluck for a table in this tiny old-town bistro.

New York, 33 quai des Belges, Marseille, 13001 Bouches-du-Rhône (tel: 91 33 60 98). Ever-popular brasserie on the old port. Bourride and bouillabaisse are constant favorite choices.

Budget
Le Bistro Latin, 18 rue de la Couronne, Aix-en-Provence, 13100 Bouches-du-Rhône (tel: 42 38 22 88). Just off the Cours Mirabeau. Excellent local dishes and wines. Very good value menus.

MASSIF CENTRAL

Accommodations
Expensive
Château de la Caze, La Malène, 48210 Lozère (tel: 66 48 51 01). Medieval atmosphere, if not comfort, in this solid castle set in shady grounds about 5.5 km from the village; there are some additional apartments set in converted farm buildings.

Manoir de Montesquiou, La Malène, 48210 Lozère (tel: 66 48 51 12). Little 15th-century manor house, with well-maintained accommodations. Well situated for exploring the Tarn gorge.

Michel Bras, Laguiole, 12210 Aveyron (tel: 65 44 32 24). A restaurant with rooms, rather than a hotel—but what a restaurant! Michel Bras, one of France's great chefs, makes dreams come true with his superb menus.

HOTELS AND RESTAURANTS

Moderate

Auberge Pré Bossu, Moudeyres, 43150 Haute-Loire (tel: 71 05 10 70). Former farmhouse, in remote village of thatched stone houses. Renowned cooking by patron/chef.

Le Castel Blanc, 15 rue Arsène Vermenouze, Vic-sur-Cère, 15800 Cantal (tel: 71 49 63 63). Gabled mansion in attractive medieval village. Excellent food.

Renaissance, rue de la Ville, Meyrueis, 48150 Lozère (tel: 66 45 60 19). Charming old building with the atmosphere of a family house. No restaurant.

Sainte-Foy, rue Principale, Conques, 12320 Aveyron (tel: 65 69 84 03). Eighteenth-century building in the heart of the village. Pretty bedrooms and two apartments in neighboring former convent.

Budget

Auberge Fleurie, place du

Riverside charm: a cottage in the Burgundy countryside

Barry, Montsalvy, 15120 Cantal (tel: 71 49 20 02). Ivy-covered auberge at the edge of the village, with cheerful country-style restaurant (excellent value).

Manoir, Arlempdes, 43490 Haute-Loire (tel: 71 57 17 14). Very simple inn in tiny village, with splendid views.

Midi-Papillon, place A. Lemasse, St-Jean-du-Bruel, 12230 Aveyron (tel: 65 62 26 04). Well-run village hotel with excellent-value menus.

Parc, 47 avenue J. Monestier, Florac, 48400 Lozère (tel: 66 45 03 05). Peaceful, large hotel in extensive grounds.

ALPS AND THE RHONE VALLEY

Accommodations

Expensive

L'Abbaye, Talloires, 74290 Haute-Savoie (tel: 50 60 77 33). Elegantly furnished and very atmospheric former abbey building in beautiful situation on Lake Annecy.

Château de Collonges, Ruffieux, 73310 Savoie (tel:

79 54 27 38). Superb château in beautiful setting near Aix-les-Bains, with good cooking.

Ostellerie du Vieux Pérouges, Pérouges, 01800 Ain (tel: 74 61 00 88). Medieval inn, a filmmaker's dream.

Moderate

Beausoleil, Lavancher, 74400 Haute-Savoie (tel: 50 54 00 78). Simple little hotel, 6 km from Chamonix, in mountain village; pretty garden, tennis.

Chalet Croix-Fry, route Col de la Croix-Fry, Manigod, 74230 Haute-Savoie (tel: 50 44 90 16). Swisslike chalet with delightful annexes (high on mountain pass).

Châteaurenard, St-Véran, 05350 Hautes-Alpes (tel: 92 45 85 43). Simple hotel with wonderful views, in mountain village.

Budget

Chalet-Hôtel du Cucheron, Col du Cucheron, Saint-Pierre-de-Chartreuse, 38380 Isère (tel: 76 88 62 06). Pass-top chalet, restaurant with rooms, in hiking country.

Grand, 60 rue de l'Hôtel de Ville, Crest, 26400 Drôme (tel: 75 25 08 17). Simple family-run town-center establishment with popular and good-value restaurant.

La Marmotte, Bonneval-sur-Arc, 73480 Savoie (tel: 79 05 94 82). Totally peaceful, in fine surroundings. Terrace, hearty mountain cooking.

Restaurants

Expensive

La Tour Rose, 22 rue du Boeuf, Lyon 69005, Rhône (tel: 78 37 25 90). Extremely elegant, in a glorious 17th-century former convent in the old town. Suitably exalted cooking.

Budget

Le Mercière, 56 rue Mercière, Lyon 69002, Rhône (tel: 78 37 67 35). One of several good restaurants/bistro in this street (Le Bistrot de Lyon and Le Bouchon aux Vins are also highly recommended).

BURGUNDY AND JURA

Accommodations
Expensive
Le Cep, 27–29 rue Maufoux, Beaune, 21200 Côte-d'Or (tel: 80 22 35 48). Beautiful Renaissance mansion with courtyard, in town center (your car is parked for you). Elegant restaurant, with terrace for eating out.

Château d'Igé, Igé 71960 Saône-et-Loire (tel: 85 33 33 99). Medieval castle appropriately converted and furnished. Spacious bedrooms and gardens.

L'Espérance, Saint-Père-sous-Vézelay, 89450 Yonne (tel: 86 33 39 10). Restaurant with rooms of one of France's top chefs, Marc Meneau. Some rooms in restored mill.

Host. du Vieux Moulin, Bouilland, 21420 Côte-d'Or (tel: 80 21 51 16). Jean-Pierre Silva offers gourmet eating and a welcome for families.

Moderate
Le Bourgogne, Cluny, 71250 Saône-et-Loire (tel: 85 59 00 58). On the abbey square, a stylish little hotel, with a well-liked restaurant.

La Fontaine aux Muses, La Celle St-Cyr, 89970 Yonne (tel: 86 73 40 22). Converted village farmhouse, near A6 motorway, with a music room (occasional concerts).

Le Paris, Arbois, 39600 Jura (tel: 84 66 05 67). Old posthouse in resort center, with a long-standing culinary reputation.

Paris et Poste, Sens, 89100 Yonne (tel: 86 65 17 43). Old-fashioned town-center hostelry (next to the cathedral).

Budget
Le Castel, Mailly-le-Château, 89660 Yonne (tel: 86 81 43 06). Turn-of-the-century village-center house, convenient for stopovers for southbound travelers. Attractive garden and shady terrace.

Castel de Valrose, Montmerle-sur-Saône,

01090 Ain (tel: 74 69 30 52). Solid 1930s house in peaceful setting near the A6 motorway and the River Saône.

Poste, Charolles, 71120 Saône-et-Loire (tel: 85 24 11 32). Right in the center of this small market town. Offers very good regional cooking.

Relais du Mâconnais, La Croix-Blanche, 71960 Saône-et-Loire (tel: 85 36 60 72). Unassuming little hotel in tiny village 14 km from Mâcon, with elegant restaurant.

ALSACE-LORRAINE AND THE NORTH

Accommodations
Expensive
Château de Montreuil, Montreuil-sur-Mer, 62170 Pas-de-Calais (tel: 21 81 53 04). Country house, English style. Excellent cooking; fine gardens.

Les Crayères, 64 boulevard Vasnier, Reims, 51100 Marne (tel: 26 82 80 80). Gérard Boyer's palatial restaurant and hotel, in a 19th-century château located in Reims's suburbs.

Grand Hôtel de la Reine, Nancy, 54000 Meurthe-et-Moselle (tel: 83 35 03 01). Eighteenth-century palace on the superb place Stanislas.

Moderate
Aux Armes de Champagne, L'Epine, 51460 Marne (tel: 26 66 30 30). Opposite the basilica, this renowned hostelry has long had a high standard of cooking.

Le Cheval Blanc, Sept-Saulx, 51400 Marne (tel: 26 03 90 27). Traditional coaching inn in quiet village center. Bedrooms (in annex) in rustic style.

Les Vosges, 2 Grande Rue, Ribeauvillé, 68150 Haut-Rhin (tel: 89 73 61 39). In the heart of a pretty wine village, an elegant restaurant with rooms.

Budget
Les Alisiers, Lapoutroie, 68650 Haut-Rhin (tel: 89 47 52 82). Converted hilltop farmhouse; small and cosy bedrooms. Robust cooking.

Grand Hôtel de l'Europe, 23–25 rue Diderot, Langres, 52200 Haute-Marne (tel: 25 87 10 88). In town center, busy and traditional, with generous cooking.

Restaurants
Moderate
Maison Kammerzell, 16 place de la Cathédrale, Strasbourg, 67000 Bas-Rhin (tel: 88 32 42 14). An excellent place for choucroutes of all kinds.

Main gate of Dijon's Palais des Ducs

283

Index

INDEX

285

INDEX

INDEX/ACKNOWLEDGMENTS

Acknowledgments

The Automobile Association would like to thank the following photographers, libraries and associations for their assistance in the preparation of this book.

J ALLAN CASH PHOTOLIBRARY Spine: Frenchman

CDT CANTAL 201 Chaines des Puys

CHAMONIX TOURIST BOARD 209 Walkers, 211 Climbers, 215 Paragliders

HAUTE SAVOIE 25 Skiing

HULTON PICTURE LIBRARY 45 Général de Gaulle, 47 François Mitterand

MARY EVANS PICTURE LIBRARY 34 Fighting Spanish, 34/5 French in Flanders, 37 Cardinal Richelieu, 39 Louis XIV, 40 Napoleon, 41 Women marching to Versailles; Napoleon, 42 Lafayette; poster, 44 Signing of Treaty of Versailles; cartoon

SCOPE 164 Gave des Oulettes de Gaube, Vignemale, 167 St Michel de Cuxa, Prieuré de Serrabone

SPECTRUM COLOUR LIBRARY 26 Lyon, 28 Carnac, 47 Lyon, 109 Tapestry, 150 St-Sernin, Toulouse

ZEFA PICTURE LIBRARY (UK) LTD 3 Monet, *Artist's Garden at Vetheuil*, 31 Megaliths, Gavrinis, 43 Yvette Gilbert, 46 Lyon, 103 Paul Gauguin, *The Gossipers*, 161 Garvanie, 168 Monet, *Cap d'Antibes*, 175 Museum of Modern Art, Nice

All remaining pictures are held in the Automobile Association's own library (© AA Photo Library), with contributions from:

P Atterbury, P Bennett, J Edmunson, P Enticknap, P Kenward (and back cover), D Noble, T Oliver, K Paterson, N Ray, B Rieger, D Robertson, C Sawyer (and front cover), M Short, B Smith, A Souter, R Strange, R Victor